W9-CBK-221

SOVIET POLICY
TOWARD THE BALTIC STATES
1918–1940

BY THE SAME AUTHOR

Lithuania and Her Independence Day
16th February 1918–1946
Hanau, 1946

Wirtschaftliche Rückständigkeit Europäischer Agrarländer
und ihr Zusammenhang mit dem Industrialisierungsgrad
Frankfurt am Main, 1947

SOVIET POLICY TOWARD THE BALTIC STATES

1918–1940

BY ALBERT N. TARULIS

University of Notre Dame Press

1959

32.47
T17s

Library of Congress Catalog Card Number 58–13608
© 1959, University of Notre Dame Press
Notre Dame, Indiana

54552

*In Commemoration
of the Fortieth Anniversary Since the
Restoration of Independence of Lithuania
on February 16, 1918*

FOREWORD

A generation ago, nascent Bolshevism found its spread from Russia to Western Europe blocked by three small but courageous Baltic peoples. The Bolsheviks did not like that. "Estonia, Latvia, and Lithuania are directly on the road from Russia to Western Europe and are, therefore, a hindrance to our revolution . . . this separating wall has to be destroyed," *Izvestiia* wrote on December 25, 1918, when Red troops were pouring into the Baltic area.

It took more than two decades for the Bolsheviks to achieve their goal. In spite of the tremendous odds against them, the Baltic peoples managed to repel the attackers, consolidate their statehood, and enjoy the fruits of independence in the ensuing period of relative peace and prosperity.

The following pages will tell how the Baltic peoples were finally overpowered and annexed to the Soviet Union and what devious methods were used to achieve this end. It is a story of broken pledges and broken treaty obligations, diplomatic duplicity, connivance between Communism and Nazism, application of force in international relations, and the most naked and brutal imperialism.

The only comforting aspect of the whole story is the fact that the Soviet westward drive over the bodies of the three riparian republics has not met with approval on the part of any of the leading democratic nations, the United States included. They have never recognized the legality of the Soviet seizure of the Baltic States and, consequently, their hands are not tied as far as re-establishment of national and human rights in that area is concerned.

The Library of Congress rules of transliteration for Russian names and terms are used in the text. Lithuanian, Latvian, and Estonian place names are given in the form officially accepted in each country concerned. The language of available translations of various documents has, as a rule, been preserved.

The author wishes to express his gratitude to all the institutions and persons who assisted in the assembly of reference material, gave advice and criticism, and took time to engage in correspondence on various problems in the course of work. The author's associates at the Library of Congress have been particularly helpful.

Carnegie Institute of Technology, Pittsburgh, Pa., to whose distinguished faculty the author had the honor to belong, is thankfully remembered here for a generous research grant which was used to visit libraries in search of material. The author is indebted to the Committee on International Relations of the University of Notre Dame for publishing the book under its auspices.

Last but not least, special thanks go to Mrs. Tarulis who spent many days and nights typing and retyping the manuscript, discussing various aspects of work, and worrying more than the undersigned himself did when something went wrong.

A. N. T.

Washington, D.C.
Spring 1959

Contents

Maps

INTRODUCTION

It so happened that shortly before the present volume there appeared an exhaustive bibliography of American publications on East Central Europe 1945–1957, edited by Professor Robert F. Byrnes. He could point out the general progress which had been achieved in that long-neglected field, but he had to admit at the same time that not all countries of that area received the same attention. And it clearly appears that the three Baltic Republics, Estonia, Latvia, and Lithuania, still are very insufficiently studied, since out of 2810 items in the bibliography only 104 deal with these three states.

Were it only for that reason, any new contributions to their better knowledge must be highly welcomed, particularly if it is a result of painstaking scholarly research. The book of Albert N. Tarulis is much more than that. Its very topic is of the greatest possible significance indeed. No other case would be more instructive for a better understanding of Soviet Russia's aggressive imperialism than the study of her policy toward the Baltic States from the proclamation of national self-determination of the small Baltic nation when in 1940 they were forced to enter the Soviet Union. This tragic story is described by Dr. Tarulis in the light of the primary sources and is particularly impressive if we remember what happened in the postwar period when, instead of being liberated after the occupation of Hitler's Germany, the unhappy Baltic peoples were once more conquered by the Red Army to suffer a ruthless oppression to the present day.

Concentrating on the danger which from the dawn of their independence threatened them from their big eastern neighbor, the author could not fail to show at the same time the threat, coming also from the German side, a threat which, in view of her geopolitical situation, was especially serious for Lithuania, as evidenced in the critical year of 1939. His book, therefore, contains a great deal of information about German policy also, taken from the official German documents, which in addition to those on Soviet foreign policy, are so frequently quoted in the numerous footnotes.

As far as Lithuania is concerned, Dr. Tarulis also had to touch upon her relations with Poland. There was indeed in the interwar period a most regrettable conflict between these two countries, both of which were threatened by the same two enemies. But the author, who in this case has not included the material coming from the other side, has oversimplified the issues which separated Lithuanians and Poles, and which cannot be compared with the basic hostility of their stronger neighbors, endangering their very existence as independent nations. An objective study of Polish-Lithuanian relations during the independent period, including the improvement of these relations in the last year before the common ordeal, could contribute to a reconciliation which today seems more desirable than ever before.

This is, however, another question, and differences of opinion regarding the controversy between one of the Baltic States and Poland, which had the best possible relations with two others, cannot affect the high appreciation of all Dr. Tarulis has so well written about the dramatic relations of the three of them with Soviet Russia. As far as this basic problem of his book is concerned, his achievement is outstanding, his conclusions are indisputable and every careful reader will share the hope expressed in the last sentence that the United States will continue to support the cause of the national independence of the Lithuanians, the Latvians, and the Estonians.

OSCAR HALECKI

Chapter One

SELF-DETERMINATION ON PAPER

The Bolshevik revolution in Russia, set off more than forty years ago, found the Baltic peoples clamoring for freedom. This was equally true of the Russian-held inhabitants of Estonia and Livonia and the German-held inhabitants of Kurland and Lithuania. Political objectives of Estonians, Latvians, and Lithuanians were identical on either side of the dividing line between the Russian and the German administration zones.

The overthrow of the Tsarist regime eight months prior to the Bolshevik revolution had provided the Baltic peoples with an excellent opportunity for restating their political objectives. The attitude of the new rulers of Russia—the Provisional Government and the Soviet of Workers' and Soldiers' Deputies—seemed to be most encouraging. For hardly had Nicholas II signed his instrument of abdication, when *Izvestiia* came out with a report on a meeting of the Soviet of Workers' and Soldiers' Deputies where the request was made to include in the program of the Provisional Government a promise of cultural and national self-determination for all peoples of Russia.[1]

In the general turmoil, the readers of Provisional Government announcements may have failed to notice that no such promise was incorporated in its program made public on March 16,[2] or in its declaration appearing in the papers on March 20.[3] Ten days later *Izvestiia* again took a stand on the problem of national oppression; this time using very emphatic language:

> We are striving not to take territory from other peoples, but to help them attain liberty, especially the peoples living in Russia. We will oppose, with arms in hand, everything that stands in the way of liberty.[4]

1

It was the Central Executive Committee of the Soviet of Workers' and Soldiers' Deputees that spoke through *Izvestiia*, its mouthpiece. The Provisional Government in those days enjoyed *Izvestiia's* support and listened carefully to what it said. A week later (April 10) the above words reappeared in the Provisional Government's statement on war aims:

> The very purpose of free Russia is not domination over other nations, or seizure of their national possessions, or forcible incorporation of foreign territories, but the establishment of stable peace on the basis of self-determination. The Russian people does not intend to increase its world power at the expense of other nations. It has no desire to enslave or degrade anyone.[5]

The declaration of the second Provisional Government, published in the papers on May 19, reiterated the same statement on national self-determination.[6] Similarly, the declaration of the third and last Provisional Government, made public on October 10, promised to "recognize for all peoples the right to self-determination on such principles as the Constituent Assembly shall determine." [7]

Finally, the First Congress of Soviets, meeting on June 14–21 and expressing its full confidence in the policies of the Provisional Government (there were but 105 Bolsheviks out of 1020 delegates), called on it to "strive persistently for the earliest conclusion of a general peace without annexation, indemnity, and on the basis of self-determination." [8]

The Central Executive Committee of the Soviets incorporated this demand in its outline of instructions guiding the Delegation to the Interallied Conference in Paris. The first condition of peace was the evacuation of Russian territory occupied by the Germans. Russia offered in exchange full self-determination to Poland, Lithuania, and Latvia, all three at that time occupied by the Germans. Russian-held Estonia was not mentioned.[9] The text of instructions was published in *Izvestiia* on October 20.

The Baltic peoples were, of course, aware of these fresh winds blowing in Russia. And they took advantage of the favorable situation.

As early as March 24–26, representatives of all Estonian countries and political organizations convened in Tartu and moved to demand autonomy from the Provisional Government of Russia.[10] As no response was forthcoming, fifteen thousand Estonians staged a demonstration in the streets of Petrograd on April 8 in support of immediate action on the Estonian demand.[11] On April 12 the *Decree on the Temporary Organization of Administration and Local Self-Determination in the Province of Estonia* was promulgated.[12] An Estonian, J. Poska, was appointed Provincial Commissioner to be in charge of administration.

On July 7–8 the Provincial Council (referred to by the Estonians as the National Council) was elected. The Council convened a week later and promptly notified the Provisional Government that it regarded the present status of Estonia as only a first step toward her transformation into an autonomous entity within a Russian federated republic. This implied a demand for the acknowledgment of Estonia as an autonomous state; being an autonomous Russian province no longer satisfied the Estonians. By September the question of Estonia's independent statehood and her complete separation from Russia came up for discussion at the National Council. The reluctance of the Provisional Government to relinquish control—despite a formal acknowledgment of autonomy—must have played an important part in it.

The Latvian-inhabited provinces of Livonia and Kurland received an identical autonomous status as the province of Estonia by virtue of the July 5, 1917, *Decree on Temporary Organization of Administration and Local Self-Government in the Provinces of Livonia and Kurland.*[13] J. Priedkalns, a Latvian, was appointed Provincial Commissioner of Livonia. No such appointment could be made for Kurland owing to her occupation by the Germans. In fact, these measures merely acknowledged the existing status of autonomy achieved by the Latvians themselves after the overthrow of the Tsarist regime.[14] The Latvian Political Conference, meeting in Riga on July 30, followed the Estonian trend and stated in its resolution that

> the Latvian nation, like other nations, has a full right to self-determination . . . Latvia shall be a political, autonomous unit within the Russian democratic republic.

The whole of Lithuania being under German occupation, there was nothing the Provisional Government of Russia could do about heeding political self-determination demands of Lithuanians. Such demands were voiced by representatives of Lithuanian political parties and Lithuanian representatives at the Russian *Duma* (Diet) meeting in Petrograd on February 21, i.e., nearly on the eve of the Russian revolution. The resolution proclaimed that "the Lithuanian nation, irrespective of class distinctions, demands the right to decide for itself its political fate and destinies."

As soon as the revolution broke out, the National Council of Lithuania was constituted in Petrograd on March 13 by the representatives of all Lithuanian political parties and the Lithuanian *Duma* representatives. The Council wasted no time in informing the Provisional Government of Russia (May 2) and the Soviet of Workers' and Soldiers' Deputies that "Lithuania was a separate ethnographic, cultural, economic, and political unit," and that only the future Constitutent Assembly of Lithuania had the right to decide her internal order and relations with the neighboring states.

This brought forth an avalanche of support resolutions adopted by Lithuanian refugees and soldiers in the Russian Army scattered all over Russia. A convention of Lithuanian soldiers, attended by 100 delegates representing 25,000 men in uniform, was held in Petrograd on May 25 and 26. Its resolution proclaimed that "Lithuania must become free." It also demanded that Lithuanian representatives be permitted to take part at the Peace Conference and that the Provisional Government of Russia state its solution of the problem of freedom for Lithuania before the convocation of the Constituent Assembly of Russia.

The Lithuanian Political Conference, attended by 320 duly-elected delegates, was held in Petrograd on May 27. Its resolution, adopted by the right-wing political parties, restated that "the whole of Lithuania must become an independent state" and that the form of her government and the internal order must be reserved to the future Constitutent Assembly of Lithuania; her external relations were to be determined by the Peace Conference, with Lithuanian representatives participating.

Thus Lithuanian demands went much farther than either Estonian or Latvian demands. The Lithuanian National Council regarded its demands for independence as a foregone conclusion and contested any right of the Constituent Assembly of Russia even to discuss such a question. A paper prepared for consideration by the latter stated the Council's opinion that the Constituent Assembly of Russia would have only to acknowledge the right of the Lithuanian people to decide its way of national life in its own Constituent Assembly while the Provisional Government would state its agreement to such an arrangement prior to the convocation of the Constituent Assembly of Russia.

The Lithuanian National Conference meeting in German-occupied Vilnius on September 18–23 expressed the same views on the future of Lithuania as those stated by the Lithuanians in Russia. Its resolution adopted by 2000 delegates read:

> In order that Lithuania may be able freely to develop, it is absolutely necessary to make the country an independent state, based upon democratic principles and having ethnographic frontiers which shall take into consideration the interests of economic life. . . . The interests of Lithuania, in normal times, are rather in the direction of the West than the East [Russia] or the South [Poland].[15]

The Conference elected a National Council (*Taryba*) and resolved to convoke the Lithuanian Constituent Assembly in Vilnius, "in order to fix the basis of independent Lithuania and her relations with neighboring countries."

Hence, the new rulers of Russia—the Bolsheviks—could entertain no doubt as to the political objectives of all three Baltic peoples: the Estonians, the Latvians, and the Lithuanians. The repeated pronouncements of their important exponents—Lenin and Stalin—indicated that no formal objection to the realization of such objectives was to be anticipated.

Lenin's first writings on national self-determination went back to 1902. In that year he prepared a draft of the program of the Russian Social Democratic Party (RSDRP) which received approval of a committee of five. The program draft included the promise that the RSDRP would work for a democratic constitution of the future republic of Russia providing, among other things, for

> the acknowledgment of the right to self-determination for all nations entering into the composition of the state.[16]

The Committee adopted this formulation, although its member, G. V. Plekhanov, suggested substitution of the words: ". . . for all nations who entered into the composition . . ." for Lenin's draft.[17] For Plekhanov feared that otherwise Russia would disintegrate. Yet Lenin's formulation prevailed, and it was included in the program as published in *Iskra* on June 14, 1902.[18]

The program was adopted by the Second Congress of the RSDRP in mid-1903.[19] Lenin commented on the program in *Iskra* in an article entitled, *Manifesto of Armenian Social Democrats:*

> The general and basic program of the Russian Social Democrats, which always remains binding, must include the demand for complete equality among the citizens (regardless of sex, language, religion, race, and other differences) as well as for the right to their free democratic self-determination . . . We, the party of the proletariat, must lead a continuous struggle in all circumstances against any attempt to exert, through oppression or injustice, external pressure on national self-determination.[20]

The revolution of 1905 in Russia gave an impetus to the discussion of national self-determination problems. Lenin took an energetic stand against suggestions to grant the oppressed nations cultural self-determination only.[21] He pointed out that every revolutionary government must put particular emphasis on complete freedom of oppressed nations, insisting on the acknowledgement of their political—not merely cultural—self-determination.[22]

In 1913 Lenin put together his *Postulates on the National Question,*[23] a rehash of the RSDPR program on that subject. He tried to explain this program, upon request from the Central Committee of the RSDRP, to audiences in Switzerland and Poland. He repeated on every occasion that the RSDRP recognized the right of every nation to self-determination and even to secession from Russia.[24] In Latvia, he assured the local Social Democrats that the RSDRP was for freedom of peoples and for freedom of secession.[25] Lenin defined the right to self-determination as the right to self-determination in a political sense, the right to a separate political existence.[26]

This interpretation also may be found in his study on the *Right of Nations to Self-Determination* published in 1914.[27] The recognition of this right in Russia seemed to him to be a matter of particular urgency owing to the fact that the "alien races" made up 57 per cent of the entire population.[28] Any interpretation of self-determination denying the right to secession was for Lenin playing into the hands of Great Russians.

In World War I Lenin saw, as one of the objectives of the Russian Social Democrats, the struggle against the Tsarist monarchy and Great Russian as well as Panslavist chauvinism. Preaching for a revolution in Russia and for liberation and self-determination of peoples oppressed by Russia was to be one of the means to express this struggle. He called a chauvinist "a socialist of the oppressor nation . . . who does not recognize the right of oppressed nations to self-determination, i.e., to freedom of secession." Such a socialist was not even a socialist in Lenin's opinion.[29]

Evidently Stalin, too, was a "chauvinist," since Lenin accused Stalin of a spiteful attitude toward "social nationalism" and laid squarely in his lap the blame for harsh measures against nationalism in Georgia in 1922. Lenin called it a "truly Great Russian nationalist campaign." Finally, he undoubtedly referred to Stalin when he spoke of "brutal Great Russian *Derzhimordas*" and Russified non-Russians who like to exaggerate when it comes to 100% Russian attitude.[30]

In general, Lenin was strongly critical of hypocrisy in the matter of national self-determination.[31] He engaged in polemics with the exponents of "the imperialist economism," who were denying the right of the people to self-determination. He demanded that every non-hypocrite be in favor of the freedom of secession from Russia for all the people oppressed by her.[32] For Lenin, "acknowledgment" (in quotation marks) could be regarded as nonhypocritical

> only when the representative of the oppressor nation has continued to demand, both before and during the war, the freedom of secession for a people who was oppressed by his own "fatherland" . . . The socialists and democrats of the oppressed nations must, in their propaganda and agitation, call scoundrels the socialists of oppressor nations (be it Great Russians or Germans, Poles in regard to the Ukrainians, etc.) who do not uphold consequently and unreservedly the freedom of secession of nations which are oppressed (or forcibly detained) by their own nations.

Lenin's Party, the Russian Social Democrats, adopted his definition of a chauvinist. An editorial in *Sotsial-Demokrat* on October 13, 1915, stated that the Social Democrats regarded as revolutionary chauvinists all those who wanted a victory over Tsarism as a stepping stone to a victory over Germany, plunder of other countries, and "consolidation of the domination of Great Russians over the other peoples in Russia." [33]

The year 1916 witnessed Lenin's summarization of his views on national self-determination. He restated his postulates in an article, *The Socialist Revolution and the Right of Nations to Self-Determination.*[34] Here he repeated that in Russia, where oppressed nations comprised at least 57% of the population

> . . . the acknowledgment of the right to freedom of secession from Russia for all nations oppressed by Tsarism is absolutely necessary for the Social Democrats because of their democratic and socialist objectives . . . the proletariat must demand the freedom of political secession for both the colonies and the nations which are oppressed by "its" nation . . . a victorious socialism must absolutely implement a full democracy, i.e., not only put in effect a complete equality of nations, but also implement the right to self-determination of oppressed nations, i.e., the right to freedom of political secession.

Another of Lenin's writings in 1916, putting together the *Results of Discussion About Self-Determination,*[35] includes a statement which Lenin's followers conveniently forgot to apply to their policies on national self-determination; namely: "A victorious proletariat cannot impose happiness on any nation whatever without thereby undermining its own victory." Lenin even quoted Karl Marx saying that "a nation which oppresses other nations cannot be free." [36]

The year 1917 was taken up in preparation for the Bolshevik revolution. There were many problems to face, of which that of national self-determination was only one. However, on several occasions Lenin found time to take a stand on these problems. The following are a few of his pronouncements of that period:

> You have to be crazy to continue the policies of [Tsar] Nicholas II . . . we must break the old, bloody, and dirty past where Russia of capitalists and oppressors played the role of executioner of other peoples . . . the proletarian party must insist, before all, on proclamation and immediate implementation of a complete freedom of secession from Russia for all nations and peoples who were either oppressed by Tsarism, forcibly attached to her, or forcibly detained within the state boundaries, i.e., annexed.[37]

Annexation for Lenin was "violation of people's right to self-determination and establishment of state boundaries against the will of the people." [38] He made it abundantly clear that he regarded the Baltic provinces as annexed to Russia. Lenin admitted that he, in order to deceive Tsarist censors, used to speak of Japan-annexed Korea when he actually meant Russian-annexed Finland, Poland, the Ukraine, Khiva, Bokhara, Kurland, Estonia[39] . . . and Lithuania, which he evidently forgot to include in this list. Kurland had been, in Lenin's opinion, "always annexed to Russia." [40] He was against Russia's "detaining Kurland by force." [41] He even strongly denounced the *Rech'*, the mouthpiece of the Russian Constitutional Democrats (*Kadets*), denying the very fact of annexation of Kurland.[42]

L. Kamenev, who played a very prominent role in the establishment of the Bolshevik state, expanded Lenin's definition of annexation to include the whole of Latvia as well as Lithuania and other non-Russian borderlands. Writing in *Izvestiia* on January 24, 1918, he stated:

> Poland, Lithuania, Latvia, and the Ukraine answered this definition perfectly; these territories were forcibly annexed and forcibly detained by Tsarist Russia.

Lenin's and Kamenev's attitude toward annexation of Kurland deserves particular scrutiny. On strictly formalistic grounds, they might have agreed that the inhabitants of the Duchy of Kurland had received from Empress Catherine II of Russia, "the favor of accepting you among our faithful subjects [upon] your sincere desire expressed in your general Diet and solemnly confirmed by your representatives." So read her Manifesto of April 15, 1795.[43]

Yet both Lenin and Kamenev must have recognized the true value of such an "expression of popular desire" in the presence of foreign troops. For it was just as genuine as the Lithuanian "thanksgiving delegations" ordered by Catherine II through her Governor General N. Repnin on the occasion of Lithuania's annexation to Russia in the same year, 1795.[44]

Lenin was willing to draw the logical consequences when it came to specific problems. A member of the Lithuanian Refugee Welfare Committee in Russia, who also served on the editorial staff of the Committee's publication, *Lietuviu Balsas,* wanted to find from Lenin what he held of Lithuanian aspirations toward independence. He saw him before the outbreak of the Bolshevik revolution. Lenin was emphatic:

> The Lithuanian people will be able to make their own decision on their destiny. Either autonomy or complete independence will be approved by Russia.[45]

Stalin's contribution to the problem of national self-determination was modest in comparison with that of Lenin. For if all of Lenin's writings and statements on the subject were combined, they would form a much more impressive volume than Stalin's *Marxism and National Question* with all the appendixes. It would be hardly an exaggeration to say that Stalin made no single statement on the problem of national self-determination that had not been made by Lenin, or included in RSDRP programs and resolutions. Only Stalin did so much later.

Stalin's main contribution to the problem of national self-determination was penned in 1913—ten years after Lenin's comments on *National Question in Our Program* published in *Iskra*. The following are a few excerpts from Stalin's work:

> Social-Democratic parties in all countries, therefore, proclaim the right of nations to self-determination . . . The right of self-determination means that a nation can arrange its life according to its own will. It has the right to arrange its life on the basis of autonomy. It has the right to enter into federal relations with other nations. It has the right to complete secession. Nations are sovereign and all nations are equal . . . Russian Marxists cannot do without the right of nations to self-determination. Thus, the right to self-determination is an essential element in the solution of the national problem.[46]

Four years later, Stalin, speaking at the Seventh Conference of the RSDRP in 1917,[47] still insisted that the oppressed nations making part of Russia should be given the right to decide freely upon the question whether to remain as a part of the Russian state or secede as an independent state. Later in the year, he declared that the Russian Social-Democrats would not be worthy of their name if they failed to acknowledge the right of the peoples of Russia to freedom of self-determination.[48] That is about all Stalin ever said *in favor* of national self-determination.

The official attitude of the RSDRP as a political organization likewise seemed favorable to the away-from-Russia drive among the non-Russian borderland people. Moreover, it could be traced back to the beginning of the century or even earlier; namely, to the 1896 International Socialist Congress in London which declared itself in favor of "a full right to autonomy [self-determination in Russian and German translations] [49] to all nationalities."

The Second Congress of the RSDRP, which convened in Brussels-London in 1903, followed the lead. It adopted Lenin's draft of the RSDRP program, including Point 9 in the list of provisions to be included in the future constitution of a democratic republic of Russia:

> The right to self-determination for all nationalities entering into the composition of the state.[50]

The RSDRP remained watchful over the propagation of the above Point 9 through the following years, and particularly so after the revolution of 1905. Its 1907 Congress in London criticized the Social Democratic faction at the *Duma* for the failure to use the *Duma* rostrum for the presentation of the national question as well as for the failure to

establish contact with the broad masses of oppressed nationalities.[51]
The 1912 Conference in Prague denounced the ruthless nationalistic
policy of Tsarism, directed against all oppressed peoples and the more
cultured borderlands; the Baltic provinces were enumerated among the
latter.[52] The 1913 Conference in Poronino resolved that the RSDRP
must defend unreservedly the right of the Tsarist monarchy-oppressed
peoples to self-determination; the Conference understood it as the right
to secession and constitution of an independent state. The decision
was motivated by the national oppression of the majority of the population on the part of the Tsarist monarchy, which the Conference called
"the most reactionary and barbarian political regime as compared to
the neighboring states in either Europe or Asia." [53]

The Conference also urged the RSDRP Central Committee, the
Party press, and the local organizations to submit the national question
to the most thorough discussion. As already mentioned, Lenin heeded
the appeal. So did Stalin.

The Seventh Conference of the RSDRP convened in Petrograd after
the overthrow of the Tsarist regime (May 7–12, 1917). Its resolution
on the national problem reiterated what had been said before:

> All nations making part of Russia must be acknowledged the right to
> secession and constitution of an independent state. Denial of such right
> and failure to take measures assuring its practical implementation would be
> identical with the endorsement of policies of seizures or annexations.[54]

By mid-May changes in the RSDRP program were discussed. One
of these was to replace the 1913 demand for the right to national self-
determination by an even more forceful declaration of "the right to
freedom of secession and constitution of its own state" for all nations
entering into the composition of the state.[55]

At the same time Lenin prepared a draft of *Instructions to the
Elected Deputees to the Soviet of Workers and Peasants,* with strict
orders regarding their expected attitude in the matter of national self-
determination:

> The Russian people—both workers and peasants—do not want and will not
> oppress any people; they do not want and will not detain, forcibly attached
> to Russia, any non-Russian (non-Great Russian) peoples . . . Great Rus-
> sians will not detain by force either Poland, or Kurland, or the Ukraine, or
> Finland, or Armenia, or any other people.[56]

The Conference of Front and Rear Military Organizations of the
RSDRP, meeting together about a month later (June 29–July 6), stated
in its resolution that the peoples of Russia had full right to self-determination and independent solution of their destiny, "including secession." [57] The Sixth Enlarged Conference of the Central Committee
of the RSDRP issued on August 25 a *Manifesto to All Russian Toilers,*

Workers, Soldiers, and Peasants.[58] The Manifesto accused the Provisional Government of resorting to armed threats against "the very right to self-determination which was so solemnly proclaimed in official declarations." On September 13 the same Committee voiced the demand for "effective implementation" of the right to self-determination for all peoples inhabiting Russia.[59]

By that time the Bolsheviks were ready to launch an armed revolt against the Provisional Government. The Central Committee of the RSDRP passed a resolution to that effect on October 23.[60] Two weeks later the revolt broke out.

The *Appeal to the Workers, Soldiers, and Peasants,*[61] issued on November 7 by the Bolshevik-dominated Second Congress of Soviets, announced the seizure of power by the Bolsheviks. It also contained the promise that they would secure "to all nationalities inhabiting Russia the right to self-determination." The *Decree on Peace,*[62] issued a day later, made it known that the Workers' and Peasants' Government was ready to begin at once negotiations leading to a just and democratic peace: a peace "without annexations (i.e., without the seizure of foreign territory and the forcible annexation of foreign nationalities) and without indemnities."

Thus, the Decree on Peace actually repeated what the First Congress of Soviets had requested in its resolution several months earlier. The only difference was that the Decree on Peace went into considerable detail explaining what was meant under the term of annexation:

> By annexation or seizure of foreign territory the government understands, in accordance with the sense of justice of democracy in general, and of the laboring classes in particular, the incorporation into a large or powerful state of a small or weak nationality, without the definitely, clearly, and voluntarily expressed consent and desire of this nationality, regardless of when this forcible incorporation took place, regardless also of the degree of development or backwardness of the nation forcibly annexed or forcibly detained within the frontiers of the given state, and finally, regardless of whether this nation is located in Europe or in distant lands beyond the seas.
>
> If any nation whatsoever is retained as part of a given state by force, if despite its expressed desire—whether expressed in the press, in popular assemblies, in the decisions of the political parties, or by rebellions and insurrections against national oppression—it has not the right of choosing freely—the troops of the annexing or, generally, the more powerful nation being completely withdrawn and without any pressure being brought to bear—the constitutional forms of its national existence, then its incorporation is an annexation, that is, seizure and coercion.

It is irrelevant here whether or not the Decree was meant to apply primarily to the colonial peoples "beyond the seas." Formally, it applied to all peoples inhabiting the annexed territories. The Russian-annexed territories made no exception. As expressly admitted by Lenin, Kurland fell into the category of such territories. Russian acquisition of the title to Estonia, Livonia, and Lithuania was based on treaties between the Russian Tsars (Peter I and Catherine II), on the one hand, and Kings of Sweden and Prussia, on the other. No one had ever asked the Baltic peoples about their consent or desire. And so they, by the letter of the Decree on Peace, were entitled to exercise their right to self-determination.

The Council of People's Commissars, appointed by the Second Congress of Soviets to implement its policies, announced a week later (November 15) how it intended to go about a practical realization of the principle of self-determination proclaimed in the Decree on Peace. The *Declaration of the Rights of the Peoples of Russia*,[63] issued by the Council of People's Commissars, spelled out the principles governing its future nationality policies. Lenin and Stalin were co-signers of the Declaration. Stalin signed in his capacity of Chairman of Nationalities, a post to which he had been appointed by the Second Congress of Soviets on November 8.

In this Declaration, the Council of People's Commissars promised to apply the following principles to its activity in the implementation of the right to national self-determination as stated by the First and the Second Congresses of Soviets:

(1) Equality and sovereignty of peoples of Russia;
(2) The right of the peoples of Russia to freedom of self-determination, including the right to secede and form independent states;
(3) Abolition of all national and national-religious privileges and restrictions whatsoever;
(4) Free development for national minorities and ethographic groups inhabiting the territory of Russia.

All concrete decrees devolving therefrom will be worked out immediately after the constitution of a Committee for Nationality Affairs.

It was "A Revolution of Oppressed Classes and Oppressed Peoples," a *Pravda* editorial hastened to assert on November 18. "A new page in the history of the peoples opened," the paper stated, and, in the same breath, accused the overthrown Provisional Government of having merely demonstrated its intention to introduce changes in the relationship between the dominating nation (the Russians) and the subjugated nations, but utterly failing to give real freedom to the "conquered" and "annexed" nations.

Thereupon official documents and statements of the same nature began pouring out in quick succession. On November 21, L. Trotsky, then People's Commissar for Foreign Affairs, addressed Allied ambassadors in Petrograd with a formal proposal for armistice and peace "without annexations and indemnities, based on national self-determination." [64] This he also repeated two days later in his notes to the ministers of neutral states in Petrograd.[65] Speaking before the Central Executive Committee of Soviets on international relations, Trotsky reiterated that the Bolshevik policy was dictated by the Decree on Peace.[66] On November 28, the Council of People's Commissars, in its *Appeal to the Peoples of the Belligerent Countries*,[67] envisaged a "people's peace . . . guaranteeing to each nation freedom for economic and cultural development."

The Brest-Litovsk Peace Conference (December 22, 1917–March 3, 1918) provided the Bolshevik government with an excellent opportunity to put all these principles in practice. A. Ioffe, Chairman of the Russian Delegation, stated at the outset[68] that the only principles of a democratic peace, which would be equally acceptable to all, were those enunciated in the Decree on Peace. He immediately proposed, in the name of the Russian Delegation, "six points" as the basis for negotiations (points 5 and 6 are omitted as irrelevant to this study):

> (1) Not to allow any forcible annexation of territory seized during the war. Troops occupying these territories to be withdrawn in the shortest possible time.
> (2) To restore in full the political independence of nations deprived of their independence during the present war.
> (3) National groups not enjoying political independence before the war to be guaranteed an opportunity to decide freely by means of a referendum whether to adhere to any given state or to be an independent state. This referendum to be so organized as to guarantee complete freedom of voting for the entire population of the given territory, not excluding emigrants and refugees.
> (4) In regard to territories inhabited by several nationalities, the right of minorities to be protected by special laws, guaranteeing them cultural national independence and, as far as practicable, administrative autonomy.

The Russian delegation also wanted both contracting parties to agree to the principle that it was not permissible for a more powerful state to exert indirect pressure upon the weaker state by means of economic boycott, economic subjugation, imposed commercial treaties, customs agreements infringing freedom of commerce of third states, and sea blockade with no direct military objectives.

After this opening, the Russian delegation enumerated its more concrete objectives. The foremost among them was the withdrawal of German, Austro-Hungarian, Bulgarian, and Turkish troops from Poland, Kurland, and other territories that fell to the Quadruple Alliance during the war. Russia was willing to withdraw her troops from Austro-Hungarian, Turkish, and Persian territories she had occupied in the course of military operations. The whole proposal, formulated as Article I of the Peace Treaty, was based on public statements of all participants

MAP NO. 1

PREMATURE RECOGNITION OF THE BALTIC SOVIET REPUBLICS

The map shows inhabited points in or near Estonia, Latvia, and Lithuania occupied by Red troops on respective dates of the recognition of Soviet Governments of the three republics by Russia. Frontiers drawn according to peace treaties with Russia. A thin line—the farthest advance of Red troops in 1919.

at the Conference that they had no designs for conquest and that they desired to conclude a peace without annexations.[69]

As far as the Baltic provinces were concerned, the military situation at the beginning of negotiations was such that Germany held all of Lithuania and Kurland as well as Riga, Iekabpils, and Daugavpils in Livonia and the Estonian islands, while Russia had retained possession of the rest of Livonia and Estonia. The river Daugava served as the dividing line between the Russian and the German zones of administration (cf. map).

The German delegation became immediately aware that Russia was offering a very poor deal for Germany; she was not yielding anything, while Germany was requested to give up considerable territory and move her troops back for hundreds of miles at some places. Von Kühlmann, Chairman of the German Delegation, flatly refused to accept the Russian draft of Article I on the ground that various representative bodies in Lithuania, Kurland, and parts of Livonia and Estonia had expressed the desire to become fully independent and secede from Russia. Von Kühlmann thereupon submitted his own draft of Article I by which Russia was to accept such declarations as "an expression of the popular will" and to draw consequences arising therefrom, i.e., renounce all claims to the German-occupied territories.[70]

The two divergent drafts set off a prolonged and at times bitter debate in a committee trying to iron out the differences of interpretation. A. Ioffe and L. Trotsky, who succeeded each other as Chairmen of the Russian delegation, refused to accept the validity of any decisions taken by "the groups of people subjected to military occupation"; evacuation of foreign troops was an absolute prerequisite for freedom of expression of the popular will; only the expression of desire based on complete freedom of voting, with no foreign troops present, was genuine.[71]

To reinforce their hand during the negotiations, the Russians brought along a number of "consultants on nationality problems." One of them, P. Stucka, subsequently Chairman of the Soviet Government of Latvia, left no trace of his activity in the Russian transcript of peace negotiations (nor is there any trace left by the Lithuanian Delegation, brought along by German negotiators to reinforce their hand).[72] Yet another Soviet "consultant" was much more active. V. Mickevicius-Kapsukas, Commissar for Lithuanian Affairs at the People's Commissariat for Nationality Affairs, submitted a lengthy statement. He denounced everybody in Lithuania trying to speak in the name of the Lithuanian people. The National Council of Lithuania (*Taryba*) in Vilnius was for him "an organ created with direct participation of occupation authorities." Mickevicius-Kapsukas also drew up a list of demands, which he regarded as an absolute prerequisite for genuine self-determination of the Lithuanian people:

> (1) Immediate withdrawal of German troops and gendarmery after the conclusion of peace with Russia, as well as closing down of all agencies established by occupation authorities;
> (2) Transfer of all administration to the local population;
> (3) Guarantee to the toiling masses of full freedom of speech, press, assembly, and unions;
> (4) Immediate repatriation of all inhabitants of Lithuania who had been forcibly expelled or evacuated or who had fled from the combat zone.[73]

If the Russians considered these demands to constitute an absolute prerequisite for self-determination of the Lithuanian people in 1918, why was their attitude entirely different in 1940? For then, just as in 1918, the Lithuanian people had to determine their future relations with another state in the presence of the latter's troops and police and deprived of freedom of speech, press, assembly, and unions. The only difference was that the Soviets had taken the place of the Germans.

In view of the Russian insistence on unconditional evacuation of German-occupied Lithuania, Kurland, and parts of Livonia and Estonia, and no word about the evacuation of the Russian-held parts of Livonia and Estonia, von Kühlmann asked Ioffe point-blank whether or not Russia would reciprocate. He argued that the withdrawal of Russian troops from Livonia and Estonia would enable the local population to give expression to its desire for reunification with the compatriots on the German side, and that the withdrawal would preclude military pressure on voting and provide for the widest-possible implementation of democratic principles. The Russian reply, given by Ioffe, was immediate and emphatic:

> The Russian government has repeatedly acknowledged the right of all peoples, without any exceptions, to freedom of self-determination. The need for a complete absence of foreign troops in the given territories— foreign with respect to the given people—has been considered as an essential prerequisite for such freedom of expression of desire. Hence, as far as the Provinces of Livonia, Kurland, and Estonia are concerned, the Russian government would undoubtedly apply the same principle, the implementation of which it demands of all those recognizing the principle of genuine and free self-determination of peoples.[74]

Possibly the Russians would not have agreed so quickly to unconditional withdrawal of their troops, had they not been mistakenly dead sure of pro-Russian sentiments among the Estonians and the Latvians in the Russian administration zone. M. Pokrovsky, a member of the Russian Delegation, had no doubt they would express the desire to join the Russian Federated Republic. He based his opinion on what the numerous spokesmen for the Estonian and Latvian popular masses had stated on various occasions.[75]

It may be pointed out that the Bolsheviks remained true to Pokrovsky's argument even after the Brest-Litovsk Peace Conference. *Izvestiia* of December 25, 1918, for example, was certain that the Latvian, Lithuanian, and Estonian proletariat had no separatist goals or desires and that it would be unanimous in favoring a merger with Soviet Russia.

L. Trotsky, Chairman of the Russian delegation after January 10, 1918, even went so far as to renounce all historical claims to the Baltic provinces. This is his statement:

> From the fact that the occupied areas formerly belonged to the Russian Empire, the present Russian government does not draw any conclusions which would impose upon the inhabitants of these areas any political or juridical obligations in regard to the Russian Republic. We undertake not to coerce these areas, either directly or indirectly, to accept any specific form of political organization and not to infringe their independence by means of any customs or military conventions concluded before they have time to complete their organization on the basis of political self-determination of peoples living there.[76]

L. Kamenev, another member of the Russian delegation, repeated Trotsky's words and added that the old frontiers of the Tsarist Empire had fallen together with Tsarism and that new frontiers for those wishing to secede from Russia would be determined by the free decision of the people concerned.[77]

The Quadruple Alliance delegates took notice of these two declarations and included them in the Brest-Litovsk Peace Treaty signed on March 3, 1918. Russia was forced to renounce sovereignty to all German-occupied territories. The Treaty also stipulated:

> No obligations whatever toward Russia shall devolve upon the territories referred to arising from the fact that they formerly belonged to Russia.[78]

Abandonment of historical rights to the former Baltic provinces subsequently was confirmed in several documents. First, there was the Decree issued by the Council of People's Commissars on August 29, 1918. It abrogated partition agreements between Russia, on one side, and Germany and Austria, on the other, in regard to Poland. Art. 3 of the Decree read:

> All agreements and acts concluded by the Government of the former Russian Empire with the Governments of the Kingdom of Prussia and the Austro-Hungarian Empire referring to the partition of Poland are irrevocably annulled by the present Decree, since they are contrary to the principle of self-determination of peoples and to the revolutionary-legal conceptions of the Russian people.[79]

Neither Latvia nor Estonia was affected in any way by the terms of this Decree. Lithuania was, however, since the Treaty of 1795 between Russia and Prussia provided for the partition not only of Poland proper, but also of the Grand Duchy of Lithuania, at that time constitutionally associated with Poland.

Renunciation of historical rights to Lithuania was reconfirmed in another document, with the only difference that both Latvia and Estonia were included this time. It was contained in the resolution of the Central Executive Committee of December 23, 1918, granting recognition of independence to the Soviet Republics of Estonia, Latvia, and Lithuania. It read in part:

> Before the Soviet Republics of Estonia, Latvia, and Lithuania, created by the revolutionary struggle of the proletarian and peasant masses, the Central Executive Committee once more declares that the fact of these countries having previously formed part of the old Tsarist Empire imposes on them no obligation whatsoever.[80]

Renunciation was once again reconfirmed in 1920, on the occasion of signing peace treaties with the three democratic Baltic republics after they had repulsed the invading Soviet troops. The pertinent parts of the respective peace treaties carried slightly different wording in each case, but the meaning was the same:

Art. 2 of the Russo-Estonian Peace Treaty of February 2, 1920—

> Russia unreservedly recognizes the independence and autonomy of the State of Estonia and renounces voluntarily and for ever all rights of sovereignty formerly held by Russia over the Estonian people by virtue of the former legal situation and by virtue of international treaties, which, in respect of such rights, shall henceforth lose their force. No obligation toward Russia devolves upon the Estonian people and territory from the fact that Estonia was formerly part of Russia.[81]

Art. 1 of the Russo-Lithuanian Peace Treaty of July 12, 1920—

> Russia recognizes without reservation the sovereign rights of the Lithuanian State with all the juridical consequences arising from such recognition and voluntarily and for all time abandons all the sovereign rights of Russia over the Lithuanian people and their territory. The fact of the past subjection of Lithuania to Russia does not impose on the Lithuanian nation and their territory any liabilities whatever toward Russia.[82]

Art. 2 of the Russo-Latvian Peace Treaty of August 11, 1920—

> Russia unreservedly recognizes the independence and sovereigny of the Latvian State and voluntarily and irrevocably renounces all sovereign rights over the Latvian people and territory which formerly belonged to Russia under the then existing constitutional law as well as under international treaties, which, in the sense here indicated, shall in the future cease to be

valid. The previous status of subjection of Latvia to Russia shall not entail any obligations toward Russia on the part of the Latvian people or territory.[83]

Twenty years later (August 1, 1940), V. Molotov, then People's Commissar for Foreign Affairs, claimed that Russia had acted under duress while signing the peace treaties with the Baltic Republics in 1920. Speaking before the Seventh Session of the Supreme Soviet, he stated that nineteen twentieths of those people used to belong to the USSR, but that the western imperialists had separated them from it at the time the USSR "was weak militarily." [84]

Perhaps it was a slip of Molotov's tongue; but in 1920 there existed no USSR at all—it did not come into formal being before 1923. This is irrelevant, however. More important is the irrefutable fact that, even if Russia (RSFSR) was acting under duress in 1920, such could not have been the case in 1918, after the Central Executive Committee renounced all claims to Lithuania, Latvia, and Estonia. For the Decree of December 23, 1918, stated:

. . . the fact of these countries having previously formed part of the old Tsarist Empire imposes on them no obligation whatsoever.

No one forced Russia to make such a declaration. She did it voluntarily. It served propaganda purposes well, and it seemed impossible that Russia would fail in setting up three puppet republics on her western frontier. A status similar to that accorded to Soviet Lithuania, Latvia, and Estonia in 1940 was in the offing in 1918.

Molotov chose not to speak about it, however. Nor did he speak about the fact that the loss of the Baltic provinces was regarded by the prominent Bolsheviks in 1920 as of no great consequence. Lenin, for example, tried to convince the Fourth Congress of Soviets (March 14–18, 1918) that the interests of socialism and the preservation of the Soviet Republic had a higher claim than the interests of the right of nations to self-determination or the liberation of Poland, Lithuania, and Kurland.[85] Lenin, reportedly, treated the Baltic provinces like mere pawns in his struggle with Trotsky. Latvia and Estonia were worth losing, in his opinion, "for the sake of a good peace with Trotsky." [86]

Trotsky, too, claimed at the Brest-Litovsk Peace Conference (although possibly for propaganda purposes only) that the separation of Poland and all Baltic provinces from Russia was not likely to create any danger to the Russian Republic; the only thing which counted was "the will of the people living in those territories." [87]

Chapter Two

SELF-DETERMINATION IN PRACTICE

The Brest-Litovsk peace treaty negotiations resounded with Bolshevik declarations about the right of people to self-determination, nonrecognition of puppet governments and institutions, complete freedom of voting in the absence of foreign troops, Russia's readiness to withdraw from Estonia and Livonia, renunciation of historical claims, etc. And yet the German delegation found it necessary to tell its Russian counterpart that Russia demanded the recognition of the right to self-determination in a form such as was unknown in their own country. The delegation specifically referred to Bolshevik repressions against national movements in the Ukraine and White Russia.[1]

The Ukrainian *Rada* (anti-Bolshevik) delegation made a blistering attack against Russia in general and the Bolsheviks in particular. M. Liubinsky, Chairman, accused all Russian governments of complete solidarity in one respect only: their greedy desire to strangle the nascent national movements and to subjugate everybody to their rule. Yet the Bolshevik government received an especially rough treatment:

> The Bolshevik government has proclaimed the principle of national self-determination only to fight its application in practice yet with greater resolution. The Bolshevik government, which disperses the Constitutional Assembly and relies on the bayonets of the hired Red Army men, will never dare to implement in Russia the just principles of self-determination . . . It is only the fear of the spreading national revolution that forces the Bolsheviks to declare, with all the inborn demagogy of theirs, both in Russia and here, at the Peace Conference, the freedom of unrestricted right of peoples to self-determination, including secession.[2]

Estonia was a special case. On January 24, 1918, *Izvestiia,* seeking for a good example, enumerated Poland, Lithuania, Latvia, and the Ukraine as countries which came under Lenin's definition of annexation. "These territories were forcibly annexed and forcibly detained by Tsarist Russia," the paper pointed out. Strangely enough, Estonia was not included among the territories fitting under the definition. The reason was very simple: while all the enumerated countries were under German occupation, Estonia was not. In fact, the Bolsheviks had high hopes by the end of January 1918 that Estonia would soon become one of the constituent parts of the Russian Federated Republic.

This must also have been the motive behind the resolution of the Petrograd Soviet on January 1, 1918. The resolution repeated the slogans about the free expression of the will of the population, non-recognition of decisions taken in the presence of foreign troops, repatriation of evacuees, etc., but only Poland, Lithuania, and Kurland were included among the provinces where the Soviet "stood for effective self-determination." [3] Estonia's case was considered settled.

Bolshevik duplicity in the matter of recognition of the right to self-determination in practice was in full conformity with their theoretical attitude toward the problem. Lenin, for one, introduced qualifications of the right as such at the very beginning of discussion of the problem of self-determination.

Writing in *Iskra* in 1903, Lenin gave support to the RSDRP promise to provide in the constitution of the future democratic republic of Russia for "the right to self-determination of all peoples entering into composition of the state"; he did not neglect, however, to leave an escape clause:

> Unconditional acknowledgment of the struggle for the freedom of the right to national self-determination does not obligate us [the Social Democrats] to support all demands for it . . . A Marxist cannot acknowledge the demand for national independence unconditionally.[4]

Lenin even suggested a substitute for national self-determination: "self-determination of the proletariat." He called on fellow Social Democrats to work toward this latter objective. Only in isolated cases was there any support to be given to demands aimed at creating a new "class" state.

The 1913 RSDRP Conference in Poronino took up the problem of national self-determination as well. It confirmed that the RSDRP must defend unqualifiedly the right to self-determination, but it also introduced a qualification in the same resolution:

> The question of the right of peoples to self-determination (i.e., constitutional provisions ensuring a completely unfettered and democratic manner of deciding on the question of secession) may not be confused with the question

of expediency of secession for a given nation. This question must be solved by the Social Democratic Party completely independently in every individual case, bearing in mind the interests of the whole social development and the interests of the class struggle of the proletariat for socialism.[5]

Commenting on this resolution, Lenin stated that the recognition of the right to self-determination, including secession, did not bar propaganda and agitation against secession. He went so far as to proclaim his Party's and his own opposition to secession:

> Secession is not at all our plan. We do not by any means advocate secession. In general, we are against secession . . . Class-conscious workers do not advocate secession . . . We, Social Democrats, are inimical to all kinds of nationalism.[6]

While agreeing that the right to self-determination implied the right to secession and to complete freedom of agitation in favor of secession, Lenin wanted to convince the "toiling strata" that secession was by no means advantageous to them:

> Class-conscious workers do not propagate secession; they are aware of advantages of large states and unity of large masses of workers . . . the other conditions being the same, large states can solve much more successfully than the small ones all the problems associated with economic progress and the tasks evolving from the struggle of the proletariat against the bourgeoisie.[7]

In World War I Lenin worked out a formula for a "voluntary union" to be suggested instead of secession. He repeatedly advised the Social Democrats in small and/or oppressed nations to stress in their propaganda the principle of "voluntary union" among the nations and among the workers of oppressed and oppressor nations:

> The proletarian party strives to create as large a state as possible, for this is of advantage to the toilers; it strives to bring closer and merge further the nations, yet it wants to attain this goal not by force, but only by voluntary, fraternal union between the workers and masses of toilers of all nations . . . We want a free union and, therefore, we have to acknowledge the freedom of secession (no union can be termed free if there is no freedom of secession).[8]

Here Lenin was merely following in the footsteps of Russian liberals. They did not oppose separatist tendencies among the non-Russians, in the belief the latter would never go so far as to seek secession from Russia. They felt the non-Russians were fighting against Tsarist autocracy and national persecution, not against Russia as such. They never held it possible the non-Russians would place their own national interests above the rights and interests of the whole of Russia after the overthrow of autocracy.[9]

The Menshevik faction of the RSDRP, as an example, included in their 1906 Election Platform to the State *Duma* the demand:

All peoples living in Russia shall enjoy equal rights and freedom of self-determination. There is no place in free Russia for a forcible oppression of peoples by each other.[10]

As Lenin spoke in favor of "voluntary union" among the peoples, he at the same time advocated fighting against narrow nationalism and separatism and for subordination of private interests to common interests. Education of workers in the spirit of "indifference" to national distinctions, was his idea. He believed that mankind would eventually come to the unavoidable stage of the merger of nations. This would not occur, however, immediately, but after a transition period necessitating the acknowledgment of the freedom of secession.[11] Lenin was convinced that democratization of Russia would stop the away-from-Russia drive:

> The closer the democratic system of the state to a complete freedom of secession, the less frequent and strong actually will be the urge to secession . . . The more democratic the Russian Republic, the greater success with which it is organized into a republic of Soviets of workers' and peasants' deputies, the greater will be the force of voluntary attraction of masses of toilers of all nations to such a republic . . . where the state boundary runs is of no consequence to us; it is important that the union between the toilers of all nations be preserved for a fight against the bourgeoisie of any nation.[12]

So sure was Lenin of the infallibility of this theory that he strongly urged the Seventh Conference of the RSDRP (May 12, 1917) to come out in open support of complete freedom of Finland. He saw nothing wrong if Finland seceded. And he believed Finland would actually abstain from secession if given such freedom. "Only then will they have trust in Russian democracy," Lenin argued.[13]

Stalin's views were identical with those of Lenin. He also claimed that the acknowledgment of the right to self-determination was "a way toward a genuine union of peoples" and that only a voluntary union of peoples was both genuine and lasting. It seemed to him that nine tenths of all the peoples formerly oppressed by Tsarism would show no desire to secede from Russia when Tsarism was overthrown. The right to self-determination was to be enjoyed by the toiling masses, not by the bourgeoisie, and thus would become a means of struggle for socialism—the primary objective. He even disapproved of cultural and national autonomy. These he found to be artificial, nonviable, and to lead toward the ultimate evil—nationalism.[14]

Stalin agreed, point by point, with Lenin that neither autonomy nor secession were to be sought by the toilers:

> A nation has the right to arrange its life on autonomous lines. It even has the right to secede. But this does not mean that it should do so under

all circumstances, that autonomy or secession will everywhere and always be advantageous for a nation, for the majority of its population, for the toiling strata . . . We are by no means for dismemberment of large states into small ones; for it is obvious that the merger of small states into large ones is one of prerequisites facilitating the implementation of socialism.[15]

Stalin repeated the same line of thought at the Seventh Conference of the RSDRP in 1917. In fact, he paraphrased the text of the RSDRP resolution on the same subject passed in 1913. This time Stalin said:

> The question of the right of nations to secede freely must not be confused with the question that a nation must necessarily secede at any given moment. This latter question must be settled by the party of the proletariat in each particular case independently, according to circumstances. When we recognize the right of oppressed peoples to secede, the right to determine their political destiny, we do not hereby settle the question of whether particular nations should secede from the Russian state at the given moment. I may recognize the right of a nation to secede, but it may or may not exercise that right, according to circumstances. Thus we are at liberty to agitate for or against secession, according to the interests of the proletariat, of the proletarian revolution . . . for this reason, the question of the recognition of the right to secession must not be confused with the expediency of secession in any given circumstances.[16]

In its resolution of May 12, 1917, the Conference gave unqualified approval of Lenin's and Stalin's position on secession:

> The question of the right of nations to secede freely must not be confused with the question of expediency of secession for a given nation at any given moment. This latter question must be settled by the party of the proletariat in each particular case entirely independently, from the viewpoint of the interests of the social development and the interests of the class struggle of the proletariat for socialism.[17]

The Conference also rejected the notion of "cultural-national" autonomy. It stated that the interests of the working class demanded merger of workers in common political, professional, cooperative, educational, and other proletarian organizations.

A reflection on Lenin's and Stalin's views on the advantages of "a voluntary union" can be found in the resolution of the Conference of Front and Rear Military organization of the RSDRP, meeting on June 20–July 6, 1917:

> Only a resolute and irrevocable acknowledgment of the right of nations to self-determination—acknowledgment by deeds, not only by words—could strengthen brotherly trust among the peoples of Russia and thereby pave the way toward their real merger voluntary, not forced—into political entity.[18]

Similarly, the *Declaration of the Rights of the Peoples of Russia,* promulgated on November 15, 1917, contained several references to "voluntary and honest cooperation," "honest and lasting union," etc. The declaration read:

Only as the result of such union can the workers and peasants of Russia be welded into a revolutionary power capable of resisting all attempts on the part of the imperialist-annexationist bourgeoisie.[19]

The Third Congress of the Soviets (January 23–31, 1918) also "whole-heartedly" approved the policy of the People's Commissars on nationality problems based on the principle of self-determination of nations "in the sense of self-determination of the toiling masses of all nationalities living in Russia." In addition, the Congress expressed hope that the Soviet government would transform the former Russian Empire into "a brotherly union of Russian Soviet Republics, freely united on federation principles." [20]

During the debate, Bolshevik delegates openly called the nationalist movement a threat to the very existence of the Soviet government. They claimed that the nationalist movement was progressive and deserved support only when it was directed against imperialism and reaction. The bourgeoisie was accused of exploiting the principle of self-determination to carry on counterrevolutionary propaganda and build up a White Guard. Delegate E. Preobrazhensky was particularly outspoken in his opposition to self-determination:

Now that Russia is a socialist republic and the champion of the great ideal of liberation of oppressed classes over the world, there is no longer any reason for secession from Great Russia . . . Insofar as bourgeoisie gives chauvinistic and imperialistic interpretation to the principle of self-determination and uses it to detract the ignorant masses of the border nationalities from class war, the Soviet government will do all in its power to prevent its application.[21]

Nearly a year later Stalin, in an article in *Pravda* of November 6, 1918, practically repeated Preobrazhensky's words. He emphasized that bourgeois-nationalists had interpreted the right of nations to self-determination "as the right of bourgeoisie in the border regions to assume power and misuse the February [1917] revolution for the formation of 'their own' nationalist state."

In general, Stalin was very much against the "revolutionary bourgeois-nationalist" governments of Estonia, Latvia, and Lithuania. He time and again condemned them in *Zhizn' natsional'nostei,* the mouthpiece of the People's Commissariat for Nationality Affairs, of which he was in charge.[22]

Commenting on the debate at the Third Congress of Soviets, *Izvestiia* gleefully reported on January 29 that the speakers had called the principle of self-determination "antiquated" and had urged the Soviet government to oppose decentralization tendencies "which would make an independent republic out of every *guberniia* (province)."

Izvestiia, in general, was pursuing its own peculiar line of reporting on the attitude of the Baltic peoples toward Russia. Thus, on January 28, the paper said that representatives of Polish and Lithuanian Social Democrats had assured the Central Executive Committee they had no desire to secede from Russia. Two days later there was a report from Riga claiming that the Latvian proletariat had expressed at no time and at no place any desire to secede from Russia and have its "tiny country fenced in by the boundaries of an independent state." A week later (February 7) another report from Riga repeated that the Democrats in Latvia "had no other desire, but to remain united with the Russian Soviet Republic." And so forth. The tendency was clear enough.

A Soviet historian of that period has given the following reasons for the Russian desire to restrict the away-from-Russia drive.

> Interests of socialism demanded that the Ukraine as well as the other national border regions of Russia remain united with revolutionary Russia . . . Separation of border regions from Russia would have undermined the economic and political might of the young Soviet Republic, the focus of the world-wide proletarian revolution and the mainstay of the national liberation movement both in the west and in the east. Central Soviet Russia would not have been able to survive for any length of time without assistance on the part of the border regions supplying her with raw materials, fuel, and food products. The border regions, on secession from Russia and deprived of Central Russia's political, military, and organizational help, would have unavoidably become enslaved by international imperialism. This is the reason why the demand of the bourgeois nationalists for separation of the border regions from Central Russia was counterrevolutionary throughout.[23]

To be sure, there were people, besides the German Peace Delegation at Brest-Litovsk, who saw duplicity in the Bolshevik proclamation of the principle of self-determination and its application. One of the delegates at the Third Congress of Soviets, L. Martov, a Menshevik, stated his bewilderment that the Bolsheviks were demanding a referendum in the German-occupied Poland, Kurland, and Lithuania and insisting that in the Russian-held Ukraine, Finland, and the Caucasus only the toilers were to be granted the right to vote. He saw in it duplicity and contradiction. "Why not let each nationality have what it likes?" he wondered. Each nationality, he argued, should be allowed to settle its own affairs without any outside interference.[24]

A reply to L. Martov was given by Lenin long ago. Lenin was aware of criticism to that effect in 1916. Yet he dismissed it nonchalantly:

> There is no "contradiction" between the propaganda for freedom of secession for peoples and a firm resolution to implement such freedom when we assume the rule, on the one hand, and the propaganda for rapprochement and merger of peoples, on the other; there cannot be any "contradiction." [25]

At the Seventh Conference of the RSDRP (May 12, 1917), Lenin repeated it even more emphatically:

> People refuse to comprehend that, in order to strengthen internationalism, there is no need to repeat the very same words; one has to stress in Russia the freedom of secession for oppressed nations and in Poland, the freedom of merger. Freedom of merger presupposes freedom of secession. We Russians have to stress [here] freedom of secession, but in Poland [we have to stress] freedom of merger.[26]

This, of course, equally applied to the Baltic peoples. The Bolsheviks were only biding their time. The revolution of November 7, 1917, furnished a convincing proof.

Having escaped German occupation and thus having remained under Russian administration until February 1918, the Estonians were the first among the Baltic peoples to discover from bitter experience that the Bolsheviks had no intention of letting them secede from Russia—whatever the resounding declarations to the contrary.[27]

The Bolshevik revolution found the Estonians enjoying territorial autonomy, accorded them by the *Decree on Temporary Organization of Administration and Local Self-government in the Province of Estonia* of April 12, 1917. The Decree, among other things, provided for administration through elected representatives of the Estonian people.

Elections to the Provincial Council (referred to by the Estonians as the National Council) took place on July 7–8. They furnished incontestable proof that the Bolsheviks enjoyed little popularity among the Estonian people—they won but 5 out of 62 seats. No wonder Bolshevik representatives offered strong opposition to the National Council, particularly after the latter began discussing the problem of outright secession from Russia and membership in a Balto-Scandian bloc instead. The Bolshevik faction even introduced a motion on the floor (October 9) requesting the Council to disown itself and proclaim new elections. The motion was rejected.

The Estonian Bolsheviks, however, scored a victory shortly thereafter by gaining control of the Estonian Soviets of Workers', Peasants', and Soldiers' Deputees. As soon as the Russian Bolsheviks seized power in Petrograd, the Tallinn Soviet, acting under the name of the Military Revolutionary Committee headed by J. Anvelt, declared itself the legal government of Estonia and took charge of the offices of the Commissioner of the Provisional Government.

In spite of this, the Estonian National Council and its agencies all over the country remained in Estonian hands, for they acted independently of the Provincial Commissioner. Seeing this situation, the Estonian Bolsheviks made an abortive attempt to destroy the authority of the National Council and its local agencies. The Council was notified on November 25 of the following decisions reached by the Executive Committee of the Estonian Soviets:

> The Executive Committee resolved on November 25, 1917, to dissolve the Provisional National Council of the Province of Estonia and to convene the Constituent Assembly on February 15; elections shall be held on January 21 and 22, 1918.
>
> The members of the Provisional Administration of the Province of Estonia shall stay on their posts and take care of the current affairs until the Constituent Assembly convenes.

In so acting, the Estonian Bolsheviks relied not on the Estonian people, who had decisively beaten them at the electoral polls on July 7–8, but on the Russian armed forces stationed in Tallinn. A Soviet-Estonian historian, J. Sepp, reviewing the events of that period from a perspective of three decades (1947) made the following admission in his book, *The Struggle for the Soviet Regime in Estonia 1917–1919:*

> The Estonian Soviets had a trustworthy force in the revolutionary sailors, soldiers, and numerous groups of the Red Guard. At the disposal of the Soviets there were the ships of the Baltic Fleet and the cannons of the fortress.

The official *History of the Estonian SSR,* published in 1952, likewise admits that the Soviet regime prevailed in Estonia in 1918–1919 only wherever Soviet troops were in control. It was the Red troops that held the Estonian Soviets in saddle. Under these conditions, widespread strikes in Tallinn as an expression of a popular rejection of the Soviet rule mattered little. It was the Red troops that swung to the Bolshevik side the elections to the Consituent Assembly of Russia on November 27–29, when the Estonian province also voted. With the ranks of voters swollen by Russian ship crews, and the workers at the naval bases (which even the Soviet sources admit readily),[28] the election results showed that 40 per cent of all ballots cast were in favor of the Bolshevik ticket. It was quite a change compared to the results of the July 7–8 elections. It seemed as if the Bolshevik popularity had soared tremendously since then.

The elections to the Constituent Assembly of Estonia on January 21–22, 1918, with only the Estonians casting the ballots, furnished proof, however, that this was not the case. Despite intense propaganda in favor of the Bolshevik candidates, the first election results indicated that they would remain in the minority, polling not more than one-third of the votes cast. The Bolsheviks, unable to take such a defeat, canceled the elections after the first day of voting. The elections have remained taboo ever since for all Soviet historians.

The Estonian National Council was fully aware of popular sentiment at the time it received the notification of its dissolution by the

Executive Committee of the Estonian Soviets. As a reply, the Council resolved on November 28, 1917, to issue a proclamation to the Estonian people and to state in it the following:

> (1) The Estonian National Council proclaims itself the sole depository of supreme power in Estonia; its regulations and resolutions are obligatory in Estonia until the convocation of the Constituent Assembly, which shall be elected without delay by democratic suffrage; after having determined the form of government, it shall establish definitely the legislative and executive branches.
>
> (2) All regulations, orders, and edicts, without regard to their source, shall be considered effective in Estonia until the convocation of the Constituent Assembly only when published by the Estonian National Council; otherwise such acts shall not be followed.
>
> (3) During the intervals between its sessions, the Estonian National Council authorizes the Presidium of the National Council and the Committee of Elders, jointly with the Administration of the country as the representative of supreme power in Estonia, to issue and put into effect, pending their definitive confirmation by the National Council, urgent regulations and orders for the regulation of public life of the country.[29]

At the same time, an appeal was issued to Estonian soldiers in the Russian Army urging all comrades in arms to get their release and hurry home, with weapons, to join the Estonian regiments. On December 19 a divisional command headquarters was set up. Although numerically much inferior to the Bolshevik forces, the National Estonian Army was instrumental in preventing the Executive Committee of Soviets from taking over local administration in all places. In fact, the Soviets complained that, where "bourgeois" cavalry units were set up, they prevented local Soviets from performing their functions and that they were even releasing political prisoners.

By that time there were hundreds of political prisoners in jails and concentration camps. A state of siege was declared in all cities. Free movement of people was restricted. Freedom of the press was curtailed and censorship was introduced. No one dared to speak of self-determination of the Estonian people. What else could be expected if the Third Congress of the Estonian Soviets condemned in a resolution "the crazy idea of an independent Estonian state"? J. Anvelt, Chairman of the Executive Committee of the Estonian Soviets, likewise spoke disdainfully of "the silly home-bred idea of an independent Estonian state." In its motivation of the rejection of the idea of independence for Estonia, the Third Congress of the Estonian Soviets followed old Lenin's ideas on advantages of large states and the necessity to merge small states into "a single brotherly state." [30]

Petrograd was highly pleased with the course of events in Estonia. *Izvestiia* on January 14 joyfully reported that the Soviets were gradually liquidating the organs of Estonian autonomy and that the National

Council and the majority of district councils already had been abolished. This was the reason why the Russian delegates at the Brest-Litovsk Peace Conference were so confident that the Estonians would express the desire to join Russia. By mid-February everything was ready to make the joining official.

Russian designs upon Estonia came into the open after the announcement of a *Plan for the Establishment of the Estonian Workers' Commune.* As announced in *Izvestiia,*[31] the plan was to operate as follows:

> (1) The Estonian Workers' Commune is an autonomous part of the Russian Soviet Republic. Relations with the Russian Soviet Republic and questions regarding external affairs of the Estonian Commune shall be decided by agreement with the central power of the Russian Soviet Republic.
> (2) The Estonian Workers' Commune is fully autonomous in all local matters and has the unconditional right to secede from Russia, at any time and without requiring any agreement on the part of other nations and governments, and to unite with any other state or declare itself independent.

Since *Izvestiia* was the organ of the All-Russian Central Executive Committee of the Soviets, its plan represented more than a newspaper's private opinion. It should be pointed out, however, that neither *Izvestiia* nor the Central Executive Committee had thought of Lenin's views on constitutional changes, which were applicable to the Estonian people just as well as to any other people Lenin might have had in mind:

> The right of self-determination means that the question must be decided upon by the parliament, the seim, or the referendum of the seceding minority, rather than by the parliament of the center.[32]

Of course, the Central Executive Committee could have complied with Lenin's requirement for an approval of the plan by the "seceding minority"; its Estonian stooges would have been more than willing to do so. Yet such an approval would have been contrary to the conditions spelled out only a few months earlier in the Decree on Peace where it was stated quite clearly that any decision regarding constitutional forms of political existence of a nation must be made under the condition that the troops of the more powerful nation are completely withdrawn and that no pressure is brought to bear upon the weaker nation. This was not the case in Estonia, where even the Soviet historians admit the decisive role played by the Red troops in 1917–1918.

Izvestiia's plan would have meant a complete abandonment of the idea of an independent Estonia. The declarative paragraph about the freedom of secession was surely included in the plan as a dead letter. One has only to think of the Constitution of the Soviet Union in which all member-republics likewise enjoy the empty right of withdrawal. For there can be little doubt that an attempt of the Estonian Workers' Commune to leave the Russian Soviet Republic would have been dealt with mercilessly in 1918 or at any time thereafter, for that matter. The revenge incurred by various lesser nationalities in the Soviet Union in World War II for expression of their desire for freedom is an instructive and terrifying example. So is the abortive anti-Soviet revolution in Hungary in 1956.

The Estonians, under different political conditions, might possibly have been satisfied—at least temporarily—with *Izvestiia's* plan. For as recently as November 28, 1917, the Estonian National Council had endorsed drafting a bill by which the future administration and local government in Estonia was to be based on the principle of Estonia's remaining "an autonomous part of a democratic federated Russian republic." By mid-February 1918 this no longer satisfied the Estonians —they were seeking complete independence.

Negotiations to that effect went on among the Estonian political parties continuously, and culminated in an agreement of January 14, 1918. All of them, with the exception of communists, resolved to make the following statement:

> We stress first of all that the entire Estonian nation considers itself sovereign and alone authorized to determine the political fate of the country, independently of the interests of great powers. On this basis, we consider a complete national independence of Estonia as necessary and as the only normal basis upon which the nation could determine its future.[33]

A similar declaration was issued on January 23. Then, on February 24, the Committee of Elders of the Estonian National Council issued a manifesto to the Estonian people, in effect a Declaration of Independence:

> As of today, Estonia, within her historical and ethnic boundaries, is proclaimed an independent democratic republic . . . The Supreme governmental power is vested in the Estonian Liberation Committee, set up by the Estonian National Council.[34]

Neither the Soviet-Estonian police nor the Russian troops were able to prevent issuance of the Manifesto. They were in full retreat before the advancing Germans. Tallinn had to be abandoned on February 23.

In Latvia the course of events approximated that in Estonia. Only the scale was much smaller, owing to the fact that but a part of Latvia proper remained exposed to Bolshevik infiltration (specifically, Livonia without Riga, Iekabpils, and Daugavpils and the Latvian-inhabited portion of Lattgalia). Here the Provincial Council of Livonia was taken over by the Soviets of Workers and Landless Peasants. Local Soviets took charge of administration in smaller localities. Lawlessness and terror spread. Expropriation made economic conditions insecure. Revolutionary tribunals filled the jails and passed death sentences on a frightening scale. Bourgeoisie and intellectuals sought escape in Petrograd.[35] The German advance, beginning on February 18, cut short this reign of terror.

By February 24 the Central Executive Committee of the Soviet of Workers', Soldiers', and Peasants' Deputies was ready to talk peace with the Germans. In less than a week the Brest-Litovsk Peace Treaty was signed.

Chapter Three

A MISSED GOAL: THE SOVIET SEA

The first Bolshevik attempt to get a foothold in Estonia and Livonia ended on March 3, 1918, with the signature of the Brest-Litovsk Peace Treaty. The Treaty exacted heavy tribute from Russia in terms of lost territory, population, and industrial and agricultural potential. It also decided, after prolonged negotiations, the fate of the Baltic peoples. Articles III and VI of the Treaty had direct bearing on the Baltic peoples:

> Article III: The territories lying to the west of the line agreed upon by the contracting parties [i.e., according to Annex I to the Treaty, all of Lithuania and Kurland, the cities of Riga, Iekabpils, and Daugavpils in Livonia, and the Estonian islands], which formerly belonged to Russia, will no longer be subject to Russian sovereignty . . . No obligations whatever toward Russia shall devolve upon the territories referred to from the fact that they formerly belonged to Russia. Russia refrains from all interference in the internal relations of these territories. Germany and Austria-Hungary purpose to determine the future status of these territories in agreement with their population.
>
> Article VI: . . . Estonia and Livonia will likewise, without delay, be cleared of Russian troops and the Russian Red Guard . . . Estonia and Livonia will be occupied by a German police force until security is insured by proper national institutions and until public order has been established. Russia will liberate at once all arrested or deported inhabitants of Estonia and Livonia and insure the safe return of all deported Estonians and Livonians.[1]

The Russian delegation at Brest-Litovsk was angry. G. Sokol'nikov, the Chairman, called the peace treaty "dictated at the point of sword . . . concluded in unprecedented circumstances, in an atmosphere of violence . . . forced upon Revolutionary Russia to accept with her teeth clenched." And he added ominously:

> We have no doubt that the triumph of imperialism and militarism over the international proletarian revolution will prove to be temporary and ephemeral.[2]

This was also the attitude of Lenin at the Fourth Congress of Soviets (March 14–18, 1918), where he spoke in favor of ratification of the Brest-Litovsk Peace Treaty. Lenin called the peace "a humiliating one," but he saw no way out:

> We had to sign the peace because of the breathing spell it affords, however brief and slight . . . We all know, whatever you say, we have no army; and no gestures will save us from the necessity to retreat, gain time, and let the army rest . . . We shall be able not only heroically to advance, but also heroically to retreat and wait until the international proletariat comes to our assistance; then we shall be able to launch another socialist revolution, but this time on a world-wide scale.[3]

But while waiting for victory over imperialism and militarism, Russia had to make further concessions. Less than six months after the signature of the Brest-Litovsk Peace Treaty, A. Ioffe, Diplomatic Representative of the Russian Socialist Federated Republic in Berlin and erstwhile Chairman of the Russian delegation at Brest-Litovsk, affixed his signature to a supplementary treaty (August 27, 1918). It concerned the fate of Estonia and Livonia, which now Germany wanted to have determined along the same lines as for Kurland and Lithuania. Article VII of the supplementary treaty read:

> Russia, taking account of the condition at present existing in Estonia and Livonia, renounces sovereignty over these regions as well as all interference in their internal affairs. Their future fate shall be decided in agreement with their inhabitants. No obligations of any kind towards Russia shall accrue to Estonia and Livonia through their former union with Russia.[4]

Yet Lenin was right about the brief duration of the breathing spell: the collapse of the German war machine was only eight months away when he made his prediction; by the end of 1918 the Red troops were to spill into Estonia, Latvia, and Lithuania in the wake of retreating German troops. Meanwhile preparations for invasion were going on unabated in Russia. In fact, they had been going on practically since the next day after the signature of the Brest-Litovsk Peace Treaty.

A Commissariat for Latvian Affairs, an organic division of the People's Commissariat for Nationality Affairs, established upon a decision of the Second Congress of Soviets in 1917 and headed by J. Stalin, was set up on March 24. The Estonian Section was organized on May 11. And the Commissariat for Lithuanian Affairs, in operation since December 8, 1917, greatly intensified its activity.[5]

The reasons for setting up these organizations were clearly outlined in a statement by the Commissariat for Lithuanian Affairs. It said that the Commissariat regarded the strengthening of the Soviet rule in Russia and propagation of such rule among the masses of Lithuanian refugees as one of its foremost objectives. The Commissariat maintained a training program for its agents, who then traveled to Lithuania. The goal was to have at least one such agent in every railroad car with refugees returning home. Newspapers, pamphlets, leaflets, and other printed material were smuggled across the border. All this was in flagrant violation of the noninterference clause in Article III of the Brest-Litovsk Peace Treaty.

On December 6, the Commissariat for Lithuanian Affairs appealed through *Izvestiia* to all specialists, urging them to go to Lithuania to help rebuild her shattered economic life. The call itself was premature, as there was no Soviet Lithuania at that time—either actually or on paper. It seemed, however, that all preparations for such an event were about complete. "The time comes closer," concluded the appeal, "for the workers and the poorest peasants to assume rule in Lithuania."

The parent-organization, the People's Commissariat for Nationality Affairs, did the same. Its leading personnel slipped into the German-occupied territories in order to be ready to take over command of the local Soviet governments and military operations when the time arrived. Surprisingly, many of those hardened Communists proved unreliable and joined forces with anti-proletarians. Such complaint was subsequently voiced by Z. Angarietis, Deputy Chairman of the Soviet Government of Lithuania.[6] On the other hand, Lithuanian units of the Russian Army, trying to reach their homeland with weapons, were disarmed.[7]

At the same time the Commissariat exerted strong pressure against war refugee organizations in Russia. Thus, the Supreme Council of Lithuanians in Russia, with its Executive Committee in Voronezh and branches in Petrograd, Moscow, and other cities, was dissolved on April 25.[8] Its identity cards issued to the Lithuanian refugees were declared null and void. All its property, correspondence, books, and documents were transferred to the Commissariat for Lithuanian Affairs. As a consequence, the latter came into possession of an excellent printing shop, from which subversive propaganda material soon began pouring out in large quantities.

The action against the Supreme Council of Lithuanians in Russia was officially motivated by the following considerations: (a) the Council was composed of reactionary, nationalist Lithuanian groups; (b) the Committee spoke in the name of a counter-revolutionary "Lithuanian Government" and entertained connections with the enemies of the

Soviet government; (c) it did not pay any attention to the Soviet government and issued passports valid for return to Lithuania.

To be sure, it was not the sole action of that sort performed by the People's Commissariat for Nationality Affairs. For one of the main purposes for which it was constituted was "to fight against nationalism in all its forms and aspects." [9] Consequently, it was instrumental in "unmasking and liquidating" many a "bourgeois-nationalist" government all over restive Russia; smashing nationalist-inspired revolts; closing down scores of "counterrevolutionary" institutions, agencies, organizations, newspapers, etc. No wonder; Stalin was at its head, and his attitude to national sentiments was well known.

Meanwhile, important changes in Russo-German relations were taking place. On November 9, German Emperor William II abdicated. The Armistice was signed on November 11, and on November 13 Russia revoked the Brest-Litovsk Peace Treaty "of violence and plunder . . . in its entirety and all its parts." [10] Cession of territories was abrogated. The toiling masses in Russia, Lithuania, Latvia, Estonia, etc., were called upon "to decide their own fate." Evacuation of all Russian territories under foreign occupation was requested. The "right of all toiling nations to self-determination" was reconfirmed, but an appeal was made to them "to form a brotherly alliance with the workers and peasants of Russia."

Soon thereafter the German troops, who had advanced to the Narva-Pskov-Polotsk-Mogilev line, began pulling out. The Red troops followed in their wake and did not stop when they reached the Estonian frontier on November 22. Here they met, however, with resolute resistance on the part of the Estonian defenders of their homeland. As war communiques published every day in *Izvestiia* show, it took a week to break through trenches and barbed-wire fences and take Narva, which fell on November 28. Another week was needed to cover a distance of less than 30 miles between Narva and Johvi, a railroad station on the Narva-Tallinn railroad line, which was overrun on December 8.

Pursuant to the Soviet "railroad strategy," with armored cars playing an important role in military operations,[11] another detachment of Soviet troops invaded Estonia along the Pskov-Valga railroad. By December 8 they managed to reach Võru, a station southwest of Lake Peipsi. One wonders in view of this situation that the Soviet government of Estonia could issue a Manifesto on November 29, on the morrow of the capture of Narva, ending in an appeal: "Comrades! We have to fight the last battle. Victory is ours." [12]

Expressed in square miles, the area occupied by the invading forces was negligible. All the rest of the country was held in firm control by the Estonian government, recognized *de facto* as such by a number of European Powers in 1918 (Great Britain, March 1; France, March 20; Italy, May 27; Germany, September 22). It was acting on the basis of the Declaration of Independence adopted by the democratically elected National Council of Estonia on February 24.

In this situation, the Council of People's Commissars, on Stalin's urging, decided to take further steps. On December 8 it promulgated the *Decree on Recognition of Independence of the Estonian Soviet Republic*.[13] It read:

> In reply to the inquiry of the Estonian Soviet Government, the Council of People's Commissars declares:
>
> (1) The Russian Soviet Government recognizes the independence of the Estonian Soviet Republic; as the supreme power in Estonia the Russian Soviet Government recognizes the Soviets of Estonia; until these Soviets meet in congress, however, it recognizes the Council of People's Commissars of Estonia, headed by their Chairman, Comrade Anvelt.
>
> (2) The Russian Soviet Government instructs all military and civilian authorities of the Russian Soviet Republic in areas adjoining Estonia to accord the Estonian Soviet Government every assistance in its struggle for liberation of Estonia from the yoke of the bourgeoisie.
>
> (3) The People's Commissariat for Finance is instructed to grant a loan of ten million rubles to the People's Bank of the Estonian Soviet Republic.
>
> (4) The People's Commissar for Food and the Supreme Economic Council are instructed to enter into agreement with the corresponding bodies of the Estonian Soviet Republic for the purpose of organizing the exchange of goods between the two Republics.

It was only on December 10 that *Izvestiia* shed some light on the background of the "Estonian Soviet Government" receiving such favors from the Council of People's Commissars. A report said it had been formed "within the last few days in Estonia" (actually in Narva on the day it was overrun by the Red troops)[14] out of the Provisional Revolutionary Committee. The Commissar for Estonian Affairs, i.e., a representative of the People's Commissariat for Nationality Affairs in Petrograd, was mentioned as the first among the members of the "Workers' and Peasants' Government." Thus, it was truly a government formed under the protection of Red Army bayonets.

Moreover, the newly-organized Soviet government of Estonia held virtually no control over the territory it claimed as that of the Estonian Soviet Republic on the day it was recognized by the Council of People's Commissars. Even *Izvestiia* admitted that it would take several weeks to reach Tallinn, the capital of Estonia.[15] In fact, the Red troops never reached Tallinn. The prediction proved as false as the report that the Estonian "reactionaries" had been cut off by December 20 and that they would be captured by revolutionary forces.

In view of the fact that the Soviet government of Estonia had gained practically no foothold in Estonia before being recognized by the Council of People's Commissars, it was a clear act of premature recognition, as understood by authorities on international law. They agree that premature recognition is an act of intervention in internal affairs of another country.[16] It so happens that the Soviet government likewise shares this view.

M. Litvinov, Soviet Commissar for Foreign Affairs, admitted this much in his address before the League of Nations Assembly on September 28, 1937. He strongly condemned General Franco's government in Spain, although his case was almost identical to that of Estonia in 1918. Litvinov said:

> A handful of officers and generals in Spain revolted against the legally constituted government. No one here will question the legality of the Spanish government. What was the duty of other governments in such circumstances? Obviously, in accordance with international law, it was to give no help to the rebels against the lawful government. Any help given to such rebels in the form of supplies of arms or, more particularly, of men, would be a flagrant breach of international law. Recognition of the head of the rebels as the head of a new Spanish government would not improve the position. If that view is held, any revolt or rebellion could be legalized by simply stating that the rebels are henceforth the government. Recognition of the rebels as a government is in itself an intervention.[17]

A comparison of the situation in Spain in 1937, of which the Soviet government was outspokenly critical, and that in Estonia in 1918, of which it highly approved, reveals that General Franco's position was relatively much stronger than the position of the Estonian Soviet government. At the time of the debate, General Franco had been fighting the leftist government of Spain for more than a year, and was firmly entrenched on Spanish soil. Fighting over Estonia had just begun at the time of recognition of its Soviet government, and the latter had barely managed to gain control over two tiny sections of Estonian territory.

The case of Lithuania was similar to that of Estonia. The Provisional Workers' and Peasants' Government of Lithuania was constituted in the Bolshevik-held Vilejka,[18] some 80 miles due east of Vilnius, the capital, on December 15. However, the newly-constituted government must have immediately moved to Daugavpils in Latvia, likewise in Bolshevik hands. V. Mickevicius-Kapsukas, head of the Soviet Lithuanian Government, also went to Daugavpils, and on December 18 he received the following telegram, signed by Lenin and Stalin:

> Message received. All of us are enjoying your news very much. Greetings. Liberate Vilnius as soon as you can.[19]

On December 22, V. Mickevicius-Kapsukas still was in Daugavpils, making speeches[20] instead of being in Lithuania. An *Appeal to the Lithuanian and White Russian Workers and Peasants,* issued on December 21, also in Daugavpils,[21] announced that "our units are entering localities you live in," meaning they were not yet there on December 21.

This also finds confirmation in the daily front communiques published in *Izvestiia* in late 1918. They show that the Red troops, advancing in the general direction of Lithuania from the north and the east, were by December 22 in or near the following places: Daugavpils, Pastovai, Molodechno, and Lyda[22] (cf. map p. 14). Here the front line curved sharply eastward toward Stolbtsy on the upper Nemunas. All territory held on that date by the Russian-sponsored government of Mickevicius-Kapsukas could hardly be called ethnographically Lithuanian, although parts of it subsequently were assigned to Lithuania by virtue of the Russo-Lithuanian Peace Treaty of July 12, 1920. It was not before December 24 that the first ethnographically Lithuanian localities were captured by Red troops.

Thus, not a foot of Lithuanian soil was under control of the Lithuanian Soviet Government on December 22, 1918, and the government itself was abroad. The political situation was not at all favorable to the Soviets. Commenting on it on the eve of the recognition of the Lithuanian Soviet Republic, *Izvestiia* had to admit that in Lithuania the actual power was vested in military authorities unreservedly supporting the bourgeois Lithuanian *Taryba* (Council) and that at some places the *Taryba* representatives wielded all power. Even the Vilnius Workers' Council had a Bolshevik minority, with only 96 seats out of 220 falling to the Bolsheviks and their sympathizers.[23] And although the Council declared itself "the sole agent of government, which all inhabitants must obey," Mickevicius-Kapsukas dismissed it as soon as he arrived in Vilnius.

In an article written in 1922, Mickevicius-Kapsukas admitted that at many a place in Lithuania in 1919 there were no Workers' Soviets at all were bourgeois committees, parish committees, etc., were sprouting everywhere; in the majority of rural districts there were no Communist organizations of any kind.[24] Later on (1935) he added that the Communist Party in Lithuania in 1919 was in general very small and extremely weak.[25] Deputy Chairman of the Council of People's Commissars and People's Commissar for Internal Affairs, Z. Angarietis, agreed with Mickevicius-Kapsukas that various bourgeois committees had sprung up throughout Lithuania in 1918, i.e., before the invasion.[26] Finally, Stalin, too, must have had precisely such a situation in mind when he wrote in *Pravda* on November 6, 1918, that during the bourgeois revolution in Russia, national movements in the border regions were "of the bourgeois-liberation type" and that these regions were dotted with "central national" institutions headed by national, bourgeois-democratic intelligentsia.

Such was the situation on December 22 when the Council of People's Commissars promulgated a *Decree on Recognition of Independence of the Lithuanian Soviet Republic.*[27] A Soviet historian has asserted, however, that a decision on recognition had been taken much earlier, on December 7,[28] i.e., at the time Red Army units were far away from the Lithuanian territory, and before a Soviet government of Lithuania had been appointed. The Decree, for all practical purposes, repeated the contents of an earlier decree concerning Estonia. And if the term "premature recognition" applied to Estonia, judging by its interpretation on the part of a high Soviet authority (M. Litvinov), it had to apply even more so to Lithuania.

There was another element in the case of Lithuania, which was nonextant in the case of Estonia. The party claiming the right to speak in the name of "the revolutionary working people of Lithuania," as the *Manifesto of the Provisional Revolutionary Workers' Government of Lithuania,*[29] published on December 22, 1918, did, was not even a purely Lithuanian political organization. For the Manifesto was issued by the Central Committee of the Communist Party of Lithuania *and* White Russia, "the only mass proletarian party in Lithuania."

The fact that the Lithuanian communists were serving two separate ethnic entities proves they were utterly alien to the national aspirations of their countrymen. "We do not recognize either a state coat of arms or state and national colors," Mickevicius-Kapsukas once said; "we have struggled too much for the Red Flag to tolerate beside it any [Lithuanian] 'stripes.' " [30] And he himself admitted subsequently that the devotion of Lithuanian communists to internationalism acted as a deterrent in gaining support among the Lithuanian people.[31]

Actually the internationalism of Lithuanian communists was but a blind subservience to Russia. In their zeal to please the masters, they wanted to include a forceful declaration to that effect even in the Manifesto of Mickevicius-Kapsukas' Government. The Russian communists, however, evidently being aware of a possible bad propaganda effect therefrom, dissuaded their Lithuanian colleagues from doing so.[32] Yet this did not stop the latter from claiming that Lithuanian workers were demanding a union with the Russian Republic.[33]

To be sure, it did not escape the attention of Lithuanian communists that they were accused of subservience to Russia. For as early as 1923, Z. Angarietis ridiculed the "fairy tales" about the Soviet Government of Lithuania being a mere Russian puppet.[34] Yet another member of the government did actually make an admission that they had arrived in Vilnius from Russia, having received proper instructions from Sverdlov, Chairman of the All-Russian Central Executive Committee. Furthermore, A. Ioffe, another prominent Bolshevik, served as Russia's advisor to the Soviet Lithuanian Government[35]—an arrangement which was reimposed on Lithuania after her reoccupation in 1940.

The subservience of Lithuanian communists was also demonstrated during the Eighth Congress of the Russian Communist Party, meeting on March 18–23, 1919. While not opposed to the existence of "independent" Lithuanian, Latvian, and other Soviet republics, the Congress refused to consider Party reorganization on federation principles. Central Party Committees in these republics could only enjoy the rights of regional committees, otherwise being "completely subordinated to the Central Committee of the Russian Communist Party." The latter's decisions were "to apply unreservedly to all Party subdivisions, regardless of their national ties." [36]

No wonder that the Communist Party of Lithuania opposed her self-determination. Mickevicius-Kapsukas made no secret of it. He was against both self-determination and secession from Russia.[37]

It was only in Latvia that the Soviet government could claim a substantial portion of Latvian territory as actually under its control on the day of recognition. The *Decree on Recognition of Independence of the Latvian Soviet Republic,*[38] similar in wording to the two other Decrees concerning Estonia and Lithuania, was promulgated on December 22, a few days after the Provisional Soviet Government of Latvia had been constituted in Valka (December 17).[39]

It is true that invasion of Latvia was crowned with more success than that of either Estonia or Lithuania. War communiques show that Red troops, after capturing Daugavpils on December 9, advanced along the right bank of the Daugava as far as Ogre, only 20 miles southeast of Riga. They also held control of the Plavinas-Aluksne railroad and all territory east of it. In the north they managed to advance past Valka, and were fighting Latvian forces in the general area of Ruiena, Valmiera, Piebalga, and Cesis.

A rough estimate indicates that on December 22 the Red rule in Latvia extended over two-fifths of the Latvian territory. But as in the case of Estonia and Lithuania, neither the capital of the country—nor any other larger city, for that matter—was in the hands of the invader.

Recognition of all three "paper" Soviet Republics by the Council of People's Commissars received a seal of approval from the Central Executive Committee on December 23. Stalin reported on the matter and moved to grant independence to the Estonian, Latvian, and Lithuanian peoples, so that they, "after assuming power, could proclaim unity of the Soviet Republic." [40] The *Resolution on Recognition of the Soviet Republics of Estonia, Lithuania, and Latvia*[41] had the following wording:

> The Central Executive Committee, having heard the report of the People's Commissar for Nationality Affairs, congratulates the peoples of Estonia, Lithuania, Latvia, and the Ukraine on their progressive liberation from the yoke of foreign conquerors.
>
> Acting on the principle of complete and genuine self-determination of the working masses of the oppressed nationalities, a principle set at naught by the imperialists of all lands, the Central Executive Committee confirms the resolution of the Council of the People's Commissars on the recognition by the Socialist Federated Soviet Republic of the Soviet republics of Estonia, Latvia, and Lithuania.
>
> Before the Soviet republics of Estonia, Latvia, and Lithuania, created by the revolutionary struggle of the proletarian and peasant masses, the Central Executive Committee once more declares that the fact of these countries having previously formed part of the old Tsarist Empire imposes on them no obligation whatever. At the same time the Central Executive Committee expresses its firm belief that only now is there being created on the basis of the recognition of full freedom of self-determination and transfer of power into the hands of the working class, a free, voluntary and inviolable alliance of the workers of all nations inhabiting the territory of the former Russian Empire.
>
> The Central Executive Committee affirms the readiness of the RSFSR to give all necessary help and support to the working class of Estonia, Latvia, Lithuania, and the Ukraine in their struggle against the regime of exploitation and oppression, and in defense of their freedom and independence from foreign attempts at conquest.

The resolution was significant because it confirmed renunciation of historical claims to Estonia, Latvia, and Lithuania. Russia had already done it once upon signing the Brest-Litovsk Peace Treaty and its supplement (March 3 and August 27, 1918, respectively). After its abrogation, however, the Baltic peoples had remained with no such assurance on Russia's part. The resolution of December 23, 1918, restored the previous situation, and, to repeat, the renunciation this time was completely voluntary.

Furthermore, the resolution promised help and support to the Soviet regimes in Estonia, Latvia, and Lithuania. The promise was a mere repetition of that contained in the November 13, 1918, decree abrogating the Brest-Litovsk Peace Treaty and assuring "the peoples in the regions freed from German imperialism" of the Soviet government's "every assistance to the very end of their struggle to establish on their soil a socialist government of workers and peasants." [42]

These were not empty promises. As the fight for supremacy was going on, the Estonian Soviet Government admitted that "only the Great

Russian Republic" was supporting nascent Soviet Estonia and giving aid to her.[43] Likewise, in 1919 the Latvian Soviet Government was expecting help from the revolutionary proletariat all over the world, but "mainly from the RSFSR." [44] The Lithuanian Soviet Government was assured of "utmost assistance from Workers' and Peasants' Soviet Russia." [45] Later on it thanked her for "brotherly aid given to the poorest peasantry of Lithuania." [46]

A Soviet historian of the 1918–1919 period states quite frankly:

> Beginning with the very first days of their existence, the independent re-
> publics of the Ukraine, White Russia, Latvia, Lithuania, and Estonia re-
> ceived from the RSFSR tremendous military, political, and economic
> assistance, which they needed very badly.[47]

The same admission continues to appear in Soviet writings. *Sovet-skaia Litva,* for example, recalled in 1952 that "it was the peoples of Soviet Russia who rendered assistance to the Lithuanian people in its heroic struggle for Soviet rule and against the Anglo-American and German imperialists and their hirelings—bourgeois nationalists." [48] A practically identical statement may also be found in *Pravda* in 1957.[49] The list of quotations could be expanded to include both Latvia and Estonia; however, it would not add anything new.

The fact remains that Russia in 1918–1919 did assist the Soviet governments of Estonia, Latvia, and Lithuania fighting against the national governments of the three newly-constituted democratic republics. Thus, she violated the basic principle of noninterference in civil strife in other countries.

Two decades later (1937), when the question of help to General Franco of Spain came up for discussion at the League of Nations General Assembly, the Soviet government seemed to have completely forgotten what its predecessors had done. Soviet People's Commissar for Foreign Affairs, M. Litvinov, had no doubts then that "any help given to such rebels in the form of arms or, more particularly, of men would be a flagrant breach of international law." [50] But it was precisely help in the form of arms and men that the Soviet governments of Estonia, Latvia, and Lithuania received from Russia in 1918–1919.

Statements about such help emanated from the highest Bolshevik sources. Stalin was one. "Our Navy, following an order of the Council of People's Commissars, is protecting Soviet Estonia from possible surprises from the sea," he wrote in *Zhizn' natsional'nostei* on December 22, 1918.[51] "With arms in hands, Soviet Russia once again is fighting her way through the White Guardist gangs to the Baltic Sea," *Izvestiia* described the nature of "help" three days later (December 25). An authoritative *History of Civil War 1918–1921* had this to say:

Soviet Russia, as the first proletarian state in the whole world, rendered active assistance in the border areas to the peasantry and masses of workers desirous of setting up Soviet republics at home. The Soviet government permitted formation of National Soviet Armies in the RSFSR for the purpose of conquest and consolidation in their hands of areas inhabited by these people.[52]

The problem of the so-called "National Soviet Armies" was first taken up by the People's Commissariat for Nationality Affairs on February 15, 1918, and again on May 7. Stalin is credited with having "personally directed formation of national units of the Red Army and their organization in the Ukrainian, White Russian, Baltic, and Transcaucasian Soviet Republics." [53] However, these national units of the Red Army were not trusted by their organizers. The Commissariat for Nationality Affairs demanded "unconditional guarantee" of their political reliability and prevention of their falling into the hands of nationalists and bourgeois. Formation of national units larger than a company, a squadron, and a battery was frowned upon.[54]

On the other hand, the national character of such units appears doubtful owing to the fact that they were directly subordinated to the Red Army ("national units of the Red Army"; "the Soviet Army, in the ranks of which the Latvian Rifles were also fighting").[55] The Commander-in-Chief of the Latvian Red Army and the Commander-in-Chief of all armed forces of the RSFSR was the same person—Comrade Vacetis. Furthermore, enlistees had to swear to obey all disciplinary rules of the Red Army, comply with all instructions given by Soviet administration, and carry out all orders issued by Soviet appointed authorities. After suffering defeat in 1919, the Latvian Red Army was absorbed by the 15th Red Army and forgotten.

The number of enlistees in the national Red Army units was small. In fact, the Soviet Lithuanian Government was unable to form an armed force of its own. It relied on the 2nd Pskov Division put at its disposal by the Red command. Neither was there a Soviet Estonian armed force to launch an attack against Narva on November 22, 1918. Instead, the 6th Rifle Division of the 7th Red Army and the Red Fleet were ordered to do the job. But the Soviet Latvian Government was more fortunate, as it commanded the Latvian Rifle Division (9 regiments in all); formation of another division was a failure, however. On the other hand, the Latvian Rifles had to assist their comrades in arms in Estonia and Lithuania. This proved to be their doom.[56]

Recruitment for the national Red Army units was evidently carried on all over Russia. *Izvestiia,* for example, reported on December 10, 1918, that several hundred Estonians had been mobilized and were departing from Samara "to join the ranks of the Red Army and fight for the re-establishment of Soviet rule in Estonia." The Latvian and Lithuanian refugees were declared subject to all mobilization laws on the same basis as the Russian citizens.[57] Nor was recruitment evidently limited to Estonians, Latvians, and Lithuanians. The proof was furnished in an official report that the Petrograd Soviet and the Russian Communist Party had proclaimed mobilization of "communists in Petrograd and its vicinity." Not fewer than 1000 "militant" communists were expected from Petrograd alone. They were urged, at all costs, "to drive the White gangs" out of Estonia and Latvia.[58]

Soviet military historians do not deny that the invading forces met stiff opposition. The following is an admission taken from two authoritative histories of civil war in Russia in 1918-1921:

> The attack met with stubborn resistance on the part of Estonian and Russian White Guardists . . . The Estonian Government was able to set up a rather large armed force of two infantry divisions and a Russian corps, all told about 25,000 men. Its resistance was not easy to overcome. The Estonians operated with a great deal of success and engaged substantial forces on our side seeking to break down their resistance . . . The attempt of the Whites to launch a counter-offensive against Narva–Iamburg and beyond was crowned with success. A similar success accompanied their campaign in the direction of Valga and Võru . . . By early April, Soviet Latvian armed forces reached the limit of endurance, and the front they were holding collapsed, after a heroic struggle, all along its length in Kurland.[59]

In addition to providing general guidance and the fighting force, the Soviet Russian Government also furnished funds and all kinds of supplies for the expeditionary corps. The *Decree on Recognition of Independence of the Estonian Soviet Republic,* dated December 8, 1918, contained a specific instruction to the People's Commissar of Finance to grant a loan of ten million rubles to Soviet Estonia. By the end of the month it was raised to fifty million rubles. Soviet Latvia was given a loan of twenty million rubles. As the Soviet governments of Latvia and Lithuania were begging for new funds within a few months, the Central Executive Committee again complied with the request.[60]

Supplies are expressly mentioned in at least one telegram dispatched by Lenin to the Ukrainian Council of People's Commissars dated January 3, 1919, at the height of the invasion. The telegram read:

> Concerning supplies to the White Russian-Lithuanian Army and generally those for the People's Food Commissariat in Minsk. I beg you not to hold them back, but to dispatch in the direction of Minsk. Do accelerate by all means . . . Lenin.[61]

Russian assistance to her stooges—Soviet governments of Estonia, Latvia, and Lithuania—was far from being unselfish. In an editorial written for *Zhizn' natsional'nostei,* the mouthpiece of the People's Commissariat for Nationality Affairs, Stalin voiced undisguised criticism of "counterrevolutionary bourgeois-nationalist" governments of Estonia, Latvia, and Lithuania. He compared the nascent Baltic States to a "partition wall between the revolutionary West and socialist Russia." Stalin expressed hope, however, that this "partition wall" would be pulled down by the mounting waves of revolution.[62]

The editorial appeared on November 17, 1918. Eleven days later, November 28, the Petrograd newspaper *Vooruzhennyi narod* took up the same "separating wall" argument:

> The world bourgeoisie desires to erect bourgeois Estonia, Latvia, and Lithuania as a wall separating us from revolutionary Germany. By restoring the power of Soviets in Estonia, Latvia, Lithuania, and White Russia, we are not only assisting our brothers, but we are also establishing for ourselves a revolutionary base for the struggle with the bandits of Allied imperialism.[63]

The paper was entirely wrong, by the way, in urging restoration of the power of the Soviets in all three Baltic countries. In Lithuania, for one, the Soviets wielded no power prior to the Russian invasion at the end of 1918. This is the unanimous admission of both the Chairman and the Deputy Chairman of the Soviet-recognized government of Lithuania.[64] Nothing could be restored which did not exist before. In Latvia the Soviets succeeded in establishing themselves only in a part of the Latvian territory, which excluded Riga, the capital. This was also the case in Estonia, where the power of Soviets met stiff resistance in Tallinn and rejection in rural communities.

It is not surprising that the Bolshevik press was as much against the "Allied imperialists" as it was against the "bourgeois nationalists." *Izvestiia* on November 30 gave rough treatment to nationalist Latvia and her newly-elected President K. Ulmanis. The paper significantly called Ulmanis "a caliph for one hour." It also reminded its readers that "the Anglo-American robbers" were staging an attack against the Russian revolution and thereby against the international revolution by way of the Latvian ports.

Two weeks later (December 14), Lithuania's turn came. *Izvestiia* bitterly denounced the creation of "a new center of counterrevolution" in Vilnius, meaning thereby the National Council of Lithuania. The paper complained that landowners and capitalists had switched allegiance to the Allied Powers and were trying to separate revolutionary Russia from revolutionary Germany and Austria-Hungary by "a blank wall." Denunciation ended in an ominous warning: "The Soviet Republic will have to expand its territory in the immediate future."

Petrogradskaia Pravda came out on December 24 with another assault against the well-worn argument of "a separating wall":

> It is plain that, after the victory of the revolution in Russia and Germany, a continued existence of the bourgeois order in the buffer states set up by

German imperialism is inconceivable. A wall has been erected between revolutionary Russia and Germany, and it must be pulled down in the interests both of the Russian and the German revolution. The Russian Red Forces will do all they can to facilitate the victory of the workers in the occupied countries.[65]

Instructions of the same nature must have gone to all Soviet newspapers. The next day (December 25) *Izvestiia* launched another in its almost countless series of blistering attacks against the nascent Baltic States, leaving no doubt as to Russia's designs:

> Soviet Russia must gain access to the Baltic coast and replant the Red Flag of the proletarian revolution there. Soviet Russia must reinforce the Baltic ports and harbors to ensure repulsion of the world-wide counterrevolution. The Baltic Sea and the former occupied territories of Lithuania, Latvia (including Kurland and Livonia), and Estonia are in the way of pressure exerted by our revolution upon Western Europe . . . This separating wall between the workers' revolution in Russia and Germany must be torn down and destroyed. Soviet troops must occupy Lithuania, Latvia, and Estonia. The Russian working class must get a possibility of exerting direct influence upon the course of German revolution, the goal being a merger of the genuine German Government, after it has been constituted, and formation of a common union in the Socialist Federation of Central Europe. The conquest of the Baltic Sea and its coast will enable Soviet Russia to exert influence upon the Scandinavian countries in the interest of the Socialist Revolution . . . The Baltic Sea must become a Soviet Sea. All efforts must be directed toward the attainment of this urgent political objective.

This was followed by an appeal published on December 29 by G. Zinov'ev, Chairman of the Petrograd "Northern Commune":

> We must at all costs drive the White gangs out of Pskov, Rezekne, Daugavpils, and Riga; all those lands of ours which have been snatched by the imperialists must belong to Soviet Russia. In addition to the region of Pskov, there is also that of Narva.[66]

References to various cities were false, as all of them, with the exception of Riga, were in Russian hands by the time the Appeal was published. Its tenor remained clear, however: Russia was on the move, and not because of the beautiful eyes of the Baltic toilers.

All this press activity coincided with increased military activity on all fronts. In Estonia, Tartu and Valga fell on December 23, and shortly thereafter Red troops were threatening Tallinn and Parnu on the Baltic coast. In Latvia, Valmiera surrendered on December 25 and Riga, on January 3. Then the invading forces crossed the Daugava and swiftly occupied all of Kurland with the exception of Ventspils and Liepaja ports where some British naval units were anchored. Next, they spilled over into Western, Northern, and Central Lithuania. Vilnius was captured on January 3. Kaunas, where the Lithuanian government had fled, was saved, although the so-called White Russian-Lithuanian Army came dangerously close to it. All other larger cities in Lithuania, such as Siauliai, Panevezys, Ukmerge, and Telsiai, saw the red flag fly over their public buildings. As a matter of fact, the red flag in the grim winter of 1919 was flying over one-half of Lithuania, three-fourths of Estonia, and seven-eights of Latvia.[67] It seemed as though the Bolshevik victory was in sight.

Sure of the ultimate victory, the Soviet governments of Estonia, Latvia, and Lithuania undertook immediate reorganization of the whole social and political life in areas under their control. The entire administration system was revamped and replaced by the Soviets on all levels. Large-scale nationalization was proclaimed. State and cooperative farms sprang up. Soviet Latvia went so far as to adopt the Constitution of Soviet Russia, "without changing its basic statutes," and introduce Russian currency.[68] The latter was also the case in Lithuania.[69]

The time seemed ripe for unification of the Baltic Soviet Republics and the Russian Socialist Federated Soviet Republics, for the former had expressed "their longing" for such a union, and both Stalin and Lenin had received thousands of messages to that effect, according to a Soviet historian.[70] The time was already overripe for the Estonian Soviet government, which lost its foothold on the Estonian soil in the first two months of 1919 and was discarded.

Consequently, the Congresses of Soviets in Latvia and Lithuania resolved on January 17 and February 22 respectively to unite with the RSFSR.[71] Furthermore, Soviet Lithuania was to lose her theoretical political independence even further by merging with Soviet White Russia into a single state.[72] Russia's interest in these developments was evidenced by Sverdlov and Kamenev, two members of the Central Committee of the Communist Party of Russia, attending the Latvian Congress of Soviets.[73] The fact that the merger resolutions were passed in both Lithuania and White Russia the very same day—February 2, 1919—was hardly accidental. Two decades later—on July 21, 1940—Lithuanian, Latvian, and Estonian "people's diets" repeated an identical deed by "voting" for a merger of their countries with the Soviet Union. The same guiding hand showed unmistakably in either case.

In implementing the Russian-conceived merger plan in 1919, representatives of Lithuanian, Latvian, White Russian, and Ukrainian Soviet Republics presented their pleas to the All-Russian Executive Committee and came out of the meeting united in a military alliance under the aegis of the RSFSR.[74] It was also decided to unify military organizations and command, national economy councils, railroad transportation, finance, and labor commissariats. RSFSR decrees pertaining to these matters received precedence.[75]

Evidently Stalin had precisely such a development in mind when he wrote in *Izvestiia* (February 9, 1919) about the peoples of Russia "reaching the stage of voluntary, fraternal unity by way of independent

Soviet republics." Similarly, the Eighth Congress of the Russian Communist (Bolshevik) Party meeting on March 18–23 no longer spoke of national self-determination. The necessity of rapprochement between proletarians and semiproletarians of all nations was emphasised. Abolition of national privileges and acknowledgment of the right to secession were regarded as a means to overcome the mistrust toward the oppressor nations. Federation of the Soviet type was only to serve as a transition to complete unity.[76]

This development was not at all surprising in view of the fact that the Baltic Soviet republics were nothing but Russian puppets. *Izvestiia* on December 25, 1918, admitted this much by stating that Soviet Russia had taken the path of least resistance and "created" these republics. The act of creation was far from being unselfish. The new republics, to quote *Izvestiia,* were to enable Russia to convert the Baltic Sea into a "Soviet Sea" or a "Sea of the World-Wide Socialist Revolution." This constituted Russia's "urgent political objective," and *Izvestiia* was not concerned whether this also constituted a political objective of the Soviet Baltic republics. These were merely to serve Russian ends.

And yet the governments of the Soviet Baltic republics were extremely anxious to show they were independent. Thus, the Soviet Latvian government hastened to lodge a protest note in Berlin as soon as it received information that the German government had complained in Moscow, instead of in Riga, following the arrest of a German diplomat in Latvia.[77] The Estonian Soviet government vigorously denied in its manifesto of December 8, 1918, that Estonia was supposedly occupied by Russia.[78] One wonders whether or not its reaction would have been the same if it had known about Lenin's telegram dispatched to the Supreme Military Headquarters on November 29, 1918, the day the Red troops pushed beyond Narva:

> As our troops advance westward and into the Ukraine, there come into being provisional Soviet governments called upon to strengthen the local Soviets. This circumstance has a certain advantage, for it deprives the Ukrainian, Lithuanian, Latvian, and Estonian chauvinists of the chance to regard the advance of our troops as [military] occupation and creates a favorable atmosphere for the further progress of our troops. Otherwise they would be placed in an impossible situation in the occupied territories. For this reason, we ask you to instruct the commanding staff of military units involved that our troops must support by all means the provisional Soviet governments of Latvia, Estonia, the Ukraine, and Lithuania; but only Soviet governments, of course.[79]

Yet the behavior of the Red troops "in the occupied territories" (using Lenin's own words) was far from being what it was supposed to be. V. Kapsukas, erstwhile Chairman of the Soviet Government of Lithuania, complained subsequently that "the Red Army units operating in Lithuania . . . often paid no attention at all to the local workers' (particularly estate workers') and small farmers' needs." They lived off the land, did what they wanted, abused their rights, and finally made enemies everywhere.[80] Kapsukas' deputy, Z. Angarietis, admitted that the Red Army simply gave orders to the Revolutionary Committees, which it sometimes also appointed.[81]

All this proves beyond a shadow of doubt that Bolshevik Russia in the early period of her history, despite all the assurances to the contrary, was far from being prepared to let the Baltic republics go their own way. On the contrary, she laid careful plans well in advance for their military occupation by her own armed forces, the occupation to be followed by a merger into a Russian-dominated political entity. To achieve these ends, Russia supplied both military and political guidance to her favored side and assisted it with men, money, and supplies.

Since the local "Soviet" and "bourgeois-nationalist" factions in the three Baltic republics were engaged in a life-or-death struggle with each other, Russia's actions violated the fundamental principle of non-interference in the internal affairs of another country, particularly in its civil war. Thus, Soviet Russia was an aggressor by virtue of the very definition of aggression which she (then the Soviet Union) submitted to the United Nations with the recommendation it be adopted as binding in international relations, to wit:

> In accordance with the Soviet concept of aggression, a state shall be found guilty of committing indirect aggression which: (a) supports subversive actions against another state (terroristic acts, sabotage, etc.); (b) contributes to the spreading of civil war in another state; or (c) encourages internal revolt in another state or a change in its policies to please the aggressor. Such actions constitute violation of the foremost principle in international law: the principle of nonintervention in internal affairs of another state. Thus, the Soviet concept of aggression declares intervention to be aggression, i.e. international crime.[82]

Russian aggression against the Baltic States, launched at the end of 1918, terminated in complete failure within less than a year. National governments succeeded in building up armed force contingents. These were ill-armed, ill-clothed, and ill-fed, but they showed courage and love of freedom. Help was received from Allied Powers. Volunteers came from Finland, Norway, and Sweden to Estonia; Germans, anti-Bolshevik Russians, and Polish legionaires joined in the fight, although their goal was not to liberate the Baltic countries and then go home. And yet this strange combination of opposing interests stopped the Bolsheviks from converting the Baltic Sea into the Sea of Social Revolution.[83]

A counteroffensive in Estonia began on January 3, 1919. It achieved resounding success. A detachment of Soviet Latvian Rifles was dispatched to the Russo-Estonian theater, but it could not change the situation. On the first aniversary of the proclamation of Estonian independence (February 24), not one Red soldier remained on Estonian soil.

At the same time resistance in Lithuania stiffened. Russian troops were unable to carry out the order of January 12, 1919, to occupy the right bank of the Nemunas between Gardinas and Kaunas. Instead, they had to begin retreat. They lost Vilnius on April 19. In a few weeks, all the important centers in Lithuania were liberated. By the end of August, Lithuania became the second Baltic State (after Estonia) to rid herself of Russian invaders.

In Latvia, the Red Army found itself in a precarious situation. Its flanks were unprotected and its lines were spread very thinly. The Russian government was unable to extend any help, as all manpower and resources were needed for decisive battles in the east and the south—the two principal theaters of the Civil War. In the words of a Soviet history of the Civil War, "the military command was hampered, therefore, in allocating any further armed forces and resources for the purpose of strengthening the front in the west." As a result, Red positions in Kurland collapsed. By early April they were taken back to the Daugava. Riga had to be abandoned on May 24. The Soviet Latvian Rifles disintegrated and their remnants were absorbed by the 15th Red Army.

Soviet military historians also supply their own reasons for the collapse of the Soviet-Russian attack against the "bourgeois" Baltic republics:

> (1) formation of a number of small bourgeois states which acted as a cordon separating the Soviets from the workers in Europe ("it prevented the German and Russian revolutions from joining hands");
> (2) inadequate attacking forces which proved their inability to cope with the locally organized armed forces;
> (3) lack of active support on the part of a peasantry constituting the bulk of the local population, receptive to the influence of the local nationalist elements, and aware of the fact that the Soviet rule failed to create any immediate material advantage;
> (4) a demoralized and decimated proletariat; and
> (5) a hatred of Tsarism and everything Russian as a result of the previous national oppression.[84]

Soviet nonmilitary historians, too, agree on some of the reasons for the failure to establish Soviet rule in the Baltic area in 1918–1919:

In Estonia—the peasants were never fully won over to the Soviet side and joined the ranks of the bourgeoisie; land reform was miscarried; farming communes in South Estonia shocked the peasants; the intelligentsia shunned the Soviets altogether.[85]

In Latvia—peasants were likewise alienated by the imposition of state and cooperative "communes" and failure to distribute land among those wanting it; as for the intelligentsia, all of it "went over to the bourgeois camp." [86]

In Lithuania—there was the failure to recognize the importance of a union between the workers and the peasantry; the creation of state farms and failure to distribute land among the landless peasants and small farmers; the withholding of voting privileges from all owners of medium-size farms; the hatred of the Red Army living off the land and indulging in outright looting; the poor performance of administration organs; the failure to set up a law enforcement apparatus (Cheka); the lack of interest on the part of the proletariat in either the Soviet rule or communism, so that even Mensheviks were acceptable for high posts in the government; the longing of landless peasants and small farmers for land of their own and the refusal to distribute the nationalized estates.[87]

No wonder that *Izvestiia,* in its comments on the situation in Lithuania (May 3, 1919), was forced to admit that "anyone who was recently in Vilnius could see easily for himself the antagonism between the population and the Soviets." The paper put a few communists on one side of the fence and, using *Izvestiia*'s terminology, the vast numbers of merchants, speculators, land-owners, intelligentsia, Catholic priests, bureaucrats, White Guardists, and proletariat on the other. "For all practical purposes, we failed in gaining control over the city."

This was also true of the entire country. The former members of the Soviet Lithuanian government were complaining subsequently that the Soviet system had lost all influence among the proletariat, farmhands, and small farmers. They paid no attention to the request to take over the local Soviets—nor did they take part in voting. Consequently, the Soviets were largely controlled by the bourgeois elements. *Komunaras,* the mouthpiece of the Soviet Lithuanian government, wrote on March 23, 1919, that "the Soviet Government is no longer recognized." Two weeks later it complained about the mass of leaflets and open anti-Soviet agitation all over Lithuania and about small farmers and workers "digging the grave for workers' rule." As late as March 18 *Komunaras* discovered that "no revolution in Lithuania had begun yet." [88]

What happened in Lithuania in 1918–1919 was best described in a few words by former Deputy Chairman of the Soviet Lithuanian Government, Z. Angarietis, three years later:

> The Soviet rule in Lithuania was not won through internal struggle, nor was it the result of a workers' revolt, although there was some sporadic workers' stirring and revolutionary activity (Vilnius, Siauliai, and elsewhere); it was the Red Army that brought the Soviet rule to Lithuania, while only a handful of class-conscious workers applied themselves to its establishment despite obstruction on the part of various parasites.[89]

Chapter Four

PEACE FOR RUSSIA; DISARMAMENT FOR OTHERS

Facing serious military difficulties caused by Russian anti-Bolshevik forces, an effective Allied economic blockade, and a strong resistance on the part of the Baltic peoples, Russia was ready to renounce her plans for converting the Baltic Sea into a "Sea of Socialist Revolution" and to talk peace instead. By mid-1919, as a Soviet historian put it, "neutralization of the Baltic area had both political and strategic sense." [1] Consequently, on July 21 the Estonian government heard over the radio the assurance that Red troops would not cross Estonian frontiers. As no reply was forthcoming for quite some time, a formal peace offer followed on August 31. Russia was willing to start peace negotiations "on the basis of irrevocable recognition of independence of the Estonian state." Estonia's conditional acceptance of the offer on September 4 prompted Russia to submit similar offers to both Latvia and Lithuania on September 11. Yet these two were not so eager to start peace talks.

Exploratory talks began in Pskov on September 17 and immediately ran into a deadlock. Estonia requested that the other Baltic States also take part in negotiations. The Soviet delegation issued a statement the next day accusing the Estonian government of reneging on its original assent to independent negotiations and disclaimed all responsibility for the further prolongation of war. At the same time it reaffirmed its readiness to resume peace talks, "either with the Tallinn government alone or simultaneously with the governments of other states now at war with the RSFSR." [2]

A few days later (September 22), both the Latvian and the Lithuanian governments received identical proposals to open negotiations "for the cessation of hostilities and for working out conditions for peaceful relations between the two countries." The Soviet government took this opportunity to assure recipients of its note that it had "sufficiently demonstrated the absence of any aggressive intentions toward the newly-established states on the borders of the former Russian Empire." [3] But could the invasion of Estonia, Latvia, and Lithuania launched by the Soviet government eight months earlier be so easily forgotten?

The proposal was immediately followed by a propaganda appeal to the workers of Great Britain and France (September 27). They were urged to demand emphatically from their respective governments that they stop opposing the reestablishment of peace in the Baltic area. The appeal also contained the assurance that "the workers' and peasants' government of Russia had always been in favor of recognition of the right of all and every people to self-determination." It went on:

> Soviet Russia of Workers and Peasants is not imposing its rule on any nation or country. It rejects all aggressive tendencies and coercive actions against other nations. It equally rejects the idea of imposing upon any other nation, against the latter's will, institutions which the nation itself had not introduced.

Despite these assurances, negotiations with Estonia proceeded slowly. She did not want to go ahead alone and was apprehensive both of adverse reaction among the Allied and Associated Powers and of Bolshevik promises and the dangers involved in peaceful coexistence. Consequently, to discuss the common problems, representatives of Estonia, Latvia, and Lithuania met together in Riga on September 10–12; in Tallinn, on September 14–15; and in Tartu, on September 29– October 1. At the conclusion of the Tartu Conference, a declaration was adopted with the intent of counteracting condemnation of the Baltic States, which were about to enter into peace negotiations with Bolshevik Russia, and secure guarantees of their independence. The declaration read in part:

> Estonia, Latvia, and Lithuania address themselves to the Allies and to the public opinion . . . At present they are prepared to enter into *pourparlers* with Russia, but in order to safeguard their future, they earnestly request the great democratic states to control the fulfilment of the treaty, should a treaty be concluded.[4]

The Latvian government was even more explicit. Its delegation to the Paris Peace Conference submitted a last-minute appeal to George Clemenceau, President of the Conference. The appeal called Clemenceau's attention to the fact that Latvia was in a precarious military situation, with German troops increasing in number every day and Bolshevik troops still stationed in Southeastern Latvia (Latgale). Latvia saw no way out, and her words sounded prophetic if one thinks of what was to happen in 1939:

> While not ignoring how little faith can be placed in treaties concluded with the Bolsheviks, the Latvian Government does not believe itself to be in a position to refuse the offer . . . The Latvian Government appeals to the representatives of Allied Powers with a view of learning what support they would be willing to accord to it in its struggle against the Germans and the Bolsheviks.[5]

The Allied Powers were in no hurry, however, to undertake any commitments of the type requested. Consequently, the Baltic States accepted the Bolshevik peace offer on October 4. They insisted, however, that the Bolsheviks not only recognize their independence, but also agree to cease all propaganda in their countries. This was to be "the first condition of peace." [6] Chicherin agreed immediately. He only wanted the talks to begin on October 12 instead of on October 25, as suggested by the Baltic States.

Yet even October 25 proved to be too early for Estonia. She requested a later date, allegedly guided by the desire to await the results of General Yudenich's offensive against Petrograd which began on October 25.[7] In his exasperation, Chicherin, on October 30, made a direct radio appeal to Estonian workers. He blamed the Allied Powers for having persuaded the Baltic peoples to attack Russia and denied all implications that Russia had been preparing to crush independent Estonia and her neighbors. She constituted no threat to them; all she wanted was peace. After telling the Estonian workers that Russia had offered peace to the Estonian government, Chicherin closed his appeal with these words:

> Russia of workers and peasants is unchanging in her desire for peace with Estonia and her neighbors . . . May the workers and peasants of Estonia cease to submit to those machinations which permit their sons to be sent into battle against us. May they clearly realize that the workers and peasants of Russia are not the enemies of Estonia but her friends, and that on the part of Soviet Russia there is nothing in the way of establishment of peace and friendship between their country and ours.[8]

Another meeting of the Baltic representatives concluded that it was necessary to start negotiating with the Bolsheviks seriously. It finally was arranged for Estonian and Russian delegates to meet in Pskov on December 5. Two weeks later (December 17) Deputy Commissar for Foreign Affairs M. Litvinov had a chance to talk things over with representatives of all three Baltic States. Russia was eager to make peace with all of them and was ready to pay a price for it. She wanted to make her western frontier safe and then go ahead with strengthening her war-damaged national economy. On the last day of 1919 an armistice with Estonia was signed, despite British, French, and American disapproval of the whole idea.[9]

The Armistice was followed by the Peace Treaty signed in Tartu on February 2, 1920.[10] Article 2 of the Treaty stipulated recognition of Estonian independence and renunciation of all sovereignty claims by Russia. The other articles dealt with cessation of the state of war; Russia's obligations to respect and guarantee the perpetual neutrality of Estonia if it were recognized internationally; establishment of diplomatic and consular relations; repatriation; and cessation of war in financial and economic fields, to be followed by conclusion of a commercial treaty based on the reciprocal application of the principle of "the most-favored nation" treatment.

Russia agreed to pay Estonia 15 million rubles in gold to cover all her claims (Estonia wanted 88 million at the start),[11] and give timber concessions. Estonia, in turn, agreed to reserve for Russia, in the free docks at Tallinn and other ports, sites for transshipment and warehousing of goods in transit. Transit goods were to be free reciprocally from import duties or taxes, while freight charges were to show no discrimination.

Signing of the Russo-Estonian Peace Treaty met with profound satisfaction among Soviet statesmen and in the Soviet press.

Lenin was glad that Great Britain had "permitted" Estonia to conclude a peace with Russia; it seemed to him "an actual break through the blockade." [12] Suggesting ratification of the Peace Treaty by the Central Executive Committee, he called it "a fact of tremendous universal historical significance," because Russia had thereby "opened a window on Europe." [13] He was convinced that "all these sacrifices would not ruin the revolution." [14] Trotsky admitted that negotiations with Estonia "produced the same effect as opium and implanted the confidence that the war [meaning the Civil War in general] was approaching its end." [15]

Chicherin reiterated Lenin's words that signing of the treaty was indeed "a fact of universal historical significance." He added that it had developed "into a dress rehearsal, so to speak, for an understanding with the *Entente,* into the first attempt to break through the blockade, and into the first experiment in peaceful coexistence with bourgeois states." [16]

A. Ioffe, Chairman of the Russian Peace Delegation at Tartu, conceded that Russia had gained political advantages. It was worthwhile giving Estonia "a bonus for being the first to conclude peace." He was pleased that Russia's desire to receive guarantees preventing the Baltic republics from transformation into the "foreposts of forces inimical to the Soviet Republic" had been satisfied. "In this respect we have attained what we wanted—we have such guarantees," Ioffe told the Central Executive Committee.[17]

Izvestiia was exuberant. In an editorial on February 3 it called the treaty "the first break through the ring of diplomatic blockade imposed on Soviet Russia not only by the *Entente,* but also by the bourgeoisie all over the world." The editorial ended with a contented statement that "the crusade of the world bourgeoisie against the Russian Republic had already been frustrated."

In general, *Izvestiia* made an ambitious propaganda undertaking out of the Russo-Estonian Peace Treaty. It did so by writing editorials, reporting extensively on ratification debates at the Seventh Session of the All-Russian Central Executive Committee, giving long official bulletins, and even reproducing the treaty itself *in extenso.*

In the next six months Russia also came to terms with both Lithuania and Latvia (on July 12 [18] and August 11 [19] respectively). Both peace treaties, as in the case of Estonia, contained unreserved recognition of the independence and sovereignty of Lithuania and Latvia as well as renunciation of all historical claims to them. There were also nearly identical articles dealing with economic matters, re-evacuation of people and goods, claims and counterclaims, etc. Payments in gold in lieu of Lithuanian and Latvian claims were substantially lower, however: three million rubles for Lithuania and four million rubles for Latvia.

Izvestiia, commenting editorially August 14 on the Russo-Latvian Peace Treaty, was glad that "another link had been punched out of the iron chain with which the world imperialism tried to tie up Workers' and Peasants' Russia." The paper also expressed satisfaction that "Russia had acquired a wide door to Europe—not just a small window—in the form of excellent Latvian ports of Riga, Liepaja, and Ventspils, through which she can freely move in and out her goods." The outstanding political significance of the treaty was that Soviet Russia had thereby reduced the number of enemy states, refuted slanderous claims about her imperialism and aggressiveness, and furnished proof that only she was a protector and liberator of oppressed nations and states.

The Russo-Lithuanian Peace Treaty was not commented on. Ioffe claimed, however, that Lithuania was rewarded more than Latvia because she "did not wage a war against Soviet Russia." [20] It should be pointed out that in doing so Ioffe was contradicting Lenin's pronouncements on the same subject. For, in one of his speeches (March 1, 1920), Lenin made it clear that no such war had been waged by the Baltic States:

> Had all these small states taken up arms against us—and they were given hundreds of millions of dollars as well as the best guns and equipment; they had war-experienced British instructors—there is no slightest doubt that we would have suffered defeat.[21]

Neither did Chicherin blame the Baltic States for their struggle against Russia. To him, they were mere tools in the hands of the *Entente,* trying to set up a number of bourgeois republics on Russia's western frontier; Russia was simply not strong enough to struggle simultaneously against the *Entente* (not the Baltic States!) and anti-Bolshevik civil war leaders—Denikin and Kolchak.[22] The reasons for Bolshevik opposition to the independence of the Baltic States were made abundantly clear in *Izvestiia* of December 25, 1918. After the plans for conversion of the Baltic Sea into a Soviet Sea or a Sea of Socialist Revolution were frustrated, Chicherin found the development fully consistent with Russia's desires. To him, the Baltic States had suddenly become a barrier *protecting* Russia against new attacks launched by the *Entente;* they were no longer a barrier impeding Russia.[23]

Besides admitting that the failure of the Baltic States to take up arms against Russia was welcome to her from a military viewpoint, Lenin also stated in the same speech that the Baltic States did so in disregard of Allied urging to start an offensive. He ridiculed the British for their failure to press fourteen small states into such an undertaking; although the names of those fourteen states were not given by the British, Lenin believed the Baltic States were among them.[24] He must also have known that the French and the Americans—not only the British—were opposed to peace talks between Estonia and Soviet Russia.[25]

Each of the peace treaties between Russia and the Baltic States invariably began with the solemn assurance that Russia, acting "on the basis of the right of all peoples to decide their own destinies and to secede completely from the state of which they form part," was renouncing "voluntarily and forever," "voluntarily and irrevocably," "voluntarily and for all times," all rights of sovereignty formerly held by Russia over the Estonian, Latvian, and Lithuanian peoples and territories. Yet renunciation was not meant seriously. Both Lenin and Stalin made blunt statements to that effect soon after the signing of the three peace treaties.

Referring to the Russo-Estonian Treaty on January 28, 1920, i.e., even before it was signed, Lenin stated what he really thought of it:

> We made numerous concessions. The principal one was the cession of disputed territory with a mixed Russian and Estonian population. But we do not want to shed workers' and Red Army soldiers' blood for a piece of land, particularly since the concession is not forever. Estonia is going through a Kerenskiade-period. The workers are beginning to realize the meanness of their established leaders . . . they will soon overthrow this Government and form Soviet Estonia which will conclude a new peace with us.[26]

Lenin's opinion on the Russo-Estonian Peace Treaty coincided with his views on international treaties in general, stated at the time the arguments for and against conclusion of the Brest-Litovsk Peace Treaty were raging in full swing:

> In war never tie your hands with considerations of formality. It is ridiculous not to know the history of war, not to know that a treaty is a means of gaining strength.[27]

Speaking on another occasion of Poland, after Russian troops were repulsed from the gates of Warsaw in the summer of 1920, Lenin said regretfully:

> Had Poland become Sovietized, the Versailles Peace would have been terminated, and the system built on victory over Germany would likewise have been destroyed.[28]

There is no doubt that Sovietization of the Baltic States—"a partition wall between Soviet Russia and revolutionary Germany," to use *Izvestiia's* definition of December 25, 1918—would have been just as welcome to Lenin.

Stalin's views were identical. Writing in *Pravda* of October 10, 1920, shortly after the conclusion of all three peace treaties with the Baltic republics, Stalin spoke strongly against the secession of border states in general:

> The demand for secession of the border regions from Russia must be rejected . . . primarily because it is fundamentally opposed to the interests of the mass of the peoples both of the center and of the border regions. Apart from the fact that secession of the border regions would undermine the revolutionary potential of Central Russia, which stimulates the emancipation movement both in the West and in the East, the seceded regions themselves would inevitably fall into bondage to international imperialism . . . the secession of the border regions at the present stage was profoundly counterrevolutionary.

It is characteristic that not only the communists, but also all other Russian political parties, were unamimous in their opposition to the independence of the secession states. However they hated each other, whatever their ideological differences, they were in full agreement on Russia's right to hold tenaciously everything she had acquired in the past.

P. Miliukov, leader of the so-called Progressive Coalition at the Russian *Duma* (the Diet) and subsequently Foreign Minister in the Provisional Government, was asked about autonomy—not independence—for the Latvians. He ironically replied, "then it would be necessary to grant autonomy even to the Samoyedes" [29] (a nomadic tribe living in the Arctic). A. Kerensky, a Revolutionary Socialist and Prime

Minister of the Provisional Government, flatly rejected any possibility that the Russians might ever grant independence to Lithuania or, for that matter, to any of the other non-Russian entities. All he offered was autonomy.[30]

A stenographic record of Kerensky's statement on Finland's struggle for independence, made at the State Conference on August 12, 1917, gives a good insight into his mentality where such problems were concerned:

> I, as Head of the Provisional Government, as War Minister, will issue appropriate orders. This will not be permitted . . . [Storm of applause. Shouts: "Bravo!"] And we hope that this decision of ours and this will of ours will be upheld by the whole might of the entire people and the entire nation.[31]

While uttering his threats, Kerensky must have had in mind the Provisional Government's declaration of April 9, 1917, which emphatically assured that the Russian people would never permit its motherland to come out of the World War humiliated and undermined in its vital resources.[32] At the same time he was wondering why the non-Russians were

> raising their heads higher and higher in an endeavor to seek salvation not in a closer unity with the vital forces of the Russian state, but in an endeavor to set their fate farther apart from it and with greater definiteness.[33]

N. Ustrialov, a cabinet member of the anti-Bolshevik Kolchak government, aptly summed up the Soviet and anti-Soviet views on the problem: "The Soviet government will strive by all means to reunite the outlying lands with the center—in the name of the world revolution; Russian patriots will fight to achieve the same objective—in the name of Great, Indivisible Russia." [34] General A. Denikin, leader of anti-Bolshevik forces in Southern Russia and the Ukraine, likewise predicted that the political bond between Russia and the borderlands would be re-established: "either soon or not so soon; voluntarily—by means of an agreement, or forcibly—by means of customs and/or economic war or invasion of armed forces"; and this, he said, would be done by "any Russia—be it 'Red,' 'Pink,' 'White,' or 'Black' . . . The time will come when 'scraps of paper' will be torn to pieces and thrown away as trash." [35]

In view of Russia's reluctance to grant rights of secession to the former Baltic Provinces, it was only logical to expect that she would try to recover the loss on the first favorable occasion. It did not take long.

While the Lithuanian delegation was engaged in peace negotiations at Moscow, Russian troops launched a successful counteroffensive against Polish armed forces who had penetrated deep into White Russia and the Ukraine. The Poles also occupied a large section of Eastern Lithuania, including the capital—Vilnius. Early in July, the Russians reached the eastern frontier of Lithuania as agreed upon at Moscow. Instead of halting there, the Russians continued westward. On July 14, 1920—two days after the signing of the Russo-Lithuanian Peace Treaty —they entered Vilnius, located some 60 to 70 miles west of the Lithuanian frontier.

A declaration issued by the Lithuanian delegation at the time of signing the Peace Treaty stated that an encroachment upon Lithuanian territory, if dictated by military emergency, was not to be regarded as violation of her territory and an unfriendly act, provided that Russian troops were removed after the emergency had passed.[36] And so the Russians took advantage of this agreement.

An excuse that Russia, guided by strategic reasons, was compelled to occupy part of the territory she had renounced "voluntarily and for all times," is hardly tenable. Lithuania was not an ally of Poland and not even neutral in the conflict. She herself was trying hard to recover possession of Vilnius and the surrounding territory lost to the Poles in the spring and early summer of 1919. A diplomatic battle was in full swing. Shortly before the conclusion of the Russo-Lithuanian Peace Treaty, Poland agreed to withdraw from the contested Lithuanian territory (the Spa Protocol of July 10, 1920).[36a]

In fact, by mid-July, both the Lithuanian and Russian troops were simultaneously converging upon the same boundary line from the west and east respectively. If the Russians feared that the Poles would not evacuate Eastern Lithuania and would thus create a threat to their right flank, the fear was unfounded. For a speedy evacuation of Eastern Lithuania would have become compulsory when the Russians penetrated the region of Belostok and exposed the Poles to the danger of being cut off.

The Russians permitted a small detachment of Lithuanian troops to enter Vilnius, but otherwise they were in no hurry to let the Lithuanian government take over administration of the city. It took more than three weeks to negotiate an agreement by which the Russian troops were to be cleared out, and another three weeks to complete the evacuation. Not until August 27 did the Lithuanian government become the master in its own house. It took another ten days to negotiate an agreement of August 6 providing for the evacuation of the occupied territory in three stages.[37]

Incidentally, it was not the only violation of the Russo-Lithuanian Peace Treaty. Despite its clearly defined obligations, the RSFSR and its successor, the Soviet Union:[38] (1) dodged repayment of prewar savings of Lithuanian citizens in Russian banks amounting to some 13 million gold rubles; (2) failed to return historical documents pertaining to the medieval state of Lithuania and even refused to grant permission to photograph them; (3) avoided putting at Lithuania's disposal 100,000 dessiatin (270,000 acres) of timber; and finally (4) violated the very spirit of that treaty by reinvading Lithuania in 1940.[39]

It is hardly conceivable that the Russians could have relinquished Vilnius in 1920 because the Russo-Lithuanian Peace Treaty compelled them to do so. Lenin's ideas on the sanctity of treaties in war have been referred to. It was rather the unfavorable military situation that forced the Russians to abandon Vilnius. In contrast to the earlier Polish military reverses, the month of August witnessed a recovery and the resumption of a successful counteroffensive. Russian forces could only avoid destruction by retreating. Sovietization of Poland had to be postponed, as was the conversion of the Baltic Sea into the Sea of Socialist Revolution. In October of the same year, the Russians conceded defeat and asked the Poles for an armistice.

The Russo-Polish Peace Treaty of March 18, 1921,[40] deprived Russia of large White Russian and Ukrainian territories. It confirmed renunciation of all her claims to the territory situated west of the frontier mutually agreed upon between the two contracting states. This frontier ran farther east (Nos. 1 & 3, map p. 135) than the one negotiated between Russia and Lithuania on July 12, 1920. Actually it ran inside the Polish-held territory. (Poland had reoccupied Vilnius on October 9, 1920, in violation of the Polish-Lithuanian Pact of October 7, 1920, leaving Vilnius on the Lithuanian side.) Russia left it to Poland and Lithuania to decide the whole problem among themselves. "The question of the attribution of these districts to one of those two States," the Russo-Polish Treaty read, "is the matter which exclusively concerns Poland and Lithuania."

Thus, Poland failed to receive from Russia the coveted acknowledgment of her claims to the contested territory. As for Lithuania, she never agreed to recognize the Polish occupation of more than a third (36%) of her land. She even refused for eighteen years, as a sign of silent protest, to maintain any diplomatic, consular, postal, commercial, and other relations with Poland. Her constitution stated that Vilnius was the capital of Lithuania. All maps showed the eastern frontier running as agreed upon between Russia and Lithuania. The actual separation line between the Lithuanian and the Polish-administered areas was referred to as an "administration line." No vehicular or rail traffic moved across this line until 1938, when Poland, under threat of taking "measures of her own" (ultimatum of March 17), forced Lithuania to agree to the normalization of relations.

Nor did Russia make any secret of her strong condemnation of Polish occupation of Eastern Lithuania. While the Russo-Polish peace negotiations were conducted in Riga, Chairman of the Russian delegation A. Ioffe repeatedly told his Polish counterparts that the invasion of Lithuania had created "an extremely alarming situation" in that area.[41] A note signed by People's Foreign Commissar G. Chicherin a year later (April 28, 1922) confirmed Russia's attitude to the Polish-Lithuanian controversy:

> The Treaty of Riga does not affect in any way the Russo-Lithuanian Peace Treaty, done in Moscow June [July] 12, 1920. By virtue of the Treaty of Riga, the question of Vilnius must be settled between Poland and Lithuania alone. This stipulation, however, does by no means contradict the Russo-Lithuanian Treaty which remains in full force after signing the Treaty of Riga. The Republic of Lithuania will exercise sovereignty over Vilnius as conceded by the Republic of Russia as long as the Republic of Lithuania itself has not decided to renounce it in favor of the Republic of Poland.[42]

When Poland remained unimpressed by such statements and kept trying to legalize the seizure of Lithuanian territory, the Soviet government warned both Poland and Lithuania that any endeavor to bring in third parties ("the so-called League of Nations") to settle their dispute would be unacceptable to Russia and that any meddling of such third powers would show a hostile attitude toward Russia and her allies.[43] The Soviet government, consequently, refused to recognize the validity of the decision reached by the Conference of Ambassadors on March 15, 1923, awarding the Polish-occupied territory in Lithuania to Poland.

On the occasion of signing the Soviet-Lithuanian Treaty of Non-aggression on September 28, 1926, the Soviet government reassured the Lithuanian government in a separate note that the *de facto* violation of Lithuanian frontiers committed against the will of the Lithuanian nation had not shaken the Soviet attitude toward the territorial sovereignty defined in Art. 2 of the Peace Treaty of July 12, 1920.[44]

The Soviet Minister in Kaunas stated in *Izvestiia* on October 13, 1926, that the Soviet government was prepared to recognize any settlement of the Vilnius problem by a voluntary agreement between Poland and Lithuania; on the other hand, it would regard as not binding any decision against the will of the Lithuanian people, no matter by whom and under what circumstances. Polish representations in Moscow to the effect that the Soviet-Lithuanian Treaty of Nonaggression violated the provisions of the Russo-Polish Peace Treaty were rejected. Poland was so upset about such an "unfriendly act" on the part of the Soviet government that Great Britain and France had to warn her not to start any military move against Lithuania.[45] It helped, but not for long.

When relations between Poland and Lithuania became dangerously tense again in 1927, the Soviet government suggested moderation to both parties. It pointed out, however, that "the maintenance of peace depended to a much larger degree on Poland than on Lithuania," and concluded the note with an unmistakable warning to the former:

> In particular public opinion in the Soviet Union is especially disturbed by the fact that reports have appeared in the responsible Polish press, and have not been authoritatively contradicted, that the Polish Government had decided on a "radical cutting of the knot of Polish-Lithuanian relations." Without entering upon an estimate of all the disturbing reports reinforcing these fears, the Government of the USSR, being the nearest neighbor of Poland and Lithuania and vitally interested in the maintenance of peace in eastern Europe, is compelled with the utmost gravity to direct the attention of the Polish Government to the immeasurable dangers of an eventual attack by Poland on the independence of Lithuania in whatever form and expresses the conviction that the Polish Government, which only recently in such solemn form declared its desire for peace, will in fact be able to remove the threatening danger of war.[46]

The Russo-Polish Peace Treaty served as an indication Russia had failed to tear down the hated "separating wall" and prevent formation of its substitute—the *cordon sanitaire*. Poland was never forgiven for it. More than two decades after the termination of the Russo-Polish war (1944), the Soviet press reminded the Poles that they in the twenties were willing to become a bastion of the West against the East and play the leading role in the struggle against the Soviet Union and in the establishment of a *cordon sanitaire* along its western frontiers.[47]

But in the early twenties, Russia could do nothing to alter the situation. Defeated militarily by the secession states, exhausted by civil war at home, she could but postpone realization of the objectives she had failed to attain by sword and subversion. All she could do was try to prevent the weak *cordon sanitaire* from becoming a strong armed camp. Hence, every attempt at closer cooperation between the secession states was looked upon with suspicion and unfriendliness.

By the end of 1921, it became clear in Moscow that Poland and the Baltic States were about to meet together in a conference at Warsaw. Their goal was to reach agreement on matters of mutual interest, after such earlier attempts had failed. The Ninth Congress of the Soviets deemed it advisable to take a stand. Its resolution of January 1, 1922,[48] stated that, despite all efforts of the Soviet government to establish friendly relations with all states, the world reaction had not abandoned its attempts to stifle the revolution in Russia; it had chosen her neighbors as instruments for achieving the goal. Although the Soviet government made all possible concessions and even sustained substantial sacrifices, military and chauvinistic parties in the neighboring states had never stopped their preparations of attacks against Russia. The governments in these countries were then accused of either giving active support to the "military parties" or being unwilling or unable to hinder them in their activities.

Referring to Finland's complaint against Russia at the League of Nations because of ill-treatment of the Finnish people in Russian-held Eastern Karelia, the resolution singled out two of Russia's Baltic neighbors for their sympathy toward the Finnish cause:

> The Estonian and Latvian Governments, closely connected with Russia by economic ties and making full use of their situation as transit states between Russia and the West, nevertheless associated themselves with Finland's appeal to the so-called League of Nations and so entered the ranks of the hostile states in favor of attacking the RSFSR. The Congress observes that the governments of the states on the western frontiers are acting in a manner which cuts across the elementary interests of their peoples, for these require the strengthening and development of friendly relations and close economic connections with the Soviet republics.

The resolution also contained a stern warning—one of the first such to be given in the years to come:

> At the same time the All-Russian Congress of Soviets addresses a serious warning to the Governments of the neighboring states and directs their attention to the fact that the Soviet republics are strong enough not to submit to the role of defenceless victims of attacks from without and of foreign violence. The Congress warns the Governments of the neighboring states that if in the future they make any attempt on the integrity of Soviet territory and the security of the Soviet republics or if they support such attempts, in that case the latter, in lawful and just defence against any attack on the security and well-being of the republics, will be compelled to retaliate, which may be fatal for the attacker and his accomplices.

Despite the warning, representatives of Poland, Latvia, Estonia and Finland (Lithuania refused to have anything to do with Poland after the seizure of Vilnius in 1920) met at Warsaw and signed a Convention on March 17, 1922.[49] Its signatories undertook: (1) to abstain from concluding any agreements to the direct or indirect disadvantage of any of the signatories and to communicate to each other those concluded between them and any other states; (2) to enter into negotiations with a view of concluding commercial treaties and various conventions; (3) to decide any controversy or dispute among the signatories by peaceful means, eventually taking recourse to arbitration in conformity with the Covenant of the League of Nations; (4) to adopt a benevolent attitude toward the signatory fallen victim to unprovoked aggression and immediately to agree upon the course of action.

Russia was unpleasantly surprised. She took the agreement reached as a military alliance directed against her.[50] This served as a sign for the Deputy Foreign Commissar M. Litvinov to act. While the Warsaw Conference was in progress, he dispatched notes to all participants, suggesting they meet together in an informal conference. They did so in Riga on March 29–30, with Lithuania absent and Finland represented by an observer.

The Riga Conference examined the following questions:[51] (a) reconstruction of economic life in Eastern Europe; (b) re-establishment of commercial relations between the countries represented; and (c) consolidation of peace in Eastern Europe. The final Protocol of the Conference, signed by Latvia, Estonia, Poland, and Russia, stated the opinion of the delegates that it would be advisable to seek to encourage freedom of financial and economic agreements both with individual states and with financial concerns and private financiers; it would be useful to guarantee mutually peace treaties between Russia, on one side, and Estonia, Latvia, and Poland, on the other; and it would be in the interest of the states represented to re-establish commercial relations among them. In the latter case, the delegates made a number of specific recommendations.

The delegates also "solemnly reaffirmed their sincere desire for universal peace as well as their determination to entertain friendly relations and to procede to the settlement of controversial questions by peaceful means." They made several recommendations to that effect, such as: protection of frontiers by regular troops and frontier guards only; limitation of the number of such troops and its equalization on either side of the frontier; prohibition of concentration of troops in the vicinity of the frontiers, of raids into the neighboring territory, and of formation of armed gangs.

Whatever the value of such declarative statements, Russia must have been much more pleased with the statement in the Protocol that (1) it would be desirable to coordinate the actions of the representatives of Estonia, Latvia, Poland, and Russia at the Economic Conference at Genoa (April 10–May 19, 1922) and (2) it would be useful if these countries worked out at Genoa precise proposals for the realization of the above principles. Russia was pleased, because she would appear at an international conference—first ever to be attended by Bolshevik Russia—as a member, or even a leader, of a bloc of Eastern European States. With these Russia professed to want to live in peace. She was satisfied with the *status quo* in Eastern Europe of the early twenties as exemplified by the peace treaties between Russia and her neighbors.

Russia must have been pleased also because the Riga Conference stated that the *de jure* recognition of the Russian Soviet government would constitute "an apropriate step in the economic reconstruction of Eastern Europe." This was to convey prestige to Russia, still awaiting recognition by capitalist countries. The *de jure* recognition seemed so important to Russia that her Foreign Commissar G. Chicherin advised the Genoa Conference that Russia was ready to make payments on financial obligations of the former Tsarist government incurred prior to August 1, 1914. She further would make payments to foreign powers and their nationals, and restore to foreigners the right to use their former property, now nationalized or requisitioned.[52]

The subsequent interpretation given by Russia to the agreements reached at the Riga Conference was that it obligated the participating states not merely to coordinate their actions at the Genoa Conference, but also to do their utmost at the Conference to induce the states which had not yet done so to recognize the Soviet Government of Russia.[53] Thus, Poland, Latvia, and Estonia, by virtue of this interpretation, were supposed to work for Russian interests.

Finally, the Riga Conference gave its full support to the principle of limitation of armaments in all countries. Chicherin hastened to state at the very first plenary session of the Genoa Conference his intent to submit a proposal to this effect.[54] Yet the disarmament problems did not come up for discussion at all. The All-Russian Central Executive Committee, therefore, had to state later on, "with deep regret," that Chicherin's proposal "did not meet with any response among the representatives of other powers at the Genoa Conference." [55]

Otherwise Russia was greatly satisfied with her achievements at the Riga Conference. An authoritative diplomatic history,[56] in evaluating its results, proudly stated that "the Soviet diplomacy succeeded in shaking somewhat the united front of the Baltic countries and taking the anti-Soviet edge off the decisions taken at the Warsaw Conference." Hence, Poland, Latvia, Estonia, and Finland were invited on June 12, 1922, to come to Moscow on November 30 and talk things over. The invitation said that the Russian government saw no obstacle "to the partial solution of the problem which was not dealt with at Genoa and which might be settled by countries sincerely anxious to live in peace and to regulate all disputes which may arise between them by pacific means, thus avoiding the necessity of maintaining excessively large armies." Lithuania, having no common frontiers with Russia after Poland had wedged herself between them in 1920, was also invited "at the last minute"—on November 23.[57]

The Conference convened on December 2.[58] Litvinov immediately suggested that the Conference draw up a plan by which the land forces of the participating countries be reduced within 1½–2 years by one-fourth; the amount of military expenditures be limited proportionately; paramilitary formations be dissolved; and frontier zones be demilitarized. Litvinov refused, however, to submit any proposal tending to limit naval armaments. He also stressed in his opening address that the proposals advanced by the Russian government could not be replaced by talks on "the so-called moral disarmament."

And yet the "moral disarmament" clause was to play a big part in ultimately wrecking the Conference. In vain the non-Russian delegations insisted that: "the material disarmament should be preceded and accompanied by political disarmament"; "the reduction of armaments alone does not provide for adequate security"; "it is necessary to begin by creating the atmosphere of moral confidence"; etc. Litvinov refused to budge from his position. He implied that the other delegations "prefer palaver on 'moral disarmament' to real work."

The material disarmament proved just as difficult. Poland, for example, reached the conclusion that Russia wanted to reduce Polish armed forces 27%; Latvian, 30%; Estonian, 40%; but Russian, only 25%. Lithuania, mindful of her territorial demands versus Poland, refused to accept the *status quo* as permanent. Poland, in turn, refused to allow arbitration of her controversy with Lithuania. There was some doubt as to whether or not certain Russian proposals were compatible with the duties of negotiating parties toward the League of Nations. These Russia bitterly opposed. The tone of the Russian press was unfriendly and caused complaints by other delegations.

By December 12 it became clear to all that the Conference was a failure. It terminated without even concluding the debate on the Treaty of Nonaggression suggested by Poland and amended by Lithuania and Russia. "As far as Russia is concerned," Litvinov declared on parting, "she keeps her army for defense purposes only. As soon as she is sure that her neighbors and other states nurture no aggressive designs, she will go about a further reduction of her armed forces, the entertainment of which will not be dictated by considerations due to the internal situation."

It deserves particular mention that the Russian draft of the Treaty of Nonaggression contained a provision whereby all differences between the contracting states were to be submitted to arbitration.[59] Never again did Russia or subsequently (the Soviet Union) agree to arbitration. Otherwise her draft provided for: (1) abstention from aggression; (2) nonsupport of an aggressor, nonsignatory to the Treaty; (3) prohibition of all treaties contradicting the spirit of the Nonaggression Treaty; (4) nonsupport of one contracting party committing aggression against the other contracting party; and (5) settlement of all differences by pacific means.

Chapter Five

NONAGGRESSION PROMOTER

Russia had no reason to complain about the political situation in Eastern Europe at the end of 1922. Although she had failed in disarming her neighbors, she also could see they presented no danger to her. A broader Baltic Union embracing all border states from Finland to Poland was as remote in 1922 as it was in 1920 when discussions to that end first began. On the other hand, Russia, herself, not fully recovered from Civil War wounds and still in the second year of her New Economic Policy (NEP), was badly in need of peace. Thus, all she needed was preservation of the *status quo* on her western frontiers.

Russia made this clear by reminding both Poland and Lithuania that she was viewing with "serious alarm" the mounting tension between them. In a note of February 17, 1923, she pointed out that any threat to general peace in that area deeply affected Russian interests, too. The note ended with this warning: "Any violation of peace in Eastern Europe may have repercussions on Soviet Russia's international position and give rise to undesirable consequences." [1]

Stability in the Klaipeda region (No. 5, map p. 135)—a sore point between Germany and Lithuania—likewise was claimed by Russia as a factor of great importance for political equilibrium on the Baltic and for Russian security.[2] Russia also showed eagerness to eliminate any third powers in the Klaipeda region[3] which came up for discussion in 1923, after Lithuania established her *de facto* administration there. (It was detached from Germany by the Peace Treaty of Versailles.) Granting of special rights to the third powers was termed by Russia as a "hostile action directed against her vital interests." The Soviet government refused to recognize such decisions and reserved for itself the right to freedom of action and the freedom to demand compensation.

The idea of transferring the Klaipeda region to a *de jure* Lithuanian administration met with a resolute Russian opposition. In several notes dispatched between 1922 and 1924 to Lithuania, Germany, Poland, Great Britain, France, and Italy (the three latter being signatories of the Klaipeda Convention of May 13, 1924), the Soviet government vigorously protested against the transfer without Russia's (the Soviet Union's) participation in the settlement. It went so far that the Lithuanian government was formally requested to check with the Soviet government before taking any further steps in that matter.

The *Treaty of Defensive Alliance* between Estonia and Latvia concluded on November 1, 1923,[4] was not likely to upset the equilibrium in the Baltic area or to present a danger to the Soviet Union. The Treaty was drawn up in the spirit of friendship and development of economic relations with all nations, "particularly with the Baltic and neighboring countries," which obviously included the Soviet Union. The two contracting parties obligated themselves to render each other military assistance and assume the state of war should either of them suffer an unprovoked attack. In such a case neither party was to negotiate or conclude separately an armistice or peace. The Treaty provided for consultation on foreign policy problems of mutual interest; communication to each other of the text of any treaties; and submission of all eventual disputes either to the Court of International Justice or to international arbitration.

The Estonian-Latvian defensive alliance, backed by a combined population of only 3,000,000 and the resources of two tiny countries the size of Ohio, could not possibly be viewed as a danger to the Soviet Union. Nonetheless, Chicherin, when asked by the *Manchester Guardian* about his views on the Estonian-Latvian agreement, expressed his profound displeasure (December 24, 1923):

> These attempts to form combinations of border states will never solve the problem of their healthy development, which can come about only through friendly economic and political agreement with Russia; of course, with complete preservation of their own independence. It is noticeable, that the Estonian-Latvian agreement was concluded just at the moment French diplomacy was particularly active in its attempts to thwart the pacific designs of Russian policy. It is unfortunate that certain leading political personages of the Baltic States should, with their eyes on France, try to make a show of hostility towards Russia, which is by no means felt by their countries as a whole.[5]

Of course, Chicherin felt differently about his own combinations, however strange they appeared to outsiders. Such was the case with his attempt, undertaken in November 1923 through his emissary V.

Kopp, to induce Lithuania, Latvia, and Estonia to sign an agreement
by which these states and the Soviet Union would accept the principle
of nonintervention in German (*sic!*) affairs and place no obstacles to
the transit of goods and food regardless of political changes in Germany.
V. Kopp offered a Soviet guarantee of integrity and independence in
exchange for neutrality. Chicherin's desire allegedly was to ensure
peace for Eastern Europe, "even in the event of a further turmoil in
the West." The real reason lies somewhere else: the Soviet Union,
anticipating a Bolshevik uprising in Germany, thought about active
intervention. The former Latvian Minister in Moscow, K. Ozols, tells
in his memoirs that Kopp made an unofficial inquiry regarding his government's willingness to let Soviet troops cross Latvia en route to
Germany.[6]

To be exact, Soviet-Estonian relations in the mid-twenties were not
too friendly for another reason. Early in 1924 Estonian communists
began to exhibit extreme agility.[7] After searching Communist headquarters in Tallinn, the Estonian police found documentary evidence
showing close connection between Estonian communists and the Soviet
Legation. An official communique of the Minister of the Interior
caused the Soviet Legation to lodge a protest. Another protest followed
the trial of 149 communists, ending in 89 jail sentences and one death
sentence. At the same time noisy demonstrations were staged in Leningrad. The Soviet press spoke highly of the defendants and saw nothing
wrong in the fact that they merely wanted "a legal incorporation of
Estonia into the Soviet Union."

All this activity culminated in an abortive communist revolt in
Tallinn on December 1, 1924. It was carefully prepared by 80 to 100
professional agitators smuggled in from the Soviet Union. Russian
employees of the Soviet Trading Agency and 60 Red Army officers
likewise took part in the revolt while Soviet naval units were cruising
within sight of Tallinn. G. Zinov'ev, Party Secretary in Leningrad and
Chairman of the Communist International, was the principal figure in the
background. He advocated an outright annexation of Estonia.

The revolt was suppressed quickly and easily. Numerous arrests
were made and some death sentences were imposed upon the leaders.
One of those shot was J. Anvelt, erstwhile Chairman of the Soviet
Government of Estonia. *Pravda* on December 11 published an angry
denunciation of Estonian actions and caused, in turn, unfavorable
comments in the Estonian press. As a result, the Soviet Legation submitted one more strongly-worded protest. Stalin also took issue in
one of his addresses half a year later (May 18, 1925) by referring to
"the campaign of calumny in connection with the insurrection in
Estonia." He dismissed the whole incident with the explanation that

imperialists had already begun their preparations to exert pressure on the Soviet Union; he saw preparations for an offensive, preliminary bombardment of public opinion, and creation of moral prerequisites for intervention. A retaliation trial of 50 "Estonian spies" was announced to take place in Leningrad in late January 1926.[8]

A simultaneous increase in communist activities in Lithuania surely was more than coincidence. To be sure, they never were at a standstill. As told in reminiscences of a prominent political figure, Msgr. Krupavicius, the Lithuanian Diet was reminded in 1921 that police had found in Kaunas large caches of communist propaganda material, explosives, arms, and passport blanks. In the fall of 1923 the Diet again was reminded that the communists were engaged in smuggling subversive persons, arms, and explosives into Lithuania, killing defectors, etc.[9] But it was only in 1926, after relaxation of certain restrictions of civil liberties, that the communists became really active. Their turbulent demonstrations in the streets of Kaunas served as one of the excuses for the overthrow of the leftist government by the rightists (December 17, 1926). Possibility of a communist revolt in Lithuania at that time was both affirmed and denied, depending on the desired interpretation. Soon after the rightist coup, a communist underground paper, *Komunistas,* stated categorically:

> We did not call for an armed revolt in 1926 for the purpose of over-throwing the bourgeois government. Under the conditions prevailing in 1926, such a call would have been but an adventure. We only called for a struggle against the reaction and fascism and at the same time gave instructions to take up arms in the event of a fascist uprising. Today, after the fascist uprising is over, we do not call for an armed revolt to over-throw the bourgeois rule in Lithuania because we do not have favorable conditions on hand.[10]

On the other hand, one of the communist underground organizers in Lithuania admitted in his memoirs that the necessity and feasibility of an armed uprising in 1926 actually had been discussed among the faithful; lists of "volunteers" were drawn up; and even some arms were available for that purpose.[11]

The new Government of Lithuania took no chances. It immediately restricted the freedom of action for any such activities, made arrests among the known communists, and drove them underground. Such was also the fate of communists in Latvia.

And so the Soviet Fifth Column in the Baltic States lay completely shattered by the mid-twenties. In fact, it never recovered sufficiently to be a danger to the existing order before the Soviet Union moved in with all its military might. As a matter of record, *Komunistas,* early in 1927, explained why the Soviet Union had not moved in earlier.[12]

Local communist organizations did discuss the pros and cons of an armed uprising. But it was felt that a further development of the international proletarian revolution demanded that the USSR become yet stronger and avoid war; its interference in Lithuanian affairs would precisely have indicated a world war.

Nevertheless, danger existed that Russia might destroy the independence not only of Estonia but of all the border states, either by attacking them directly or undermining them one by one from within. This danger induced Finland, Estonia, Latvia, and Poland to meet in another conference at Helsinki and revive discussions on mutual rapprochement. It eventually resulted in the signature of the *Arbitration and Consultation Treaty* (January 17, 1925),[13] by which the contracting parties undertook to submit to a procedure of conciliation or arbitration any disputes arising between them which had not been settled within a reasonable time through diplomatic channels. The remaining articles of the Treaty dealt with the complicated machinery and procedure of conciliation and arbitration.

That was all. The Baltic bloc under Poland's aegis was dead. Latvian Foreign Minister Z. Meierovics undoubtedly expressed the prevailing opinion in the Baltic States when he, on the eve of the Helsinki Conference, told the press: "We do not wish to become an enemy of one country by drawing closer to another."[14] This could but please the Soviet Union. For it was not long before, that Chicherin warned the Soviet Union's neighbors in the West, "not to enter into the orbit of the Western Powers and not to participate in the plan to encircle us." He also accused them of having always taken a hostile attitude toward the Soviet Union.[15] When the Estonian Foreign Minister K. Pusta failed to make a similar declaration, the Soviet Union retaliated. It stopped all its traffic of transit goods through the Estonian ports and redirected it through the Latvian ports.[16]

In his report to the Third Congress of Soviets on May 13, 1925, A. Rykov, Chairman of the Council of People's Commissars, took a strong stand against the recently concluded Helsinki Treaty and against cooperation among the Baltic States in general:

> The inhabitants of the frontier countries of these separate republics which were formed from parts of the single Tsarist Russia of that time know very well that our program of national self-determination guarantees the independence of all these countries a thousand times better than any treaty or legal declaration . . . Another fact which should not be ignored is the secret meeting recently held of the Baltic countries. But the secret leaked out, and, apparently, it was chiefly from us that the secret was kept, and not without reason . . . This and a number of other facts indicate that attempts are being made to reach an agreement directed against the USSR.[17]

At the end of 1925, Chicherin stopped in Kaunas and Riga. He took an opportunity to issue through *Izvestiia* (January 3, 1926) a statement making it clear that the Soviet Union wanted an agreement with each and all Baltic States individually, but not with their union.

The Soviet government maintained, as before, violent opposition to any endeavor of the western powers to exert influence in the Baltic area. An attempt of the League of Nations to settle the Polish-Lithuanian dispute over Vilnius was branded as carrying "traces of hostile attitude toward Russia and her allies." [18] France was repeatedly accused of anti-Soviet scheming, while the Baltic States were warned that the efforts of French diplomacy were not in the least concerned with the interests of the Baltic States, but with the prevention of formation of settled conditions in Eastern Europe.[19]

An attempt was made to discredit Great Britain by coercing the Estonian envoy in Moscow, A. Birk, into "revelation" of alleged British plotting against Soviet interests in Tallinn. Forced to resign in June 1926, Birk was detained in the Soviet Union for some nine months. Then his story made the rounds of the European press.[20]

Poland received a strong rebuke from Chicherin for a statement made by her Foreign Minister Skrzynski at the Helsinki Conference where he referred to the Baltic Union as a "barrier in defense of European civilization against Asiatic barbarism." Speaking at a press conference in Kaunas where he was visiting (December 23, 1925), Chicherin made it clear that he had no sympathy for such a union. He further claimed that its creation had been the objective of the Helsinki Conference.[21] Poland was also castigated by Chicherin's deputy, M. Litvinov, in his report on foreign affairs to the Central Executive Committee on April 24, 1926:

> Unfortunately, all our efforts to reach lasting agreement with Poland have up to now been defeated by the Polish Government's anxiety to play the part, so to speak, of the manager of external relations for all the Baltic States. We seek agreement with Poland, while Poland insists on speaking on behalf of all the Baltic States which, as far as we are aware, have never authorized it to do so. We do not, and are not prepared to recognize Poland's protectorate, open or concealed, over the Baltic. The stubborn reluctance of the Polish Government to speak only on behalf of its own state has up to now brought to nothing all our attempts at rapprochement.[22]

Similar accusations were repeated on December 8, 1926,[23] and April 18, 1927.[24]

In general, the Soviet Union held a negative attitude toward close collaboration among the Baltic States and violently disapproved of any other state showing interest in this area. In the long run, its expectations proved disappointing. On the one hand, no anti-Soviet bloc, except that of Latvia and Estonia, had become a reality—despite all negotiations, meetings, and conferences to that end. On the other hand, the Soviet Union had failed to align the neighboring states on its side or gain their confidence; it also had failed to bring about their disarmament or to assure their neutrality in event of an armed conflict between the Soviet Union and the capitalist countries or imposition of sanctions by the latter.

Such an eventuality became more likely after the League of Nations reached a multilateral agreement providing for sanctions against any state disregarding international law (Geneva Protocol of 1924). The Soviet Union was quick to realize the necessity of neutralizing all its neighbors. With this idea in mind, it proposed to them conclusion of nonaggression treaties.

Lithuania was first among the Baltic States to agree. She signed up on September 28, 1926, after considerable courting on the part of the Soviet Union and after Chicherin paid Kaunas a visit at the end of 1925. The provisions of the *Soviet-Lithuanian Treaty of Nonaggression*[25] read as follows:

> (1) The relations between the Union of Socialist Soviet Republics and the Lithuanian Republic shall continue to be based on the Treaty of Peace between Lithuania and Russia, concluded at Moscow on July 12, 1920, all the provisions of which shall retain their force and inviolability.
>
> (2) The Lithuanian Republic and the Union of Socialist Soviet Republics undertake to respect in all circumstances each other's sovereignty and territorial integrity and inviolability.
>
> (3) Each of the Contracting Parties undertakes to refrain from any act of aggression whatsoever against the other Party. Should one of the Contracting Parties, despite its peaceful attitude, be attacked by one or several third Powers, the other Contracting Party undertakes not to support the said third Power or Powers against the Contracting Power.
>
> (4) If, on the occasion of a conflict of the type mentioned in Article 3, par. 2 or at a time when neither of the Contracting Parties is engaged in warlike operations, a political agreement directed against one of the Contracting Parties is concluded between third Powers, or a coalition is formed between third Powers with a view to the economic or financial boycott of either of the Contracting Parties, the other Contracting Party undertakes not to adhere to such agreement or coalition.
>
> (5) Should a dispute arise between them, the Contracting Parties undertake to appoint conciliation commissions, if it should not prove possible to settle the dispute by diplomatic means. The composition of the said commissions, their rights, and the procedure they shall observe shall be settled in virtue of a separate agreement to be concluded between the two Parties.

The Treaty was to run for five years after the date of ratification, with the exception of Art. 1 and 2, which had no time limit. The Treaty was duly renewed for another five years on May 6, 1931, and for more than ten additional years on April 4, 1934 (it was to run until December 31, 1945).

This Treaty, in contrast to the Disarmament Convention proposed by Russia in 1922, contained no reference to arbitration. In fact, soon thereafter (December 6) Chicherin told the press that the Soviet Union would go as far as possible to meet the Baltic States, but she would not go back on the Soviet principle of rejecting arbitration pacts. "I do not doubt," he predicted, "that sooner or later all the Baltic States will sign guarantee treaties with us, without clauses about arbitration." [26] And he proved right.

As far as the Soviet-Lithuanian Treaty of Nonaggression is concerned, a substitute for arbitration was found in the form of conciliation commissions. However, such commissions, being appointed by governments in dispute, were unlikely to arrive at an impartial decision, with no third impartial party to cast a decisive vote. Furthermore, the Treaty provided that conciliation commissions' decisions would in no way bind either government. In fact, the commissions could do little more than submit their joint or separate proposals to both governments.

But even this meager substitute of arbitration remained a dead letter. There was not a single case of conciliation between the Soviet Union and Lithuania for fourteen years. When, however, in June 1940, Lithuania proposed to take recourse to conciliatory procedure for settling a dispute that had resulted from Soviet interpretation of the execution of the Soviet-Lithuanian Pact of Mutual Assistance of October 10, 1939, the Soviet Union did not consider the proposal even worthy of a reply.[27]

The Soviet Union did not oppose, however, eventual application of sanctions ordered by the League of Nations. Lithuania, as a member of that body, was under obligation to act in accordance with the majority decision no matter what her treaty with the Soviet Union said. Consequently, Lithuania, in a separate protocol, made a reservation to the effect that (1) her obligations under the Treaty of Nonagression could not in any way hinder the execution of the obligation laid upon her by Covenant of the League of Nations and that (2) her membership in the League of Nations would not constitute an obstacle to the maintenance of either friendly relations between the two countries or to the "Lithuanian nation's aspirations toward neutrality, which is the policy best suited for her vital interests."

The belief has been expressed that the Soviet-Lithuanian Treaty of Nonaggression actually dealt a fatal blow to a Baltic bloc of nations under Poland's aegis and that the Soviet Union signed the Treaty to prevent formation of such a bloc.[28] It is true that the Soviet government was highly pleased. Even before the conclusion of the Treaty, Litvinov spoke of "particularly friendly relations with Lithuania." [29] The Treaty signing was termed by Chicherin "an occasion of great strengthening of friendly relations" between the two peoples. He felt that the Treaty would make possible a further development and consolidation of these relations and a strengthening of the independence of the Lithuanian people.[30] Similar statements were made by the Soviet Ambassador in Paris[31] and the Soviet Minister in Kaunas.[32] The Soviet Union obliged further by stressing in a separate note its unchanging attitude in regard to the Polish-Lithuanian controversy over Vilnius.[33] Polish representations on that score were curtly dismissed.[34]

This did not prevent the Soviet Union from continuing active espionage in Lithuania. Its extent came to light in 1927, following the arrest of General K. Klescinskis, former Chief of Staff of the Lithuanian Army. He was apprehended with incriminating documents in his possession, found guilty of high treason, and shot. An employee of the Soviet Legation in Kaunas, found at the time of General Klescinskis' (nickname: Ivanov IV) arrest in the latter's apartment trying to destroy reports he had just received, was permitted to go home. The very next morning he took the train to Moscow.[35]

As the Soviet-Lithuanian Treaty of Nonaggression was taking shape, negotiations for the same purpose began between the Soviet Union, Estonia, and Latvia. While there was no response from Estonia, negotiations proceeded quite smoothly in the case of Latvia. On March 9, 1927, the Treaty was initialed. Yet all the efforts of the Latvian government to have it ratified were frustrated by a strong opposition, both domestic and foreign.[36] Latvian President K. Ulmanis even appealed to the Lithuanian government, urging it "to maintain a common Baltic diplomatic front." [37] The Lithuanian government chose, however, to go ahead with the ratification and succeeded in getting parliamentary action on it.

The Soviet Union, determined to complete formation of a protective belt of neutral states, refused to be discouraged by Estonian and Latvian rebuffs. A substitute for the Soviet-Latvian Treaty of Nonaggression was available in the form of the *Treaty Concerning the Settlement of Frontier Disputes,* signed on July 19, 1926.[38] A similar treaty with Estonia was signed on August 8, 1927.[39] Although these two treaties were not fully equal substitutes for the treaties of nonaggression, their principal objective was the same—elimination of friction along the 300-mile frontier zone where it was most likely to occur.

These treaties were followed by a number of other agreements on commercial, legal, civil, and other matters.[40] Litvinov, in his end-of-the-year report on foreign relations to the Central Executive Committee

(December 10, 1928), was pleased. He did not say anything bad about the Baltic States. On the contrary, he noted "a general improvement" in relations with Latvia, and "relations of unchanging friendship" with Lithuania.[41]

By that time Litvinov was engrossed in lining up the Baltic States behind his plan to extend the provisions of the so-called Briand-Kellogg Pact (the Paris Treaty) of August 27, 1928, to Eastern Europe. The Soviet Union actually begged for an invitation to take part in negotiations in Paris. ("If we were invited," Chicherin stated in *Izvestiia* on August 5, "then I repeat that the possibility of the signature of the Kellogg Pact by our government is likely.") Yet the Soviet government only received an invitation to adhere to the pact after it had been signed by fifteen original signatories[42] . . . and readily accepted.[43] It also hastened to ratify it—even before any of the original signatories.[44]

These are the main provisions of the Briand-Kellogg Pact:

> (1) The High Contracting Parties solemnly declare in the names of their respective peoples that they condemn recourse to war for the solution of international controversies, and renounce it as an instrument of national policy in their relations with one another.
> (2) The High Contracting Parties agree that the settlement or solution of all disputes or conflicts of whatever nature or of whatever orgin they may be, which may arise among them shall never be sought except by pacific means.[45]

Little over a decade later, the Soviet Union grossly violated these provisions by resorting to open threats and military demonstrations to force acceptance by the Baltic States of the dictated terms of a so-called "mutual assistance" (1939) and then staging a full scale invasion (1940).

But in 1928, the Soviet Union was so enthusiastic about the Briand-Kellogg Pact that it not only was the first to ratify it; it also wanted to see the Pact enter into force as quickly as possible, "particularly between the Soviet Union and its nearest neighbors." To effect this, the Soviet government on December 29 dispatched notes to Poland, the original signatory, and Lithuania, the first Baltic State to adhere to the Pact, suggesting the signing of a protocol whereby the Pact would enter into force between the Soviet Union, Poland, and Lithuania immediately after its ratification by these three states, i.e., without awaiting ratification by all the signatories.[46]

Within a month Litvinov rounded up Estonia, Latvia, and Rumania and induced them to sign the Moscow Protocol of February 9, 1929 (although he had to spend "a great deal of effort and time to . . . overcome resistance of certain Governments").[47] Poland signed at the same time, while Lithuania gave its adherence shortly thereafter (April 1, 1929). The principal paragraph in the Protocol stipulated:

The Treaty for the Renunciation of War as an Instrument of National Policy, signed at Paris on August 27, 1928 . . . shall come into force between the Contracting Parties after the ratification of the said Treaty of Paris of 1928 by the competent legislative bodies of the respective Contracting Parties.[48]

Despite all this hurry, the Soviet Government remained critical of the Briand-Kellogg Pact as a whole. In his report to the Fifth Congress of the Soviets on May 29, 1929, Rykov did not conceal his negative attitude to the entire matter:

The Kellogg Pact cannot be regarded as a factor in the prevention of war, as this document contains no real guarantees against war; in particular it says nothing about disarmament or even the limitation of armaments. It would, therefore, be erroneous to connect the question of real prevention of war with the Kellogg Pact. It contains no guarantees that war will not break out. War destroys all treaties, because these are concluded between contracting parties in times of peace . . . This was our estimate of the Kellogg Pact from the very beginning.[49]

Rykov did not deny, however, that the Pact, by imposing a moral obligation to abstain from war, would make psychological preparations for war more difficult. Referring to the Baltic States, Rykov said the Moscow Protocol had made for considerable improvement in their relations with the Soviet Union. As an after-thought, he added: "But we think the signature of the Protocol should be followed by acts which strengthen and reinforce it."

Evidently the general situation improved as expected. Litvinov at the end of 1929 noted, for the second time in a row, that there were no important changes in relations with the Baltic States in the past year, except "the undoubted progress" in relations with Estonia.[50] Nor was there much movement in 1930. So trivial an incident as the Estonian protest against repeated violation of her territory by Soviet reconnaissance planes did not count.[51]

Reconnaissance from the air was supplemented by espionage under diplomatic cover. The role of an employee of the Soviet Legation in Kaunas, who became involved in General Klescinskis' affair, was already mentioned. Yet other means were found to seek the same objectives. On August 29, 1931, the Lithuanian government was forced to sign a protocol by which the Soviet Trade Mission in Kaunas acquired exterritoriality and its personnel diplomatic immunity, thus augmenting the number of agents permitted to operate under the safety of a diplomatic cloak.

It was the first such agreement between the Soviet Union and other states. The Soviet government had it recorded at the League of Nations[52] and used it as a model for subsequent agreements. This writer had a chance to witness in 1940 how the Soviet Trade Mission in

Kaunas prepared plans for nationalization of Lithuanian industry and trade[53]—the pro-Soviet Lithuanian "diet" had only to vote for their enactment, without changing an iota.

Turning back to 1931, this year witnessed renewed Soviet efforts to consummate treaties of nonaggression with all neighboring states. Offers to that effect, made in 1926, still held. By mid-1931 rumors were spread that negotiations with Poland, dormant for five years, were about to be resumed.[54] Litvinov, having in the meantime succeeded Chicherin as People's Commissar for Foreign Affairs, pointed out that the Soviet government still regarded the conclusion of such treaties desirable.

Latvia and Estonia, as well as certain other states, took the hint seriously. Litvinov was able to report at the beginning of 1932 that agreement had been reached on treaties of nonaggression with Finland and Poland; neither Latvia nor Estonia was expected to present any special difficulties in that respect.[55] He was right: Latvia signed up on February 5;[56] Estonia, on May 4.[57]

The Soviet-Latvian and Soviet-Estonian treaties of nonaggression, based on corresponding peace treaties with Russia and on the Briand-Kellogg Pact, were to run for three years. Principal provisions of the Soviet-Latvian treaty (which were *mutatis mutandis* identical with those of the Soviet-Estonian treaty) read:

> (1) Each of the High Contracting Parties undertakes to refrain from any act of aggression directed against the other, and also from any acts of violence directed against the territorial integrity and inviolability of the political independence of the other Contracting Party, regardless of whether such aggression or such acts are committed separately or together with other Powers, with or without declaration of war.
>
> (2) Each of the Contracting Parties undertakes not to be a party to any military or political treaties, conventions, or agreements directed against the independence, territorial integrity, or political security of the other Party, or to any treaties, conventions, or agreements aiming at an economic or financial boycott of either of the Contracting Parties.
>
> (3) The obligations provided for in the present Treaty may not in any way limit or change the international rights and obligations devolving on the High Contracting Parties from treaties concluded by them before the coming into force of the present Treaty and duly published in the official publications of each Party, insofar as such treaties do not include any elements of aggression within the meaning of the present Treaty.
>
> (4) In view of the obligations assumed in the present Treaty, the High Contracting Parties undertake to submit all disputes, whatever their kind or origin, which may arise between them after the signature of the present Treaty and which cannot be settled within a reasonable period by ordinary diplomatic procedure, to a procedure of conciliation in a joint conciliation commission of which the composition, powers, and procedure are to be fixed by a special Convention which the two Parties undertake to conclude as early as possible, and which shall come into force at the same time as the present Treaty.

Thus, here, in contrast to the Soviet-Lithuanian Treaty of Non-aggression of September 28, 1926, no special protocols were needed to permit the signatories to discharge their international obligations, specifically those devolving from the Covenant of the League of Nations. The Soviet Union maintained its negative attitude with regard to arbitration clauses. Instead, it stuck to conciliation commissions. But, in contrast with the case of Lithuania, where nothing was done about setting up conciliation procedure provided in the Treaty, both Estonia and Latvia signed conventions with the Soviet Union involving such procedure (on June 16 and 18, 1932, respectively).[58]

As Finland and Poland also signed treaties of nonaggression with the Soviet Union (January 21 and July 15 respectively), V. Molotov, Chairman of the Council of People's Commissars since 1930, happily reported to the Central Executive Committee on January 23, 1933, that the Soviet Union's international position had been "substantially strengthened." He considered the signature and ratification of non-aggression pacts with Poland, Finland, Latvia, and Estonia "among the assets of the Soviet Government;" these pacts were "important for the consolidation of peace." Yet, turning around, Molotov saw the Soviet Union surrounded by "hostile bourgeois states." [59]

The Soviet government felt, however, that the nonaggression obligation was not of great value because it lacked a generally accepted, precise definition of nonaggression. Without such a definition, it would be difficult to place the blame for violation of nonaggression clauses. There were no generally recognized international authorities to give judgment in such cases. Even if there were, they would have no criteria upon which to base their judgment.[60]

These considerations induced the Soviet government to formulate a detailed definition of aggression and submit it to the League of Nations early in 1933. The Soviet draft ran into considerable opposition, however. Thereupon Litvinov conceived the idea of reaching an agreement with a limited number of states; first of all with the neighbors—a repetition of how the Briand-Kellogg Pact was handled.

Litvinov's idea received support among all the neighbors of the Soviet Union, from Estonia in the north to Afghanistan in the south. On July 3, 1933, the *London Convention for the Definition of Aggression*[61] was signed. Lithuania, not being a neighbor of the Soviet Union *de facto,* adhered to the London Convention by a separate treaty signed two days later,[62] but she still refused to be a party to any agreement with Poland.

The London Convention, as stated in its preamble, was necessitated by the desire to define aggression as specifically as possible in order to obviate any pretext for its justification. It was based on the Soviet proposals submitted to the Conference for the Reduction and Limitation of Armaments. Litvinov could feel proud.

By the terms of the Convention, the signatories undertook to accept the following definition of aggression (Article II):

> The aggressor in an international conflict shall, subject to the agreements in force between the parties to the dispute, be considered to be that State which is the first to commit any of the following actions: (1) declaration of war upon another State; (2) invasion by its armed forces, with or without a declaration of war, of the territory of another State; (3) attack by its land, naval or air forces, with or without a declaration of war, on the territory, vessels or aircraft of another State; (4) naval blockade of the coasts or ports of another State; (5) provision of support to armed bands formed in its territory which have invaded the territory of another State, or refusal, notwithstanding the request of invaded State, to take, in its own territory, all the measures in its power to deprive those bands of all assistance or protection . . . No political, military, economic or other consideration may serve as an excuse or justification for the aggression referred to in Article II.

The Annex to the Convention enumerated specific examples where aggression was not justified on two grounds, namely:

> A. The internal condition of a State: e.g., its political, economic or social structure: alleged defects in its administration; disturbances due to strikes, revolutions, counterrevolutions, or civil war.
>
> B. The international conduct of a State: e.g., the violation of the material or moral rights or interests of a foreign State or its nationals; the rupture of diplomatic or economic relations; economic or financial boycotts; disputes relating to economic, financial or other obligations towards foreign States; frontier incidents not forming any of the cases of aggression specified in Article II . . . the present Convention can never legitimate any violation of international law that may be implied in the circumstances comprised in the above list.

The London Convention contained an excellent definition of aggression covering all possible loopholes. This made the Briand-Kellogg Pact workable.[63] In his comments on the Convention a few days after its signature, Litvinov underscored the peaceful intentions of the Soviet Union and declared it was ready to sign similar conventions with all states, regardless of their geographical situation or relations with the Soviet Union. He took the occasion to expound on some basic tenets of Soviet foreign policy:

> In order to understand the Soviet Union's foreign policy, it must be realized that its essence is and always had been peace. Since it has no imperialist aims, no desire for new territories outside its established frontiers, since it considers the subjection to itself of other peoples undesirable and out of keeping with its basic principles, and stands solidly for their complete independence, the Soviet Union cannot gain any advantage from war, and that alone is enough to make it avoid war.[64]

A few months later K. Voroshilov, People's Commissar for Military and Naval Affairs, took up the subject of the Soviet Union's peaceful intentions by giving assurance that the Soviet Union had no desire to conquer foreign lands. "Our armies are factors making for peace," he said.[65] To which Molotov added: "Nobody can ask for further proofs of the pacific nature of our policy." [66]

This prompted a student of Soviet foreign relations to observe that the conclusion of treaties with its western neighbors in the late twenties and early thirties "seemed to imply a definite acceptance of Russia's new boundaries." [67]

Whatever the Soviet Union's original intentions might have been while promoting extension of the Briand-Kellogg Pact to Eastern Europe and supplementing it with a loophole-proof definition of aggression in the form of the London Convention, both documents became just another scrap of paper, along with all the nonaggression pacts, after the Soviet Union resorted to force in its relations with Poland, Finland, and the Baltic States (1939).

Yet international rewards for the Soviet Union in the mid-thirties were rich. On November 16, 1933, the United States extended *de jure* recognition to the Soviet Union and was quickly followed by Czechoslovakia, Bulgaria, Rumania, Hungary, and Austria. On September 18, 1934, the Soviet Union became a full-fledged member of the League of Nations. The three Baltic States were among those members of the League of Nations who signed a formal invitation to the Soviet Union.

Chapter Six

PROTECTION OVERTURES

In his report to the Central Executive Committee at the end of 1933, Molotov stated that the Soviet Union had achieved substantial success in its foreign policy and had consolidated its international position. "The facts speak for themselves," he pointed out with pride.[1]

Yet Molotov could not help seeing "growing aggressive intentions of ruling circles in certain countries." He meant Germany, where Adolf Hitler became Chancellor of the German Reich on January 30, 1933. Everybody could read the following passage in Hitler's book *Mein Kampf:*

> We National-Socialists deliberately draw a line through the prewar foreign policy of Germany. We begin again where Germany left off six hundred years ago. We stop the eternal German march to the South and West of Europe and direct our gaze to the land in the East. We finally put an end to the colonial and commercial policy of prewar times and pass to the policy of territorial conquest of the future. But when we now speak of new lands in Europe today, we can only think in the first instance of Russia and her border states. Destiny itself seems to be pointing to this road.

The Soviet Union became genuinely alarmed. It was not because of what Hitler said in his book, but because of deeds which followed each other in quick succession in 1933, shortly after his ascent to power. Already on June 20 and 24 *Izvestiia* gave its readers the gist of statements made by Litvinov at the World Economic Conference in London and by the Soviet Ambassador in Berlin. Both vigorously protested against the so-called Hugenberg's memorandum submitted by Germany to the World Economic Conference with a paragraph bearing directly on the Soviet Union:

> The second step consists in placing at the disposal of a people without *Lebensraum* new territories where this energetic race can found colonies and carry out great peaceful works. We are suffering not from over-production, but from forced under-consumption. War, revolution, and internal disruption have found a starting point in Russia, in the vast regions of the east. This process of destruction is still going on. The time has now come to stop it.[2]

These objectives were unlikely to be brought closer to realization unless Germany rid herself of armament restrictions imposed by the Peace Treaty of Versailles. This she requested at the Disarmament Conference in Geneva, but received a cold shoulder. By October 14 Germany was out of both the World Disarmament Conference and the League of Nations. "Idle talk of disarmament is giving way to 'businesslike' talk about armament and rearmament,"[3] such was Stalin's apt description of the general atmosphere of that period.

The Soviet government became apprehensive that Hitler, after building up German armed forces, would turn his attention to the Soviet Union. They reasoned that an eventual invasion could be carried out either across Poland or across the Baltic States; an invasion across the unprotected and unallied Baltic States was more likely as Poland, allied with France since 1921, was not so safe to touch.

Stalin put it rather bluntly in a statement to the Seventeenth Congress of the Communist Party of the Soviet Union. He believed the "old" policy in Germany had been losing ground to a "new" policy. This was reminiscent of "the policy of the former German Kaiser, who at one time occupied the Ukraine, marched against Leningrad, and converted the Baltic countries into a *place d'armes* for this march."[4] Stalin implied thereby that the same *place d'armes* still lay open for Germany to use. What was needed now was to close this invasion road.

Strangely enough, the Soviet Union sought an ally in Poland. Toward the end of 1933, the Soviet government approached the Polish government, suggesting they sign a joint declaration of their "determination to protect and defend peace in Eastern Europe." The declaration was also to recognize that the two states considered as a necessary condition of such peace "the integrity and complete economic and political independence of the new political entities that have been formed out of the former Russian Empire."[5]

Thus, the Soviet Union changed from an opponent to a supporter of the so-often denounced and ridiculed Versailles Treaty. "It is not for us, who have experienced the shame of the Brest-Litovsk peace, to sing the praises of the Versailles Treaty," Stalin stated at the Seventeenth Congress of the Communist Party of the Soviet Union; "we merely do not agree to the world being flung into the abyss of a new war on account of this Treaty." [6]

The whole Soviet undertaking sounded strange indeed in view of the fact that on November 15, 1933, the Polish Ambassador in Berlin had discussed with Hitler the problem of German-Polish relations. A German communique, the text of which was agreed upon with the Polish Ambassador, should have shown Litvinov that something was brewing:

> The Chancellor of the German Reich this morning received a first visit from the Polish Minister, in the presence of the Reich Minister for Foreign Affairs. Discussion of German-Polish relations revealed the complete agreement of both governments in their intention to deal with the questions affecting both countries by way of direct negotiation, and further to renounce all application of force in their mutual relations, with a view to strengthening European peace.[7]

On January 26, 1934, Germany and Poland signed a declaration laying down the principles for the future development of their mutual relations. These were to be based on maintenance of a lasting peace between the two countries, application of the Briand-Kellogg Pact provisions, and settlement of all disputes by peaceful means only.[8]

The Baltic States were astonished that the Soviet Union had taken up the question of their security with another state without previously consulting them.[9] A guarantee of their security by the Soviet Union and Poland alone, with the exclusion of Germany and thus obviously directed against her, must have seemed not too enticing to them. They also must have been apprehensive of angering Germany for purely economic reasons. Germany was buying 30 to 40 per cent of their export goods while the Soviet Union's share was negligible.

The Polish-Lithuanian conflict over Vilnius would also have become a stumbling block as Lithuania was unlikely to accept the Soviet-suggested Polish guarantee of the territorial *status quo* in Eastern Lithuania with which she thoroughly disagreed.

After the conclusion of the Polish-German agreement of January 26, 1934, *Izvestiia* immediately asked whether Germany was not expecting some compensation for the voluntary renunciation of her designs on Poland, and if so, at whose expense. *Lietuvos Zinios,* a Lithuanian Socialist daily, bluntly declared that Germany had postponed her attack on Poland for ten years but that she now was preparing an attack on the Baltic States and through them on the Soviet Union.[10]

Taking the bull by the horns, Litvinov on March 28 indicated to the German Ambassador in Moscow that the Soviet government was seeking to normalize mutual relations. He suggested that they sign a protocol whereby both governments would undertake "to be invariably guided in their foreign policy by the obligation to preserve the independence and integrity of the Baltic States and to refrain from any action capable of directly or indirectly violating their independence." The protocol should be open to other interested countries.[11]

Aside from other implications, the note deserves attention for its reference to a "direct or indirect violation." The formula of "indirect aggression," as sought by the Soviet Union to apply to the Baltic States in 1934, was to become a stumbling block in the 1939 diplomatic negotiations between the Soviet Union, Great Britain, and France.

In a further display of its peaceful intentions toward the Baltic States, the Soviet Union on April 4 extended the validity of all three treaties of nonaggression until December 31, 1945.[12] The Soviet-Lithuanian Treaty, in 1931 prolonged for another five years, was in no immediate need of such extension, but what the Soviet government needed was a demonstration. As a matter of fact, Litvinov's original idea was to continue the treaties for an indefinite period, but even Litvinov felt that this would have indicated an abstract or a philosophical concept rather than a concrete action.[13]

A demonstration of peaceful intentions was underscored in Litvinov's statement issued on the occasion of the signature of the prolongation of treaties:

> The Soviet state had never demanded revision of existing treaties and never intends to demand it. The Soviet state, which is a stranger to chauvinism, nationalism, or racial and national prejudice, perceives its state duties to lie, not in conquest, not in expansion of territory.[14]

Germany remained unimpressed. On April 14 she rejected the Soviet proposal. Neither the territorial integrity nor the independence of the Baltic States was threatened by anyone, Germany and the Soviet Union included, the German note pointed out. Consequently, there was no need that the Soviet Union and Germany act as protectors of the Baltic States. Germany simply felt that no protocol of the kind proposed by the Soviet Union could serve a useful purpose. The Soviet proposal was one previously rejected by Poland. Furthermore, it had not been discussed beforehand with the Baltic States.[15] To prove that Germany acted differently, contents of the note were transmitted through channels to Kaunas, Riga, and Tallinn.

In his verbal reply to the German Ambassador in Moscow, Litvinov agreed that no threat existed to the independence and integrity of the Baltic States. At the same time he reminded the German government that violation of peace in Eastern Europe in all probability would prove a prelude to the outbreak of a new world war. Otherwise he found "not a single convincing reason or argument" against his proposal. Yet Litvinov felt uncomfortable over his failure to consult the Baltic States. "It goes without saying," he belatedly assured the German Ambassador, "the Baltic States would have been previously informed." [16]

Who knows? In 1939 the same powers—Germany and the Soviet Union—reached an agreement at the expense of the Baltic States. Molotov, who by then replaced Litvinov as People's Commissar for Foreign Affairs, chose not to divulge any information to them.

In the second half of May 1934, i.e., shortly after receiving the German brush-off in the matter of imposing a protectorate over the Baltic States, Litvinov went to Geneva as head of the Soviet Delegation to the Disarmament Conference. Here he met French Foreign Minister L. Barthou and exchanged with him ideas on an Eastern Pact. This was conceived as a mutual security system comprised of the Soviet Union, Finland, the three Baltic States, Poland, Germany, and Czechoslovakia. When asked by *Paris-Soir* on June 23 what he thought of the Eastern Pact, Litvinov replied that the Soviet Union was not only interested, but already had agreed to participate in it. He expected, however, that it would take time to bring all the problems to a final solution.[17] He was right.

On his way home, Litvinov stopped in Berlin and tried to persuade his German colleague, Baron von Neurath, to join the pact (June 13).[18] Von Neurath remained noncommittal, however. He postponed his reply until September 8. In an identical note delivered in Moscow, Warsaw, Tallinn, and Kaunas on that date, the German government stated it was unable to undertake the far-reaching obligations that would result from its signing the Soviet-proposed pact. Poland's refusal followed on September 27.

Only the Baltic States were ready to go along, despite the trip in July of Polish Foreign Minister J. Beck to both Riga and Tallinn, in an effort to dissuade both the Latvian and Estonian governments from agreeing to the pact.[19] Litvinov was happy to receive the Estonian and Lithuanian Foreign Ministers in Moscow at the end of July and in early August, respectively, to hear them approve of the idea of the Eastern Pact.[20] The Latvian Minister in Moscow associated himself with these statements.[21]

Such an attitude of the Baltic States is not astonishing. They had signed a number of agreements with the Soviet Union and felt at least formally secure from that side. It was not so with Germany. For she not only kept open the problem of the Klaipeda Territory (a number of local Nazis were arrested by the Lithuanian authorities and found in court guilty of high treason in 1934); she also suggested to Poland the idea of partitioning certain areas in the Soviet Union.[22] This prospect meant conversion of the Baltic States into a battleground. On the other hand, a multilateral security agreement promised to tie the hands of both rival powers—Germany and the Soviet Union. This must have seemed to the Baltic States better than either bilateral nonaggression treaties with no arbitration permitted, or the resounding, but otherwise empty, declarations of good intent, such as renunciation of war or definition of aggression, on which their security was based. Even several years later (1937), Latvian Foreign Minister V. Munters tried to impress upon United States Ambassador in Moscow J. E. Davies ideas which were highly reminiscent of the Eastern Pact of a few years ago, and which the Ambassador called "an English and French plan for preservation of peace in Eastern Europe":

> The solution for the peace of Eastern Europe may be found under an arrangement between Germany and the Baltic States, Poland, and Rumania, whereby Germany would enter into the same kind of treaties with these states, respectively, which the USSR had with these states. With such pacts of nonaggression, together with a clear definition of what constitutes the aggressor, peace would be assured as far as treaties could effect that end.[23]

It should be noted that the Eastern Pact draft provided for automatic assistance to the victim of an attack by a third Power. Germany was against it. Although giving preference to bilateral nonaggression treaties, in general, she was of the opinion that multilateral treaties ought to be based on consultation rather than on automatic assistance (note of September 8, 1934).[24] The Soviet Union thought differently, however. This may be seen from its demand for the recognition of the principle of "automatic assistance," persistently brought forth during the negotiations with Great Britain and France in 1939.

Upon the collapse of diplomatic negotiations between Germany and the Soviet Union, security of the Baltic States remained, as before, solely dependent on Germany's good will and the Soviet Union's signature under several treaties, referred to in the foregoing. Collaboration among the Baltic States was of minor importance in view of their physical limitations. Nevertheless, some progress was achieved in this respect.

The Latvian-Estonian *Treaty of Defensive Alliance* of November 1, 1923, was amended on February 17, 1934. It provided for the signatories (1) to act together at international conferences and to have a common delegation; (2) to hold regular conferences of foreign ministers; and (3) to establish a joint council for the coordination of legal, political, and economic matters.[25]

Two months later (April 25), the Lithuanian government expressed the desire to join the Latvian-Estonian Alliance. Although such initiative was welcomed in both Riga and Tallinn, negotiations did not proceed smoothly. The main difficulty presented itself in Lithuania's involvement in territorial disputes with Germany and Poland. Only after it became known that Germany had declined to join the Eastern Pact, did the three foreign ministers come to agreement.

The *Treaty of Good Understanding and Cooperation* between Estonia, Latvia, and Lithuania, signed in Geneva on September 12, 1934,[26] contained the following undertakings of the signatories:

(a) To confer together on questions of foreign policy which are of common concern and to afford one another mutual political and diplomatic assistance in their international relations;

(b) to institute periodical conferences of the Ministers for Foreign Affairs of the three countries, to take place at regular intervals, at least twice a year, in the territories of each of the three states in turn;

(c) to settle amicably and in a spirit of justice and equity any questions in respect of which their interests may clash and also to do so in the shortest possible time (and) to negotiate with each other such agreements as may appear suitable for attaining this end;

(d) to give instructions to their diplomatic and consular representatives abroad and to their delegates to international conferences to establish appropriate contact;

(e) to communicate to one another forthwith the text of the treaties concluded between one of them and one or more other states;

(f) to foster the growth and general diffusion in their respective countries of the spirit of mutual understanding and friendship among the three nations and . . . to take or to promote all suitable measures and efforts to that end.

The signatories also took cognizance of the territorial disputes between Lithuania, on the one hand, and Germany and Poland, on the other. This was done in a separate article of the Treaty:

The High Contracting Parties recognize the existence of the specific problems which make a concerted attitude with regard to them difficult. They agree that such problems constitute an exception to the undertakings laid down in Article 1 of the present Treaty.

The Treaty was to remain in force for ten years. In its implementation,[27] the three foreign ministers met regularly in conferences to discuss problems of mutual concern, such as the Eastern Pact, neutrality, legislation, economic matters, etc. A Bureau for the Promotion of Cooperation between Estonia, Latvia, and Lithuania was set up in 1935. It worked out a plan for common action in cultural and economic matters and was instrumental in arranging several conferences on cultural cooperation. A trilingual publication, the *Baltic Review,* devoted to cooperation among the Baltic States, made its appearance in February 1940.

Although for several years the Soviet Union raised no objections to these activities, they were to play an important role in its ultimatums presented to Lithuania, Latvia, and Estonia in 1940.

While cooperation between the Baltic States was being pushed off the dead spot where it had been stuck since 1920, the Soviet Union refused to give up hope of extending its unwelcome protection over the

Baltic States. It had to be a unilateral act after Poland and Germany rejected Soviet overtures to that end. German refusal either to guarantee the territorial integrity and independence of the Baltic States or join the Eastern Pact—both advocated by the Soviet Union—must have produced uneasiness in Moscow. In his report to the Seventh Congress of the Soviets on January 28, 1935, Molotov[28] quoted extensively from Hitler's book to show his aggressive tendencies. He warned that neither the Soviet government nor its citizens could ignore Hitler's pronouncement: "We shall reckon with the fact and draw the necessary conclusions."

At the same time Molotov indicated the Soviet Union was fully aware how important was the need for a reliable defense of its frontiers. He pointed out that a few fortified areas with necessary equipment had been built on the western frontier and that both the numerical strength of the Red Army and its equipment had grown at considerable expense and sacrifice. He implied this was not aimed against the Baltic States, as relations with them had developed normally.

In doing this, Molotov did not miss the chance to emphasize that the Soviet Union had never held out the threat of annexation to a single state—large or small. He stressed that the Soviet government proved the friendliness of its policy toward the Baltic States in a special declaration recognizing their inviolability and complete economic and political independence. He only regretted that Poland and Germany had declined to participate.

Evidently seeking to strengthen further the Soviet Union's western frontier, Litvinov on April 6, 1935, made inquiries in Tallinn, Riga, and Kaunas regarding the willingness of these states to conclude bilateral treaties of mutual assistance.[29] Litvinov's inquiry was preceded by Marshal Tukhachevsky's article in *Pravda* (March 31) where he referred to Hitler's purported demand for the "weakening of the western frontier of the Soviet Union." Although Lithuania *de facto* had not had common frontiers with the Soviet Union since 1920, Litvinov also included her in his offer.

As could have been expected, the Conference of the Baltic Foreign Ministers, meeting on May 6, reached the conclusion that the Baltic States should observe strict neutrality and avoid close ties with any great power.[30] The three ministers were perfectly aware of the dangers involved in such treaties. Their acceptance would have turned them into allies of the Soviet Union and foes of Germany.

The fact that Hitler on May 25 expressed his readiness to conclude nonaggression treaties with all European countries except Lithuania, thus posing a direct threat to the latter, did not bring about a reversal in the decision. Formally, none could be expected in view of the fact that the Treaty of Good Understanding and Cooperation between the Baltic States excluded solidarity in such "purely Lithuanian" affairs.

But even had they acceded to the Soviet proposals in 1935, as they did under pressure in 1939, their ultimate fate hardly would have been different. For the signature of the treaties of mutual assistance in 1939 served only as a pretext to establish Soviet land, naval, and air bases all over the Baltic. It also prepared an outright invasion with huge forces. An earlier signature of those treaties would possibly have resulted in mere abbreviation of the period of independence.

The beginning of the year 1936 bore witness to the Soviet Union's anxiety about the situation in the Baltic area. While making a report to the Central Executive Committee on January 10, Molotov accused Germany of continuing to espouse her "plans of aggrandizement at the expense of the Soviet Union" and specifically of "feverishly preparing to occupy a dominant position in the Baltic region." After mentioning that the Soviet Union's defenses had been placed "on a proper footing" and that "not a little" had been done in this direction in the past few years, Molotov included a warning:

> Whoever launches into a new imperialist war may succeed in breaking his neck before accomplishing his plans of conquest . . . We shall take every measure to frustrate every possibility of an attack on our country by the imperialists. But if they do attack us, we have no doubt that our Red Army will inflict the repulse they deserve.[31]

In an apparent endeavor to show the Soviet Union's continued interest in the Baltic area, its planes flew demonstratively over the Estonian town of Tartu in February 1936.[32] This caused considerable concern and nervousness, although only a month before Molotov had stated that "not a single one of these states has had any cause for anxiety as far as we are concerned." Another demonstration, this time of a peaceful nature, was staged on May 1, when the Chiefs of Staff of the Baltic States watched the huge military parade on the Red Square in Moscow among the highest Soviet Party and Army men. Finally, a Soviet warship *Marat* visited the Estonian port of Tallinn and the Latvian port of Riga.

Evidently the Soviet government felt that intimidation was also needed. For there is no other explanation for the verbal attack upon the Baltic States launched by A. Zhdanov, Leningrad Party Secretary, during the Eighth Congress of the Soviets (November 29, 1936):

> As you know, the Leningrad region marks the Soviet frontier with Finland, Estonia, and Latvia, countries with whose peoples the USSR has normal peaceful relations. And if, in some of these little countries, for example Finland, feelings of hostility to the USSR are being kindled by larger and more adventurist countries, and preparations are being made to make their

territory available for aggressive action by fascist powers, in the long run it is these little countries alone which will be the losers. It does not pay for little countries to get entangled in big adventures, and if fascism dares to seek military victories on the northwest frontier of the Soviet Union, then we in Leningrad, placing at the service of defense all the technical strength we can command, shall deal it such a crushing blow that the enemy will never again turn his eyes on Leningrad.[33]

The impression Zhdanov produced in the Baltic States was one of profound shock.[34] *Tass* hastened to issue a rectified version of his speech in which fascism, and not the Baltic States, was blamed. The Soviet Minister in Riga called on the Latvian Foreign Minister and assured him that Zhdanov's speech was not directed against any of the Baltic States and that the Soviet press had given a false version of it. Similar assurances must also have been given both in Tallinn and Kaunas.

Zhdanov's boasting about the preparedness of the Red Army was not an empty one. While he was talking, the General Staff of the Red Army was busy printing military maps of the Baltic States. One such map, covering a certain area in Lithuania to the scale of 1:100,000, was brought to the United States in 1951. The legend on the map says that it was in preparation from October 26 until December 27, 1936.[35]

In addition to the preparation of maps, other measures of military nature were taken along the Estonian and Latvian frontiers. Strategic railroad spurs were built. Forest strips were burnt down. Entire villages were evacuated. Even frontier incidents were deliberately provoked, as at Lake Peipsi where the Soviet police tried to kidnap Estonian citizens within Estonian territory. In the ensuing gun battle, three Soviet police were killed, whereupon their colleagues returned, seized three Estonian nationals, took them over the border, and shot them in cold-blooded reprisal.[36]

Military preparations were accompanied by subtle reminders that the Baltic States had better look up to the Soviet Union for protection. For the Soviet Union was not uninterested in what was happening there. As an example, Soviet Minister in Kaunas, M. Karsky, while calling on Lithuanian Minister S. Lozoraitis to smooth out the bad impression created by Zhdanov's speech, did not content himself with assurances of unchanging Soviet friendliness. He reminded Lozoraitis that neither Lithuania nor any other Baltic State, for that matter, could remain outside a European conflict and that in such an event only the Soviet Union could protect them.[37] Litvinov, who saw Latvian Foreign Minister K. Munters in mid-June 1937, made it clear that Latvia's geographical position was such that the USSR could not help being interested in the preservation of her complete independence.[38] A visit of Soviet Chief of Staff Marshal Egorov to all three Baltic capitals in the same year apparently was meant to put greater emphasis on Litvinov's words.

Despite these threats, military demonstrations, and sweet persuasion, the Soviet Union was far from being prepared to protect the existing *status quo* in Eastern Europe. This came to light twice in 1938; first, in the case of the Polish ultimatum to Lithuania, and second, in the case of the territorial rearrangement in Czechoslovakia.

Throughout the twenties and thirties, the Soviet Union repeatedly warned Poland not to use force in her relations with Lithuania. This attitude came to an acid test in mid-March 1938. At that time, emboldened by the lack of real opposition among the European powers to Hitler's invasion of Austria (March 11), Poland used a minor incident at the Polish-Lithuanian frontier (the "demarcation line" in Lithuanian terminology) to normalize her relations with Lithuania by force.[39]

As a consequence, Warsaw served an ultimatum on March 17. It rejected a Lithuanian offer to settle the incident amicably and requested, instead, immediate establishment of normal diplomatic relations; specifically, accreditation of diplomatic representatives at Kaunas and Warsaw not later than March 31. The Lithuanian government was given 48 hours to accept the terms of the ultimatum—*ne varietur*. The ultimatum was worded in such a way as to present this time a real threat to peace in Eastern Europe:

> Failure to reply or the proposal of any supplements or reservations whatever will be considered by the Polish Government as a refusal. In this negative case, the Polish Government will guarantee the just interests of their State by measures of their own.

While presenting the ultimatum, supported by heavy concentration of troops along the disputed frontier, Warsaw seemed little concerned that Poland was the original signatory of the Briand-Kellogg Pact of August 27, 1928, which obligated her "never to seek the settlement or solution of all disputes or conflicts of whatever origin they may be except by pacific means." Poland's endeavor to settle a dispute with Lithuania by force made her an outright aggressor by virtue of the London Convention of July 3, 1933, of which she likewise was a signatory.

It would be wrong to assume that Poland resorted to the threat of force solely because she was influenced by Germany, which since 1933 had broken her international obligations one after another and managed to provoke only minor reprimands. Poland, too, had already broken one agreement with Lithuania, the so-called Treaty of Suvalki of October 7, 1920, establishing a provisional *modus vivendi* between the two states. Although this caused Lithuania to sever all relations with Poland for a period of seventeen and a half years, Poland kept possession of the occupied territory. Now the time seemed ripe for another drastic solution of the impasse in Polish-Lithuanian relations.

The Lithuanian government complied with the ultimatum. Lithuania was too weak to resist a Polish attack, and all diplomatic representatives accredited to the Lithuanian government urged acceptance of the ultimatum.[40] The Soviet diplomats played a strange role. When the Lithuanian Minister in Moscow tried to get Soviet advice, Litvinov remained unavailable to him for 24 hours, and Litvinov's office "knew nothing" of his whereabouts. When he finally showed up on March 19, it was too late for any advice—the Lithuanian government already had complied with both the terms and the deadline stipulated in the ultimatum.[41]

Litvinov's advice this time differed from the previous Soviet attitude toward the Polish-Lithuanian disagreement. He "strongly urged" the Lithuanian government to accede to Polish demands.[42] It must have been a great disappointment in this respect at Kaunas. The Germans were quick to detect "considerable coolness" in Soviet-Lithuanian relations as a result of Soviet failure to extend help—or even moral support—to Lithuania during her crisis with Poland.[43] A prediction made in 1937 by United States Ambassador in Moscow J. E. Davies that "Lithuania would find her most effective protector, in case of war with either Poland or Germany, in the Soviet Union," [44] proved false.

Litvinov might have suspected that a war between Poland and Lithuania was likely to involve Germany. The latter made no secret of her determination to regain the Klaipeda Territory. A Polish-Lithuanian conflict would have furnished an excellent opportunity to go ahead with incorporation plans.

As a matter of fact, Germany foresaw such an eventuality. While Foreign Minister Ribbentrop suggested to the Lithuanian Minister in Berlin "unconditional acceptance" of the Polish ultimatum (and flatly refused mediation),[45] he also signed a memorandum giving his views on the German attitude toward the incident. He considered the occupation of the Klaipeda Territory, in case of a Polish-Lithuanian conflict, "necessary within the first few hours." Ribbentrop's memorandum also revealed that appropriate preparations for the occupation had been made.[46]

Ribbentrop was evidently referring to Hitler's orders of March 18 to the German High Command of the Armed Forces to prepare plans for the occupation of the Klaipeda Territory ("I intend, if the Poles march into Lithuania, to reunite the German Klaipeda with Germany. I shall decide time for this.")[47] The High Command, however, in such an event would have sought to establish "a demarcation line" in the

Lithuanian Territory. A sketch on the map[48] showed it running along the Nemunas to the mouth of the Dubysa, thence northward, along the river, to the vicinity of Siauliai, and thence westward to the Baltic Sea. Thus, the High Command was eyeing a block of Lithuanian territory covering an area of about 6,000 sq. miles (larger than Connecticut). Since only 1100 sq. miles belonged to the Klaipeda Territory, German plans went far beyond reincorporation of what she lost by virtue of the Versailles Peace Treaty.

At the same time economists at the German Foreign Ministry were ordered to work on the problem of eventual aid to Lithuania in her development of a substitute port as well as rail and water connection. The directive spoke of the possibility that a situation might arise in which Lithuania could be confronted with the demand for reincorporation of the Klaipeda Territory.[49] Acceptance of the Polish ultimatum by Lithuania made things easier all around.

Another test of Soviet readiness to uphold, by force if necessary, the existing *status quo* in Eastern Europe, came in the fall of 1938, during the crisis over Czechoslovakia. It was also a test of Soviet readiness to honor its treaty obligations, since Czechoslovakia and the Soviet Union had signed a Treaty of Mutual Assistance on May 16, 1935.

While the crisis was still building up, Chairman of the Supreme Soviet of the USSR, M. Kalinin, told a Czech Labor Delegation (May 11) that the Soviet Union had invariably fulfilled all its treaties concluded with other states in all their consequences and that it would, if called upon, "fulfill to the last letter all its obigations to Czechoslovakia and France." [50] Speaking at the League of Nations on September 21, Litvinov confirmed that the Soviet Union intended to fulfill its obligations to afford assistance to Czechoslovakia.[51] Two days later the Soviet government issued a warning to Poland:

> Should Polish troops in fact cross the frontier of Czechoslovakia and occupy her territory, the Soviet Government thinks it expedient and necessary to warn the Polish Government that, in virtue of Article 2 of the non-aggression pact concluded between the USSR and Poland on July 25, 1932, the Soviet Government, faced with a Polish act of aggression against Czechoslovakia, would be compelled to denounce the said pact without further notice.[52]

When Poland, after the Munich Conference (September 29–30), did "cross the frontier of Czechoslovakia and occupy her territory" (about 400 sq. miles containing one quarter of a million inhabitants), the Soviet Union neither denounced its Nonaggression Treaty with Poland nor afforded any assistance to the victim. Its excuse was that France, likewise bound to Czechoslovakia by a Treaty of Mutual Assistance, rendered no aid either.[53] However, the Soviet-Czechoslovak Treaty did not call for such consultation, since Art. 2 and 3 provided for "immediate" aid and assistance.

In Great Britain, Lord Winterton, Chancellor of the Duchy of Lancaster, suspected the truth. He was bold enough to tell the Upper Chamber of the British Parliament: "At the time of the crisis, the Soviet Union made no offer of help but, because of its military weakness, confined itself to promises." [54] An angry denial in *Pravda* (October 14) and the Soviet Ambassador's protest in London could not alter the impression left by Soviet inaction. Even half a year later Stalin felt obliged to take a stand (March 10, 1939) against "vociferous lies" in the foreign press about "the weakness of the Russian Army" and "the demoralization of the Russian Air Force." [55]

The German Foreign Ministry must have shared Lord Winterton's views. It did not anticipate, shortly after the Czechoslovak crisis, any military aid from the Soviet Union to Lithuania in case of a German-Lithuanian conflict over Klaipeda.[56] Nor did the Polish Minister in Kaunas, who reported to his superiors on November 7 that the Lithuanians had abandoned all hope for Soviet aid.[57]

This is not astonishing. The commanding staff of the Red Army was greatly weakened as a result of Stalin's purges in 1937–1938, beginning with the execution of Deputy People's Commissar of Defense Marshal M. Tukhachevsky and seven high-placed generals and going through the ranks of other high officers. The Soviet Union was unlikely to risk involvement in a war.

Uneasiness prevailed, however, among the Soviet neighbors. A British student of Baltic policies, Robert Machray, who visited the Baltic States in September 1938, found a feeling in the air that "the destinies of the little nations, not excepting the Baltic States, were in the balance." [58] The situation was much different from what United States Ambassador J. E. Davies had found on his trip in 1937. Although even then he saw them "walking the tight rope" between Germany and the Soviet Union," Estonia seemed to him to lie "outside of the danger zone" in event of a Soviet-German war.[59]

In 1938, the Estonian Chief of Staff, Major General Reek, did not share this view. On the contrary, in a conversation with the German Minister and Military Attaché in Tallinn, he expressed fear the Soviet Union might occupy Estonia on the grounds that she could serve as a supply base to the enemy. In such a case, the Soviet Union would never leave the country, making Estonian independence illusory. According to Major General Reek, Estonia was firmly resolved to oppose any attempt to march Soviet troops and was ready to fight to the limit of her capabilities. He seemed over-optimistic, however, in evaluating the effectiveness of such opposition—Estonia would be able to put up

200,000 men, and the Red Army better "think twice" before embarking on any similar operation.[60]

Neutrality, which the Baltic States professed for several years and reconfirmed at the end of 1938 and in early 1939, no longer satisfied the Soviet Union. "Escape into neutrality," *Pravda* reminded them (June 21, 1938), "does not assure for the small states safety from danger which would arise in the event of a war between the great powers."

But in the meantime one "great power," the Soviet Union, steered clearly away from any involvement in an armed conflict with another "great power," Germany. In the fall of 1938, there were some signs of reconciliation between these two powers. Soon rumors began spreading that they were about ready to partition Poland and the Baltic States. No wonder that Hitler, under these conditions, was left free to undertake a slight expansion in the Baltic area by taking the Klaipeda Territory away from Lithuania. This was a goal toward which Hitler had worked since assuming power in 1933.

Throughout those years, Hitler was alternately putting pressure on Lithuania and taking it off. In the fall of 1934, enraged by the trial of Klaipeda Nazis which ended in imposition of heavy sentences upon a number of them, he broke off commercial relations with Lithuania. As a result, she lost her only market for geese. The plight of farmers was alleviated by forcing government employees to purchase a certain number of geese in proportion to each one's pay grade. But the country, as a whole, lost a substantial amount of foreign currency.

The fall of 1938 seemed to be different. On September 26 Hitler declared that, after the solution of the Sudeten-German problem in Czechoslovakia, "there will be for Germany no further territorial problems in Europe." But these were only words. Tension mounted rapidly toward the end of the year. By early December, the Lithuanian Foreign Minister became convinced that the Nazis were seriously contemplating taking Klaipeda away. He then ordered the Lithuanian ministers in both London and Paris to advise the governments they were accredited to, which were signatories of the Klaipeda Convention, about the impending danger.[61]

"It is too late to save Klaipeda for Lithuania," the British Ambassador in Berlin cabled to London on December 8.[62] A *démarche* he and his French colleague made at the German Foreign Ministry on December 12 requesting assurance of respect for the *status quo* remained fruitless.[63] By the end of January 1939, the British Foreign Office knew that the *Anschluss* of Klaipeda was to take place around March 15.[64] However, neither the British nor the French governments offered help. Lithuania was advised to act on her own; another *démarche* in Berlin was considered useless.[65]

For the time being, Hitler was preoccupied with Czechoslovakian affairs. Their solution was ready by March 15 when he entered Prague and took the Czech people "under the protection of the German Reich." [66] The Soviet Union failed again to intervene in behalf of its partner in a mutual assistance pact. All it did was to submit a strongly-worded protest to the German government (March 18).[67]

Then came Lithuania's turn. On March 20 Ribbentrop summoned Foreign Minister Urbsys and told him that the Lithuanian Government must transfer the Klaipeda Territory to Germany on its own accord, or else the German Army might do it.[68] Urbsys realized that Ribbentrop meant business when he stated Germany "could not look idly on" if uprisings and shootings broke out in the Klaipeda Territory. "Nobody could predict what the development would then be and what frontiers would be decided upon," Ribbentrop warned; "once the Army should start moving, there was no means of knowing or telling where it would stop." [69] Evidently, this time Ribbentrop's plans went farther than a modest occupation of 6000 sq. miles of Lithuanian territory the year before.

Despite the warning not to seek support elsewhere, Urbsys, on his way home for consultation with the Lithuanian government, stopped in Warsaw to see the British Ambassador to Poland and the Polish Vice-Minister of Foreign Affairs. Both remained noncommittal.[70] When approached by the Lithuanian Minister in London, the Foreign Office could not offer anything but assurances of "deep sympathy" to Lithuania "in this painful situation." [71] Warsaw came to the conclusion "there was nothing to be done" about the whole matter.[72] No support could be expected from either Latvia or Estonia in view of their neutrality in regard to these "specific problems" of Lithuania.

As for the Soviet Union, the British Chargé in Kaunas cabled to his home office that there had been some talk at Kaunas of Soviet assistance in the event of a war. He thought the consensus was that to ask Russia for assistance would be "like asking the devil for help against the devil." Otherwise he believed, on the strength of Foreign Minister Urbsys' assurances, that Lithuanian policy henceforth would be "to preserve neutrality at all cost, defending herself against all aggressors no matter from what direction." [73]

No one wanted to fight Germany over such a small piece of land, particularly since it belonged to somebody else. Austria and Czechoslovakia undoubtedly had been of much greater significance, yet Hitler was permitted to swallow them up. It would have been illogical to expect that the general appeasement trend could suddenly be changed because of the Klaipeda Territory.

It has been subsequently noted that the Lithuanian government did not appeal to the Soviet Union.[74] This could be attributed to two reasons. First, the Soviet Union was not a signatory to the Klaipeda Convention and consequently neither could Lithuania appeal nor the Soviet Union intervene in her behalf on formal grounds. Secondly, asking was not expected to produce any results anyway in view of Litvinov's hide-and-seek play during the Polish-Lithuanian tension a year earlier, and in view of the Soviet failure to intervene in Czechoslovakia's behalf. Either the Soviet Union was displaying its continuing military unpreparedness or it did not wish to jeopardize an eventual reconciliation with Germany. (The first direct contacts to that end were made in less than a month thereafter.)

As a matter of fact, the Lithuanian Minister did inform Litvinov about the German ultimatum and the Lithuanian government's compliance with it. Yet this time, too, the Lithuanian Minister had difficulty in seeing Litvinov. The latter had seemingly forgotten his negative attitude toward the German move, which he had considered grave and had termed aggression to be countered by collective action and mutual assistance to the victim.[75]

Anticipation of Soviet inactivity at the time of crisis proved right. Three weeks later (April 7), Italy invaded Albania. *Pravda* was quick to accuse the British and French governments of inactivity (April 10). As the rumors spread to the effect that Soviet naval forces were hurrying to assist Albania, *Pravda* hastened to assert (April 14) that "not a single Soviet Black Sea Fleet destroyer or cruiser had, in the last two weeks, weighed anchor and passed through the Bosphorus."

Consequently Lithuania could but comply with the ultimatum. A German-Lithuanian Agreement, signed on March 22[76] and intended "to strengthen their decision to assure the friendly development of relations," deprived Lithuania of sovereignty over the Klaipeda Territory (1,100 sq. miles and 154,000 inhabitants). It also took away her only sea port. Although Germany agreed to accord Lithuania a free zone in the port, it was feared in Kaunas that she might any time repudiate the agreement. Futhermore, even if the agreement proved workable, no one was to repay Lithuania for her huge outlay in money incurred while modernizing and expanding Klaipeda's port and industry.

In view of all this, it is rather hard to believe German Secretary of State Weizsäcker's claim that Lithuania had renounced her sovereignty over the Klaipeda Territory "half voluntarily and half involuntarily" or that her Foreign Minister Urbsys "seemed himself to be relieved and well content" after having signed an agreement to that effect.[77]

Chapter Seven

THE WEST OPPOSES STALIN'S AIMS

Absorption of Czechoslovakia and incorporation of Klaipeda by Germany as well as invasion of Albania by Italy, all taking place in the spring of 1939, were clear signs of lawlessness prevailing in international relations in Europe. The ethnographic principle of the twenties and thirties was unmistakably giving way to imperialism. Although the Soviet Union had not made any moves detrimental to the security of its neighbors, diplomatic observers in Moscow feared that the fate of the Baltic States posed a grave question.

It was indicative of the general spirit making itself felt in Europe in the eventful year of 1939 that even representatives of the lesser powers were unable to resist the lure of such impunity as was enjoyed by aggressors. As an example, Polish Ambassador in Moscow W. Grzybowski was advocating the idea of partition of the Baltic States between Poland and the Soviet Union. He reasoned that if they were to lose their independence, it would be better to see it bring advantage to Poland and the Soviet Union rather than to see Germany and the Soviet Union "split the loot." [1]

What Ambassador Grzybowski failed to foresee was that Poland herself would be partitioned within five months between Germany and the Soviet Union. Those five months were filled with fear and false hopes for millions of Europeans, but particularly for the Lithuanians, Latvians, and Estonians caught between the two giants.

The fate of the Baltic States came under discussion shortly after the absorption of Czechoslovakia by Germany on March 18, 1939. The British Government asked Soviet Ambassador in London I. Maisky what his country would do if Germany attacked Rumania. Would it be willing to sign a four-power declaration condemning further aggression and providing for consultation among the signatories? The Soviet government in turn suggested calling a conference of representatives of the four powers plus Rumania and Turkey. It believed that such a conference would afford the greatest possibility for the clarification of the real situation and the determination of the position of all its participants. A statement to that effect issued by *Tass* on March 22 ended in a regretful announcement that the British government had found the Soviet proposal "premature." [2]

In the first half of April, the governments of Great Britain and France assumed guarantee obligations in regard to Poland, Rumania, and Greece. Thereupon London asked Moscow whether the Soviet government would be willing to give unilateral guarantees to Poland and Rumania. Moscow replied with a proposal of its own (April 18).[3] It called for an undertaking on the part of Great Britain, France, and the Soviet Union to render all kinds of assistance, including that of a military nature, in case of aggression against any of the three contracting powers or any eastern European state between the Baltic and the Black Seas bordering the Soviet Union.

Consequently, the Soviet draft applied only to Latvia and Estonia among the Baltic States. It did not apply to Lithuania because she was separated from the Soviet Union by a strip of the Polish-held territory. The draft also applied to Finland. In the course of negotiations, Finland was counted among the Baltic States, contrary to the existing practice whereby only Estonia, Latvia, and Lithuania were called the Baltic States.

The Baltic States, well-experienced in Soviet offers of protection since 1933, became suspicious at once. On April 21 the British Minister in Tallinn was asked whether or not conversations between London and Moscow affected the Baltic States and whether Great Britain had offered to the Soviet Union a free hand in the Baltic States "as an inducement to act against Germany." [4] The Estonian government had heard disquieting rumors in Tallinn on that score and wanted to know what the rumors were about. The British reply was evasive. The Estonian attitude had been indicated three days earlier (April 18) by her Foreign Minister Selter. He assured the Parliament that "Estonia would remain neutral in case of war and fight for her neutrality if it were violated."

The Franco-British counterproposals, received in Moscow on May 8, were found unacceptable by the Soviet government.[5] Moscow was visibly displeased that the counterproposals, while providing for Soviet guarantees to Poland and Rumania, said nothing of any help which was to be received on a reciprocal basis by the Soviet Union from France and Great Britain, should the Soviet Union be drawn into hostilities in carrying out its obligations in regard to any eastern European state.

As no mention of the Baltic States was made and nothing else transpired from either Moscow, London, or Paris, Selter, on May 15, requested the British Minister in Tallinn to find out from his government whether the latter would exert any influence on the Soviet government to abstain from aggressive policy towards Estonia in the case of a general conflagration.[6] He was told that the British government would naturally be interested in dissuading the Soviet government from aggression against Estonia; however, an Anglo-Soviet understanding, if reached, would reduce such danger.[7]

The agility of the Estonian diplomats made an impression in London. When Maisky called at the British Foreign Office on May 16 and impatiently requested the British government "to make up its mind" in regard to the inclusion of the Baltic States in the tripartite agreement, he was told by Viscount Halifax that the Baltic States did not want to be included.[8] Viscount Halifax was fully supported in this reply by his French colleague, who, by early May, had arrived at the conclusion that an extension of the guarantee to cover the Baltic States "would be excessive" at the present stage.[9]

While calling on Viscount Halifax, Maisky also had with him the text of the Soviet reply, dated May 15,[10] to the Franco-British proposals of May 8. The Soviet government reiterated that it had found the latest proposals inadequate as a basis for organization of a front of resistance against further extension of aggression in Europe. The note gave the following reasons:

> (1) The English proposals do not contain principle of reciprocity with regard to USSR and place the latter in a position of inequality inasmuch as they do not contemplate an obligation by England and France to guarantee the USSR in the event of a direct attack on the latter by aggressors.
> (2) English proposals only extend guarantee to Eastern European States bordering on USSR to Poland and to Rumania, as a consequence of which north western frontier of USSR towards Finland, Estonia, and Latvia remains uncovered.
> (3) On the one hand, absence of guarantee to USSR on the part of England and France in the event of a direct attack by aggressors, and, on the other hand, the fact that north western frontier of USSR remains uncovered may serve to provoke aggression in the direction of Soviet Union.

The Soviet government stipulated "three indispensable conditions for creation of an effective barrier by pacific states against a further extension of aggression in Europe," namely: (1) conclusion of an effective tripartite pact of mutual assistance; (2) guarantee by all three powers of Latvia, Estonia, and Finland; (3) conclusion of a formal agreement on forms and extent of assistance to be rendered reciprocally.

Following the exchange of views between Viscount Halifax and Maisky, the Estonian Chargé in London was summoned to the Foreign Office and informed that the Soviet government insisted on inclusion of Estonia and Latvia. However, the British government did not entertain this idea and was not anticipating a change of attitude.[11]

Estonia was not alone in fearing Soviet guarantees. Its fear was shared by Finland, Poland, and Rumania. However, the Baltic States seemed to lie in the first line of fire. They were anxious to preserve their precarious balance between Germany and the Soviet Union. This could be achieved only as long as they remained neutral. As a consequence, they were afraid to provoke Germany by accepting a tripartite guarantee of their neutrality without her participation and, at the same time, as the *London Times* pointed out (May 2), they were "suspicious of Soviet intervention." The *New York Times* fully concurred when it said a few days later (May 6) that the Soviet Union was resolved to occupy the Baltic States in case of any threat of German aggression. Moreover, according to certain diplomatic observers, such an eventuality was imminent, and the Baltic States were "scared to death." [12]

All these considerations undoubtedly played a role in British Prime Minister Neville Chamberlain's statement in the House of Commons (May 19) to the effect that certain countries were reluctant to agree to the Soviet Union's participation in an agreement guaranteeing their integrity. He was also aware that British public opinion was wholeheartedly in support of the policy protecting weaker European states.[13]

After Chamberlain's statement, the British Foreign Office found that there was no alternative between agreeing to a three-power pact such as the Soviet government advocated or allowing the present negotiations to fail.[14] At this juncture, however, Latvian Foreign Minister V. Munters stepped into the picture with a proposal that found acceptance in London. He suggested to Halifax in Geneva on May 23 that the tripartite agreement, if it covered the Baltic States, should take the form of some kind of guarantee of their neutrality.[15]

A new draft of the joint Franco-British proposals to the Soviet Union was forthcoming. The Latvian and Estonian governments were advised by the British diplomatic missions in Riga and Tallinn that in the new draft there would be no idea of inserting in the formula any unsolicited guarantee of the Baltic States, which would not be mentioned by name.[16]

The British draft proposal of May 25,[17] with France concurring,[18] contained the obligation to render mutual support and assistance to any of the three contracting states engaged in hostilities with a European power in consequence of (1) aggression by that power against another European state which the USSR had, in conformity with the wishes of that state, undertaken to assist against such aggression; (2) assistance given by the USSR to another European state which had requested such assistance in order to resist a violation of its neutrality; or (3) aggression by a European power against the USSR, France, and the United Kingdom.

There was to be consultation before rendering assistance, but this would be "without prejudice to the rights and position of other powers." Both the Estonian and the Latvian governments were informed of the Franco-British proposal.[19] Munters found it "entirely satisfactory from the Latvian point of view." [20] Halifax in turn readily agreed that the second provision was inserted as a result of Munters' suggestion.[21]

The draft was submitted to Molotov, who unexpectedly had replaced Litvinov as People's Commissar for Foreign Affairs, on May 27.[22] His reaction was unfavorable, amounting to outright rejection. "The Soviet government wanted effective guarantee of action, not words and conversations," he said. Molotov specifically objected that assistance would be rendered "without prejudice" to other states assisted. "Why was this necessary," he wondered; "would we not be helping them in their own interest"? Sir W. Seeds, British Ambassador in Moscow, replied that the British government recognized the right to limit even friendly intervention in such matters as the passage of troops.

Another conversation between Seeds and Molotov on May 29 did not bring them any closer.[23] Once again Molotov raised the question of the Baltic States. "What would happen if they came to an understanding with Germany on Czechoslovakian precedent?" he wanted to know. "Neither His Majesty's Government nor British public opinion," Seeds replied, "would consider imposing on independent nations guarantees of protection against their will: such guarantees would amount to menaces, not protection against aggression . . . any change in that attitude would be repugnant to the fundamental spirit of the British people."

Molotov evidently was not convinced. The next day he received the French Ambassador and told him that the Soviet Union would be compelled to "come to the assistance" of the three Baltic States, even without their request, "if one or more of them were to sell itself to Germany and admit German troops without resisting." [24] He must have known, however, that these three Baltic States had been negotiating nonaggression treaties with Germany and were determined to resist aggression from whatever direction it might come.

Molotov objected to Seeds' argumentation on the ground he feared the prospect of Germany appearing within a few miles of Leningrad.

He evidently did not accept or forgot the British contention stated to Maisky on May 16 to the effect that a German attack on Soviet Russia via the Baltic States only was the least likely; the front would be far too narrow for any effective result; no German attack on the Soviet Union was conceivable except by the broader front of Poland and Rumania.[25]

Two years later, on June 22, 1941, when the Germans poured across the entire length of the Soviet frontier from the Baltic to the Black Sea, Molotov learned from bitter experience that the British were right and he was wrong. But in the spring of 1939 he obstinately stuck to his guns. The British and French Ambassadors in Moscow were forced to conclude that the question of German aggression through the Baltic States constituted a fundamental difference in their and Molotov's viewpoints, which, in Seeds' words, "a mere argument may well be unable to remove." [26]

If any hope remained that differences between Great Britain and France on one side and the Soviet Union on the other might somehow be overcome, Molotov shattered this in his report to the Supreme Soviet on May 31.[27] He surveyed the negotiations up to the latest Franco-British proposals, which he found to be "a step forward," but otherwise showing "no advance if the question is looked at from the viewpoint of reciprocity." His main criticism concerned the fact that the proposals implied Soviet assistance to Belgium, Greece, Turkey, Rumania, and Poland, to which the British and the French had already promised guarantees, but said nothing about their assistance to "the three countries on the northwestern frontier of the USSR [Finland, Estonia, and Latvia]." Molotov feared these three countries might prove unable to defend their neutrality in the event of aggression. He insisted on complete reciprocity and pointed out the Soviet Union would not assume any obligations toward the five above countries, "if it does not get guarantees in regard to the three countries on its northwestern frontier."

The report received additional emphasis by being reprinted in *Pravda* and *Izvestiia* on June 1. Commenting on it, Seeds expressed the opinion that

> Soviet assistance is not worth purchasing at the price of extra hostility on the part of the Baltic States and other countries (not to mention the effect on Britain and probably American opinion) which we should earn by yielding to Soviet demands for what amounts to compulsory guarantees imposed on States who violently object to Soviet help.[28]

The next day (June 2) Molotov handed the British and French Ambassadors a new Soviet draft of the tripartite agreement. The draft clearly stipulated that the three contracting states had agreed to defend Belgium, Turkey, Rumania, Poland, Latvia, Estonia, and Finland against aggression. Molotov inserted a whole new article, likely to meet with opposition on the part of the Baltic States. It read:

> In the event of circumstances arising which, in the opinion of one of the contracting parties, create a threat of aggression by a European power, the three states will immediately consult together to examine the situation and in case of necessity to establish in common moment for putting into immediate effect mechanism of mutual assistance and manner of its application independently of any procedure applied by the League of Nations to examination of questions.[29]

In a dispatch from Moscow, dated June 2 and dealing with Soviet assistance to the Baltic States "even if they refused it," the London *Times* stressed that "the Soviet government did not wish to let the Baltic States make that choice and that it was generally thought in Moscow the Soviet Union would send armed forces to prevent the extension of German hegemony over them." As for the concept of violation of neutrality, the *New York Times* soon (June 7) found out in Paris that every signatory of the tripartite agreement would be entitled to define it unilaterally.

It did not take long for Estonian and Latvian reaction to become manifest. The Estonian Foreign Minister stated (June 2) that any system whereby a great power assumed the role of defender of the Baltic States would be regarded as aggression, whether such a power would act as a representative of a collective system or defend its own interests. "The Baltic States are prepared to fight with all their forces against such aggression," he said emphatically.[30] The Estonian Minister in London pointed out that any such proposals would be considered as "an unfriendly act directed against the neutrality of Estonia."[31] His Latvian colleague communicated his government's refusal to accept any guarantee in view of Latvia's professed neutrality.[32]

It was at this point (June 7) that Latvia and Estonia signed non-aggression treaties with Germany. The British Ambassador in Berlin observed that British advances to the Soviet Union were to blame for the fact these two republics had "reinsured" with Germany.[33] A Latvian diplomat called it an act of "self-preservation," especially so after nationalistic Molotov replaced Litvinov, who, on the whole, used to be "well disposed" to the Baltic States.[34]

Energetic protestations of countries fearing any kind of Soviet protection were reflected in Chamberlain's statement to the House of Commons on June 7, where he spoke of "certain states which do not want to receive a guarantee on the ground that it would compromise the strict neutrality which they desire to preserve." As much as Chamberlain wanted an agreement with the Soviet Union, he had to admit that "it is manifestly impossible to impose a guarantee on states which do not desire it." He hoped, however, that means would be found by which the present obstacles on the way to the agreement with the Soviet Union might be overcome.[35] Viscount Halifax, speaking the next day, sounded almost apologetic when he explained to the House of Commons that the delay in negotiations had been caused by the British government's desire "not only to take account of the particular circumstances of the government with which it was negotiating [the Soviet Union], but also to have regard to the situation and the wishes of the third countries." [36]

The Soviet government, speaking through the controlled press, entertained different views. On June 7 *Pravda* mentioned that Molotov's proposal of May 31 constituted the "minimum" conditions for the organization of a defensive front against further development of aggression in Europe. The article was liberally interspersed with quotations from the foreign press. These were selected in order to show the interest the Soviet Union attached to the guarantee of the Baltic States.

On June 13 *Pravda* took up the question of protection of the Baltic States. The paper dealt editorially with all objections—one by one. It was wrong for the foreign press to claim this question was of no vital importance either to the Soviet Union or Great Britain and France, *Pravda* claimed. The Baltic States could not defend themselves alone nor would they lose independence by accepting guarantees of the "peace-loving" states. Their refusal to accept such offers was based on either misunderstanding, a desire to break up the peace front, underestimation of the threat of aggression, or foreign influence. Only the Soviet attitude was right, *Pravda* concluded, and this attitude corresponded to the wishes of the Baltic peoples.

This editorial greeted the arrival of W. Strang from the British Foreign Office to strengthen Sir Seeds' hand in negotiations with the Soviets. Surprisingly enough, *Pravda* did not say a word about the recently concluded nonaggression treaties between Germany on one side and Latvia and Estonia on the other, although it did quote extensively from the French press that opposition of the Baltic States to assistance meant they had entered the German orbit.

Pravda's attitude likely would not have been different had the editors waited three more days for the new Franco-British proposal (June 15) offering slight modifications. Molotov rejected them the next day.[37] He suggested that the guarantee to all eight states be altogether forgotten, if Latvia, Estonia, and Finland refused to go along. He reiterated his rejection of all suggested modifications on June 22 and kept insisting on enumeration of all guaranteed states.[38] This, the British and French tried to avoid.

Viscount Halifax became exasperated. On June 23 he asked Maisky point-blank whether the Soviet government really wanted a treaty,

since it "had not budged a single inch" while the British government
had made "all the advances and concessions." [39] Sir Seeds thought that
the Soviet government wanted to be "the sole judge" of the question
whether the circumstances required them to assist the Baltic States, if
for reasons of their own they felt obliged to do so, irrespective of
whether the Baltic States desired such assistance or not.[40]

The Soviet government's attitude was quite different. An article
in *Pravda* of June 29, written by A. Zhdanov, Member of the Central
Committee of the Communist Party and First Secretary of its Leningrad
region, revealed the utter irreconcilability between the Soviet and the
Franco-British views. In his article, Zhdanov admitted that British-
French-Soviet negotiations had reached stagnation and deadlock. He
accused negotiation partners of showing no desire to conclude a treaty
on terms of equality. He spoke of intolerable delays, endless procrasti-
nation, lack of sincerity and goodwill, piling up of artificial difficulties,
etc. He stated the following with reference to the Baltic States:

> It is known, for instance, that the question of a tripartite guarantee of im-
> mediate assistance to Latvia, Estonia, and Finland, in the event of violation
> of their neutrality by aggressors, forms just such an artificially invented
> "stumbling block" in the negotiations. Statements to the effect that the
> said Baltic States do not desire these guarantees and that precisely this cir-
> cumstance allegedly hinders England and France from accepting the Soviet
> proposal, are obviously unsubstantial and could only be inspired by one
> intention: to hamper the negotiations in order to disrupt them . . . It
> seems to me that the English and French desire not a real treaty acceptable
> to the USSR, but only talks about a treaty in order to speculate before public
> opinion in their countries on the allegedly unyielding attitude of the USSR,
> and thus make easier for themselves the road to a deal with the aggressors.
> The next few days will show whether this is so or not.[41]

In the apparent belief that mere words were not enough, Soviet
naval units went on a three-day cruise along the Baltic coast, all the
way from Kronstadt to Liepaja.[42]

Since "the next few days" did not produce a complete reversal of
the Franco-British position, Molotov, on July 4, proposed a modification of his proposal of June 2. The new Soviet draft of the tripartite
agreement provided that the contracting powers would immediately render each other effective assistance should one of them become involved
in hostilities as a result of "direct or indirect aggression" against any
European state, "whose independence or neutrality one of the three
countries concerned felt obliged to defend." By the term "direct or
indirect aggression," the Soviet government understood "an internal
coup d'état or a reversal of policy in the interests of the aggression, in
Estonia, Latvia, Finland, Poland, Rumania, Turkey, Greece, and
Belgium." However, this definition was not to be made public.[43]

This new Soviet draft was extremely important as it introduced the concept of "indirect aggression," first mentioned by Stalin on March 10. It was to become a real "artificially invented stumbling block," using Zhdanov's words, in the further course of negotiations.

In a message to Sir Seeds dated July 6, Viscount Halifax rejected the Soviet definition of "indirect aggression" as "completely unacceptable." Its use, he said, would confirm the worst suspicions of the Baltic States, whose objection to the proposed treaty rested largely on their fear of Soviet interference in their internal affairs.[44] This he also told Maisky. The inclusion of the term "indirect aggression" and its Soviet definition could be represented as authorizing almost unlimited interference in the affairs of the Baltic States, Viscount Halifax stressed. "We had gone as far as we possibly could in dealing with the Baltic States and we could not accept a formula of this nature." Maisky merely thanked him for this information, but also added that "the fuss made by the Baltic States was about 75 per cent for purposes of show." Maisky had heard from people prominent in the Baltic countries that they would not really object to guarantees. However, they could neither ask for nor accept them openly.[45]

On July 9 Molotov submitted another secret definition of the term "indirect aggression." It was to cover action accepted by the guaranteed states under threat of force or even without such threat, but involving the use of their territory of forces for aggression and resulting in the loss of their independence or violation of their neutrality. Orally Molotov explained that Latvia or Estonia might make an agreement with Germany inconsistent with their independence or neutrality, yet without any threat of force by Germany; or they might employ German officers or military instructors, thus converting their armies into instruments of aggression against the Soviet Union.[46]

News about the unyielding Soviet attitude filtered to the press. On July 5th the London *Times,* for example, reported on the controversy in regard to the interpretation of the term "indirect aggression" which, the paper believed, amounted to "a potential interference in the internal policies of other states."

The Baltic diplomats evidently had their own, though not always accurate, information sources.

Thus, Estonian Foreign Minister Selter informed the British Minister in Tallinn that it would be impossible for Estonia to accept unasked protection even in theory. "If a Soviet guarantee were accepted," he said, "Estonian neutrality would disappear." He also remarked that Soviet interference in strictly internal Estonian affairs, such as a *putsch,* would inevitably bring into power a government with pro-German tendencies.[47]

Latvia, in Munters' words, wanted to be entirely left out of any Anglo-Franco-Soviet agreement.[48] His directive to Latvian missions abroad reiterated that there had been no change in determination "to oppose by all means the entry of any foreign army." [49]

Even the Lithuanian Minister in Moscow was anxious to find out from Sir Seeds whether or not Lithuania had been mentioned in current negotiations. He had heard that negotiations had already been completed (July 5!) and that the Soviet demand for inclusion of Lithuania among the guaranteed states had been accepted.[50]

The Lithuanian Minister must have been glad to hear that the rumors were not true. He had recently had a talk with an officer of the People's Commissariat for Foreign Affairs. When he told him that Lithuania did not seem to be included among the states to be guaranteed, the representative of the Commissariat immediately replied this could be arranged if such was the desire of the Lithuanian government.[51] In fact, Molotov had been trying since May 31 to find out about the British and French attitude toward the inclusion of Lithuania in the system of guarantees. Zhdanov likewise mentioned Lithuania in his article.[52]

There was no progress in negotiations throughout the whole month of July. The Soviet negotiation partners were getting weary. Around July 20 press reports appeared in both Paris and London intimating that the French were ready to accept Soviet proposals on all points.[53] Sir Seeds also noticed that the French Ambassador in Moscow became "increasingly reluctant" and "lukewarm" in supporting him during the protracted negotiations.[54]

According to French sources, differences were ironed out in the second half of July, and a draft of the British-French-Soviet political agreement was initialed on July 24.[55] It contained the Soviet version of assistance in the event of "direct or indirect aggression." The published French and British texts of the agreement differ chiefly in minor details only. However, the French text also lists Lithuania among the states to be covered by guarantees. The British text omits Lithuania entirely.

Although G. Bonnet, French Minister of Foreign Affairs at the time of negotiations, stated that initialing the agreement had removed all difficulties and that even Molotov was satisfied, the interpretation of the concept of "indirect aggression" remained unsolved. This may be judged from the debate in the British House of Commons on July 31, i.e., hardly a week after the alleged initialing of the British-French-Soviet agreement.

The House was informed by Parliamentary Undersecretary for Foreign Affairs R. Butler that the three governments had not been able to agree upon a definition, satisfactory to all parties, of the term "indirect aggression." He gave assurance that the British government was "extremely anxious not even to appear to be desirous of encroaching upon the independence of other states." The Soviet-favored formula seemed to him "to carry that precise signification." Butler concluded the debate by stating that the British government had proceeded with utmost vigor in discussing with the Soviet Union whether or not one should encroach upon the independence of the Baltic States. "We are in agreement . . . that we should not do so," he pointed out.[56]

The Soviet government did not like Butler's statement. *Tass* on August 2 issued a communique thereon:

> The difference is not whether to encroach or not to encroach on the independence of the Baltic States, because both sides stand for guaranteeing this independence, but whether any loophole should be left in the formula "indirect aggression" for aggressors making an attempt on the independence of the Baltic States. One of the reasons for the delay in the negotiations is that the British formula leaves such a loophole for the aggressor.[57]

Sir Seeds saw Molotov the same day the *Tass* statement appeared in the papers. He found him indignant and just as unyielding. In fact, Molotov refused to budge an inch from the Soviet definition of "indirect aggression." Sir Seeds reported to the Foreign Office that negotiations received "a severe set-back," and that he foresaw no new proposals from either side in the near future. Consequently, Sir Seeds suggested the recall to London of W. Strang who had been sent by the Foreign Office to help in negotiations and had been staying in Moscow since June 14.[58] Viscount Halifax agreed.[59]

It was only on August 17 that Viscount Halifax suggested to Sir Seeds continuation of discussions with the Soviets on the outstanding political points, including that of indirect aggression.[60] Sir Seeds, however, wanted a postponement of political discussions until the resumption of military discussions begun on August 12.[61] But while cables went back and forth between the British Foreign Office and its diplomatic representative in Moscow, the time to reach an agreement with the Soviet Union—either political or military—grew shorter and shorter.

On August 21 *Tass* announced cryptically that a trade and credit agreement between the USSR and Germany had been signed in Berlin.[62] Marshal K. Voroshilov, People's Commissar of War, who acted as the Chairman of the Soviet Military Delegation then meeting with its British and French counterparts in Moscow, suggested the adjourning of military talks until reply had been received from British and French governments.[63] Sir Seeds' telegram to London was dispatched at 1:10 A.M. on August 22. A few hours later *Tass* made an announcement confirming what was suspected for months:

> After the conclusion of the Soviet-German trade and credit agreements there arose the question of improving political relations between Germany

and the USSR. An exchange of views on this subject, which took place between the Governments of Germany and the USSR, established that both parties desire to relieve the tension in their political relations, eliminate the danger of war, and conclude a nonaggression pact. Consequently the German Minister for Foreign Affairs, Herr von Ribbentrop, will shortly arrive in Moscow for the relevant negotiations.[64]

An announcement about the termination of both political and military talks with the British and French was made simultaneously by Molotov and Voroshilov on August 25. They failed to see any sense in continuing such talks in view of the new political situation.[65] On August 31 Molotov took the case to the Supreme Soviet, meeting together in a special session. He, of course, blamed only Great Britain and France for breakdown of negotiations. The Baltic States were not mentioned. Molotov only complained that Great Britain and France, while offering military assistance to the Soviet Union on the basis of reciprocity, hedged their assistance round with such reservations regarding indirect aggression as might convert this assistance into a myth, and provide them with a formal legal excuse for evading assistance and placing the USSR in a position of isolation in face of the aggressor.[66]

Slightly over a decade later (June 20, 1950) the London *Times* admitted that, back in 1939, even the British shared to some extent Molotov's views on the "guilt" of the Baltic States:

> Many in this country believed that the British Government were wrong, during the abortive negotiations with the Soviet Union in 1939, to resist the Soviet claim for bases in the three countries; they maintained that Russia had a right to safeguard its security. The dreadful sequence of events presents its own warning.

The Baltic States thought differently at the very outset. This may be seen from a statement made by the Estonian Minister in London on August 25. In it he transmitted his government's "sincere thanks for the understanding shown by His Majesty's Government, during these last months, for Estonia's policy of neutrality." At the same time he expressed his conviction that the Soviet-German pact would not worsen the position of Estonia. He believed—as many did in the Baltic States— that there still was considerable latent hostility between the Russians and the Germans and that neither side wished to see the other side occupying the Baltic States.[67]

The Estonian Minister was basically wrong. The Soviet-German agreement not only worsened the position of Estonia—it also set the stage for a complete suppression of her independence, alongside that of Latvia and Lithuania, despite the "considerable latent hostility" between the two gravediggers. To be sure, the agreement was not reached without negotiations. They actually began at the same time as the negotiations with Great Britain and France. In this case, however, the Soviet partner was not so scrupulous.

Chapter Eight

STALIN GETS FREE HAND FROM HITLER

Failure of British-French-Soviet negotiations was not unexpected either in London or in Paris. As early as the beginning of May, diplomats in Berlin suspected the possibility of a Soviet-German nonaggression pact.[1] By the end of May, it seemed to them that Ribbentrop was "pressing hard" for an understanding with the Soviet Union.[2] Neither was such a development unexpected in the Baltic capitals. At the beginning of June Estonian Foreign Minister Selter transmitted to the British Minister in Tallinn information he had received from German sources to the effect that the Soviet Union would avoid signing an agreement with Great Britain and France, even if the question of the Baltic States was settled.[3] At the same time the Estonian Minister in Berlin told State Secretary of Foreign Affairs E. Weizsäcker that the Soviet Union entertained greater mistrust toward the democratic states than toward the totalitarian ones, and that it only was waiting for a friendly public gesture from that direction before giving expression to these sentiments.[4]

Weizsäcker was undoubtedly glad to hear it. It was he who on May 25 stated that it should be the German aim to prevent British-French-Soviet relations from assuming a still more binding character and becoming intensified any further.[5] Weizsäcker was one of the high officers in the German Foreign Ministry instructed by Ribbentrop early in April[6] to find out from Soviet diplomats residing in Berlin what Stalin really meant by his emphatic assurance at the Eighteenth Congress of the Communist Party on March 10, 1939, when he said:

> We stand for peace and the strengthening of business relations with all countries. That is our position; and we shall adhere to this position so long

as these countries maintain like relations with the Soviet Union, and so long as they make no attempt to trespass on the interests of our country.[7]

The ensuing Soviet-German negotiations had direct bearing on the Baltic States, yet it was not until the end of July that the Soviets brought them into the negotiations for the first time. The story can very well begin on March 22, 1939, when Lithuania lost the Klaipeda Territory to Germany.

Acquisition of Klaipeda was insignificant to Germany, both in terms of area and population. Its strategic importance as a potential naval base, some 100 miles closer to the Soviet Union than Pillau in East Prussia, was incontestable. Moreover, the incorporation of the Klaipeda Territory was accompanied by an agreement between Germany and Lithuania "not to use force in their mutual relations, and not to encourage any use of force directed against either of the Contracting Parties by a Third Party." [8] This in reality represented the first treaty of non-aggression concluded by Germany with any of the Baltic States. German reluctance to conclude such a treaty with Lithuania was well known, and as recently as mid-1938 Ribbentrop replied in the negative to Lithuanian Foreign Minister S. Lozoraitis' inquiry as to Germany's willingness to conclude a nonaggression treaty between the two countries.[9]

The Soviet Union must have feared that some far-reaching suggestions might also be extended to, and accepted by, both Latvia and Estonia, as a result of which the Baltic Sea would turn into a mere German lake, as was the case between 1914 and 1918. Moscow witnessed visits of high German officers in the Baltic capitals; a German submarine detachment called on Estonian ports; German bombers flew training missions along the Baltic coast, reaching Tallinn and Helsinki. The British General Staff also was very active.[10]

Less than a week after the signature of the German-Lithuanian Treaty, Litvinov summoned the Latvian and Estonian Ministers in Moscow (March 28) and handed them identical *notes verbales*.[11] The notes called to the attention of the two recipient governments the efforts exerted by the Soviet government during the past fifteen years to ensure the inviolability of the frontiers of both Latvia and Estonia. The Soviet government was vitally concerned about the preservation of their complete independence because this was in conformity with their own interests as well as with those of the Soviet state. Although the notes contained assurance that they were presented in the spirit of sincere benevolence to the Latvian and Estonian peoples, there was also a showing of teeth:

From this it should be clear that no matter what kind of agreements were signed, "voluntary" or concluded under outside pressure, should they result even only in the abatement or restriction of the independence and self-determination of the Republic of Latvia/Estonia, permitting in it the political, economic or other domination of a third state, and granting to the latter any exceptional rights and privileges, both within the territory of Latvia/Estonia and in its ports, this would be recognized by the Soviet Government as insufferable and contradictory to the stipulations and spirit of the above-mentioned treaties and agreements regulating at present its mutual relations with Latvia/Estonia, and even as a violation of these agreements with all the consequences arising therefrom.

The notes ended with the assurance they were made in the spirit of sincere benevolence toward the Latvian and Estonian peoples as well as for the purpose of enhancing in them the feeling of security. The Soviet Union was ready "to prove with deeds, in case of need," its interest in preserving the political and economic independence of Latvia and Estonia. By the same token, it would be unable "to remain an idle bystander of open or masked attempts to destroy their self-determination and independence."

Less than three weeks prior to the issuance of these notes, Stalin had assured (March 10) all the neighbors of the Soviet Union that the latter was standing for "peaceful, close, and friendly relations" with all of them.[12] The tone of Litvinov's note was hardly compatible with the assurance given by Stalin, especially since there was no justification whatsoever for Litvinov's outburst in regard to Latvia and Estonia. They were not negotiating agreements that could possibly meet objections listed in Litvinov's declaration, nor were they willing to abate or restrict their independence and self-determination. Was all this a plain intimidation of the two tiny Soviet neighbors despite the professed "close and friendly" relations?

The Lithuanian government was not among the recipients of the note. This probably was because she had no common frontiers with the Soviet Union. The reaction in both Latvia and Estonia was one of apprehension. The Estonian Deputy Foreign Minister termed the note "a powerful threat aimed at the occupation of Estonia." [13] Latvia must have felt the same, although Foreign Minister Munters did not believe the Soviet Union would actually march into Latvia to forestall the Germans. "They have no sufficient interest here," he told the British Minister in Riga.[14]

There is no indication whether or not Germany did offer encouragement to either Estonia or Latvia at that time. (She did later.) Rumors, both officially denied and confirmed, made the rounds in Estonia to the effect that the latter had received from Great Britain an offer guaranteeing her independence. The Soviet Union responded by massing troops at the Estonian frontier and then staging a military demonstration under the disguise of military maneuvers in the Leningrad area. This created considerable concern among the Estonians.[15] Ultimately, however, both

Latvia and Estonia rejected the Soviet note. The Latvian reply, dated April 7, read in part:

> The Latvian people will always and with all means at their disposal defend their national freedom and state independence. Being guided by the vital interests of Latvia, the Latvian government has never permitted and will never permit restrictions of any kind whatsoever to be placed upon the sovereign will of the people. In the same way the Latvian government does not recognize the right of any foreign state whatsoever, directly or indirectly, to exert its influence upon the foreign, domestic or economic policy of the state, and in all its actions reserves complete freedom of decision, being fully prepared to defend this freedom and to bear all responsibility for its decisions. Conscious of this responsibility, Latvia cannot share with any state its rights and its obligation to take care of the defense of its self-determination and independence, strictly observing in this respect all international obligations undertaken by it.[16]

The Estonian reply was of the same nature and date.[17] At this point Germany came into the act, and this time Lithuania received special favors.[18] On April 20 Commander-in-Chief of the Lithuanian Army, General S. Rastikis, was Hitler's honor guest at a huge military parade in Berlin.[19] Hitler, Ribbentrop, and high German generals engaged him in conversation. He was also received by Colonel General Halder, Chief of the Army Staff. An offer of arms in repayment of Lithuanian investments in Klaipeda was made, but the Lithuanian government rejected it lest her neutrality might be compromised.[20] Trade negotiations suddenly began to proceed very favorably for the Lithuanians. In a burst of magnanimity, Hitler decreed that all Lithuanian interests in the Klaipeda Territory be preserved and that Lithuania suffer no material losses from the transfer of Klaipeda to Germany. All measures against Lithuanian enterprises already taken were to be canceled and the German commissioners withdrawn forthwith; requisitioned goods, warehouses, etc., were to be returned. "The Lithuanians are to be convinced that their economic activity in the Klaipeda Territory will offer them more opportunities after cession than before," the directive pointed out.[21]

On May 22 Urbsys was received by Hitler. The latter assured him that Lithuania could "count upon Germany." Hitler hoped in return, however, that she would not enter into any commitments directed against German interests, particularly vis-à-vis Poland. He was suspicious of a report in the London *Sunday Times* of April 4 to the effect that Great Britain had undertaken to render assistance to Poland should she find herself at war because of invasion of either Danzig or Lithuania. Urbsys also had to explain the purpose of General Rastikis' visit to Warsaw on May 9–10, right after a visit to Berlin. (It had been dictated by the desire to emphasize the policy of neutrality pursued by Lithuania.) [22]

The German Foreign Office noted with satisfaction that the Lithuanian and Estonian governments answered in the negative when asked whether they felt threatened in any way by Germany; and whether they had authorized the President of the United States, F. D. Roosevelt, to seek Hitler's (April 15) assurance that his armed forces would not attack or invade the territory or possessions of Estonia, Latvia, Lithuania, and more than a score of other states. Latvia's reply was at first evasive, but finally came out to Germany's satisfaction.[23]

The Estonian government must have been frightened, however. For on April 21 the German Minister in Tallinn was approached with an inquiry whether or not Germany would be willing to counteract Soviet efforts to establish "a kind of protectorate over Estonia" under the excuse of purported German intentions to attack the Baltic region; a joint German-Estonian action was suggested. The official reply of the German government was that Germany could not do so for the time being.[24]

A week later, Germany changed her attitude. On April 28, she proposed nonaggression treaties to a number of states, including the Baltic States.[25] Germany seemed to be in a hurry. The German Minister in Tallinn was instructed to reach an agreement at once.[26] On June 7, Latvia and Estonia signed (there being no need for Lithuania to sign after the treaty of March 22), with their foreign ministers, Munters and Selter, attending. On this occasion, Hitler told Munters that Germany now was anxious to back both Latvia and Estonia and safeguard their interests; she was not at all afraid of the Soviet Union.[27]

This *Treaty of Nonaggression between Latvia and Germany* was concluded for a period of ten years, and was based on a firm resolution "to maintain peace between Latvia and Germany in all circumstances." (The treaty between Estonia and Germany was identical.)[28] Its main provision, Article 1, read:

> The Republic of Latvia and the German Reich shall in no case resort to war or to any other use of force one against the other.
> Should any action of the kind referred to in paragraph 1 be taken by a third Power against one of the Contracting Parties, the other Contracting Party shall not support such action in any way.

A Protocol of Signature of the same date was appended to the Treaty:

> The Contracting Party which is not participating in the conflict shall not be deemed to be giving support within the meaning of paragraph 2 of Article 1 of the Treaty if the attitude of that Party is in harmony with the general rules of neutrality. Therefore, the fact of a normal exchange of goods and transit of goods continuing between the Contracting Party not involved in the conflict and the third Power shall not be regarded as constituting illicit support.

It did not seem reasonable to expect the Soviet Union to raise any objections to these two treaties, even after Litvinov's warning on March 28. After all, neither Latvia nor Estonia was abating or restricting her self-determination or independence; nor was she granting Germany any rights or privileges likely to lead to her political or economic domination.

Of course, rights and privileges, objectionable from the Soviet point of view, could have been included in secret protocols had they been signed simultaneously with nonaggression treaties. No such protocols have even been published, however, and their existence has never been intimated by the Soviet Union—not even at the time when the latter resorted to ultimatums full of completely unfounded accusations.

Nevertheless, the Latvian and Estonian Ministers in Moscow called on Molotov. They characterized the nonaggression treaties with Germany as guarantees of peace and as entirely natural in view of the fact that both Latvia and Estonia had had similar treaties with the Soviet Union since 1932. Molotov, however, took the position that these treaties indicated an inclination toward Germany. He could not be moved from this position.[29]

United States sources indicate that Molotov, in the course of his talks with the Baltic Ministers, told them he had discussed a guarantee of the Baltic States "in principle only." He gave assurance that, when the discussions were completed, Latvia and Estonia would be informed of the results.[30] This procedure, used by the Soviet government in its discussions with the Polish and German governments in 1933–1934, showed that Molotov was continuing his predecessor Litvinov's policy of trying to make deals behind somebody else's back. It is not clear, however, whether Molotov spoke of British-French-Soviet or German-Soviet discussions.

In general, Latvia and Estonia were much concerned about Soviet reaction to their nonaggression treaties with Germany. The Latvian Government hastened to assure the British Minister in Riga that it had not incurred vis-à-vis Germany any obligations other than those contained in the Soviet-Latvian Nonaggression Treaty of February 5, 1932.[31] Estonian Foreign Minister Selter found it advisable to inquire of the British Minister in Tallinn whether or not the British government could use its influence on the Soviet government so that the latter would not view the Estonian-German Nonaggression Treaty with disapproval. He probably suspected that the Soviet government regarded the Treaty as one "concluded between cat and mouse." [32]

The Germans spared no efforts in representing these treaties as an instrument of peace. In vain, however, German Ambassador in Moscow, F. W. Schulenburg, tried to convince Molotov (June 28) that they provided the Baltic States with the additional security in which the Soviet Union itself was interested. Molotov retorted that Germany had concluded these treaties in her own interest and not for the love of the Soviet Union; they concerned only Germany and the countries participating, but not the Soviet Union. Furthermore, Molotov doubted the permanence of German treaties with the Baltic States "after the experience which Poland had had." [33] Molotov undoubtedly was referring to the recent (April 28) abrogation of the German-Polish Nonaggression Treaty by Germany.

It was hard for Schulenburg to understand Molotov's attitude. At the time nonaggression treaties between Germany and the Baltic States were signed, he believed the Soviet Union had received from Germany, "free of charge, increased security and thereby a German political down payment." [34] On the other hand, Schulenburg's efforts to represent these treaties as an instrument of peace could have been prompted by a Soviet hint that Moscow was considering a rapprochement with Germany, but feared a German attack either via the Baltic States or via Rumania.

Such a hint was given by the Soviet Chargé Astakhov to the Bulgarian Minister in Berlin sometime around the middle of June. The conversation was reported to the German Foreign Ministry, which obviously constituted the original idea behind the hint. At the same time the Soviet Chargé in Rome hinted that his Government would remain completely unyielding on its demands regarding the Baltic States.[35]

Furthermore, while Molotov was exchanging views with Schulenburg, he had in his possession a cable from the Soviet Chargé in Rome. The cable contained information about a German plan to achieve a decisive improvement in German-Soviet relations. This information had been obtained from Italian Foreign Minister G. Ciano who in turn had received it from his Ambassador in Berlin, Rosso. The plan envisaged a joint guarantee of the Baltic States, in addition to a nonaggression pact and a broad economic treaty with the Soviet Union.[36] The veracity of information sources being very high, the Soviet government had only to be patient and wait for the Germans to speak up. It took about a month.

On July 26 Astakhov had exploratory conversation with K. Schnurre, Director of the Economic Department of the German Foreign Ministry. Astakhov was given to understand that a close collaboration and community of interests in foreign policy appeared to be obtainable, if the Soviet government considered it desirable. Schnurre assured Astakhov that controversial problems of foreign policy, which would prevent an arrangement that might take account of the vital political interests of both political parties, "did not exist anywhere along the line from the Baltic Sea to the Black Sea." [37]

Was this an open, considered invitation for the Soviet Union to stake its claims in regard to the Baltic States? Germany knew very well from official statements and press reports in London, Paris, and Moscow that the Soviet Union was insisting with particular obstinacy on its right to guarantee the Baltic States. A memorandum prepared by the German Embassy in Moscow on June 7 was devoted largely to various measures to be eventually taken with respect to the Baltic States. These measures were to constitute elements of a "political basis" for the Soviet-German negotiations, as requested by Molotov on May 20. The memorandum suggested a statement to the effect that there existed no issues between Germany and the Soviet Union affecting vital questions. A greater stress was to be placed on the fact that the Soviet Union had obtained increased security after nonaggression treaties between Germany and the Baltic States were signed, and safeguards of trade routes in the Baltic were to be emphasized.[38] Evidently these suggestions received a thorough examination at the German Foreign Office. Now Schnurre was letting Astakhov peek into the German cards.

Astakhov seized the idea immediately. He stated frankly that the Soviet Union regarded the Baltic States, as well as Finland and Rumania, as its sphere of interest. He also wanted to know whether Germany had any far-reaching political aims in the Baltic States, in addition to economic penetration. Schnurre merely assured Astakhov that no German-Soviet clash of interest would result in that area.

There was no doubt that Germany would have to pay a high price for an agreement with the Soviet Union. Renunciation of German influence in the Baltic area was rather hard to swallow. It was likely to entail a complete abandonment of German cultural positions acquired there since the thirteenth century. It might cause an abandonment of intense commercial relations with the three Baltic States. The advance of Soviet airfields to the very doorstep of East Prussia was likely to be looked upon with disapproval by the German High Command.

Political considerations must have outweighed, however, cultural, economic, and strategic considerations. The German government made up its mind in a few days. On July 28 Hitler told J. Tiso, Minister President of Slovakia, that the attitude of the Baltic States had resulted in a German decision to make a settlement with the Soviet Union.[39]

Consequently, Schulenburg received on July 29 instructions to seek an interview with Molotov and tell him, among other things, that Germany was prepared "to safeguard all Soviet interests and to come to an understanding with the Government in Moscow." The price of the Baltic States seemed not too high for her: "In the Baltic question, too, if the talks took a positive course, the idea could be advanced for so adjusting our attitude to the Baltic States as to respect vital Soviet interests in the Baltic Sea." [40]

Despite the secrecy of talks between Germany and the Soviet Union

(Astakhov admitted that not even his colleagues at the Soviet Embassy in Berlin were informed about it),[41] rumors began spreading in the countries concerned. On July 26 the Foreign Minister of Finland inquired of the German Minister in Helsinki whether or not there was any truth to the rumor that Germany intended to concede to the Soviet Union the Baltic States as a sphere of interest. The German Minister pointed out the untrustworthiness of such "propaganda fairy-tales," but asked Berlin for instructions.[42]

In his reply, the Director of the Political Department in the German Foreign Ministry suggested that the following language be used in all such conversations:

> The rumor that Germany intends to concede the Baltic States to the Soviet Union as a sphere of interest is based on malevolent invention, the obvious aim of which is to disturb Germany's relations with the Baltic States. German-Soviet talks are confined to the attempt to guide economic relations into more normal channels. The Soviet Union is known to have tried, in the Moscow negotiations with Britain and France, by means of the well-known formula about indirect aggression, to create for itself opportunities for interference in Baltic affairs.[43]

Before Schulenburg had a chance to carry out instructions of July 29 and see Molotov,[44] Ribbentrop himself had a talk with Astakhov (August 2). He told him that Germany was favorably disposed toward the Soviet Union, and if the latter took a positive attitude, "there was no problem from the Baltic to the Black Sea that could not be solved between the two of us . . . there was room for two of us on the Baltic, and the Soviet interests by no means needed to clash with ours there." [45]

Schulenburg repeated substantially the same things to Molotov on August 4. The latter already had digested Astakhov's report. Speaking of the Baltic States, Schulenburg stressed once again that Germany's conclusion of nonaggression treaties with them proved her determination to respect their integrity. He also added that Germany was ready "to adopt such an attitude to the Baltic States, if occasion arose, as would safeguard vital Soviet interests in the Baltic Sea." On hearing this, Molotov was interested in learning what states Germany meant by the term and whether Lithuania was also one of them. He evidently was thinking of his negotiations with the British and the French where this term applied to Latvia, Estonia, and Finland. Schulenburg's report does not say what the reply was.[46]

Germany's readiness to "safeguard vital Soviet interests in the Baltic area" and the Soviet desire to learn more details about it coincided with the stalemate in the British-French-Soviet negotiations. In general, the German attitude toward the independence of the Baltic States was entirely different from the British anxiety "not even to appear encroaching upon the independence of other states." (R. Butler's statement in the House of Commons on July 31.) Molotov seemed not to doubt Germany's willingness to write off both Latvia and Estonia. He only wanted to know whether this also included Lithuania.

Strangely enough, the Estonian government, even at this late hour, was still thinking of requesting German guarantee of her independence, even though an identical request made back in April had been rejected. Now again (August 7) the same idea was brought up by the Estonian Chargé and the German Minister in Moscow. Schulenburg's comment was: "I am of the opinion that the Soviets no longer want such a guarantee to be given by us." [47] In other words, the Soviet Union's, not Germany's, wishes took precedence in the Baltic area at the beginning of August. Germany took seriously her promise "to respect vital Soviet interests" there.

There were no further developments for about two weeks. The question of the delimitation of spheres of German and Soviet interests in the Baltic area was discussed by Hitler on August 14. He seemed to have no second thought about conceding either Estonia or Latvia and spoke quite nonchalantly about the Soviet desire "to widen its outlet to the Baltic." He recognized Lithuania as an issue, however.[48]

Otherwise, August 14 was the day on which the German government decided to drop all reserves and press for an agreement with the Soviet Union. Ribbentrop's telegram to Moscow, addressed "For the Ambassador Personally," stated: "There is no doubt that German-Soviet policy today has come to an historic turning point." Consequently, Schulenburg was instructed to call upon Molotov and communicate to him the following:

> There exist no real conflicts of interest between Germany and the USSR. The living spaces of Germany and the USSR touch each other, but in their natural requirements they do not conflict. Thus there is lacking all cause for an aggressive attitude on the part of one country against the other. Germany has no aggressive intentions against the USSR. The Reich Government is of the opinion that there is no question between the Baltic and the Black Seas which cannot be settled to the complete satisfaction of both countries. Among these are such questions as: the Baltic Sea, the Baltic area, Poland, Southeastern questions, etc. In such matters political co-operation between the two countries can have only a beneficial effect. The same applies to German and Soviet economy, which can be expanded in any direction.[49]

Ribbentrop was in a hurry to make a speedy clarification of German-Soviet relations. He feared that "otherwise these matters, without any German initiative, might take a turn which would deprive both Governments of the possibility of clearing up jointly the territorial questions of Eastern Europe." Since clarification could be achieved but slowly, and only through the usual diplomatic channels, Ribbentrop, therefore, reasoned that the best thing for him to do would be to go to Moscow and there "set forth the Führer's views to Herr Stalin."

Molotov saw Schulenburg on August 15. He wanted to know whether Germany was prepared to conclude a nonaggression pact with the Soviet Union; if so, more concrete discussions should take place at once. Despite all his efforts, Schulenburg did not succeed in ascertaining entirely clearly what Molotov desired in the matter of the Baltic States. Molotov only quoted from the report he had received from the Soviet Chargé in Rome at the end of June stating that Germany had had at that time a plan to make a joint guarantee of the Baltic States. In general, however, Schulenburg was rubbing his hands in sheer content. "It actually looks at the moment as if we would achieve the desired results in the negotiations here," his message to Secretary of State Weizäcker ended.[50]

Schulenburg's telegram was dispatched from Moscow at 2:30 A.M. on August 16. The very same afternoon Ribbentrop instructed Schulenburg to call again upon Molotov and communicate to him the following:

> The points brought up by Herr Molotov are in accordance with German desires. That is, Germany is ready to conclude a nonaggression pact with the Soviet Union and, if the Soviet Government so desires, one which would be irrevocable for a term of twenty-five years. Further, Germany is ready to guarantee the Baltic States jointly with the Soviet Union.[51]

In his reply (August 17) Molotov suggested conclusion of (1) a trade and credit agreement; (2) a nonaggression pact; and (3) a special protocol which would define the interests of the signatory parties in specific questions of foreign policy. Molotov thought the Germans should begin working at once on the draft of the nonaggression treaty and the protocol; the Soviets would do the same.[52] There was no reference to the Baltic States.

Molotov's leisurely handling of the entire matter exasperated Ribbentrop. The latter wired once again on August 18 instructing Schulenburg to get another appointment with Molotov and tell him that Ribbentrop was in a position to arrange details in oral discussions at Moscow and, "if occasion arises, to comply with Soviet wishes." He would also be in a position to sign a special protocol regulating the interests of both parties in questions of foreign policy of one kind or another; "for instance, the settlement of spheres of interest in the Baltic area, the problem of the Baltic States, etc." [53]

As Molotov remained unmoved by Ribbentrop's arguments and suggested August 26 or 27 as the earliest date for his arrival in Moscow,[54] Hitler dispatched a personal telegram to Stalin in which he asked him to receive Ribbentrop either on August 22 or 23. "The tension between Germany and Poland has become intolerable; Polish demeanor toward a great power is such that a crisis may arise any day," Hitler argued.[55] Stalin agreed to August 23.[56]

The haste of the entire action is well illustrated by the fact that as late as August 19 Molotov was requesting the German government to state more specifically what points were to be covered in the proto- col regarding the division of Eastern Europe into spheres of influence. To be sure, Molotov submitted the Soviet draft of the treaty of non- aggression the same afternoon of August 19, but there is no record of any protocol being submitted at the same time.[57]

The Estonian government seems not to have suspected the Soviet- German deal to the very last moment. As late as August 20, the Ger- man Minister in Tallinn reported a hint from the Secretary of the Estonian Foreign Ministry in regard to the possibility of help from Ger- many should the Soviet Union attack Estonia. She would defend her neutrality. But he did not believe in her ability "to hold out for very long." [58]

When Ribbentrop met both Stalin and Molotov for the first time at the Kremlin, he found that Soviet aims in the Baltic area went much farther than he had anticipated. There was no discussion about joint guarantees of the Baltic States. All of Eastern Europe was to be di- vided between Germany and the Soviet Union into clearly defined spheres of interest.[59] Ribbentrop became convinced that neither Great Britain nor France would interfere in such a deal, having already "sold" the Baltic States to the Soviet Union.[60] Hitler declared in his instructions that "all the problems of Eastern Europe are to be regarded as belong- ing exclusively to the spheres of interest of Germany and the Soviet Union," and requested that such a statement be put into the record.[61]

Ribbentrop had previously assured the Soviets that the living spaces of the two countries "touched each other, but in their natural require- ments they did not conflict" (August 15). Yet he was quite surprised to learn that the Soviet concept of "natural requirements" was so much at variance with his own. While the Germans had visualized the northern boundary of their sphere of influence running along the Daugava and the western shore of the Gulf of Riga (cf. map p. 14), the Soviets wanted to have all of Latvia, including the ports of Riga, Ventspils and Liepaja, at their disposal (thus bringing Soviet bases some 200 miles closer to East Prussia).

The three-hour conference ended with neither party yielding on that particular point. It looked as if the boundaries of "the living spaces" conflicted after all. Desiring to reach an agreement at any half-way acceptable price, Ribbentrop cabled home asking Hitler's assent to Soviet territorial demands. He obtained it [62]—this was not the German land they were bartering away.

The very same night both the Soviet-German *Treaty of Nonaggression* and the *Secret Supplementary Protocol* to it were signed.[63] While the treaty itself did not contain provisions directly affecting the Baltic area and was made public, such was not the case with its integral part, the Secret Supplementary Protocol. Signed after "strictly confidential conversations" concerning the question of the boundary of the German and the Soviet spheres of influence in Eastern Europe, the Protocol contained the following provision which affected all three Baltic States:

> In the event of a territorial and political rearrangement in the areas belonging to the Baltic States (Finland, Estonia, Latvia, Lithuania), the northern boundary of Lithuania shall represent the boundary of the spheres of influence of Germany and the USSR. In this connection the interest of Lithuania in the Vilnius area is recognized by each party.

The signature of the Secret Supplementary Protocol constituted a gross violation of nonaggression treaties concluded between the Soviet Union on one side and the Baltic States on the other. The corresponding provisions read as follows:

> *For Lithuania:* "If a political agreement directed against one of the Contracting Parties is concluded between third Powers . . . the other Contracting Party undertakes not to adhere to such agreement" (September 28, 1926);
> *For Latvia:* "Each of the High Contracting Parties undertakes not to be a party to any military or political treaties, conventions or agreements directed against the independence, territorial integrity or political security of the other Party, or to any treaties, conventions, or agreements aiming at an economic or financial boycott of either of the Contracting Parties" (February 5, 1932);
> *For Estonia:* "Each of the High Contracting Parties undertakes not to take part in political agreements manifestly directed in an aggressive sense against the other Party" (May 4, 1932).

The question may arise whether or not the provisions of the Secret Supplementary Protocol were actually directed against the Baltic States. Had the two powers simply stated their interest in particular areas, but with no further designs? The answer to this question was given by Stalin on September 25, during a meeting with Schulenburg. In asking Germany's consent to a territorial swap (of which there will be more later), Stalin announced that, if German consent was given,

> the Soviet Union would immediately take up the solution of the problem of the Baltic countries in accordance with the Protocol of August 23, and expected in this matter the unstinting support of the German Government.[64]

The solution contemplated by Stalin came into evidence the next day in a "Very Urgent" telegram, signed jointly by the German Minister and the Military Attaché in Estonia. They had received information from the Estonian Chief of Staff that the Soviet Union had demanded an alliance with Estonia, a naval base, and an air base and that Soviet airmen had carried out extensive flights over Estonian territory on September 25 and 26,[65] i.e., even before announcing the impending "solution of the problem of the Baltic countries."

In another "Very Urgent" telegram from Tallinn of the same date, the German Minister in Estonia transmitted information received from the Estonian Foreign Minister that the Estonian government was prepared to accept a military alliance with the Soviet Union "under the gravest threat of imminent attack." [66] Finally, in a document dated October 8, which referred to Lithuania, Molotov openly spoke about the eventuality that "the forces of the Red Army should be stationed" in Lithuanian territory.[67]

This was the kind of "territorial and political arrangement in the areas belonging to the Baltic States," agreed upon by Germany and the Soviet Union on August 23. It is difficult to see, even by the widest stretch of imagination, how it could be construed as compatible with the Soviet-Baltic nonaggression treaties.

In less than a week after Germany signed an agreement with the Soviet Union to partition all of Eastern Europe into their respective spheres of influence, she began gathering its fruit. On September 1 German troops invaded Poland and thus ignited World War II. It was to end five and a half years later with the partition of Germany herself. The Soviet Union followed the lead on September 17 by launching a simultaneous invasion of Poland and Lithuania (the Polish-occupied part of it). What the Soviet neighbors had been in constant fear of finally happened: the Red troops were again, as in 1918–1919, rolling westward, along the entire 500-mile line from Polotzk to Kamenetz-Podolsk.

Chapter Nine

QUARRELS OVER LITHUANIA

Until the conclusion of the Soviet-German Nonaggression Treaty on August 23, Lithuania was left alone in negotiations among the great powers. She did not play any role in the British-French-Soviet talks. The Soviet Union did not bother her with threatening notes as in the case of Latvia and Estonia; nor was Lithuania claimed during the Soviet-German talks as belonging to the Soviet sphere of interest. Her inviolability and territorial integrity were secured by nonaggression treaties with both the Soviet Union and Germany (September 28, 1926, and March 22, 1939, respectively) as well as by the guarantee implied in the assurance given by British Prime Minister N. Chamberlain in the House of Commons on March 31, 1939. Since Great Britain and France were to give support to Poland in the event of any action which threatened Polish independence and which the Polish government considered vital to resist, it was felt that a German attack on Lithuania would be considered by Poland as a move to encircle her and would cause the Franco-British guarantees to come into action.[1]

In fact, Latvia and Estonia were looking upon Lithuania with envy. The Latvian Minister in Kaunas, for example, once told his United States colleague that both Latvia and Estonia would be pleased to have the sort of guarantee from the Western Powers that Lithuania already had. He considered an implied guarantee of this kind to be the finest one "the small countries in this part of the world could have." And it seemed to him that Lithuania already had all she could wish in the way of guarantees.[2]

What the Latvian Minister in Kaunas did not foresee, however, was the eventuality of a partition of the Baltic States between the Soviet Union and Germany instead of a fight over them. The Secret Supplementary Protocol of August 23, 1939, created all prerequisites for that; only the implementation was lacking. Lithuania, by virtue of this agreement, was assigned to the German sphere of interest, and the Germans wasted no time in drawing obvious consequences. The alignment of Lithuania on the German side appeared to carry so much weight that Ribbentrop himself took charge of it—practically immediately on his return from Moscow.

On August 29 he instructed German Minister in Kaunas Zechlin to advise the Lithuanian Government that Germany would abide unconditionally by the terms of the German-Lithuanian treaty of March 22, 1939, but expected that in any eventual conflict Lithuania would observe a completely unimpeachable neutrality toward Germany. This would include Lithuania's refusal to tolerate any territorial infringement and her resistance to it. Failure or inability to do so would force Germany to safeguard her interests in such a way as the resulting situation required.[3]

Zechlin spoke to Deputy Minister President K. Bizauskas the same day and received from him assurance that Lithuania would pursue the policy of strictest neutrality and would resist with all means in her power any violation of the same by a third party. Such an attitude was dictated by her own particular interests, and she fully realized the consequences likely to arise otherwise.[4]

Thereupon, in a surprising move which could hardly be reconciled with German insistence on Lithuanian neutrality, Zechlin was requested to sound out the Lithuanian government cautiously as to whether or not it would be prepared to stage a demonstration on the Polish frontier, "perhaps by means of troop concentrations." As a reward, Germany promised to support Lithuanian claims to Vilnius.[5]

Ribbentrop was well aware that the foremost objective of the Lithuanian foreign policy since 1920 had been the recovery of her capital Vilnius and all of the Polish-occupied territory as delineated by the Russo-Lithuanian Peace Treaty of July 12, 1920. He also knew that the establishment of diplomatic relations with Poland, as a result of her March 18, 1938 ultimatum, had not produced any formal change in this attitude.

Germany's diplomatic interest in Lithuania coincided with her military interest. The problem of integrating Lithuania into the military plans occupied the minds of the planners of the German attack on Poland, literally to the last minute. Thus, Colonel General Halder, Chief of the Army Staff, wrote in his diary on August 29: "Lithuania?" The next day he jotted down that Lithuania was preparing three divisions, but that she had not extended official feelers until then.[6]

As a matter of record, General Halder's interest in Lithuania was of long standing. As far back as April 20, 1939, he was trying to find out from General S. Rastikis, Commander-in-Chief of the Lithuanian Army, then visiting Berlin, if Lithuania was still interested in Vilnius.[7] Later on the German Military Attaché in Kaunas repeatedly approached General Rastikis, urging him to take Vilnius away from the Poles. He promised German support with aircraft, tanks, and heavy artillery, and he made no secret he was speaking on behalf of General Halder and General Brauchitsch, Commander-in-Chief of the German Army.[8]

As the first attempt failed, Zechlin was instructed on August 30 "to express still more clearly" German sympathies with Lithuanian aspirations regarding Vilnius and to state that, in the event of a territorial rearrangement taking place between Germany and Poland, any Lithuanian claims to the Vilnius area might also be taken into consideration.[9]

Ribbentrop's efforts to align Lithuania on the German side prompted several statements on the part of military men and government heads in Lithuania. First, General Rastikis stated to the German Military Attaché in Kaunas that Lithuanian troops on the Polish-Lithuanian demarcation line had been reinforced, but that strictest secrecy was observed to avoid any outward demonstration against Poland.[10] This was exactly the opposite of what Ribbentrop wanted. Then, on August 31, on the eve of the German attack against Poland, Minister President General J. Cernius asserted that Lithuania would "preserve her neutrality and defend Lithuanian territory against any aggressor with all her means" and that necessary military measures had been taken. Finally, Deputy Minister President K. Bizauskas tried to avoid discussing with Zechlin Ribbentrop's suggestion of a military demonstration against Poland. So did President A. Smetona.[11] Zechlin, therefore, had to conclude that the Lithuanian government would not take such action, although public opinion in Lithuania, he believed, was divided in regard to the prudence of such an attitude.[12]

Consequently, Germany attacked Poland in the early morning of September 1, 1939, unassisted by Lithuania. Ribbentrop, however, was not to be so easily discouraged.

As Polish armed resistance was rapidly disintegrating and Soviet military action in Poland was promised "within the next few days"[13] Ribbentrop asked the German Minister in Kaunas and his military Attaché to take up the Vilnius problem with the members of the Lithuanian government "who favor the matter" and also with the army commanders respectively. Ribbentrop's decision was reached after consultation with Hitler,[14] which is indicative of the importance the German government attributed to Lithuania's participation in war against Poland. It was September 9, the date on which Molotov conveyed to the German government his congratulations on the entry of German troops into Warsaw.[15]

It seems, however, that Ribbentrop's move was to some extent precipitated by Lithuanian Minister in Berlin Colonel K. Skirpa.[16] Since the beginning of the Polish-German war he had been arguing with his government about the necessity for Lithuania to take back from Poland Vilnius and the surrounding territory as rightfully belonging to Lithuania. On September 8 he submitted a detailed plan outlining military and diplomatic moves to be undertaken. By that time, only token Polish forces remained in and around Vilnius. Finding little response in Kaunas, Skirpa then, on the morning of September 9, gave a hint to Dr. P. Kleist, an officer of the German Foreign Ministry, who was all ears. The latter must have reported immediately to his superiors, and was thus instrumental in arranging a hasty conference between Hitler and Ribbentrop. The result of this conference was the cable to the German Minister in Kaunas, dispatched on September 9 at 2:45 P.M.

The same night Kleist saw Skirpa again. He sought more information about Skirpa's ideas and who was behind them. This time Skirpa revealed that he had urged the Lithuanian government to attack Poland immediately and hoped his suggestion would be accepted. Ribbentrop, after receiving Kleist's report, wrote on the margin: "I have had Skirpa told that Lithuania should immediately take Vilnius, but nothing more." Otherwise, he expected from Zechlin an immediate report on conversations with the Lithuanian government regarding its attitude to the Vilnius problem.[17]

Contrary to Skirpa's expectation, the Lithuanian government was in no hurry to commit itself. On September 11 he had to admit to Kleist that the acceptance of his suggestions was delayed due to the professed neutrality of Lithuania and uncertainty about Soviet intentions.[18] A confirmation of this statement was also received from Zechlin. He had talked to General Rastikis, who felt that Lithuania would be handicapped if she abandoned her neutrality, and that Great Britain and France were urging her not to. Zechlin had heard from other sources that such was also the attitude of the Soviet Union.[19]

Nevertheless, the German government continued putting pressure on the Lithuanian government through Skirpa. Kleist again called on him on September 11 and 13. This time he intimated that Germany could offer diplomatic assistance in regard to the Soviet Union and military assistance—tanks and planes—to overcome possible Polish resistance, although he did not anticipate any. On his last call on Skirpa, Kleist advised that the Lithuanian government should act quickly in view of very important political and military events to take place within a few days.

As the Lithuanian government delayed its reply, the news began spreading in London and Paris that Germany was pressuring Lithuania in the strongest possible way into marching against Poland and retrieving Vilnius.[20] Ribbentrop recognized he had failed in inducing Lithuania to join in an attack against Poland. On September 14 Kleist was instructed to drop the subject and not to discuss it, even if it should be taken up by the Lithuanian side.[21]

The apprehension of the latter regarding the Soviet attitude toward the march of the Lithuanian armed forces to retake Vilnius found its substantiation in the strange change in the behavior of the Soviet diplomats between September 6 and 12. According to Skirpa, the Soviet Ambassador in Berlin called on him on September 6 and, without further ado, stated rather undiplomatically that he had been at a loss to understand why the Lithuanian government delayed its order for the armed forces to cross the Polish-Lithuanian demarcation line and take Vilnius. He even gave advice not to lose time lest the Germans get there first.[22]

On receiving Skirpa's report, the Lithuanian Foreign Ministry instructed him to seek further clarification. This time, however (September 8), the Soviet Ambassador displayed an entirely different attitude. He volunteered no additional information and generally was reluctant to speak about the whole matter. Skirpa concluded thereupon that Moscow, in the meantime, must have learned that the Lithuanian government had, on September 5, decided not to take Vilnius by force. The Soviet Minister in Kaunas must have also received identical instructions, since he, on September 12, unofficially warned an officer of the Lithuanian Foreign Ministry against "sticking the finger in the door."

This is why Skirpa could not receive a favorable consideration of his plan to take Vilnius. On the contrary, he received instructions from Kaunas advising him to comply strictly with the May 11 directive. This directive advised Lithuanian missions abroad to avoid any unguarded statements and to point out that unreserved observance of neutrality constituted one of the basic tenets of Lithuanian foreign policy which Lithuania was determined to uphold and defend if necessary.

Nevertheless, the Soviet government remained not entirely sure of what Lithuania might do in regard to the reoccupation of Vilnius and the surrounding territory she claimed as her own. On the eve of the Soviet invasion of Poland, which began at dawn on September 17, Molotov asked Schulenburg for an urgent explanation of what was to become of Vilnius, whether some agreement had been reached with Lithuania on that matter, and who was to occupy the city. He also emphasized that the Soviet Union absolutely wanted to avoid a clash with Lithuania, yet he was not precise as to where such a clash would occur if the Lithuanian troops moved eastward.[23]

To be sure, Molotov could have obtained the desired information on Lithuanian moves directly from the Lithuanian government instead of querying Schulenburg (either by inquiring of the Lithuanian Minister in Moscow or advising the Soviet Minister in Kaunas to do so). The reasons for his choosing an indirect approach became clear a few weeks later. The Soviet Union needed to occupy Vilnius in order to subject Lithuania to blackmail. Possession of her capital surely represented an asset, and the Soviet government knew that Lithuania would buy it back at a very high price—admission of a Trojan Horse at first and loss of independence ten months later.

Thus, an attempt by Lithuania to move eastward and meet the Soviet troops at the Soviet-Lithuanian frontier as agreed upon on July 12, 1920, could have easily caused a clash. As a matter of fact, the Soviet Military Attaché in Riga, undoubtedly speaking not on his own presumption, told his United States colleagues that the German endeavor to incite Lithuania to raise claims to Vilnius was regarded as unfriendly to the Soviet Union.[24]

Molotov's uncertainty about Lithuanian moves terminated when General Cernius, Prime Minister of Lithuania, in a broadcast on September 17, announced that Lithuania had her aspirations in regard to Vilnius, but hoped to achieve her objectives by peaceful means. In an exchange of views with the United States Minister in Kaunas the same evening, K. Bizauskas, Deputy Prime Minister, expressed his conviction that the Soviet Union would retake Estonia and Latvia, but that Lithuania and Poland would form a buffer between the Soviet Union and Germany.[25]

Whatever the motives, Lithuania did not take advantage of Poland's defeat, however angry she was over Polish behavior in the past. Lithuania had signed the Briand-Kellogg Pact by which she undertook never to seek the settlement or solution of international controversies or disputes except by pacific means. She wanted even now, at this trying moment, to keep her record clean by strict adherence to all obligations she had incurred. Some men were called to the colors as protection against all eventualities, but they remained deployed behind the demarcation line which they did not cross while the Poles were fighting both the Germans and the Soviets.

This attitude remained unchanged even after the Polish Military Commandant of Vilnius, shortly before abandoning the city to the advancing Soviet armed forces, called in person on the Consul General of Lithuania and implored him to send an urgent appeal to his government requesting it to take Vilnius immediately.[26] The Lithuanian government chose to remain neutral to the last, thus keeping its neutrality record unblemished, but provoking considerable criticism in Lithuania, where many believed that such a policy was detrimental to the national interests.

When the Red tanks moved into Vilnius on September 19, the fleeing Polish detachments found refuge in Lithuania. And so did the civilian population. The Lithuanians held no grudge against Poland for depriving them of their capital for twenty years and for trying to "normalize" diplomatic relations by means of an ultimatum. Eventually the number of military internees and civilian refugees reached a figure as high as 50,000,[27] an equivalent of some 3 million refugees in the United States.

The Soviet troops, having crossed the eastern boundary of Poland on September 17, did not halt in their advance upon reaching the eastern boundary of Lithuania as stipulated in the Russo-Lithuanian Peace Treaty of July 12, 1920. On the contrary, they continued advancing westward, and on the third day of their offensive occupied Vilnius—for the third time since 1919. In fact, the advance was not called off before the Soviet troops reached the Polish-Lithuanian demarcation line (Nos. 1 & 2 on the map p. 135).

There can be no doubt that the territory situated west of the line agreed upon on July 12, 1920, was, by all standards of international law, under Lithuanian sovereignty at the time of invasion. Russia (the Soviet Union), on signing the Peace Treaty with Lithuania, had renounced, "voluntarily and forever," all her former sovereign rights to that territory and consistently refused in a number of declarations to recognize its seizure by Poland as legal. The fact that the Conference of Ambassadors had assigned the contested territory to Poland (1923) did not change the legal status, as Lithuania refused to recognize the validity of such a decision and was subsequently upheld by the Hague Tribunal (1931). Finally, Poland herself did not request Lithuania to renounce her sovereignty over the contested territory at the time of acceptance of the Polish ultimatum (1938).

The Soviet action thus violated not only the provisions of the Russo-Lithuanian Peace Treaty of July 12, 1920, but also the provisions of the Treaty of Nonaggression of September 28, 1926, containing the obligation "to respect in all circumstances the sovereignty and territorial inviolability" of, and "to refrain from any aggressive action whatsoever" against, the other Contracting Party—Lithuania.

That this constituted an act of aggression is clear from the Convention on Definition of Aggression (July 3, 1933), signed by both the Soviet Union and Lithuania. The convention branded as an aggressor that state which was the first to invade or attack with its land, naval or air forces the territory of another state, with or without declaration

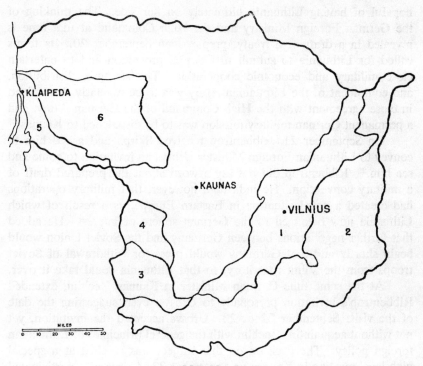

MAP No. 2

ACTUAL AND CONTEMPLATED CHANGES IN LITHUANIAN
TERRITORY IN 1920–1940

Solid line—Frontier with Russia (the Soviet Union) and Poland according to the
Peace Treaty of July 12, 1920, and with Germany according to the decision of
the Conference of Allied Ambassadors of February 16, 1923; Nos. 1, 2 & 3—
occupied by Poland 1920–1939; No. 1—occupied by the Soviet Union in 1939
and restored to Lithuania; No. 2—ditto, but annexed to the Soviet Union; No.
3 & 5— occupied by Germany in 1939; No. 4—awarded to Germany in 1939, but
occupied by the Soviet Union in 1940; No. 6—considered by the German General
Staff for annexation in 1938.

of war, while no political, military, economic or other considerations
were to be accepted as an excuse or justification for the aggression.

Aggression against Poland and Lithuania launched on September
17, 1939, was the first link in the long chain of treaty violations committed by the Soviet Union during World War II and after. Evidently the good name of the Soviet Union was considered worth
less than the acquisition, by sheer force, of a strip of land without any
particular economic or strategic value. This strip covered only an area
of about 12,500 miles, i.e., about 0.15 per cent of the Soviet territory
before World War II. But Stalin and Molotov knew what they were
doing and what were their plans regarding Lithuania.

It is surprising that Germany, even under these conditions, still was hopeful of having Lithuania ultimately on her side. The thinking of the German Foreign Ministry and the High Command at that time is revealed in a draft of a treaty, prepared on September 20. Its terms called for Lithuania to submit to German protection and to entertain close military and economic cooperation. The strength, distribution, and equipment of the Lithuanian Army was to be regularly determined in close agreement with the High Command of the German Army, and a permanent German military mission was to be dispatched to Kaunas.[28]

On September 21, Ribbentrop received Skirpa and asked him to convey to Lithuanian Foreign Minister Urbsys an invitation to come and see him.[29] Ribbentrop did not say a word about the prepared draft of a military convention. He indicated, however, that military operations had created a novel situation in Eastern Europe, as a result of which Lithuania now belonged to the German sphere of interest. He added that further negotiations between Germany and the Soviet Union would begin shortly and that Germany would press for withdrawal of Soviet troops from the Vilnius territory, so that Lithuania could take it over.

At the same time German Minister in Kaunas, Zechlin, extended Ribbentrop's invitation personally to Urbsys, even suggesting the date of the visit: September 22 or 23. Urbsys accepted the invitation, yet not without acquainting Zechlin with the general principles of Lithuanian foreign policy. The decision on that subject was reached at a special high-level meeting in Kaunas on September 22. Skirpa also participated and was given a *pro memoria* under Urbsys' signature, summarizing the decisions reached:

(1) Lithuania wishes and is firmly determined to maintain fully good neighbor relations with Germany. The recent events in Eastern Europe did not change this attitude of Lithuania.

(2) Lithuania, in the presence of actual war and after a sober estimate of her own forces, decided to maintain her neutrality. She will also maintain this attitude in the future. Her neutrality means the determination to be a free and independent state.

(3) In accordance with this policy, Lithuania wishes to maintain and is maintaining at the present time good relations with all states, especially with neighboring states.

(4) Lithuania has some unrealized national aspirations, but she seeks their realization only by peaceful measures. This was confirmed recently by a public statement of the Council of Ministers.

(5) Lithuania is grateful to Germany for her recently expressed approval of Lithuanian aspirations.

These principles were established in connection with the invitation of the Reich Foreign Minister addressed to me [J. Urbsys] to see him.[30]

This meant an open rejection of Ribbentrop's overtures. Lithuania was determined to remain neutral despite the bait offered in exchange for the reversal of these policies. Furthermore, Urbsys found it necessary to inform the Soviet Minister in Kaunas of Ribbentrop's invitation. The same night Zechlin knew about it.[31] Another rebuff came from Moscow. Molotov flatly rejected all German mediation in the Vilnius problem on the ground that the time was not ripe for discussion of all the details. These details were to be taken into consideration at the time of the final settlement of the entire Baltic complex.

Ribbentrop, under these conditions, asked for a delay of Urbsys' visit for a few days, but then failed to set up a definite date. In vain Zechlin urged no delay of the trip; it was too late to do anything about Lithuania. On September 25 Stalin requested the transfer of Lithuania to the Soviet sphere of interest. Two days later Ribbentrop was in Moscow. The day before, Zechlin informed the Lithuanian government that Urbsys' visit was no longer practicable since Lithuania had chosen not to follow German suggestions regarding her protection.

The transfer of Lithuania from the German to the Soviet sphere of interest was not to be an outright extortion act. The Soviet Union offered to barter Lithuania against all of the Polish Province of Lublin, a part of the Province of Warsaw extending to the Bug, and a small parcel of land around Suvalkai and Augustavas,[32] although Lithuania had a perfect title to the latter by virtue of the Russo-Lithuanian Peace Treaty of July 12, 1920.

Germany did not like the suggested deal. Despite the outwardly amicable relations between the two countries, it was felt in Germany that it would be desirable to keep Red troops as far as possible from East Prussia.[33] Furthermore, the area offered to Germany was substantially smaller than the territory of Lithuania to be given up. Finally, Germany was also to withdraw from oil fields around Drohobycz and Boryslav in the Soviet zone, occupied by the German troops on their dash across Poland.[34] The marshy, sparsely populated, and little industrialized territory between the Vistula and the Bug offered by the Soviet Union in exchange was in no way equal to what Germany was losing.

Consequently, Ribbentrop did his best on his second trip to Moscow to retain Lithuania—or at least a part of it (west of Kaunas)—in the German sphere of interest. All his efforts were futile, however. "When Herr von Ribbentrop was summoned to Moscow," British Prime Minister W. Churchill said in his broadcast on October 1, "it was to learn the fact, and to accept the fact, that the Nazi denizens upon the Baltic States and upon the Ukraine must come to a dead stop." Ribbentrop finally had to ask Hitler's consent to the renunciation of German "rights" to Lithuania. It would be advisable to insist on the delineation of the zones of interest as agreed upon on August 23, he argued in a message to Hitler; on the other hand, the expected annexation of Latvia and Estonia by the Soviet Union would force Germany to assume protection of Lithuania, which the world would interpret as a veiled annexation and which would cause friction with the Soviet Union.[35] Hitler must have consented, although no record of his reply was found in German archives.

The formal aspect of the transfer was effected in a Secret Supplementary Protocol to the Soviet-German Boundary and Friendship Treaty of September 28, 1939. Its provisions affecting Lithuania stipulated the following:

> The Secret Supplementary Protocol signed on August 23, 1939, shall be amended in item 1 to the effect that the territory of the Lithuanian state falls to the sphere of influence of the USSR while, on the other hand, the province of Lublin and parts of the province of Warsaw fall to the sphere of influence of Germany.[36]

British Foreign Secretary, Viscount Halifax, was correct when shortly thereafter (December 5) he told the House of Lords that "Herr Hitler had bartered away what was not his property to barter—the liberties of the Baltic peoples." In just nine months the Baltic peoples became Soviet slaves. Stalin, of course, felt differently about it. He proudly told Latvian Foreign Minister Munters (October 3) that the Soviets had prevented Latvia from becoming split into two parts, along the River Daugava (cf. map p. 14), as suggested by the Germans during the negotiations. "Nations cannot be treated this way," he said.[37] Simultaneously he told Lithuanian Foreign Minister Urbsys he also had saved Lithuania from German designs aimed at splitting her into two parts along the Nemunas.[38]

Contrary to Molotov's promise to keep the Baltic governments informed about the negotiations where the affairs of their countries were involved,[39] they were kept in complete darkness on the partition of the Baltic area into a German and a Soviet zone. The Lithuanian government reportedly suspected the deal between the two powers regarding Lithuania, but did not know the exact terms of the agreement for nearly a week.[40]

Only a year later it came into the open that the barter deal involving Lithuania was entirely unsatisfactory to Germany. In the course of a meeting between Hitler, Ribbentrop, and Molotov in Berlin on November 12–13, 1940,[41] Hitler complained that there were departures from the conception of the spheres of interest as agreed upon by Stalin and Ribbentrop. In a number of cases, on calm consideration of German and Soviet interests, Hitler said, he had not been ready "to make concessions." He had realized, however, that it was desirable to meet the needs of the Soviet Union half-way, as in the case of Lithuania. Changes from the original German-Soviet agreements were essentially due to Soviet initiative, and the Province of Lublin was no compensation, economically, for Lithuania.

Hitler's remark touched off a bitter controversy between Hitler and Ribbentrop on one side and Molotov on the other. Molotov said the Soviet Union would not have insisted on the revision of the agreement of August 23 relative to Lithuania, "if Germany had not wanted it." Ribbentrop retorted that the Soviet Union had urged such a revision "very strongly." But Molotov kept on reiterating that the Soviets "would not have refused to leave matters as provided for in the original agreement."

"Injustice" sustained by Germany on September 28, 1939, served also as one of the excuses for the German attack on the Soviet Union nearly two years later. "As we were marching victoriously into Poland," Hitler said on June 22, 1941, the day the Soviet-German war started, "Soviet leaders suddenly began to set aside the agreement with regard to Lithuania." But to be exact, disagreement over Lithuania began to cause bad blood between Germany and the Soviet Union much earlier.

The Secret Supplementary Protocol of September 28, 1939, also contained the following provision:

> As soon as the Government of the USSR shall take special measures on Lithuanian territory to protect its interests, the present German-Lithuanian border, for the purpose of a natural and simple boundary delineation, shall be rectified in such a way that the Lithuanian territory situated to the southwest of the line marked on the attached map should fall to Germany.

It is indicative of the haste with which this document was drawn that the outline of the strip of the Lithuanian territory to be ceded to Germany was *not* marked on the map attached to the Protocol and featuring signatures of both Stalin and Ribbentrop.[42] It is known, however, from another document (report of the German Minister in Kaunas dated October 5)[43] that the outline included the city and district of Naumiestis and the territory west of Marijampole, an odd rectangle stretching along the River Sesupe for about 50 miles in length and 35 miles in width, and covering some 700 square miles.

The cession of the strip was motivated by the necessity of "a natural and simple boundary delineation." But a look at the map (No. 4) does not show that the new boundary would have been any more natural or simpler than the old German-Lithuanian boundary; not even after the addition to Germany of the formerly Polish-held Lithuanian territory around Suvalkai and Augustavas (No 3; it actually should have been restored to Lithuania). The real reason for Germany's claim to this particular piece of land must have been her desire to incorporate a territory with a substantial ethnic German population (possibly some 15,000) settled there during the period of its German administration (1795–1807) and even thereafter.

The agreement was to be kept secret until the time when the Soviet government took "special measures." Before this happened, however, Molotov summoned Schulenburg on October 3 and informed him[44] about his plan to tell the Lithuanian Foreign Minister, arriving in Moscow the same day, that the Soviet government was willing to cede Vilnius and its environs to Lithuania, and that the Lithuanian government "must cede the well-known portion of her territory to Germany." Molotov thought a German-Lithuanian protocol to that end ought to be signed simultaneously with a Soviet-Lithuanian protocol providing for the cession of Vilnius and its environs.

Molotov's reasoning was indeed astonishing. The Soviet government "was willing to cede" a portion of territory that rightfully, by virtue of a mutual agreement (Peace Treaty of July 12, 1920), belonged to Lithuania, although she had been prevented by Poland from taking actual possession of it. At the same time Moscow intended to order the Lithuanian government that it "must cede" a portion of her own territory held in her uninterrupted possession since the re-establishment of independence.

Schulenburg grasped the situation immediately. Would not it be more logical, he wondered, for the Soviet government to exchange Vilnius for the strip of the territory to be ceded to Germany and then hand the latter over to Germany? Molotov disagreed, but was willing to wait for the reply until the next morning (the meeting took place at 2 P.M.). Schulenburg's personal opinion stated in his telegram to Berlin shows that he, like Molotov, was not affected by moral inhibitions regarding the entire matter:

> Molotov's suggestion seems to me harmful, as in the eyes of the world it would make us appear as "robbers" of Lithuanian territory, while the Soviet government figures as the donor. As I see it, only my suggestion enters into consideration at all. However, I would ask you to consider whether it might not be advisable for us, by a separate secret German-Soviet protocol, to forego the cession of the Lithuanian strip of territory until the Soviet Union actually incorporates Lithuania, an idea on which, I believe, the arrangement concerning Lithuania was originally based.

Ribbentrop himself answered Schulenburg's telegram on October 4 and had it telephoned to Moscow:

> I, too, do not consider the method Molotov suggested for the cession of the Lithuanian strip of territory as suitable. On the contrary, please ask Molotov not to discuss this cession of territory with the Lithuanians at present, but rather to have the Soviet government assume the obligation toward Germany

to leave this strip of territory unoccupied in the event of a posting of Soviet forces in Lithuania, which may possibly be contemplated, and furthermore to leave it to Germany to determine the date on which the cession of the territory should be formally affected. An understanding to this effect should be set forth in a secret exchange of letters between yourself and Molotov.[45]

It was too late—Molotov had already double-crossed Ribbentrop. Without awaiting German reply, as promised, he informed the Lithuanian Foreign Minister then in Moscow of the confidential understanding in regard to the strip of the Lithuanian territory. Molotov admitted that the minister and the other members of the Lithuanian delegation were "extremely dismayed and sad." Otherwise Molotov felt uneasy and even called on Stalin for support, who then let it be known he personally was requesting the German government "not to insist for the moment" upon the cession of the territory involved.[46]

This took place on October 4. The secret Soviet-German deal behind the back of Lithuania now became known to the latter. Thereupon Ribbentrop decided the least he could do was to place the blame on the Soviet Union. Early on October 5 he instructed Zechlin to get in touch with the Lithuanian government and inform it, "orally and in strict confidence," of what the Soviet-German understanding was, emphasizing that he, Ribbentrop, had repeatedly demanded that Vilnius be returned to Lithuania. Furthermore, the German government did not consider the question of such border revision timely at the moment.[47] The same reply was also given to the Lithuanian Minister in Berlin.[48]

As Ribbentrop's instructions went to Zechlin, Schulenburg was directed to request of Molotov that the border strip of Lithuanian territory involved be left free in the event of a possible posting of Soviet troops in Lithuania and also that it be left to Germany to determine the date of the implementing of the agreement concerning the cession to Germany of the territory involved.

The compromise was acceptable to the Soviet government. On October 8 Molotov delivered to Schulenburg a note that, concerning Lithuania, the following understanding existed between the Soviet Union and Germany:

> (1) The Lithuanian territory mentioned in the protocol and marked on the map attached to the protocol shall not be occupied in case forces of the Red Army should be stationed [in Lithuania];
> (2) It shall be left to Germany to determine the date for the implementing of the agreement concerning the cession to Germany of the above-mentioned Lithuanian territory.[49]

This terminated the matter, but for the time being only. It was to cause even greater disagreement between the two powers eight months hence. In the meantime the German government seemed reluctant to accept the finality of the Soviet-German arrangement concerning Lithuania as a whole. It was demonstrated with particular clarity in the handling of German repatriates in Estonia and Latvia, on the one hand, and Lithuania, on the other.

It was agreed in a separate Confidential Protocol signed on September 28:

> The Government of the USSR shall place no obstacles in the way of Reich nationals and other persons of German descent residing in the territories under its jurisdiction, if they desire to migrate to Germany or to the territories under German jurisdiction.

To implement this agreement, Germany concluded repatriation treaties with Estonia and Latvia on October 15 and 30 respectively. Although repatriation plans for Lithuanian Germans were also prepared in October,[50] no treaty was signed for more than a year (not until January 10, 1941), when Lithuania had ceased to exist as an independent state.

It is known that the German government took under renewed consideration the problem of the resettlement of German nationals from Lithuania shortly after she fell victim to Soviet aggression (June 15, 1940).[51] Three weeks later, Berlin became concerned about the safety of German nationals. The Soviet Union was reportedly taking the most drastic measures in the Baltic area and either liquidating people outright or deporting them to Siberia.[52] On this disquieting news, the German government was ready to approach the Soviet-appointed government of Lithuania and talk about repatriation (July 9).[53] Yet, no action was taken; not even after Molotov hinted (July 13) that Germany could move out of Lithuania the population of German origin whenever she wished.[54]

The delay in the case of Lithuania is all the more significant since German nationals in both Latvia and Estonia were actually urged by German organizations to follow Hitler's call home, and the argument of an impending Soviet occupation was freely circulated.[55] The repatriation action, in fact, was carried out by Germany with such impact as to cause Molotov to remark that Germany was evidently promoting a panicky emigration, turning it into a flight.[56]

This writer's attempt to secure information from former German officials, who should have known the reasons for the delay, failed to produce a uniform answer. The consensus was that Hitler expected to finish off Great Britain and France and then jump on the Soviet Union. If everything had progressed as planned, there would have been no need to move thousands of German nationals, and perhaps they could have played a useful role in the preparation of military operations.

The final disagreement between Germany and the Soviet Union over Lithuania occurred after the occupation of the latter by Soviet troops on June 15, 1940. Despite Molotov's declaration of October 8 that the strip of the Lithuanian territory allocated to Germany would not be occupied in case of stationing the Red Army in Lithuania, the Soviet troops did occupy it after all. The Germans waited patiently for more than three weeks, evidently expecting that the Soviet troops would withdraw behind the line as agreed upon on September 28, 1939. As nothing happened, Schulenburg was instructed on July 8 to take up the matter with Molotov.[57]

The latter, upon consultation with Stalin, agreed (July 13) that the German claim to the strip of Lithuanian territory and the Soviet obligation to cede it were incontestable.[58] Yet its cession at this time, Molotov pleaded, would be "extremely inconvenient and difficult for the Soviet government." Hence, Molotov requested, in Stalin's name, to consider if a way could be found to leave the strip of territory in question permanently with Lithuania[59] (which at that time officially still remained independent).

In transmitting this request, Schulenburg wondered whether it could be used "to put through German economic and financial demands with respect to the Baltic States." Ribbentrop agreed (August 2), but wanted to know what *quid pro quo* the Soviet government would propose.[60]

It did not take long for the pressure to materialize. On August 9 Schulenburg was advised that the German government was discontinuing privileges which Lithuania had been enjoying in the Klaipeda free port zone. The motivation was that the Soviet Union, with a number of Baltic ports at its disposal, did not need shipping facilities in Klaipeda and that continuation of preferential treatment accorded Lithuania would lead to politically dangerous privileges for the Soviet Union in German territory. Molotov was to be told that promises given to Lithuania in 1939 were no longer applicable after she had been incorporated in the Soviet Union.[61] As a consequence of this decision, German troops were stationed in the Klaipeda free zone, the customs office was closed, and an order was issued to remove all Lithuanian goods forthwith.[62]

Molotov took the hint. Within a few days (August 13) he offered 3,860,000 gold dollars for the cession of the strip of Lithuanian territory by Germany, payable within two years in gold or in goods at Germany's preference.[63] The sum offered was half of the amount paid to Russia for the cession of Alaska in 1867.

Berlin remained silent. The offer was neither accepted nor rejected, and the Klaipeda free port zone was not reopened for the

Soviet Union. On August 30 Molotov lodged a protest against the
"violation of rights and interests of the Lithuanian Soviet Republic."
He insisted that all rights and privileges accorded Lithuania were still
applicable and that the German authorities in Klaipeda had "seriously
affected" her economic situation and commercial possibilities.[64] In
general, the Soviet Union felt resentful and, according to Schulenburg,
made much more difficult further pursuit of German interests in the
Baltic area.[65]

Instead of complying with this demand, Ribbentrop, on September 3, reproached the Soviet government for its failure to consult with
the German government in regard to its contemplated action in the
Baltic States, and particularly in Lithuania—not only did the Soviet
Union occupy the strip of Lithuanian territory that was to be treated
as German territory; it remained silent about it, and it took German
representations to reopen the question. Ribbentrop also rejected
Molotov's offer for compensation, which he found inadequate. He
promised, however, to draw up a German counterproposal soon. As
for Klaipeda, Ribbentrop instructed Schulenburg not to broach the question at all while talking to Molotov: "We must persist in our view that
we cannot grant the Soviet government a free port zone in Klaipeda." [66]

The final settlement for the strip of Lithuanian territory was reached
on January 10, 1941, in a Secret Protocol signed by Molotov and
Schulenburg. The Soviet Union agreed to nearly double its original
offer and pay 7,500,000 gold dollars as follows: one-eighth in nonferrous metals within three months; seven-eighths in gold immediately,
by deducting from German payments in gold to the Soviet Union due on
February 11, 1941.[67]

An agreement on repatriation of German nationals from Lithuania and Soviet nationals from Germany was reached at the same
time. This signified the termination of quarrels between Germany and
the Soviet Union over Lithuania. Henceforth Lithuanian problems in
regard to the Soviet Union became exactly the same as those in either
Latvia or Estonia.

Chapter Ten

MUTUAL ASSISTANCE IMPOSED

Throughout the entire period of their independence, the Baltic States had geared their foreign policy toward preservation of neutrality in the event of a conflict between the Soviet Union and Germany—the two rival powers in Eastern Europe. They hoped to be left alone when and if the latter should start fighting each other. For this reason, they had carefully avoided taking sides with either of them and gladly signed treaties of nonaggression with both of them. "Estonia needs a strong Soviet Union and a strong Germany and has no desire to aid either to overcome the other," the Estonian Minister to Lithuania told the United States Chargé in Kaunas in early June 1939.[1] World War II furnished proof that the Baltic States lived in a state of self-deception.

This came into the open upon the conclusion of the Soviet-German Nonaggression Treaty of August 23, 1939. Provided there was no exaggeration by the local German missions, representatives of each Baltic government hastened to express their satisfaction with the turn of events.

In Tallinn, Foreign Minister Selter offered congratulations to the German government (August 28) and stated his conviction that Germany, by her nonaggression treaties with Estonia and the Soviet Union, had "prepared ground for Estonian security." He also dismissed as "completely without foundation" hints in the Western press regarding alleged dangers to the Baltic States created by the Soviet-German agreement.[2]

The same was also reported about Lithuanian Deputy Prime Minister Bizauskas, who assured the German Minister in Kaunas (August 29) that the Soviet-German treaty had been welcomed in

Lithuania as "a valuable contribution to the pacification of Eastern Europe." [3]

Only Latvian Foreign Minister Munters showed much more restraint in his comments to the German Minister in Riga. He merely stated (August 21) that the Latvian government did not feel affected by the Soviet-German agreement.[4] Yet the day before he instructed the Latvian Minister in Berlin to check at the Foreign Ministry as to whether there had been any agreements about the Baltic States. He had read in the press, including the German press, rumors regarding the partition of Eastern Europe between Germany and the Soviet Union. Under-Secretary E. Woermann, Director of the Political Department, denied any such agreements.[5]

Woermann's assurance did not satisfy Munters, however. He wanted a formal pronouncement from the German government that the conclusion of the Soviet-German Nonaggression Treaty had not lessened the independence, integrity, and security of the Baltic States and that it was not connected with any agreements affecting them.[6] The German Minister in Riga could not give a reply to such a question, and he had to wait for further instructions from Berlin.

After a consultation between the German and the Soviet governments,[7] it was agreed to tell Munters that Germany "naturally" had not entered into any kind of arrangements which would be contrary to the Nonaggression Treaty of June 7, 1939.[8] Lithuania was given a similarly-worded assurance on August 29,[9] i.e., before the Polish-German war began. This induced the Estonian government to request an assurance from Germany patterned after that given to Lithuania.[10] The German government complied with the request.[11]

The Soviet government displayed a similar attitude by declaring on the day military operations opened against Poland that "the USSR will conduct a policy of neutrality in the relations between the USSR and your country." The declaration was given to a score of states in Europe and Asia, including Lithuania, Latvia, and Estonia.[12] The Soviet Military Attaché in Tallinn also assured the Estonian General Staff that military operations against Poland had no consequences whatsoever for Estonia, with which the Soviet Union wanted to continue friendly relations.[13] On the other hand, it was intimated by Soviet spokesmen that Molotov's declaration of neutrality was by no means without reservations. He reportedly had stated that the independence of the Baltic States would be respected by the Soviet Union, if they observed "favorable" neutrality. The Soviet Military Attaché in Riga, who spoke along these lines to Major Huthsteiner of the United States Legation in Latvia, added, as an example, that concentration of Latvian troops on the Soviet frontier would be resented.[14]

In spite of the fact that the Baltic States had brought into force their neutrality laws as soon as the Polish-German war broke out, and in spite of the Soviet declaration of neutrality, the Baltic governments felt uneasy. They did not dare seek clarification in Moscow, which had demonstrated its designs on the Baltic States during the tripartite negotiations in the summer of 1939. And so they turned to Berlin as soon as the Soviet Union attacked Poland.

In Latvia, Munters wanted to find out from German Minister Kotze (September 18) whether he knew to what point the Soviets would advance and whether "unintentional" border violations were to be expected. He had no doubt that an agreement between Germany and the Soviet Union had been made. Lacking proper instructions, Kotze could only refer to the mutual nonaggression treaties and ask his home office for guidance in his conversations.[15] He was advised that Munters' question primarily concerned the Soviet Union. However, the German government believed the latter did not intend to violate the border of either Latvia, Estonia, or Lithuania, "so long as actions of these states give no occasion for it." [16]

In Estonia, Selter expressed to German Minister Frohwein (October 19) his great concern about the Soviet invasion of Poland. He was afraid that the Soviet Union might direct its expansion against the Baltic States. The Estonian General Staff was of the opinion that Germany had given the Soviet Union a free hand in this region; rumors were spreading from Moscow to that effect, he said. At the same time, Selter wanted to know whether or not Germany still would be willing and able to assist the Baltic States if need arose. Frohwein denied such rumors as pure provocation emanating from British sources and assured Selter that "the recent events had not effected any change in German-Estonian relations as defined by the nonaggression treaty." [17]

Finnish Minister in Berlin Wuorimaa had a slightly different comment on the situation which had evolved from Germany's willingness to pay a price for the short-lived peace in Eastern Europe. "By virtue of the developments in the Baltic States," Wuorimaa told the German Foreign Office on October 3, "Russia had now penetrated so far into the Baltic that the balance of power there has been upset, and predominance threatens to pass to Russia." [18]

At the same time an entry in the official diary of the German Navy, dated October 5, remarked that the increase of Soviet influence in the Baltic is happening "with the full accord of German political policy." The diary also noted some misunderstandings with the Soviets, but every effort was to be made to prevent Soviet distrust in exchange for collaboration in naval matters. The German Naval Attaché in Moscow even advised an immediate stoppage of espionage against the Soviet

Union (an ally!) through neutral states.[19] Germany, in the fall of 1939, was doing her utmost "for the love of peace at any price," according to Ribbentrop (June 22, 1941).

In the meantime events were taking their predetermined course in the Baltic area. On September 25 Molotov informed Schulenburg that the Soviet Union would immediately take up the solution of the problem of the Baltic countries in accordance with the Protocol of August 23; in this matter it expected the unstinting support of the German government.[20] In fact, the solution began much earlier.

In his subsequent testimony given under oath before a Congressional Committee in the United States, Selter revealed that the concentration of Soviet troops along the Soviet-Estonian frontier began as soon as the Soviet Union had reached an agreement with Germany in regard to the partition of Eastern Europe into respective spheres of interest. By mid-September, the number of such troops attained one quarter of a million men equipped with artillery, tanks, and planes. "It was evident that they were preparing an attack against us," was Selter's estimate of the situation.[21] Another similar testimony was furnished by the *Associated Press* at the time of the actual crisis. A report from Moscow on September 18 said the diplomatic circles in the Soviet capital were openly discussing the possibility of Soviet troops marching into Estonia.[22]

If an excuse for these military preparations was needed, such presented itself quite unexpectedly. On September 14, a disabled Polish submarine *Orzel* called at the port of Tallinn for repairs.[23] Instead of allowing the boat to leave the port in 24 hours in accordance with international law, the Estonian authorities decided to intern it. They posted sentries aboard and started disarming the vessel. It managed to escape, however, taking along the sentries and eluding the fire of Estonian coastal batteries and naval units. It was the night of September 17, the date the Soviet troops invaded Poland.

On September 19 a strongly-worded accusation was published in Soviet papers. It said the Estonian government had assisted in the escape of the Polish submarine; the Baltic ports were harboring submarines which endangered the safety of the Soviet Union; and the Soviet Baltic Fleet had received orders "to take measures."

On the same date, the Estonian Minister in Moscow was summoned to Molotov. He was told that, in view of the inability of the Estonian government to guarantee her neutrality, the Soviet Baltic Fleet would assume protection of Estonian waters by tracking down and annihilating the Polish submarine—"even in waters near Tallinn." Molotov added, however, that the measure was in no way directed against Estonia.

Thereupon the Soviet warships blockaded the port of Tallinn and subjected all Estonian sea traffic to their control. Some entered Estonian waters and even fired at Estonian planes flying over the mainland. All this was taking place despite the promise of the Estonian government to support the Soviet action with its own naval craft. These craft had to be recalled, however; Estonia feared a possible incident with the Soviet Navy.[24]

Soviet accusations were, of course, groundless. The United States Ambassador in Moscow, after examining the situation, reported to his government (September 21) that there was "no foundation whatsoever" to the Soviet accusations that submarines of other states were allegedly finding refuge in the Baltic ports.[25] The German Minister in Tallinn likewise raised no objections, while repeatedly discussing the incident with the Estonian Foreign Minister.

Violation of Estonian territorial waters was followed by violation of her air space, beginning on September 20. Soviet planes flew in formation, doing open reconnaissance. The Estonian government issued orders not to shoot at the planes under any circumstances in order not to prejudice the situation.[26] Flights on September 25 and 26 were especially heavy. Soviet infantry, cavalry, artillery, and armored units, reportedly, received battle orders and "just could not wait for the order to destroy Estonia as military base of western imperialists."

The reason was obvious. On September 22 Selter was invited to come to Moscow for the signature of the Estonian-Soviet trade agreement under discussion for some time. The Estonian government asked him to find out about the Soviet designs on Estonia "because the situation was such that somewhere every moment shooting was breaking out." Having arrived in Moscow on September 24, Selter was immediately confronted by Molotov with an accusation that the Estonian government was either unwilling or unable to maintain order and security at home and thus was endangering Soviet security as well. The Soviet government had, therefore, decided to seek further security guarantees from Estonia in the form of a mutual assistance pact. This pact would provide for the establishment of Soviet air and naval bases on Estonian territory.

Selter was taken aback by this unexpected news. For even on the eve of his departure, the Estonian Legation in Moscow had been unaware of Soviet demands, although they suspected that political questions also might come up for discussion.[27] Selter replied he had no authority to discuss such matters; furthermore, the proposed pact would violate Estonian declarations of neutrality; the Estonian government did not want it and was prepared to defend its neutrality, etc. Molotov would not listen:

> The situation needs immediate solution. We cannot wait long. I advise you to accede to the wishes of the Soviet Union in order to avoid something worse. Do not compel the Soviet Union to use force in order to achieve its

aims . . . At present all hope for foreign assistance would be an illusion. Thus, you can be sure that the Soviet Union in one way or another will see to its security. If you would not acquiesce in our proposal, the Soviet Union would carry out the safeguarding of its security in another way, according to its own discretion, without Estonia's assent.[28]

The Estonian Minister in Moscow, who also was present at the Molotov-Selter conversation, found suitable words to describe the nature of Molotov's proposals:

. . . no room for doubt was left by Molotov's proposal and by the warning, which he added orally, that the Soviet proposal, if not in its form then in its substance, was an ultimatum and that Molotov's words forced one to conclude that very grave steps would have to be feared of the Soviet Union in case Estonia should not agree to sign the treaty . . . Especially in view of the situation which had been created before that conversation, it was impossible to interpret Molotov's expressions as anything but a threat to use military force in order to enforce the Soviet demands.[29]

This was difficult to reconcile with Soviet pledges "never to seek the settlement or solution of all disputes or conflicts, of whatever nature or origin, except by pacific means" (Briand-Kellogg Pact) and "to refrain from any act of aggression or any violent measures directed against the political independence of the other Contracting Party" (Soviet-Estonian Treaty of Nonaggression). The Soviet Union also had agreed that "no political, military, economic or other considerations may serve as an excuse or justification for the aggression" (London Convention). Finally, as recently as March 10, 1939, Stalin had assured all Soviet neighbors that Moscow was standing for "peaceful, close, and friendly relations" with all of them.

Molotov tried to allay the fears of the Estonian government by giving reassuring promises:

The assistance pact with the Soviet Union would not bring any perils. We do not want to impair your sovereignty or form of government. We are not going to force communism upon Estonia. We do not want to hurt the economic system of Estonia. Estonia will retain her independence, her government, parliament, foreign and domestic policy, army and economic system. We are not going to touch all this . . . You may be sure that you will never regret you signed this pact with us. Our Bolshevik word is like steel . . . When the Bolsheviks promise something, we shall keep it.[30]

To Selter's objection that the proposed treaty would be incompatible with the German-Estonian Nonaggression Treaty of June 7, 1939, Molotov replied: "I can assure that Germany will give her consent . . . If you wish, I will procure this consent." He also dismissed all arguments that the Soviet-Estonian Mutual Assistance Treaty was not wanted: "Who does not want? That you do not want, that we know;

that the government does not want, that we know, too; but we know that the large public masses want it." Molotov agreed, however reluctantly, to Selter's returning home for consultation. The same night the latter was given the draft of the treaty with a warning not to discuss it publicly in Parliament.

Back in Tallinn on September 25, Selter received the German Minister, whom he told about the Soviet demands. The German Minister offered no suggestions.[31] He had no precise instructions from Berlin, nor did his colleagues in Riga and Kaunas. When instructions finally arrived (October 3), they requested the three German ministers to be most discreet about the German-Soviet relations and their possible effects on the Baltic States and to make no statement on this subject.[32] Molotov's interpretation of the Soviet-German agreement of August 23, 1939, was right from the very outset: "The hands of none of the partners were tied in their sphere of influence." [33]

While Selter was making his report to the Estonian government, violations of Estonian waters and air space, and Soviet troop demonstrations on the Soviet-Estonian frontier became extremely intense, causing the German Military Attaché in Tallinn to report it to the High Command of the German Army.[34] It seemed that Molotov's threat was not an empty one. The Commander-in-Chief of the Estonian Army was of the opinion that any military resistance Estonia could offer would be brief. Soviet superiority in the air made even the question of an orderly mobilization doubtful.

After weighing the entire situation, the General Staff recommended acceptance of Soviet demands (September 27). The Estonian Cabinet concurred. The approval of the Foreign Affairs Committee of the State Council was secured. The comment of the Estonian government read: "The Estonian government, under the greatest threat of imminent attack, is prepared to accept a military alliance with the Soviet Union." The German Minister in Tallinn, who was kept well informed about the events, agreed that the Estonian government did so "under great pressure, in order to avert the threat of obliteration." [35]

Selter and his staff returned to Moscow on September 27 and were surprised to read a *Tass* communique in Moscow papers rejecting the Estonian explanations about the escape of the Polish submarine. The communique ended on an ominous note:

> Taking into consideration that, according to reports received from Leningrad today, the periscopes of unknown submarines have been seen in two places in the region of the Gulf of Luga, it is possible to reach the conclusion that somewhere not far from the Estonian shores some unknown submarines have a secret base. Under these circumstances the question of safeguarding the security of Soviet waters against diversionist acts on the part of submarines in hiding acquires great importance.

Later in the day, *Tass* issued another communique in which tor-pedoing and sinking of the Soviet steamer *Metallist* by an unidentified submarine was reported. Information from various other sources pointed, however, to a premeditated fabrication of the entire story, beginning with the sighted periscopes. It developed that on the same date the Soviets deliberately caused the explosion, near the Estonian coast, of a barge loaded with ship repair equipment. (The *Metallist,* safe and sound, was seen in the Estonian port of Paldiski two years later.) The Estonian government at first wanted to issue a formal *dementi,* but then decided against it on account of the gravity of the situation.[36]

Molotov now used this story (which was never again repeated by the Soviets) to demand the right to station 35,000 Soviet troops on Estonian territory, although his original draft called for only 25,000. They were to be deployed all over Estonia, including Tallinn. But Selter remained adamant. Even Stalin's appearance at the conference failed to change his attitude. The conferees finally agreed on the follow-ing terms of the *Soviet-Estonian Treaty of Mutual Assistance* of Septem-ber 28, 1939:[37]

> Article 1. The two Contracting Parties undertake to render each other as-sistance of every kind, including military assistance, in the event of direct aggression or threat of aggression on the part of a European Great Power against the maritime frontiers of the Contracting Parties in the Baltic Sea, or against their land frontiers across the territory of the Republic of Latvia, and also against the bases provided for in Article 3.
>
> Article 2. The Union of Soviet Socialist Republics undertakes to assist the Estonian army, on advantageous terms, with armaments or other war material.
>
> Article 3. The Republic of Estonia grants the Union of Soviet Socialist Republics the right to have naval bases on the Estonian islands of Saaremaa and Hiiumaa and in the town of Paldiski, together with a number of aero-dromes for air forces, on lease at reasonable rates. The exact sites of the bases and aerodromes in question shall be assigned, and the limits thereof defined, by common accord. With a view to the defense of the naval bases and aerodromes in question, the Union of Soviet Socialist Republics shall be entitled, at its own expense, to maintain strictly limited numbers of Soviet land and air armed forces, up to a maximum to be determined by special agreement, within the areas allotted for the said bases and aerodromes.
>
> Article 4. The two Contracting Parties undertake not to conclude alliances or to take part in coalitions directed against either of the Contracting Parties.
>
> Article 5. The enforcement of the present Pact may in no way impair the sovereign rights of the Contracting Parties or, more especially, their economic system or political structure. The areas allotted for the bases and aerodromes (Art. 3) shall remain territory of the Republic of Estonia.

The Mutual Assistance Treaty was based on the Peace Treaty of February 2, 1920, and the Nonaggression Treaty of May 4, 1932.

They were to remain, as stated in the preamble, "a solid foundation of their reciprocal relations and obligations," including "recognition of independent political existence and nonintervention by either Contracting Party in the internal affairs of the other Contracting Party." The Soviet Union also agreed to drop the demand for mutual assistance in the field of economics, foreign policy, and diplomacy originally included in Molotov's draft. Nevertheless, the United States Ambassador in Moscow found no better term for the Treaty than "a military protectorate over Estonia." [38]

The Treaty was signed simultaneously with a Confidential Protocol which determined the number of Soviet troops stationed on Estonian territory for the duration of World War II to be 25,000. It also stipulated that assistance would not be automatic. It was to be rendered "at the express desire of the other Party." Neutrality was also permitted, if the other Party was engaged in war.[39]

The Confidential Protocol contained no reference either to the Estonian-Latvian Treaty of Defensive Alliance signed on November 1, 1923, or to the Treaty of Good Understanding and Cooperation between Estonia, Latvia, and Lithuania, signed on November 10, 1934. Nor was there any objection made by the Soviet side during the negotiations. On the contrary, both Stalin and Molotov assured Selter: "We are not against it. The present pact does not affect the Estonian-Latvian Treaty of Alliance. It can remain in force . . . there is no need to make reservations." [40]

The signing of the Treaty and the Confidential Protocol stopped, virtually at the last moment, the prepared invasion of Estonia by Soviet armed forces. It was to begin on September 29. An order to call it off was telephoned Marshal K. Voroshilov straight from the Kremlin, as soon as the Estonian delegation gave in. Soviet tanks at the Estonian frontier were heard to roll back in the early hours of that day.[41]

The signing of these two instruments coincided with the signing of the Soviet-German Boundary and Friendship Treaty. The German diplomatic service took credit for the fact that Soviet demands on Estonia were somewhat toned down in the course of negotiations. It was Ribbentrop's intercession with Stalin and Molotov which supposedly did the trick. The report of the German Minister in Tallinn (September 29) read:

> Informed persons regard Germany as the only power which by its weight saved the country from Soviet pressure and which alone is capable of giving protection in the future as well.[42]

The American Minister in Riga, after visiting Tallinn, also thought along the same lines.[43] What they did not know about at that time was Hitler's order to begin at once the task of evacuating German nationals from both Estonia and Latvia.[44] Nor was Ribbentrop acting as a representative of such an influential power when he was forced to give up Lithuania in spite of his reluctance to do so. It seemed that Germany's weight in regard to an eventual protection of the Baltic States was grossly overrated.

So thought Selter. He complained to Munters that the great concessions made to the Soviet Union were unavoidable because Germany had refrained from exercising any political influence on the Soviet-Estonian negotiations. She even failed to reply upon Estonian request, made on the basis of the German-Estonian Nonaggression Treaty, to state her position.[45] The German Minister in Riga feared that Munters might tell the Latvian public about Germany's having given up all political influence in the Baltic area, thus exposing Latvia to seizure by the Soviets.[46]

As if seeking to prove this point, Molotov on September 30 asked Munters to come to Moscow for negotiations of an undisclosed, though easily predictable, nature. When Munters met Stalin and Molotov (October 2),[47] he was immediately told that the Soviet government desired to discuss the settlement of Soviet-Latvian relations. The Soviet Union needed naval bases that remained open all year. He suggested the Estonian example as a basis for discussions. Stalin tried to soften Molotov's harsh approach to the whole problem:

> I think that you will not swear at us. Twenty years have passed: we are stronger, and you also are stronger. We want to discuss these same airfields and military defense. We do not encroach upon either your constitution, organs, ministries, foreign policy, financial policy, or economic system. Our demands are based upon the war between Germany, England, and France . . . The war will be very involved, and neutrals will be drawn into it. Great pressure will be brought to bear upon the neutrals . . . I tell you frankly: a division of spheres of interest has already taken place. As far as Germany is concerned, we could occupy you. However, we want no abuse—Ribbentrop is a sensible person . . . The territory having a Russian minority could also be taken away from you, but we do not raise that question.

(However, Stalin thought differently after the invasion of Latvia eight and a half months later, and took away the Jaunlatgale district of some 500 sq. mi. inhabited by a Russian minority. Estonia also lost nearly 1000 sq. mi. north and south of Lake Peipsi. Only Lithuania was lucky to get back a little over 1000 sq. mi. with a predominantly Lithuanian population.)

Molotov seconded: the Soviet Union and Germany had agreed on all basic questions, thus eliminating problems likely to cause struggle or even friction; their views in regard to the Baltic States did not differ. Then he continued:

We think that in relations with you, there is not yet a true guarantee. That is not safe for you, but we are principally thinking of ourselves. That which was determined in 1920 cannot remain for eternity. Peter the Great saw to it that an outlet to the sea was gained. We are now without an exit, and the situation in which we are now cannot remain. We, therefore, wish to ensure ourselves the use of ports, roads to these ports, and their defense . . . We cannot permit small states to be used against the USSR. Neutral Baltic States—that is too insecure.

Munters argued that Latvia was not threatened by Germany since she had a nonaggression treaty with her, as did the Soviet Union; and that no other state could possibly attack Latvia in view of Soviet and German domination of the Baltic Sea. His objections were summarily dismissed. Then presentation and discussion of Soviet demands began. The Soviets wanted Liepaja, Ventspils, and Pitrags for their naval bases; four air force bases; and a garrison of 50,000 men, i.e., two and one-half times the Latvian peace time army.

This the Latvians could not accept without consulting Riga, and the first meeting broke off. They were requested to reply within 48 hours, or necessary measures would be taken. The massing of Soviet troops on the Latvian frontier, with tanks, armored vehicles, and artillery,[48] and the presence, during the negotiations, of People's Commissar of Defense, Marshal K. Voroshilov, and Chief of Staff, B. Shaposhnikov,[49] lent the necessary weight to Soviet demands.

As soon as the news about the extent of Soviet demands became known in Riga, an outright paralysis of the government was feared.[50] Munters met Stalin and Molotov again on October 3. He found them in sour mood. Molotov refused to listen to Munters' counterproposals. He called them a retreat from the previous agreements, depriving the treaty of its value and entirely unacceptable. "Weigh the situation," he warned; "our concession of yesterday was final." Then Stalin took up the discussion:

You do not trust us, and we don't quite trust you either. You believe that we wish to seize you. We could do that now, but we do not do it. Riga is the center of anti-Soviet propaganda . . . A German attack is also possible. For six years German fascists and the communists cursed each other. Now an unexpected turn took place; that happens in the course of history. But one cannot rely upon it. We must be prepared in time. Others who were not ready paid the price . . . We do not wish to delay.

The *Soviet-Latvian Treaty of Mutual Assistance*[51] and the accompanying Secret Protocol were signed on October 5.[52] They were similar to the same instruments signed by Estonia a week earlier. The Soviet Union obtained the right to maintain naval bases in Liepaja and Ventspils, a coastal artillery base between Ventspils and Pitrags, several air force bases, and a garrison of 25,000 men.

Lithuania's turn came practically at the same time as Latvia's. On October 1 Foreign Minister Urbsys received Molotov's invitation to come to Moscow. No military demonstration was needed in this case, as strong Soviet forces were stationed along the entire formerly Polish-Lithuanian demarcation line. Urbsys undoubtedly suspected what he would hear in Moscow. There was little comfort in Molotov's assurance given beforehand that the Soviet Union was not contemplating any Sovietization of Lithuania.[53]

On October 3 Urbsys arrived in Moscow and the same night had his first conference with Stalin and Molotov.[54] He learned that Lithuania, like Estonia and Latvia, was to sign a treaty of mutual assistance on similar terms, except that the number of troops to be garrisoned was to run as high as 50,000–75,000. In vain Urbsys tried to present his arguments. Neither Stalin nor Molotov would listen: "It is to your own best interests to accept our proposals . . . with our garrisons on your territory, the entire 'tail' would move should anyone touch you." Urbsys was given to understand that the Soviet Union had saved Lithuania from German designs upon her. "If Lithuania had fallen under German rule, she undoubtedly would have become a German protectorate," Stalin said. He did not make clear, however, why the Soviet protectorate he offered would be better for Lithuania.

Yet the strongest ace Stalin held was possession of the Lithuanian capital Vilnius and a third of her territory. He was well aware how much the Lithuanian people longed to regain the historical capital. It was hardly possible to wish for a better chance for blackmail. Stalin even tried to prove that the Soviet government acted on its own responsibility in showing its readiness to transfer Vilnius and the surrounding territory to Lithuania: it was guided by the desire "of consolidation of friendly relations," but this could be resented by the Soviet people after they learned of the unauthorized action of their government!

The Soviets were so sure of ultimate acceptance of their demands that they did not deem it necessary to postpone the announcement that Lithuania was to give Germany a portion of her territory (Secret Supplementary Protocol of September 28, 1939). Molotov admitted to Schulenburg that the Lithuanian delegation, on hearing this news, became "extremely dismayed and sad." They complained that the loss of this area would be especially hard to bear, since many prominent leaders of the Lithuanian people had come from that part of Lithuania.[55]

This went beyond Urbsys' authority to discuss. In the early morning of October 4, he flew back to Kaunas to report to his government. Here he cleared up two things: first, the German Minister in Kaunas transmitted his government's declaration that it did not consider the question of the border revision on Lithuanian territory timely at the moment;[56] second, the Lithuanian Minister in Berlin got nowhere after diplomatically inquiring whether the German government had any ideas or suggestions to give in regard to the terms of the mutual assistance part proposed to Lithuania in Moscow. He was told only that German interests had not been claimed beyond the Soviet-German line in the east.[57] Evidently Stalin's statement to Munters a few days earlier ("As far as Germany is concerned, we could occupy you") equally applied to Lithuania.

On October 7 Urbsys returned to Moscow. His aim was to persuade the Soviet government to accede to the Lithuanian counterproposals he had brought along. While accepting, in principle, the idea of a treaty of mutual assistance with the Soviet Union, Lithuania wanted to restrict military assistance in manpower to the event of aggression either against Lithuania or against the Soviet Union across the Lithuanian territory. On the other hand, she was ready to collaborate fully with the Soviet Union in military matters, to double her actual military establishment, and to build defensive fortifications in places agreed upon by both states and assisted by the Soviet Union financially as well as with arms and raw materials.

Urbsys was soon to learn, however, that he must abandon all hope of persuading the Soviets to meet the Lithuanians half-way. All his counter proposals were summarily rejected. The following is a description of the general atmosphere of negotiations as reported by a high official of the Lithuanian Foreign Ministry, E. Turauskas:

> It became painfully clear that the Muscovites tenaciously clung to their own dictates . . . The Soviet delegates did not justify their insistence. Stalin was evasive. He spoke incoherently; at times our delegates could not understand him . . . The very atmosphere of the 'negotiations' rapidly disintegrated. Stalin and his aides were clearly impatient and dissatisfied over the delay. They did not conceal that the negative attitude of the Lithuanian government would make itself felt in Soviet-Lithuanian relations.[58]

Another member of the Lithuanian delegation, General Rastikis, fully concurred in the above description:

> All Russian demands were of the nature of an ultimatum. The Russians dictated, threatened, and objected to our obstinacy. During one of the conferences, Molotov stated in an unfriendly manner that it had been much easier to agree with either Estonia or Latvia, although neither was as good a friend of the Soviet Union as Lithuania . . . When Urbsys at one time, after presenting all his arguments, half-jokingly asked Stalin to have mercy on him, as a most unhappy foreign minister who now had to receive and transmit to his government another ultimatum, Stalin did not like mentioning an ultimatum.[59]

After three more sessions at the Kremlin and another trip to Kaunas for consultation, the *Soviet-Lithuanian Treaty of Mutual Assistance* was signed on October 10.[60] The Treaty was almost identical in its wording with the two previous treaties of the same nature with Estonia and Latvia. It differed only in that this treaty contained a special article on transfer of Vilnius and its region and was concluded for the duration of fifteen years as compared to ten years in the case of the two other treaties. Furthermore, the Lithuanians were able to bring the Soviet garrisons down to 20,000 (as compared to 25,000 in both Estonia and Latvia) and to reduce the number of bases to four instead of more than a dozen as originally requested.

The transfer of Vilnius could have been accomplished in a much simpler manner, without the resounding declaration in the preamble about "a just settlement of the questions of state appurtenance of the city of Vilnius and the Vilnius region." It was legally a part of Lithuanian —not Soviet—territory. And the transfer of its administration from the Soviet military authorities to the Lithuanian authorities could have been as simple an act as it was in July 1920 when the Russian troops also were in Vilnius.

However, nineteen years later, in a similar situation but under different conditions (there was no longer any danger that the Polish legionnaires might force the Soviet troops to beat a retreat), Moscow was following purely opportunistic policies. Taking unscrupulous advantage of the situation, the Soviet Union transferred to Lithuania only one-fifth of the territory to which the latter had a clear title by virtue of the Peace Treaty of July 12, 1920. This, the Soviet Union itself had never before contested. The Soviets turned a deaf ear to all arguments that they were excluding, in this manner, the districts predominantly settled by Lithuanians. "The Soviet Union does not need to give Lithuania any part of the Vilnius area," was their surprising answer. They also refused to make any adjustment of the frontiers they had drawn in Urbsys' words, "with firm hand."

The transfer itself took place only on October 28, two and a half weeks after the agreement to that effect was signed and after the Soviets had bought up all that was for sale, and had looted factories, offices, and even private homes.[61] Machines, tools, home furnishings, doors, window frames, plumbing, telephone and telegraph wire, books, and historical documents were shipped to the Soviet Union. In some instances, women slept in factories to prevent looting by Soviet soldiers. A complaint in Moscow produced no results. It was felt in Kaunas that a formal protest would be just as useless, although the Lithuanian government was compiling a list of damages. Diplomatic circles in Lithuania wondered if the belated transfer of Vilnius to the Lithuanian authorities was not a deliberate action having for its purpose the gaining of enough time for looting.[62]

The transfer of Vilnius and its region to Lithuania did not terminate the troubles with Poland that started back in 1919. On October 18 the Polish Government-in-Exile presented to the Lithuanian government a formal protest "against the acceptance of any territory ceded by the USSR which does not belong to that Union." [63] Then the Polish Minister to Lithuania departed, leaving all affairs in the care of the British Consulate in Kaunas.[64] He chose to disregard the Lithuanian government's assurances that he still was considered as having retained all diplomatic rights and privileges.[65]

Later on the Poles tried hard at Moscow, Washington, and London to obtain confirmation of their alleged rights to Vilnius.[66] They met with no success. The Soviet government considered the whole matter as settled and kept on referring to Vilnius as Lithuania's capital and a Lithuanian city (e.g., *Pravda*, July 16, 1944). The United States government declined to commit itself and referred to its traditional policy of giving no guarantees of specific frontiers. The British government stated it had never given a precise guarantee of the eastern frontiers of Poland or inclusion of Vilnius and urged the Poles to accept the so-called Curzon Line as Poland's eastern frontier.

The Yalta Conference likewise ended in an agreement (February 11, 1945) on the Curzon Line, leaving Vilnius on the Lithuanian side. The Polish Provisional Government of National Unity, composed on June 28, 1945, of representatives of both pro-Communist and anti-Communist political parties (among the latter Stanislaw Mikolayczyk, leader of the influential Polish Peasant Party and former Prime Minister of the Polish Government-in-Exile), accepted the Yalta decision.

Finally, renunciation of all claims to Vilnius was formally confirmed in the Soviet-Polish Boundary Treaty of August 16, 1945, signed by the Polish Provisional Government of National Unity on behalf of Poland. By virtue of this Treaty, the boundary was to follow the Curzon Line with digressions up to 19 miles in favor of Poland. The fact that the Polish Government-in-Exile did not recognize the validity of the above Treaty does not change the legal situation.

Chapter Eleven

THE TROJAN HORSE

After signing the three treaties of mutual assistance between the Soviet Union on the one side and Estonia, Latvia, and Lithuania on the other, the "contracting parties" began to take stock. The Soviet press went overboard describing advantages for the Baltic States after the conclusion of these treaties. Editorials in both *Pravda* and *Izvestiia* asserted that the treaties evidenced the Soviet peace policy by safeguarding the Baltic States against any aggression on the part "of imperialist powers"; especially at a time when the latter had been inciting country against country and looking for justification of the continuation of war. *Izvestiia* accused "the London politicians" of trying to use Latvia as a *place d'armes* for their aggressive designs against the Soviet Union. The paper saw the mutual assistance as proof that the Soviet government "had never used its advantage as a great and powerful country against little countries." [1]

The Soviet press was also generous in reporting favorable comments in the Estonian, Latvian, Lithuanian, and German press. [2] Yet it remained utterly silent about unfavorable comments in the French, British, American, and other free papers. It was Molotov who took care of that. On October 31, while addressing the Supreme Council, he said:

> The pacts with the Baltic States in no way imply the intrusion of the Soviet Union in the internal affairs of Estonia, Latvia, and Lithuania, as some foreign interests are trying to make believe . . . These pacts are inspired by mutual respect for the governmental, social, and economic system of each of the contracting parties. We stand for an exact and honest fulfillment

of agreements signed by us on a basis of reciprocity and declare that foolish talks of Sovietization of the Baltic States is useful only to our common enemies and to all kind of anti-Soviet provocators.[3]

The comments emanating from the three Baltic capitals were much less enthusiastic. Munters, for example, "had none of his usual optimism," when the United States Minister in Riga saw him.[4] He could not foresee how long Latvia would survive. He also feared that the Soviet Union might foment internal difficulties despite the assurance with regard to the integrity of Latvia. He had gone to Moscow on invitation at once in order to avoid any incident or unpleasant pressure. Latvian Minister in Washington A. Bilmanis had no doubts[5] that the situation of Latvia and the two other Baltic States was "precarious." They had to conduct themselves in such a manner as to avoid the Soviet Union's charge they were failing to live up to the spirit of their agreements with the Soviet Union.

Bilmanis' interviewer in Washington observed that the Minister this time (December 20) was much less "cheerful" than he was right after the signature of the pact with the Soviet Union, when he saw another high officer of the Department of State (October 7).[6] On his first visit, Bilmanis said he had feared something worse. He deplored stationing of Soviet garrisons on Latvian soil, but accepted it with philosophical resignation and was glad that Latvia still existed. In Bilmanis' opinion,

> it would have been far worse had Latvia and Estonia been sold out by England and France during their negotiations with the Soviet Union in the spring of 1939. As it was, the two countries had signed agreements of their own free will (?), they had maintained their independence; and even had received Soviet pledges to accept and not to overthrow their type of capitalistic government.

On his second visit to the Department of State, Bilmanis repeated that Latvia had not given up her independence or the hope of retaining it. She was struggling with all the resources at her disposal against being swallowed up by her great neighbors. Yet the Soviet government thus far had not interfered with the internal life in the Baltic States. At the same time Bilmanis had to reject allegations that Latvia, Lithuania, and Estonia already had become mere Soviet satellites. He declared emphatically that Latvia would not accede to any Soviet demands indicating her eventual Sovietization or reduction to a mere Soviet appanage.

The Estonian government likewise feared that Estonia had gained but a breathing spell of uncertain duration and that the Soviet Union might soon impose additional demands, particularly if Germany should be tied up in the West. The general outlook was somewhat better, however, than in the face of original Soviet demands when an extremely grave threat to the very existence of the whole state was believed to exist.[7] In contrast to Latvia, no greater danger of communist contamination was anticipated in Estonia. On the other hand, the Estonian press unanimously agreed it was impossible to disregard the Soviet desire that its fleet be released from the Gulf of Finland.

In his comments on the events, Urbsys did not hide his concern about future developments while talking to the German Minister in Kaunas. He only emphasized that the Lithuanian government would continue working in the future for the country's independence.[8] Urbsys' conversation with the United States Minister was along the same lines. The Lithuanian government found little joy in the prospect of Soviet garrisons and felt it had no guarantee they would leave the country after the war. Only Article 1 in the pact with the Soviets (the transfer of Vilnius) aroused genuine joy in Lithuania; the other articles in the pact were "because the Soviets wanted them." Urbsys' only consolation was that Stalin and Molotov had repeatedly stated that the Soviet Union did not wish Sovietization of Lithuania.[9] Vice-Prime Minister K. Bizauskas was, however, sceptical about Sovietization prospects: "One cannot be too sure of anything in these days" (October 13).[10] Of course, no one in Lithuania took seriously Molotov's advice to shoot local communists if necessary or call upon Soviet garrisons for help.[11]

There was another point on which the three Baltic governments were in complete agreement: the unavoidability of a clash between the Soviet Union and Germany, and the anti-German character of the mutual assistance pacts.[12] General Rastikis got the impression during the negotiations in Moscow that the Soviets were not even attempting to conceal their real reason for insistence on military bases—the fear of a German attack.[13] All Lithuanian objections against Soviet wishes for bases and garrisons were suspected of being German-prompted.[14] Munters also spoke about the great frankness prevailing in Moscow on the subject of Soviet-German "friendship" and on the length of time it might endure. He believed the Soviet-German relations, based on mutual mistrust, were affected by the Soviet Union's waiting for either a revolution or exhaustion in Germany, while Germany was only waiting for favorable circumstances in order to turn east.[15]

The German Ambassador in Moscow did not go so far. Yet he admitted in the course of a conversation with his United States colleague that Germany, in view of her involvement in the West, was "in no position to oppose legitimate Soviet interests in those regions." As for the future role of Estonia and Latvia, the German Ambassador was of the opinion that they would occupy the same status vis-à-vis the Soviet Union as Egypt occupied with Great Britain.[16]

The fear the Soviet Union might impose additional demands received its confirmation practically on the morrow of the signature of the Soviet-Estonian Treaty of Mutual Assistance. On October 2 a Soviet military technical committee, established in accordance with Article 4 of the Confidential Protocol of September 28, arrived in Tallinn. It included six generals, two admirals, and thirteen other officers and engineers.[17] The committee immediately requested two additional military bases, two additional airfields, and additional naval facilities.

Since these demands exceeded the provision of Article 3 of the Mutual Assistance Pact, the matter was referred to the Estonian Minister in Moscow for clarification. He was successful in persuading Molotov to instruct the Soviet committee in Tallinn not to press its demands for additional bases. This move was interpreted in Tallinn as the Soviet desire not to disturb the atmosphere for completion of negotiations with the Latvian and Lithuanian governments. Molotov's intercession resulted in reduction in some of the demands. Yet the Estonian government was forced to accede, in view of strong Soviet forces concentrated at the Soviet-Estonian border, to additional airfields and military bases. An agreement to that effect was signed on October 12.

The agreement did not prevent the Soviets from demanding more sites for airfields and military bases, rail traffic control, storage facilities, etc. In most instances, the Estonian government had no choice but to comply. "Everything happens in the common interest of both Estonia and the Soviet Union," was the usual excuse. The demands were accompanied by open violation of the agreements entered into. The contingents of Soviet troops that began pouring into Estonia by rail and sea on October 18 soon numbered at least 30,000, although the agreement stipulated "up to 25,000 men." (Exactly the same thing happened in Latvia.)[18] Reinforcements continued, and the figure reached 40,000 by June 1940, the date of an outright occupation of Estonia.

The Soviet-Estonian agreement also called for granting the Soviet Union the right to maintain naval, air, and other bases "on lease at reasonable rates." In fact, the Soviets never paid any rent or reimbursement to the people who had to be evacuated from the sites for Soviet bases. "Do you really think the Russians would pay rent to some Estonian government?" a Soviet major, member of the mixed committee, told his Estonian counterpart. "The Red Army knows only one government and that is the government of the Soviet Union."

A further gross violation of the agreement resulted when the Soviet

Air Force made extensive use of its bases in Estonia for the purpose of bombing Finland[19]—attacked by the Soviet Union on November 30, 1939.

Article 1 of the Soviet-Estonian Treaty of Mutual Assistance provided for rendering military assistance to the contracting parties only "in the event of direct aggression or threat of aggression on the part of a European Great Power against the maritime frontiers of the Contracting Parties in the Baltic Sea, or against their land frontiers across the territory of the Republic of Latvia, and also against the bases provided for in Article 3."

None of these elements was present in the Soviet-Finnish war. Finland was not a "European Great Power." She did not attack or even threaten to attack either Soviet or Estonian frontiers or military bases. However, all protestations by the Estonian Foreign Ministry were disregarded, and the Soviet planes continued taking off from Estonian airfields for bombing missions in Finland.

In view of the fact that Soviet troops in all three Baltic States were under the same military command and received the same orders, there is no doubt that similar violations of agreements must also have taken place in both Lithuania and Latvia, although no such detailed sworn reports regarding these two states have been published. It is known, however, that in Lithuania, too, the Soviets made it impossible to reach agreement on any points under discussion, since they used such tactics as offering one-tenth of the customary rate for land leased for their bases.[20] Their demands in regard to dislocation of Soviet garrisons were far too excessive, as even the best barracks offered by Lithuania would not satisfy them.[21]

On the other hand, Soviet troops gave little ground for complaints. They were inconspicuous and generally well-behaved.[22] In Lithuania, fraternization between them and the local population was not permitted by Soviet military authorities. As a result, many of the Soviet troops, according to a statement by a United States investigator, did not even know where they were.[23] In Latvia, they rode in special railroad cars and needed special permits to leave the confines of Soviet bases. But this did not prevent the officers and enlisted men alike from indulging in an endless shopping spree.[24]

The Baltic governments did their utmost to avoid incidents and, if they became known, to conceal them from the public or smooth them over. Traffic accidents due to reckless driving, drunken brawls, petty robberies, and even occasional murders were always settled amicably, but usually so that the Soviets remained blameless and paid no damages. The normalcy of relations was not seriously disrupted by Soviet actions, such as sinking an Estonian merchant vessel or firing upon an Estonian aircraft from Soviet warships.[25] The press was requested to avoid subjects that might conceivably displease the Soviet Union (such as its poor showing in the Soviet-Finnish war). Heavy fines were imposed in case of noncompliance.

Soviet ministers in all three Baltic capitals at the beginning likewise tried to live up to Stalin's and Molotov's promises of noninterference in internal affairs. In Latvia, for example, the Soviet Legation in Riga advised the local communists to avoid provocations and to lie low.[26] Yet on the other hand, Soviet ministers used extensively much more subtle means of propaganda, such as propaganda-laden books, periodicals, newspapers, films, records, lectures, exhibitions, singers, conductors, etc. The Baltic governments were helpless to resist this avalanche because of the continuous emphasis of friendship. However, there was no reciprocity on the Soviet side. The Baltic peoples were short-changed.

Considerable reorientation in the matters of foreign policy also took place in the Baltic capitals. As early as the first part of October, opinion was expressed in Tallinn that the Estonian Foreign Ministry and its foreign outposts would diminish in importance and that the latter would perhaps remain only as "listening posts." [27] The Latvian Minister in Washington, although greatly displeased that the Baltic States were labeled "Soviet satellites" (see, for example, the Washington *Star* of December 15, 1939), agreed that, in the field of foreign policies, the three countries were "compelled to act with great caution." [28]

If further proof was needed, it was furnished during the Tenth Conference of the Baltic Foreign Ministers in Tallinn on December 7–8, 1939. The three ministers met together a week before the League of Nations voted to expel the Soviet Union because of its unprovoked attack on Finland. The conference, naturally, took up this ticklish problem and decided to abstain from voting, although there was no question as to where their sympathies lay. In the report to his government, the United States Minister in Riga said that "the lack of independence of the Baltic States in matters of foreign policy was clearly to be seen in this incident." [29]

The Soviet press took no note of this action, although it did carry a brief report on the Eleventh Conference held in Riga on March 14–16, 1940.[30] However, not a word was said about the resolutions of the Conference. As it was held five to five and a half months after the conclusion of the mutual assistance treaties, the Conference took a look at the experience with Soviet troops stationed at a score of assorted bases in the Baltic States. Naturally, the Conference evaluated it positively:

The experience up to the present time has led the Ministers of the three countries to the conclusion that the policy of practical neutrality of the Baltic States, as well as international agreements concluded by these states, and, in general, the attitude they have taken in view of the problems the international situation had actually raised are in complete agreement with their firm resolution to stay out of armed conflicts and to guarantee their independence and their security.[31]

Molotov fully agreed with this evaluation while addressing the Supreme Soviet of the USSR on March 29, 1940:

> After the experience of half a year which has passed since the conclusion of Mutual Assistance Pacts with Estonia, Latvia, and Lithuania, it is possible to draw definitive and positive conclusion regarding the treaties with the Baltic countries. It must be admitted that the pacts of the Soviet Union with Estonia, Latvia, and Lithuania have furthered the consolidation of the international position of the Soviet Union as well as of Estonia, Latvia, and Lithuania. Despite the intimidation practiced by imperialistic circles, hostile to the Soviet Union, the national independence of Estonia, Latvia, and Lithuania and their autonomous policies have in no way suffered, while the economic relations of these countries with the Soviet Union have undergone considerable expansion. The execution of the pacts with Estonia, Latvia, and Lithuania is proceeding satisfactorily and creating prerequisites for a further improvement of relations between the Soviet Union and these states.[32]

This was the last friendly statement uttered by Molotov about the Baltic States. On March 12, 1940, the Soviet Union signed a peace treaty with Finland and thereby untied its hands "to take up the solution of the problem of the Baltic countries," as intimated by Molotov nearly six months earlier (September 25, 1939). At that time the Soviet government spoke of "special measures" which would be taken in regard to the Baltic States. Molotov envisaged their occupation (October 8, 1939).

Despite the lack of freedom of decisions in many a field of domestic and foreign policies, the Baltic States, in the spring of 1940, outwardly remained independent. They could by no means be regarded as Soviet-occupied countries. Stationing Soviet garrisons did not produce the effect Molotov was expecting. Termination of the Soviet-Finnish war freed the Soviet government to take the next step— outright military occupation of the Baltic States as a prerequisite for incorporation. Its coming had been foreseen by the German Ambassador in Moscow as soon as the Protocol of September 28, 1939, was signed. United States Ambassador J. Davies likewise believed that Moscow agreements envisaged a "complete restoration of the geographical and political spheres of Tsarist Russia to the Soviets." [33]

Preparations to this end were going on in Moscow uninterruptedly. On October 11, 1939, the next day after the signature of the Soviet-

Lithuanian Treaty of Mutual Assistance—the last in the series of three—, the People's Commissariat for Internal Affairs (NKVD) issued its directive No. 001223. It dealt with "counterrevolutionary elements subject to operative accounting, regardless of their anti-Soviet activities." The directive formed the basis for arrests and deportations of the Baltic people after the Soviet occupation. A United States Congressional Committee, after examining all the available evidence, concluded that this directive was issued specifically for the Baltic States,[34] even though their occupation was eight months away.

Long-range preparations are further exemplified by a map the Latvians found when the Soviets fled in 1941.[35] It was an ordinary map of the General Staff of the Workers' and Peasants' Red Army (RKKA), to a scale of 5 km. to 1 cm., marked: "Vilnius, Lithuanian SSR, Latvian SSR, Belorussian SSR." This was nothing strange. General Staff maps are printed and reprinted everywhere. It was revealing that this map carried the inscription: "First Edition, 1939," i.e., when neither Lithuanian nor Latvian Soviet Socialist Republics existed. Evidently the General Staff of RKKA knew very well that the establishment of such republics was a foregone conclusion.

The attitude of Soviet troops garrisoned in the Baltic States was just as indicative. They freely made such statements as: "You, too, will be a part of the Soviet Union pretty soon"; "The entire Baltic seacoast as far as Königsberg belongs to the Soviet Union"; "The Red Army knows only one government and that is the government of the Soviet Union"; "The Red Army will never leave when it had entered once, and you, too, will experience it." [36]

The last statement is particularly interesting. It reflects the general attitude of the Soviet government toward the behavior of its troops in occupied territories. "All military men are loath to give up occupied territories," Stalin once told the German Ambassador in Moscow.[37] This explains the printing of General Staff maps and issuance of Directive No. 001223 ahead of time, yet in strict adherence to the plan.

By February 1940, the Lithuanian military intelligence had information that the Soviets had begun massing troops at the Soviet-Lithuanian frontier.[38] Shortly thereafter, the Lithuanian Minister in Moscow reported to his government that "a black cat had crossed the road of Soviet-Lithuanian relations." He saw proof in a sudden coldness of official attitude toward him, a representative of a friendly nation. The Minister also reported he had been subjected to intense questioning on Lithuania's attitude toward the war; toward Germany; toward neutrality; etc.[39]

By the second half of April 1940, the High Command of the German Navy became fully convinced the Soviet Union was ready to take over the Baltic area.[40] The German Ambassador in Moscow also noted a change in Soviet attitude.[41]

As if by coincidence, sporadic communist-instigated strikes broke out in both Lithuania and Latvia. Leaflets denouncing government policies appeared suddenly in great numbers in urban and rural communities. Rumors were spread about impending Sovietization of the Baltic States. Even liquor addicts and criminals were used as Soviet agents.[42] By May the Lithuanian Military Command had information that strong Soviet armed forces (the 8th and the 11th armies) were concentrated near the Soviet-Lithuanian frontier.[43]

The avowed neutrality of the Baltic States no longer satisfied Moscow. The Soviet press paid no attention to the communique of the Eleventh Conference of Baltic Foreign Ministers. It also disregarded a statement by Estonian Foreign Minister A. Piip, made on April 17:

> The Government firmly intends to continue its policy of neutrality, which it has pursued during the present European war. We, as a small nation, cannot and do not want to mix in the quarrels of great powers, and the aim of our foreign policy will remain as hitherto, to preserve the integrity and political independence of our country, and develop, with this aim in mind, friendly relations with all countries, equally in the field of politics, economics, and culture. Quite naturally, our great eastern neighbor, with whom we created stable relations on the basis of the Mutual Assistance Pact, signed in Moscow six months ago, assumes a particularly prominent place.[44]

The "great eastern neighbor" should have been highly pleased with such an assertion of its preeminence in Estonian policies. What it really wanted, however, was a complete domination over the Baltic States, not merely their neutrality. "Neutral Baltic States—that is too insecure," were Molotov's words uttered in October 1939 during the discussion of the proposed terms of the Soviet-Latvian Mutual Assistance Treaty. Soviet views did not change in the intervening seven months. This came into the open in an article published in *Izvestiia* on May 16, 1940:

> The recent war events (occupation of Belgium, the Netherlands, and Luxemburg) once more proved that neutrality of small states, which do not have power to support it, is a mere phantasy. Therefore, there are very few chances for small countries to survive and to maintain their independence. All considerations of small countries in the question of justice and injustice in relations with the Big Powers, which are in the war "to determine if they are to be or not to be," are at least naive . . . We should once more remind them that the policy of neutrality of some small countries could not be called anything but suicide.

Characteristically, this article appeared less than a week after the beginning of the German offensive in the West (May 10). Molotov, when informed of it by the German Ambassador, stated that he appreciated the news and understood Germany's desire to protect herself against Anglo-French attack.[45] The western diplomatic observers, however, took a different view. Thus, the United States Minister to Latvia intimated in his cables to Washington that the Soviet Union was greatly disturbed over France's collapse. It was feared in Moscow that Hitler, after his statement that he had no desire to destroy the British Empire, might attempt to solve his problems at Soviet expense.[46]

The western press shared these views. The Moscow correspondent of the *New York Times* reported on May 19 that "the Kremlin officials are shaking in their boots [because] they realize that a Germany dominating all Europe would have Russia at her mercy." Perhaps the Soviets recalled President Roosevelt's warning to Soviet Ambassador in Washington, C. Oumansky, in the summer of 1939, that, if the Soviet government joined up with Hitler [which they did], "it was as certain as that the night followed the day that as soon as Hitler had conquered France, he would turn on Russia." [47]

Having in the fall of 1939 refused to accept the proposed collaboration of the Baltic States on questions of mutual defense against eventual aggression (at least such was the Lithuanian counterproposal), the Soviet Union could only strengthen its position on the Baltic by pouring in more men and materiel and by pushing its first lines of defense somewhat farther from either Moscow or Leningrad. The number of Soviet troops stationed in the whole Baltic area in accordance with the treaties of mutual assistance (70,000) represented a heavy burden for the "assisted" states. But this number was small as compared to 18 to 20 divisions (300–350,000 men) to be poured into the Baltic States upon their occupation.[48]

On the other hand, there could be no better opportunity to do so, with Germany involved up to her neck in war with the West. The time had arrived for taking special measures and posting Soviet troops on the Baltic, of which both Stalin and Molotov spoke as early as September and October 1939.

Chapter Twelve

Preparations for Invasion

A seemingly innocuous occurrence in Lithuania involving Soviet garrisons was indicative of the change that took place in the Balto-Soviet relations after the termination of the Finnish-Soviet war and the beginning of the German offensive in the West. On May 14, 1940, the Lithuanian Minister in Moscow informed the People's Commissariat for Foreign Affairs that a Soviet soldier, Butaev, had committed suicide. The Minister was asked to have the soldier's body delivered to Soviet military authorities in Lithuania. It seemed that the case was taken care of and forgotten. It was not so.[1]

Beginning on May 18, the Soviets began moving tanks, planes, artillery, munitions, and supplies from Naujoji Vilnia, a Soviet military base located near the Soviet-Lithuanian frontier, to Gaizunai, another base located in Central Lithuania. Within a week, about 100 tanks and 250 loaded trucks were moved. Gaizunai was only a short distance (20 miles) from Kaunas, the provisional capital of Lithuania. After completing this operation, the Soviet government on May 25 presented a note.

The note stated that two more Soviet soldiers, Nosor and Shmavgonets, had disappeared from Soviet bases in Lithuania. After accusing Lithuanian authorities of having engineered the disappearance of the two soldiers, the note ended with a threat:

> The Soviet government proposes to the Lithuanian government to halt such provocative action, to take the necessary steps immediately to search for the Soviet soldiers who disappeared, and to transfer them to the military authorities of the Soviet bases in Lithuania. The Soviet Government hopes that the Lithuanian Government will take the necessary measures to comply with the Soviet proposals and will not force it to take other measures.

170

A threat "to take other measures," in disregard of all pledges to the contrary signed by the Soviet Union, was impressive enough to move the Lithuanian Foreign Minister to reply immediately to Molotov's note. On the other hand, the Lithuanian government knew nothing about the persons and events mentioned in the note. So the reply ended with a request for additional information and evidence which would accelerate and facilitate the investigation; especially to indicate persons and authorities which Molotov had in mind in his statement. The Lithuanian government gave orders to search energetically for the two soldiers; and if found, to arrest them and deliver them to Soviet military authorities in Lithuania.

The reply was given the Soviet Minister in Kaunas on May 26. Before the Soviet side reacted, Soviet Deputy Commissar for Military Affairs General Loktionov appeared in Kaunas on May 27. He unexpectedly called on the Foreign Minister and Defense Minister and complained to them of the alleged disappearances of Soviet soldiers from their barracks in Lithuania. One of them, Shmavgonets by name, General Loktionov said, had returned to his barracks on the previous night. He had been seized several days before, questioned and tortured, and escaped by way of sewers. Another soldier, Shumov, was still missing. Butaev had been killed in cold blood. General Loktionov ended by accusing Lithuanian military and civilian authorities of deliberate kidnaping of, and spying on, Soviet troops. The General's behavior was very rude. He violated several rules of diplomatic etiquette and also refused to accept hospitality offered by Lithuanian military authorities.

It was unbelievable that the Lithuanian government, sitting on a powder keg, would dare irritate "protectors" by such foolish deeds. The explanation given to General Loktionov was simple: Lithuanian authorities had no need to kidnap Soviet soldiers or spy on them because Soviet liaison officers provided all the information desired. As for the deserters, General Loktionov was promised that everything would be done to apprehend them. However, the only such case reported by the Soviets to the proper Lithuanian authorities was that of Butaev.

Now the Butaev incident, at first believed settled, looked serious. Without awaiting Moscow's reply to the request of May 26, the Lithuanian government dispatched another note on May 28. The note stated that a special commission to investigate the charges made against the agencies of the Lithuanian government and its officials had been appointed. It also repeated the request for more detailed information from the Soviet side. Shmavgonets, mentioned in the note, had in the meantime been returned to his unit. He was found in the company of another soldier, Pisarev, the disappearance of whom had neither been reported to the Lithuanian government nor mentioned by Molotov. The note ended by suggesting that both Shmavgonets and Pisarev testify before a special commission, with the representatives of the Soviet Military Command in Lithuania participating, to ascertain where they had been kept between the time of their disappearance and return. As for Shumov, mentioned by General Loktionov, it was necessary to have additional information.

Instead of replying to these two notes through diplomatic channels, Molotov chose to issue a communique given to the Soviet press on May 30. The communique contained a direct accusation of the Lithuanian government:

> Recently there have been many disappearances of soldiers from Soviet military bases located on Lithuanian territory under the Soviet-Lithuanian Treaty of Mutual Assistance. From information gathered by the People's Commissariat for Foreign Affairs, it appears that these disappearances have been arranged with the support of the Lithuanian Government.

Thereupon the Soviet version of circumstances accompanying the disappearance of Shmavgonets, Pisarev, and Butaev was given.

Shmavgonets was kidnaped on May 18, then taken to a house somewhere in the town, and kept in the basement for seven days, with nothing to eat or drink. He was tortured and threatened while questioned about his unit and armament. On the night of May 25, he was blindfolded, taken out of the town, and released, returning to his unit on May 26. Pisarev was on May 24 attacked by a gang of six, gagged, and taken, with a bag over his head, to a basement, where he was kept for three days, tortured and interrogated without water or food. He escaped through a sewer main. Both Shmavgonets and Pisarev returned to their units tired and exhausted, bearing marks of harsh treatment. Butaev's suicide appeared doubtful to the Soviet authorities upon examining the corpse and because of contradicting information supplied by Lithuanian authorities. And there were two more cases involving the disappearance of Soviet soldiers in Lithuania.

The communique ended with a repetition of threats contained in Molotov's note of May 25.

Despite the willingness of the Lithuanian government to do all in its power to round up the deserters and learn all the facts mentioned in Molotov's note, General Loktionov's accusation, and *Tass'* communique, Soviet military authorities in Lithuania deliberately sabotaged the entire investigation. They refused to lend support to all efforts of Lithuanian authorities seeking to clarify the situation. A commission set up especially for that purpose was not permitted to question the alleged victims of kidnaping. Nor was it furnished with any additional proof except what General Loktionov had told during his brief visit at Kaunas and what appeared in the *Tass* communique. The commission was able, however, to establish beyond doubt these facts:

On May 7, three Red Army soldiers came to a farm and asked for food. They were offered a good meal, during which they got drunk. Two of the soldiers returned immediately after the meal to their base. The third, Shmavgonets, remained for two more days at a girl friend's apartment, where he left his photograph and several of his personal effects. The third day, one of his comrades came to look for him. Upon his refusal to return to camp, ten other soldiers came and took him away by force. The Soviet military authorities refused permission to cross-examine Shmavgonets; his girl friend was one of the first to be arrested when the Soviets invaded Lithuania shortly thereafter.

On May 10, two Red Army soldiers entered a restaurant in Alytus. After a heavy drinking session, they went to a house of ill fame and stayed there for four days. On the fourth day they left. Among them was Pisarev. Permission to cross-examine him was likewise refused.

On March 4, the Lithuanian authorities received a communication from the Commandant of a Soviet base, informing them of the disappearance of a soldier, Butaev, and asking them to take necessary measures for his arrest. On May 12, the Commissioner of Police of the City of Vilnius was notified that an unknown Soviet soldier had been living for several days with a woman in Vilnius. Lithuanian police were even able to produce photographs of him with his "date." Surrounded by agents of the Lithuanian police, Butaev committed suicide. Red Army representatives participated in the autopsy which established this fact beyond doubt. On May 14, Moscow was duly informed about Butaev's suicide, and then the events followed as already described.

In order to prevent any further incidents of the same type, Lithuanian military and police authorities imposed tight restrictive and control measures on all intercourse between the Soviet garrisons and the civilian population. But this also angered Moscow, as became apparent a few weeks later.

All these facts were known only to a small group of Lithuanians and Soviets, who were directly concerned with the incidents. Consequently, the Soviet communique, as reported by the German Ambassador to the Soviet Union on May 30,[2] caused "a sensational stir" in political and diplomatic circles in Moscow. They believed the present demands could be the first move toward energetic Soviet action against Lithuania and possibly also against the other Baltic States.

On the same day (May 30), the Lithuanian Minister in Berlin urged the German Foreign Ministry to tell the truth about the disappearance of Soviet soldiers, the Soviet version of which was already given to the German press; and also to inquire whether Berlin knew what was behind these Soviet actions. The Minister was particularly concerned about the strong language of both Soviet radio and press. The German reply was in the negative, possibly because the home office had not yet received Schulenburg's cable of the same date. The German Foreign Ministry remained just as uncommunicative regarding the Minister's inquiry about the background of Soviet demands on the Baltic States put forward shortly after the conclusion of the Soviet-German treaty. The Director of the Political Department "had no knowledge of the events." [3]

In the meantime, a ferocious anti-Lithuanian campaign in the press and over the radio was followed by anti-Lithuanian rallies in Moscow, Leningrad, and Minsk. The underground communist press in Lithuania already spoke of the impending end to the Lithuanian government and of her joining the "happy family" of other Soviet republics.[4] The danger looming on the horizon appeared more and more serious with every passing day, and the shadow cast by the Soviet Union grew longer and longer.

Fearing the worst, the Lithuanian government authorized Foreign Minister Urbsys, in the last days of May, to cable to the missions abroad instructions to be followed in the event Lithuania should lose freedom of action and independence. The cable read:

> We are deeply concerned about the possibility that Moscow's accusations may conceal something much more important, something perhaps very dangerous to Lithuania. Should a catastrophe engulf us and should all contacts between the Foreign Ministry home office and the legations be temporarily interrupted, you are advised to regard S. Lozoraitis [Minister in Rome] as Chief of Lithuanian diplomats remaining abroad.[5]

The Latvian government took a similar step two weeks earlier, on May 16. In a secret decision, the Cabinet of Ministers provided for the continuity of state functions abroad in case it should no longer be possible to communicate with Latvia's diplomatic and consular missions abroad. In such an event, Latvian Minister in London K. Zarins was to exercise the state authority. A. Bilmanis, Latvian Minister in Washington, was designated as his substitute. By virtue of these emergency powers, Zarins had the right to appoint, remove, and transfer Latvian representatives abroad. He also had full authority to handle all Latvian state funds, as well as movable and immovable property of Latvian diplomatic and consular missions; to give the missions binding orders; and to defend the interests of Latvia.[6]

No information is available on similar measures in Estonia. This does not mean, however, that the Soviet Union was not casting its shadow upon her, too. A report in *Pravda* of May 28, written by the paper's Tallinn correspondent under the headline, "Political Feelings in

Estonia," was just as ominous as Molotov's notes to the Lithuanian government and *Tass'* communique on the subject of the alleged kidnaping of Soviet soldiers in Lithuania. The report accused "a certain part of the Estonian intelligentsia," the University of Tartu faculty, and the press of pro-British and anti-German feelings. They were accused of regarding the occupation of Norway and Denmark as German aggression and enslavement of small nations; of loyalty to Great Britain and hatred of Germany and everything German; of extolling trade relations with Great Britain and deprecating German goods; of spreading rumors that war between Germany and the Soviet Union was inevitable; etc. The report also took issue with Soviet-Estonian relations:

> The ruling circles of Estonia are trying to remain neutral with regard to the events in the West. The political figures neither condemn nor approve Germany's actions in their speeches. They try not to refer at all to the Soviet Union. No facts concerning the trade between Estonia and the USSR are published. In all these precautions there transpires the endeavor to tone down and conceal from public opinion the role of the USSR with regard to Estonia and Estonia's fear of England for her relations with the USSR.

It was not the first time that the Soviet government had showed its friendly concern about German affairs. As reported by the United States Chargé in Riga on December 11, 1939, the Soviet government was at that time pressuring the Latvian government to accede to all demands made by Germany in connection with the Latvian-German trade negotiations going on in Berlin. Since the Soviet Union was unable to meet all German demands for foodstuffs, Latvia was requested to contribute as much as possible.[7]

Coincidentally with the *Pravda* report, a Baltic book exhibition opened in Moscow on May 26, as a friendly gesture on the part of the Soviet Union. A special Estonian delegation attended it and, during the first days, enjoyed a most friendly reception. But this attitude changed after the *Pravda* article was published. Soviet officials were now hostile. Entries made in the visitors' book at the exhibition, which before had been laudatory and sympathetic, now were insulting, sharply critical, and abusive. The Estonian delegation returned home ahead of schedule.[8]

In the meantime the Lithuanian government was doing its best to clear up misunderstandings with the Soviet government. On May 30 it informed the Soviet Minister in Kaunas of the decision to send Foreign Minister Urbsys to Moscow, who would try to settle the differences and establish procedures which would prevent recurrences.

No reply followed. Then on June 4 Molotov informed Lithuanian Minister in Moscow L. Natkevicius that, instead, he wished to see

Prime Minister A. Merkys. Molotov's reason was that the happenings in Lithuania concerned domestic, rather than foreign affairs.

Prospects for Merkys' visit did not look too bad. On June 4, Natke-vicius had an opportunity to meet socially Marshal Timoshenko, People's Commissar of Defense (since May 7, 1940). The latter appeared undisturbed about the tension between Lithuania and the Soviet Union and failed to see any tragedy in the situation. He called Butaev a scoundrel, admitting that the Red Army might also have been at fault because of the lack of security on its own part. "We will settle the incidents in a peaceful manner," he assured. "I am very calm and dislike making a fuss."

The Estonian Minister in Moscow likewise was of the opinion that the Soviet-Lithuanian difficulties would be settled, while his German colleague commented on June 5 that he had heard nothing which contradicted this view. On May 31 he had received assurance from Molotov himself that the latter hoped for a settlement, "provided the Lithuanian government showed good will." As a precondition, Molotov demanded that abuses criticized by the Soviet government be absolutely stopped.[9]

Merkys left for Moscow by train on June 6. The conditions of his trip could be construed as a bad omen. All woods and inhabited places near the Soviet-Lithuanian frontier were full of troops, complete with tanks and artillery. The trip itself was very unpleasant, if not ostensibly insulting. No one welcomed the official visitors upon crossing the Soviet frontier; they had to drag their luggage from one train to another; heavily-armed NKVD-police unceremoniously checked all the compartments on the train, etc.[10]

On arrival to the Soviet capital Natkevicius, who met Merkys at the station, together with a group of lesser officials of the People's Commissariat for Foreign Affairs, immediately expressed his concern about the outcome of the visit. He strongly believed, he said, that the fate of the Baltic States had already been decided upon so that only a miracle could possibly save their independence. Subsequent events proved how right he was.

During the first meeting on June 7,[11] Molotov refused to listen to Merkys' explanations of what really happened and what preventive measures had been taken. "Stop kidding," he interrupted Merkys. "If my government desired, I could produce a thousand of such investigations." In general, Molotov spoke in harsh, uncivilized words, cursing and uttering threats against Lithuania. He found that the two explanatory notes received by the Soviet government were unsatisfactory. ("They did not produce a good impression.") He expressed his surprise at the harsh treatment of Soviet soldiers and accused Lithuanian security organs of outright hostility toward the Soviet Union, provocations, and kidnaping. Molotov enumerated additional instances aggravating the Soviet-Lithuanian relations. He complained that the Soviet policy toward Lithuania had been pro-Lithuanian while the Lithuanian policy toward the Soviet Union had been far from pro-Soviet. "We gave back Vilnius, but the Lithuanians do not appreciate it."

The meeting ended with Molotov's request that the guilty persons be punished. He indicated precisely that he had in mind the Minister of the Interior and the Director of the Security Department. This meant a clear intervention in the internal affairs of Lithuania. Molotov also stressed that the Lithuanian government itself should decide upon the proper measures and let the Soviet government hear its proposals at another meeting. Natkevicius, who participated at the meeting, reported the following conclusions to the home office:

> (1) The Soviets are filled with much bitterness against us which they want to express;
> (2) they are less concerned about the results of the investigation, justice, and the finding of clues in the alleged kidnaping of the Red Army men;
> (3) there is a desire to have renewed affirmations of our good will and a hundred per cent pro-Soviet policy in our relations with them;
> (4) one of the principal measures to be taken should be the replacement of the Minister of the Interior and the Director of the Security Department.

The second meeting took place on June 9. It began with Merkys' additional explanations about the incidents and with the assurance that the Director of the Security Department would be replaced. He wanted to read a long prepared statement, but Molotov rudely interrupted, telling Merkys that these explanations did not satisfy him. Thereupon he brought forth an entirely new accusation—Lithuania was organizing a Baltic military alliance against the Soviet Union. This he based on Merkys' article in *Revue Baltique* in which Merkys spoke about collaboration between the Baltic States, but failed to mention the Soviet Union, "which is also a Baltic state." In supporting his allegations, Molotov also mentioned the visits of Lithuanian generals in Riga and Tallinn; the appointment of the Lithuanian Military Attaché to Estonia; and more frequent conferences of the Baltic foreign ministers. "All those measures have been taking place behind the back of the Soviet Union; we have not even been informed about it," were Molotov's words.

Merkys denied any ill will in such moves, but Molotov said he was not convinced. He would report the conversation to the Soviet government, but he did not believe the arguments would convince them. Molotov wanted the Lithuanian government to give full assurance that no military convention had been concluded by the Baltic States. He also emphasized the necessity of a thorough discussion of all outstanding questions. The general impression retained by Merkys and Natkevicius was that the head of the government himself now had become the object of discussion. Natkevicius believed Molotov was only picking a quarrel to show dissatisfaction with the policy of Merkys' government. The suspicion also remained that the Soviets were determined to occupy Lithuania in the near future.

Because Molotov's accusations this time mainly concerned foreign policy matters, Merkys decided to call to Moscow Foreign Minister Urbsys. He also suggested that Urbsys bring a message from the President of the Republic of Lithuania, A. Smetona, to the Chairman of the Presidium of the Supreme Soviet of the USSR, M. Kalinin, giving assurances of Lithuania's good will and the most loyal execution of the Mutual Assistance Treaty of October 10, 1939.

The wisdom of such a message was questioned in Kaunas by President Smetona on the ground that nothing could help if the Soviet Union decided to take violent measures against Lithuania. On the other hand, members of the Cabinet expressed hope that the Soviet Union, distrustful of Merkys' government as it was, might possibly take a different view of the entire situation when given such a loyalty message. This view won, and Urbsys left for Moscow. He, together with Merkys and Natkevicius, saw Molotov on June 11 and gave him a declaration of the Lithuanian government stating the following:

> The Lithuanian Government regrets that, in spite of its best intentions, there were cases which could affect the tested friendly Lithuanian-Soviet relations which had been strengthened by the Mutual Assistance Pact and the return to Lithuania of her eternal capital. The Government reaffirms its unquestioned and firm loyalty and its friendly relations with the Soviet Union and also to all treaties concluded between the Lithuanian Republic and the Soviet Union. The Government has adopted a series of measures designed to strengthen the security of the Soviet troops in Lithuania; it has been decided to continue energetically the investigations of cases involving Soviet soldiers in Lithuania and to take measures to punish the persons who have committed offenses of laxity and carelessness. In connection with the Soviet Government's expressed opinion that the Lithuanian Government has a military convention with Estonia and Latvia, the Government gives its assurances that Lithuania does not have such a treaty. . . . In connection with complications arising in the relations between the Soviet Union and the Lithuanian Republic, the President of the Lithuanian Republic has decided to make changes in the composition of the government.

After making this statement, Urbsys expressed surprise at the complete unexpectedness of tension, first revealed in the Soviet note of May 25. Until that time, the Lithuanian government had been convinced that the Soviet-Lithuanian relations were very good and had also received repeated assurances to the same effect from various Soviet officials. "On May 25 a storm broke out without warning and it brought to Lithuania a certain feeling of confusion because what had happened was neither known nor understood," Urbsys said. The Baltic Entente had been set up in 1934, and there were no secret agreements between Lithuania, Latvia, and Estonia. The Soviet Union had never complained because of collaboration among the Baltic States. In conclusion, Urbsys expressed the desire to know Soviet views on international policy, so that the Lithuanian government could adapt itself to them. If the Soviet Union, for example, would make known that it disliked exchange of visits between Lithuania and the two other Baltic States, such visits could be discontinued.

Yet Molotov stubbornly repeated his accusations over and over again. He wondered why the Minister of the Interior and the Director of the Security Department had not been dismissed. He summed up the discussions by stating that the assurances of the Lithuanian government with regard to the nonexistence of a military convention between Lithuania, Latvia, and Estonia had not convinced him; measures taken by the Lithuanian government did not correspond to the circumstances; while a bureaucratic investigation of the commission was only a means to postpone the decision.

Molotov's statement indicated a complete failure of the Lithuanian government's efforts to change the Soviet attitude. The Soviet government simply did not want any settlement. Merkys decided to return to Kaunas. His farewell with Molotov was decidedly cool; so was his reply to the customary courtesy telegram. Urbsys stayed in Moscow to see what he could do, and to learn the Soviet reaction to the loyalty declaration by President Smetona. On June 14, Natkevicius was given the chance to hand it to Kalinin.

The declaration was liberally interspersed with references to various treaties between Lithuania and the Soviet Union; to the "traditions of loyalty and friendship"; to collaboration in international policies of peace, security, and honoring of treaties, etc. The declaration closed as follows:

> The treaty of October 10, 1939, especially cleared up and settled relations between the two states which have been based upon traditional friendship and confidence. The Government of the Republic of Lithuania and myself have always made, are making now, and will continue to make efforts to execute this treaty in the most loyal way.
>
> Therefore, on this occasion I have the honor once again to assure the Government of the USSR through you that the Government of the Republic of Lithuania and I by no means intended to enter into any public or secret commitments with any other state because that would be incompatible with existing treaties and traditions of long standing of real friendship between our countries.

Permit me to add that not only the Government of the Republic of Lithuania and I, but also the entire Lithuanian nation appreciate very much the present conditions of peace in our country which are so closely connected with the whole peace policy of the USSR, the expression of which is the Treaty of Mutual Assistance concluded by our countries.

Firmly believing in the continuation of the tested friendship of the USSR in regard to Lithuania, I can on my part give assurance in the name of all Lithuania that for such friendship Lithuania will know how to repay the Soviet Union.

Kalinin accepted the declaration and listened to the explanations supplied by Natkevicius without comment. He promised to study the contents and give a reply. He said nothing about relieving tension in Soviet-Lithuanian relations, yet he found "signs of disloyalty" of the Lithuanian government regarding Soviet troops. "Your president will hear from us," he added on parting.[12] This sounded ominous.

On the same day, June 14, Natkevicius and Urbsys saw V. G. Dekanozov, Deputy People's Commissar for Foreign Affairs, but only to hear the same groundless accusations repeated. In his report on the talks with Molotov, Kalinin, and Dekanozov, Natkevicius concluded that the political situation required radical steps. Lithuania was going through a moment too dangerous, and everything was to be done to satisfy the big neighbor. And satisfaction seemed difficult to attain. The disappearance and the alleged ill treatment of Soviet soldiers became a minor matter. Molotov no longer placed confidence in the present government of Lithuania.

To reinforce Molotov's hand, 12 to 15 Soviet divisions, i.e., at least 200,000 men, were concentrated along the Soviet-Lithuanian frontier. They could be seen by all traveling by rail to Moscow.[13] The Soviet military command evidently was eager to learn what was the strength of Lithuanian troops on the other side of the frontier. As the Merkys-Urbsys talks in Moscow were approaching an end, the Soviets kidnaped two Lithuanian border guards and grilled them in regard to the concentration of Lithuanian troops. The guards were released unharmed. (Their files were subsequently taken to Moscow where they vanished.)[14]

There were unmistakable signs that something was also readied against Latvia and Estonia. Killing and kidnaping of Latvian border guards and the border zone population began on June 9, and culminated in a grave incident on the dawn of June 15.[15] Soviet troops attacked a guard house, killed two border guards and one woman, seriously wounded a woman and a child, and carried across the border ten guards and a number of civilians. No witnesses were left behind, except Soviet-made empty cartridges. The Latvian government lodged a protest, and Moscow agreed to a formal investigation, but time grew short. On the same June 15, Latvian ports were blockaded by Soviet naval units which ordered Latvian naval units back to their ports. Among the Soviet ships was the *Marat,* a cruiser which had visited Riga on a good will tour of Baltic ports in 1936. With her heavy guns aimed at the city, the *Marat*'s second visit meant anything but good will.

Soviet naval units also sealed Estonia from the outside world. They stopped and searched Estonian merchantmen. A movement of Soviet troops along the Soviet-Estonian frontier was noted from June 10 on. On this same date the work of the mixed military commissions was interrupted. No telephone connection with the Soviet commands on Estonian bases could be established. A few days later concentrations of Soviet troops along the railroad Paldiski-Keila (about 30 miles west of Tallinn) were reported. All Soviet bases had been alerted for several days, and the troops were given indoctrination lectures. They were told that the Estonian people wanted to join the Red Army. At the same time new Soviet troop concentrations behind the Estonian border were observed. All these troops were in battle order, and their strength was estimated at about 90,000 men.[16]

Then, in the early afternoon of June 15, an airliner on its way from Tallinn to Helsinki was shot down by two Soviet fighter planes over the sea north of Tallinn, without previous warning. Its crew and passengers were killed. The presence of a Soviet submarine at the scene lent strength to the report the attack had been planned well in advance. Estonian fishing boats went immediately to the scene and picked up mailbags and other items from the plane. The Soviet submarine stopped them and seized what the fishermen had found.

On June 5 the German Minister in Moscow reported to his home office that the Soviet government was acquiring considerable sums of Baltic currency. He wondered whether or not the Soviet government had in mind the destruction of the existence of the Baltic countries as states, or was anticipating large expenditures there for barracks, airfields, etc.[17]

All these signs clearly indicated that "I" (Invasion) Day had arrived.

Chapter Thirteen

THREE ULTIMATUMS

It was nearly midnight of June 14 when Urbsys and Natkevicius were asked to come to the Kremlin where Molotov was waiting for them. When they arrived twenty minutes later, Molotov announced gravely he had a very important statement to make. Then he read an ultimatum to the Lithuanian government.[1]

The ultimatum restated the old, often repeated and disproved[2] accusations:

(1) The alleged kidnaping of Soviet soldiers, their torture in quest of intelligence information, and Butaev's killing were seen as proof that the organs of the Lithuanian government wished to make the presence of the detachments of the Soviet Army in Lithuania impossible.

(2) Arrests among the Lithuanian citizens serving, or working for, the Soviet garrisons were termed "unbridled and unmotivated repressions of Lithuanian citizens in the employment of the detachments of the Soviet Army, calculated not only to make their presence in Lithuania impossible, but also to create antagonism against the Soviet soldiers in preparation of an attack against these military detachments."

(3) Lithuania's adherence to a military alliance with Latvia and Estonia, allegedly exemplified by the strengthening of mutual relations between the military staffs, secret conferences of foreign ministers of the three countries, appointment of a Lithuanian Military Attaché in Tallinn, and publication of the *Revue Baltique,* "an organ of the Baltic Military Entente," was regarded by the Soviet government as proof "that the Lithuanian government was grossly violating the Mutual As-

182

sistance Pact signed with the Soviet Union and preparing to attack against the Soviet garrisons stationed in Lithuania by virtue of the Pact."

These charges could have been dismissed and the ultimatum rejected had it not been backed by the tremendous military machine of a state whose population was sixty times that of Lithuania and whose garrisons, numbering as many men as the entire Lithuanian Army, but incomparably better armed and equipped, were stationed at strategically selected locations.

Point (1) charges received no further substantiation after the seizure of Lithuanian military and police archives by the Soviets. At the time when everything was used to discredit the former government, any proof showing its disloyalty to the Soviet Union and sabotage of the Mutual Assistance Treaty would have been made widely known. Since no proofs were available or could be forged, nothing was produced.

Point (2) charges were based on deliberate and disproportionate exaggeration of a few arrests of criminals and communist agitators milling around the Soviet bases. In contrast to Soviet custom, no mass arrests in Lithuania had taken place throughout the entire period of her independence. But even if this were true, the Lithuanian government was free to apprehend criminals or common law offenders. No legal provision granted them impunity because they were employed by Soviet troops. The mutual noninterference in internal affairs of another contracting party was expressly stipulated in the Soviet-Lithuanian Mutual Assistance Treaty. It was repeatedly confirmed, both privately and from the public rostrum, by Stalin and Molotov. Finally, it seems downright ridiculous to charge that the arrests had anything to do with preparation of attacks against Soviet garrisons.

The existence of a "Baltic Military Entente" (Point 3) was vigorously denied by both Merkys and Urbsys as soon as they heard about it from Molotov. The Latvian Government joined in the denial when the accusation became officially known. An official communique issued by the Latvian Telegraph Agency (LTA) on June 15 categorically stated that Lithuania had not joined the military treaty signed between Latvia and Estonia on November 1, 1923, and no other military agreement existed between the three Baltic States.[3]

An indirect denial may also be found in the archives of the German Foreign Office, which was undoubtedly well-informed about what was going on in the Baltic States. A special memorandum prepared for Ribbentrop on June 17 states:

> The assertion now made by the Soviet Union that Lithuania had joined the Estonian-Latvian military pact is, according to information available here, without any foundation . . . Since the conclusion of the Soviet Mutual Assistance Pact with the Baltic countries, in September-October 1939,

there has been no closer cooperation in an anti-Soviet sense among the Baltic States. In view of the occupation of their countries by Soviet troops, the three Baltic governments were aware of the danger of such a policy.[4]

Although it cannot be denied that high-ranking Lithuanian officers did go to Riga and Tallinn in the winter of 1939/1940, it was not for the purpose of plotting an anti-Soviet alliance. As Merkys explained to Molotov on June 9, it was simply to consult on various common problems resulting from the war in Europe and the presence of Soviet garrisons in the Baltic countries. This also was the only reason for Colonel Meskauskas' appointment as Lithuanian Military Attaché in Tallinn—a move which had been promised long before.

It is possible that the military command in Lithuania and Latvia, if given free rein, would have gone far in an attempt to establish close cooperation between the two armed forces. Former Commander-in-Chief of the Lithuanian Army General Rastikis recalls in his memoirs that Latvian Defense Minister General Balodis in 1939 advocated in private conversations the idea of a joint command, concerted defense plans, unification of arms, joint maneuvers, and close cooperation in all fields. While General Rastikis was receptive, the Lithuanian Government displayed no enthusiasm, and the whole matter did not progress beyond the stage of informal talks.[4a]

Had Molotov looked back a few years, he would have discovered that Chief of Staff of the Red Army Marshal Egorov and high-ranking Baltic officers exchanged visits in 1936. Estonian Commander-in-Chief General Laidoner visited Moscow in December 1939 and received a very friendly reception. In June 1940, when Molotov was slinging mud at Lithuania, Latvian Chief of Staff General Berkis visited Moscow to discuss problems of common interest to both countries. No one implied that these visits meant plotting aggression against any state.[5]

Conferences of the Baltic foreign ministers, likewise displeasing to Molotov, were neither secret nor extraordinary.[6] A special provision to that effect was incorporated in the Treaty of Good Understanding and Cooperation concluded among the Baltic States on September 12, 1934. Thereafter their foreign ministers met together semiannually for several years. There was no change in this undertaking after the conclusion of mutual assistance pacts with the Soviet Union. The *Revue Baltique* published communiques of both the 10th and the 11th conferences as well as the place and the date of future conferences. These were the only two conferences held after the conclusion of the mutual assistance pacts, the exact dates being December 6–8, 1939, and March 14–16, 1940. The Latvian *Valdibas Vestnesis* (Official Gazette) likewise published the communique of the 11th Conference along with its opening date and agenda.

To ascribe Anti-Soviet tendencies to the *Revue Baltique* was beyond belief. This strictly informative magazine (published in French, English, and German) was devoted to propagation of political, economic, and cultural collaboration among the Baltic States. Only two issues of the magazine appeared. Neither contained a single article which justified Molotov's interpretation. On the contrary, the first issue carried an editorial written by Munters and stating that relations with the Soviet Union had proved "most satisfactory from both political and economic points of view." Selter shared this view fully by asserting that those relations had been developing "in a spirit of mutual trust and respect."

What Molotov objected to, however, was an article by Merkys in the first issue of the magazine, where he said that, "political obstacles to a full Baltic collaboration [Klaipeda and Vilnius disputes] have now disappeared, and a wider field, on the contrary, offers itself to a sincere collaboration." From this Molotov deduced that Merkys had in mind conclusion of a military convention making collaboration complete. He was also enraged that Merkys had not once mentioned the Soviet Union in his article, although the latter "was also a Baltic State."

These were the "facts" upon which the Soviet government had based its ultimatum. They could not, even by the widest stretch of imagination, be construed as "proofs" that the Lithuanian government had violated the Soviet-Lithuanian Treaty of Mutual Assistance or was engaged in "the preparation of aggression against the Soviet garrisons." Neither the Soviet government nor the Soviet press referred to these accusations after the occupation of the Baltic States and capture of all military and other archives. The first weeks after the occupation were largely devoted to invectives hurled against the former "bourgeois" governments. Had proofs of a military anti-Soviet alliance been found, they most certainly would have been brought to light for propaganda purposes. Nothing happened, however, because there was no fire generating the smoke. In fact, it was a smoke screen for the impending Soviet aggression against Lithuania.

The Soviet government was least concerned with the credibility of the alleged facts upon which its ultimatum was based. Annexation of Lithuania and the two other Baltic States had been decided upon in August-September 1939. By mid-June 1940 all preliminary steps had been taken to proceed with "special measures." This included impressive military concentrations, diplomatic notes, a press and radio campaign, and mob gatherings. Under these conditions, any argument was good.[7]

It was surprising, therefore, that the ultimatum spoke of the "exceptionally favorable and clearly pro-Lithuanian" policy of the Soviet Union toward Lithuania. The ultimatum saw proof of it in the fact that the Soviet Union, "on its own initiative," had returned Lithuania the territory and the city of Vilnius. Since the Lithuanian government allegedly did not reciprocate, the Soviet government considered "continuation of this situation impossible."

The Soviet ultimatum read by Molotov at midnight of June 14/15, ended in enumeration of measures to be taken by the Lithuanian government which the Soviet government considered as absolutely necessary and urgent:

> (1) Minister for Internal Affairs Skucas and Director of the Security Department Povilaitis shall be prosecuted as directly responsible for the provocations perpetrated against the Soviet garrisons in Lithuania;
>
> (2) there shall be immediately formed a new government of Lithuania, capable and willing to guarantee the execution of the Mutual Assistance Pact between the Soviet Union and Lithuania and determined to stifle the enemies of the treaty;
>
> (3) a free entry of detachments of Soviet armed forces into Lithuania and their stationing at the most important centers in Lithuania shall be immediately assured in sufficiently large numbers so as to guarantee the possibility of execution of the Mutual Assistance Pact between the Soviet Union and Lithuania and to stop acts of provocation directed against the garrisons of the Soviet Army in Lithuania.

The ultimatum made it clear in concluding that the Soviet government held the fulfillment of these demands as the foremost prerequisite for a loyal and honorable execution of the Mutual Assistance Treaty. The answer was expected by 10:00 A.M. of June 15. "If no answer is received by the specified time, this shall be regarded as a refusal to comply with the above demands of the Soviet Union."

After the demands were read to the perplexed representatives of the Lithuanian government, Urbsys wanted a prolongation of the time limit. Molotov declined on the ground it was the decision of the Soviet government which he could not change. In reply to Urbsys' query if all members of the present government were unacceptable, he stated that some were acceptable, but he had no confidence in the present government, and agreement would be necessary in regard to the composition of the new one. "It is important that the Lithuanian government be pro-Soviet, just as ours is pro-Lithuanian," Molotov added. "But irrespective of the answer received, Soviet troops will enter Lithuania."

Molotov further specified that between three and four corps of Soviet troops would enter Lithuania and would conduct themselves as they wished. The Soviet jurists would also know how to find provisions in Lithuanian laws by which the Minister of the Interior and the Director of the Security Department could be prosecuted for treason to Lithuanian interests, since the Lithuanian jurists were unable to find such provisions.

In bidding farewell, Urbsys regretted that the Mutual Assistance Treaty, on which he had worked, was being brought to such a finale within just eight months; he feared for Lithuania's fate. To this Molotov retorted that Lithuania's fate was endangered by her own provocateurs.

Since the ultimatum was wilfully construed around either nonexistent or grossly distorted facts, it should have been rejected as a whole by the Lithuanian government. There had been no acts of provocation directed against the Soviet garrisons, and logically there was no reason whatsoever for dragging to court either the Minister of Internal Affairs General Skucas or Director of the Security Department Povilaitis. For Skucas was the last member of the Lithuanian government who could be accused of any provocations against the Soviet Union. His secret instructions to the press requested it to "soft-pedal the tone and employ self-restraint" in evaluating relations with the big neighbor.[8] Povilaitis was Skucas' closest associate, but he had nothing to do with establishing government policies. Anyway, both men, Skucas and Povilaitis, though entirely guiltless by Lithuanian standards, had resigned on June 12, immediately after Merkys' return to Kaunas and his report on talks with Molotov.[9] It was no longer justice that Molotov wanted done; he desired their heads.

If the first request—to prosecute Skucas and Povilaitis—represented an open attempt of the Soviet Union to dictate administrative measures of another sovereign country, the second request—to form a government of Lithuania that would please the Soviets—was entirely incompatible with the Constitution of Lithuania, international law, and the treaties in force between the two countries.

Art. 97 of the Constitution of Lithuania provided that only the President of the Republic had the right to nominate or dismiss the Head of the Government. A request to dismiss her constitutionally appointed government and replace it by persons acceptable to the Soviet government represented the most flagrant violation of the fundamental sovereignty rights of Lithuania. This is one of the basic principles of international law adopted by all civilized nations.

Furthermore, the Russo-Lithuanian Peace Treaty of July 12, 1920, expressly stated that Russia had unreservedly recognized "the sovereign rights and independence of the Lithuanian State, with all the juridical consequences arising from such a recognition." Similarly, the Treaty of Nonaggression of September 28, 1926, contained mutual obligation "to respect in all circumstances the sovereignty and territorial integrity and inviolability of each other." Finally, Art. VII of the Treaty of Mutual Assistance of October 10, 1939, read: "Fulfillment of this treaty shall not affect in any way the sovereign rights of the contracting parties, in particular their state organization, economic and social system, military measures, and generally the principles of nonintervention in internal affairs."

But these two requests, however insulting and unjustified, could bear no comparison with the request to admit an unlimited number of Soviet troops (Molotov's oral reference to three or four corps was not binding). In fact, the Soviet government was arrogating to itself not only the right to prescribe the composition of the Lithuanian government and its future policies, but also the right to supervise the latter in all its actions. This was to be the task of Soviet troops stationed throughout Lithuania "in such numbers that would prove sufficient to assure the execution of the Treaty [of Mutual Assistance] and to put an end to acts of provocation directed against Soviet garrisons." What the Soviet government had in mind was an outright military occupation of Lithuania.

The gist of the ultimatum was immediately telephoned to Kaunas where a meeting of the Council of Ministers and top army officers was called in the early hours of June 15.[10] The President of the Republic presided. Because of the difference in time, less than eight hours remained to comply with the ultimatum after the telegram was decoded and read. The President of the Republic favored rejection of all demands. They represented interference in internal affairs, and prosecution of Lithuanian officials requested by Moscow, would mean acknowledgment of baseless Soviet accusations. If need be, Lithuania should defend herself.

Some of the ministers supported this view, if only because of its high moral value for the nation's future. For everybody agreed that the struggle would be hopeless and brief, particularly with Soviet troops already garrisoned inside the country. Furthermore, it happened that all heavy equipment had been sent to the shooting ranges. Mobilization was impossible because of expiration of the time limit set for acceptance or rejection of the ultimatum. Mobilization itself was fraught with great dangers.[11]

The majority, however, felt strongly that Points (1) and (2) should be accepted in the hope that the Soviets, seeing the good will shown, would be more lenient on Point (3). The new government would be formed by General S. Rastikis. He had recently resigned as Commander-in-Chief, which fact was unfavorably commented on by Molotov during his first meeting with Merkys (June 7). As Molotov said he thought Rastikis' resignation was enforced because he had shown a certain sympathy toward the Soviets, it seemed, therefore, that he would be acceptable to Moscow. As for the President of the

Republic, he would transfer his duties to the new Prime Minister, take leave, and go abroad (which he did).

This fateful meeting ended shortly before 7:00 A.M. Its decisions, unconditional acceptance of the Soviet ultimatum and designation of Rastikis as the new head of government, were at once communicated to Moscow. In the meantime the President of the Republic accepted the resignation of Merkys' cabinet with the request that it continue in office until a new government was constituted. Thereupon Rastikis began to select cabinet members and prepared to fly to Moscow to talk the Soviets out of sending any additional troops. At this time, however, a telegram was received in the forenoon from Urbsys, still in Moscow, saying that General Rastikis was unacceptable to the Soviet government and that Deputy People's Commissar for Foreign Affairs V. G. Dekanozov would arrive in Kaunas "to take care of the formation of the new cabinet." By then Soviet troops in Lithuania and those concentrated along the Soviet-Lithuanian border had begun to move.

At 2:00 P.M. Urbsys sent another telegram from Moscow announcing that the Soviet troops would cross the Lithuanian frontier at 3:00 P.M. and enter Vilnius, Kaunas, Raseiniai, Panevezys, and Siauliai. The telegram also stated that General Vitkauskas, Commander-in-Chief of the Lithuanian Army, was requested to meet at 8:00 P.M. with Soviet General Pavlov to agree on further points of dislocation of Soviet troops; the Lithuanian government was requested to order the population and armed forces not to interfere with movements of Soviet troops so as to avoid all unnecessary conflicts and misunderstandings.[12]

Although such orders were issued, and no resistance was offered, Soviet troops showed themselves trigger-happy by killing one border guard and wounding another. At 4:00 P.M. the first Soviet Air Force detachments flew over Lithuanian towns. Soon thereafter tanks from nearby bases rumbled through the streets of the provisional capital of Lithuania, Kaunas, and took up strategic positions in front of government buildings and other points.[13] The United States Minister to Lithuania recalls that "one of these points was conveniently close to the American Legation." [14]

That night and the next day, a dozen or so towns throughout Lithuania received Soviet garrisons. For reasons of their own, the Soviet military command avoided stationing their troops along the Lithuanian-German frontier. During negotiations with General Pavlov, as requested in the Soviet note on June 15, stationing of Soviet troops in that area and its protection were not even mentioned.[15] Nor did the German Minister in Kaunas fail to note this fact.[16] The Minister felt, however, that the mood in Lithuania was "very pessimistic." [17]

On the other hand, the German government did nothing to oppose the new situation. The Lithuanian Minister in Berlin bitterly complained to the German Foreign Ministry on June 16 that the German press was giving only the Soviet version of events in Lithuania and showing her no sympathy. The Director of the Political Department refused comment.[18] Ribbentrop permitted unauthorized crossing of the border to all Lithuanians, including Lithuanian troops, who wished to cross. Yet he did not want to encourage it and ordered to intern the troops and high functionaries of the Lithuanian government.[19] He also decreed the breaking off of all connections with Director of the Lithuanian Security Department Povilaitis,[20] whose dismissal was demanded by the Soviet government. Movements of German troops in East Prussia were to be avoided so as to create no misinterpretation.[21]

Ribbentrop was curious to know, however, whether or not a tendency of the Baltic States to seek support from Germany had been observed and whether or not an attempt to form a bloc had been made (June 16). In reply to a query to this effect, the Head of Political Division VI in the German Foreign Ministry informed Ribbentrop on June 17 that "there can be no question—during the last few months— of dependence in foreign policy on Germany by the Baltic States." [22]

The fact that the German-Lithuanian frontier remained unposted by Soviet troops should truly have given little consolation to the Germans in view of large invasion forces stationed elsewhere in Lithuania. At the time of communication of the terms of the ultimatum, Molotov spoke about three to four corps of troops to be transferred to Lithuania. Subsequent estimates by high Lithuanian officers put the actual strength at 12–15 divisions[23] or, more precisely, at two infantry corps, one cavalry division, two to three tank brigades, and a large number of aircraft and ground personnel.[24] These two estimates tally accurately with Molotov's figures. They show that the invading forces numbered about 200,000 men, ten times the strength of the Lithuanian Army in peacetime.

All this mass of men and materiel rolled across Lithuania. In the early afternoon of June 16, hundreds of tanks, supported by strong artillery and mechanized infantry units, took positions along the Lithuanian-Latvian border. The Latvian government, sensing the danger, tried to believe that the concentration of Soviet tanks just beyond the frontier was another intimidation attempt.[25] On the other hand, the government must have been apprehensive after the Latvian Foreign Minister on June 12 had a lengthy talk with the Lithuanian Prime Minister, returning from Moscow by air via Riga.[26]

Since the ultimatum to Lithuania also implicated Latvia as a member of "the Baltic Military Entente," the Latvian government hastened to state, as already mentioned in the foregoing, that Lithuania had not joined the military treaty signed between Latvia and Estonia on November 1, 1923, and that no other military agreement existed between the three Baltic States.[27]

The announcement whitewashed Lithuania in regard to a part of the Soviet charges, but failed to produce any effect upon the predetermined course of events. Now it was Latvia's turn to receive an ultimatum, and on June 16, at 2:00 P.M., the Latvian Minister in Moscow was summoned to meet Molotov.[28] The ultimatum accused the Latvian government not only of failing to liquidate the military alliance with Estonia aimed against the Soviet Union, but also of enticing Lithuania into the alliance. Then the ultimatum went on:

> Until the conclusion of the Latvian-Soviet pact of mutual assistance in the fall of 1939, the Soviet Government could view casually the existence of such a military alliance, although, as a matter of fact, it was contrary to the pact of nonaggression previously signed between the Soviet Union and Latvia. But after the conclusion of the pact of mutual assistance, the Soviet Government considers the existence of the military alliance between Latvia, Estonia, and Lithuania and aimed against the Soviet Union not only nonpermissible and unbearable, but also seriously dangerous and menacing to the security of the frontiers of the Soviet Union.

The following "proofs" already known from the ultimatum to the Lithuanian government were brought forth: (1) two secret conferences of the Baltic States in December 1939 and March 1940; (2) the enhancement of relations between the General Staffs of Latvia, Estonia, and Lithuania, secretly from the Soviet Union; and (3) the creation of a special press organ of the Baltic Military Entente, the *Revue Baltique,* etc. (?)

After accusing the Latvian government of gross violation of the provisions included in the Soviet-Latvian Mutual Assistance Pact "at a time when the Soviet Union had conducted and continues to conduct a supremely favorable and definitely pro-Latvian policy," the ultimatum ended with several demands that were the same as those contained in the ultimatum to the Lithuanian government:

> The Soviet Government finds that it can no longer suffer such a state of affairs [and] considers the following completely indispensable and not to be postponed: (1) the establishment in Latvia immediately of a government capable of and ready to ensure the honest execution of the Latvian-Soviet pact of mutual assistance; (2) to ensure without delay the free entry of Soviet troops into Latvian territory, in order to place them in the most important centers of Latvia in such numbers as to secure the possibility of realizing the Latvian-Soviet pact of mutual assistance and to avoid possible provocatory acts against Soviet garrisons in Latvia. The Soviet Government considers compliance with this demand to be the elementary stipulation without which it is impossible to achieve the honest and loyal execution of the Latvian-Soviet pact of mutual assistance.

After delivering the ultimatum, Molotov added orally that it must be answered by 10:00 P.M. the same day. In case of rejection or delay, Soviet armed forces would cross the Latvian border and smash any resistance.

The Latvian Cabinet, with President of the Republic K. Ulmanis presiding, assembled in the afternoon to consider the ultimatum.[29] As in the case of Lithuania, it could have been rejected outright because of the sheer groundlessness of charges contained therein. Collaboration between the Baltic States, reaching as far back as 1920, had not inconvenienced the Soviet Union for two decades. The new objectionable Latvian-Estonian Treaty of Defensive Alliance of November 1, 1923, had never caused Soviet complaints, not even in the course of Soviet-Estonian negotiations in the fall of 1939.[30]

While talking to the new Prime Minister of Lithuania V. Kreve, nine months later (June 30, 1940), Molotov revealed that the Soviet government had even suggested to the Lithuanian government that it form a union with the other Baltic nations. It also had used its influence with the Latvian and Estonian governments to prevent their resistance to such union. The motive behind this suggestion lay in the belief that such a union would strengthen Lithuania's resistance to possible German aggression. "It is true that we were obliged to liquidate the Baltic Union, but not because it had gone astray," Molotov admitted, in complete opposition to what he had claimed two weeks earlier. "It is no longer necessary; we have assumed the task of protecting the independence of the Baltic States." [31]

Refutation of other charges brought forth against the Latvian government is the same as in the case of the ultimatum presented to the Lithuanian government the day before. Counterarguments were identical in either case.

The allegation that the Soviet government considered the non-existent anti-Soviet military alliance between Estonia, Latvia, and Lithuania "not only insufferable and intolerable, but even extremely dangerous and menacing to the security of the frontiers of the Soviet Union" stood in sheer contrast to the boasting about the Soviet might but a few years before. For it was late in 1936 that Comrade Zhdanov threatened to open a Soviet window on the Baltic with the aid of the Red Army. In this short time the Soviet Union could not possibly have grown so weak.

Perhaps the Soviet government feared the Baltic States could appeal, either individually or collectively, for support to other powers, for example, Germany or Great Britain. This possibility must, however, be ruled out entirely. Having renounced her aspirations in the Baltic area in the fall of 1939, Germany appeared to keep her word. "Ger-

man interests had not been claimed beyond the Russo-German line in
the east," the State Secretary in the German Foreign Office advised the
Lithuanian Minister in Berlin on October 5, when the latter inquired if
the German government had any suggestions in regard to Lithuania.[32]
At that time Lithuania was being forced to sign a mutual assistance pact
with the Soviet Union. The State Secretary's answer applied to either
Latvia or Estonia. The German Foreign Ministry confirmed its attitude
in a circular telegram to all German Missions dated June 17 while
Soviet troops were pouring into the Baltic States. The telegram read:

> The unresisted reinforcement of Soviet troops in Lithuania, Latvia, and
> Estonia and the reorganization of the governments of the Baltic States,
> sought by the Soviet government to bring about more reliable cooperation
> with the Soviet Union, are the concern of the Soviet Union and the Baltic
> States. Therefore, in view of our unaltered friendly relations with the Soviet
> Union, there is no reason for nervousness on our part . . . [however] please
> refrain from making any statement during conversations which could be in-
> terpreted as partisan.[33]

Information received from German diplomatic representatives in
the Baltic capitals supported the official German line. Thus, the German Minister in Kaunas recommended resettlement of all German
nationals to serve as the strongest proof that Germany was finally uninterested in Lithuania (he also believed the Soviets would welcome
the resettlement because they considered all Germans in Lithuania as
spies).[34] His colleague in Riga likewise felt that there existed no reason
for fear, since the Soviet action, although "directed against Germany,"
was "of defensive nature." [35]

On the other hand, Germany regretted very much the loss of
economic relations with the Baltic States. A Foreign Office memorandum of June 17 admitted that the consolidation of Soviet influence
in the Baltic area would "seriously endanger" the necessary imports of
food products, raw materials, and petroleum (from Estonia), since
the economic importance of the Baltic States for the German war effort
had become considerable.[36]

As for Great Britain, which, according to *Pravda* supposedly enjoyed the deep sympathy of Estonians (and by implication of Latvians
and Lithuanians as well), there was very little likelihood that help might
be expected from that side either. Great Britain was virtually barred
from the Baltic Sea after Germany occupied both Denmark and Norway.
Molotov, well aware of the predicament of the Baltic States, triumphantly
warned Latvia in the fall of 1939 that the Soviet Union could seize her if
it wanted to. ("We could do that now, but we do not do it.").[37]

Under these circumstances, it was utterly incomprehensible how
any military alliance between the three Baltic States—even if it had

actually existed—backed by the combined population of 6,000,000 (against 170,000,000 in the Soviet Union), could have been "seriously dangerous and menacing to the security of the frontiers of the Soviet Union." Unless, of course, the Soviet government believed in the fable about an elephant running away from a tiny mouse.

As in the case of Lithuania, the Latvian government discussed rejection of the ultimatum on the ground it lacked foundation in fact and constituted a breach of the Mutual Assistance Pact by the Soviet Union. First, the numerical strength of the defenders was very low and their armament inferior compared to the Red troops stationed in Latvia and massed just beyond the frontiers. Munitions could have been barely adequate for six or seven days of fighting.[38] Second, a nation of two million was physically unable to muster an army large enough to offer anything but token resistance. Third, it was manifestly impossible to effect general mobilization, as but a few hours remained until the vastly superior Red troops would begin to march in force in case of noncompliance with the terms set forth in the ultimatum. All things considered, resistance would have amounted to national suicide. A Latvian writer appropriately states:

> Such a magnificent gesture would assuredly have remained in the annals as a matchless legend. Only there would have been no Latvian people left to pay tribute to the memory of such glorious forebears.[39]

Consequently, the Latvian government stated in its reply that it was giving consent to the Soviet demand for the admission of Soviet military forces upon Latvian territory "in the same spirit of mutual trust in which it had hitherto fulfilled the stipulation of the Mutual Assistance Treaty."

The actual invasion began on June 17. The first Soviet military detachments came in from Lithuania. They reached Riga by 3:30 P.M. and proceeded immediately to occupy all communication centers, thus cutting Latvia off from the rest of the world. A protest of the Latvian Minister of Public Affairs against arbitrary interference in Latvian broadcasts was to no avail. The Commander of the Soviet occupation forces permitted musical programs only, but exercised censorship over all lectures and newscasts.[40]

In general, the invading troops behaved haughtily. Thus, when the Latvian Army officers met a Soviet tank column at the border and inquired of the commander whether any assistance was needed, they received the reply that none was needed and that he, the commander, had his orders. It proved not so, however. In Riga, a wildly cheering communist-organized mob of some 2000 met the Soviet tanks. As it seriously interfered with traffic, the Soviet command asked the Latvian authorities to disperse the mob. This brought out stones and knives against the police. Finally, Army units had to be called to restore order. But then the Soviet Minister in Riga made a strong verbal protest in which he accused the Latvian government of "preventing people from displaying their sympathy for the Soviet forces." [41]

In contrast to what happened in Lithuania, President of the Republic of Latvia K. Ulmanis remained in the country. The guns of a Soviet warship, anchored in the Daugava River, pointed straight at his castle. As the rumors began spreading around noon of June 17 that the President had left the country, he rode through the streets of Riga in an open car. Late in the evening, he addressed the people over the radio assuring them he would stay at his place. He also asked everybody to do the same. The address had a soothing effect, and it seemed that the Latvian government was still free to act. [42]

Now only Estonia remained to be occupied. The Estonian government became apprehensive as soon as *Tass* published the text of the Soviet ultimatum to Lithuania (June 16). Following Latvian example, the Estonian news agency immediately issued a statement denying that any military alliance between Estonia, Latvia, and Lithuania had been concluded and declaring that relations between the three Baltic States were based on treaties signed before the conclusion of mutual assistance pacts with the Soviet Union. [43] The statement proved as fruitless as that issued by the Latvian government.

For hardly had the Latvian Minister in Moscow left Molotov's office, bearing the ultimatum, when his Estonian colleague was summoned to Molotov and handed an identical ultimatum. The Estonian Minister was also told that the ultimatum had to be answered by 11:00 P.M. the same day, i.e., within eight and one-half hours, including time needed for transmitting the text, receiving an answer, and communicating it to Molotov. The latter added a warning: in case of noncompliance or delay, the Red Army units concentrated at the Estonian frontier would be ordered to cross it and suppress any resistance by armed force. [44]

In Tallinn, as in Kaunas and Riga, the President of the Republic and the members of the Cabinet went through the motions of considering a rejection of the ultimatum and then agreeing to its unconditioned acceptance. A member of the gathering subsequently said:

> We stood absolutely alone, unable to resist Soviet demands made under the threat of force. We had no alternative but to accept the ultimatum, hoping that in the development of world events we would one day be able to claim our rights. [45]

The actual invasion began in the early hours of June 17. [46] Soviet troops crossed the frontier, even without awaiting the arrival of Estonian

Commander-in-Chief General Laidoner, who had come to discuss the details of the entry. There were no such discussions. General Laidoner was merely informed that five infantry divisions (90,000 men) would be brought into Estonia. It already had been determined where they would be stationed. He had to sign on a dotted line, and no counter-proposals were accepted. The Soviet officers behaved in an extremely humiliating manner; they used threats and insults; the Estonian delegation was offered no seats; General Laidoner, Chairman of the delegation, was given a lower rank in the agreement despite his protestations.

The haste with which Soviet troops occupied airports, coastal batteries, and other installations of the Estonian defense seemed incomprehensible to the Estonian government.[47] They took over barracks and camps of the Estonian armed forces which then had to be housed in schoolhouses and similar buildings. In Tallinn, they also demanded evacuation of all dockyards, almost all warehouses, and numerous public and office buildings, as well as control of telephone exchanges, authorization for Soviet quartermasters to purchase food locally, etc. And they did not feel safe until all shotguns and pistols were collected from the population, and the Home Guard was disarmed.

Occupation of all three Baltic States was virtually completed by June 17. By then huge masses of Soviet land, air, and naval forces had been transferred to that area. Molotov assured the German Minister in Moscow that it had become necessary to put an end to all the intrigues by which England and France had tried to sow discord and mistrust between Germany and the Soviet Union in the Baltic States.[48]

The German Minister, however, thought differently. He reported to the home office that, in his opinion, the possibility of a quick ending of war after the fall of Paris made it appear expedient to the Soviet Union to create accomplished facts with respect to relations with the Baltic States and go ahead with their occupation.[49]

Foreign observers believed as many as 100 to 150 divisions had been moved into the Baltic area. To this *Tass* replied that no more than 18 to 20 divisions had been stationed in the Baltic Republics, to guarantee execution of the mutual assistance treaties.[50] Even if *Tass* was right, the officially acknowledged number of Soviet troops— 250,000 to 300,000—was four to five times as large as the aggregate strength of the Baltic armed forces; moreover, it greatly surpassed them in terms of armament and equipment.

In this connection, the question has been raised whether the Baltic peoples should not have rejected Soviet demands and resisted invasion as the Finns did in the winter of 1939/40. This would have demonstrated their love for freedom and their readiness to protect it with their very lives.

As a matter of record, the same question was also discussed by the governments of the Baltic peoples. A year before the invasion, the Latvian Foreign Ministry advised its diplomatic representatives abroad that there had been no change in the determination "to oppose by all means the entry of any foreign army whatsoever into our territory." [51] The Lithuanian Minister in Berlin, as late as on June 11, 1940, four days before the actual invasion began, hinted to the German Foreign Ministry that, "if the Soviet Union now made broader political or military demands, the Lithuanian government could not take the responsibility for their acceptance." [52] He surely was not acting on his own initiative.

There is sufficient testimony that, when the crucial moment came, the question of armed resistance was taken up for discussion on the highest level in Lithuania, Latvia, and Estonia. United States Minister in Kaunas, O. Norem, who had remained at his post until the end of July 1940, recalls in his memoirs that President of the Republic A. Smetona asked for Lithuanian resistance to the "unprovoked aggression of Soviet hordes," when members of his Government and the highest-ranking army officers met together in an emergency session in the early hours of June 15.[53] Latvian Minister for Public Affairs A. Berzinsh likewise testified that several of the Cabinet members were tempted to advocate a heroic act of national suicide rather than yield to the brutal Soviet ultimatum.[54]

Yet, in the final analysis, none of the Baltic States resisted the invaders. There were several reasons, and they must be considered before passing judgment on the behavior of the Baltic peoples in those tragic days.

None of the Baltic States was in a position to offer effective resistance. Finland's example is not conclusive. Nowhere on the Baltic south of the Gulf of Finland were there natural obstacles, similar to the wide swamps and thick woods in Karelia. Nor were there man-made fortifications like the Mannerheim Line stretching across the narrow isthmus between Lake Ladoga and the Gulf of Finland. Furthermore, the Baltic States were completely isolated from the rest of the world by the Soviet Union, with its naval bases all the way from Hangoe to Liepaja. The German Navy had agreed to confine its operations in the vicinity of the Baltic coast to 20° E, while Great Britain had its hands full fighting for its own survival. The situation in Finland in the winter of 1939/40 was not similar at all.

As a result of these disadvantages, the Baltic nations could but rely on their own strength. It was negligible compared to that of the Soviet Union. The numerical ratio between the Baltic nations and all the nations in the Soviet Union as of summer 1940 (after the inclusion of prewar Eastern Poland) was about 1:30. Thus, had the Baltic States succeeded in mobilizing 20 per cent of their male population, the total would not have been larger than 600,000. At the same rate, the Soviet Union could have called 18,000,000 men to the colors. Mobilization was utterly impossible, however, because it could not have been executed prior to the actual presentation of ultimatums without drawing Soviet attention and immediate reprisals, or within those few hours granted by the Soviet Union to make an affirmative reply.

Moreover, the Soviet Union had rendered military discussions among the Baltic States impossible by singling out Lithuania as the first victim. Lithuania was tendered an ultimatum 38 hours earlier than either Latvia or Estonia. There was no time left even to get in touch with the two other Baltic States as provided for by the Treaty of Good Understanding and Cooperation of September 12, 1934; for it was nearly dawn when the ultimatum was decoded in Kaunas, yet it expired at 9:00 o'clock that morning.

Even if it were possible to establish such a contact immediately, the Treaty of Good Understanding and Cooperation only called for political and diplomatic assistance. Lithuania could not possibly request military assistance, even for defense purposes, as she was not a party to the Estonian-Latvian Defensive Alliance, in spite of Soviet accusations. On the other hand, how could either Latvia or Estonia set in motion their mobilization machinery, without provoking Soviet suspicion? How could they afford to render military assistance to their neighbor, if their own borders were already besieged by Soviet troops?

After completion of the occupation of Lithuania before Molotov had tendered the ultimatums to both Latvia and Estonia, the latter found themselves surrounded by the Soviet Union on all four sides. In fact, invasion of Latvia was launched across the Lithuanian border, rather than across the Soviet border.

It appears, however, that these elaborate preparations of the Soviet Union were hardly necessary. Soviet garrisons alone were strong enough to overpower the poorly-armed local forces. They actually played the role of the Trojan Horse, as they were the first to enter Vilnius and Kaunas, the two principal cities in Lithuania. Strategically located in the vicinity of those two centers, they did it in no time. Their role in Latvia and Estonia must have been the same.

The ultimate judgment on the failure of the Baltic nations to offer resistance to the Soviet Union on June 15–17, 1940, must be reserved for history. Military and political leaders of the Baltic nations who took the fateful decision not to resist the invaders were certainly fully aware of their responsibility. None of these leaders was a Soviet stooge or traitor. On the contrary, most of them had been opposing Bolsheviks back in those decisive years of 1917 to 1920 and throughout the relatively peaceful period of independence between 1920 and 1940. They were fully aware that ultimately they would pay for this opposition with their very lives despite the decision to accept Soviet terms. In fact, the presidents of Latvia and Estonia and the foreign ministers of all three Baltic republics and scores of ministers and generals were deported to the Soviet Union within the first month after the invasion.

What all those national leaders had been concerned with was the ultimate fate of the people they served. None had the slightest doubt than an attempt to oppose the invaders by force would be futile, and that a cruel retaliation would inevitably follow. Not only would it mean extermination of all those who had raised their arms, but also thousands upon thousands of non-combatants—men, women, and children— would meet the same fate.

The execution of 11,000 Polish officers at Katyn in the spring of 1941, as well as the disappearance of entire peoples in the Soviet Union who had believed they had an opportunity to be freed from the Soviet yoke in World War II, prove that the Baltic leaders were not wrong in their darkest forebodings. They made a mistake, however, in assuming that a passive acceptance of Soviet terms would at least save uncounted thousands from physical extermination, if not from the great sorrow and misery inherent to the Soviet system.

Retaliation began in the very first week under Soviet occupation, despite the fact that Soviet terms were accepted "in the same spirit of mutual trust in which it [Latvia] had hitherto fulfilled the stipulation of the Treaty of Mutual Assistance," as the Latvian reply read. Thousands were arrested and eventually executed or deported without trial as it is understood in all the civilized world. A week before the outbreak of hostilities between Germany and Russia on June 22, 1941, the first mass deportations in the Baltic (by then Soviet) Republics were staged. Their reoccupation by the Soviet Union in 1944 was followed by yet more severe retaliatory measures. And no one knows how many tens or even hundreds of thousands of peaceful Baltic people have already perished or are awaiting slow death from exhaustion and privation among the millions of slaves in the Arctic or Asiatic regions of the Soviet Union.

Chapter Fourteen

MOLOTOV PREDICTS INCORPORATION

Upon learning the terms of the Soviet ultimatum to the Lithuanian government, President Smetona felt he no longer would be able to exercise his constitutional prerogatives under the new political conditions. He feared his presence would be misused for legalization of Soviet designs on Lithuania. And he believed the best thing for him to do was to go abroad and carry on the struggle against the occupation of Lithuania by the Soviet Union from there.[1]

President Smetona made his decision known to government members and high army officers in the course of the fateful conference at dawn on June 15. Prime Minister A. Merkys was to take over, even though he had resigned and his resignation had been accepted by the President. In fact, the announcement was given to the press and radio in the forenoon of June 15, to be retracted shortly thereafter, however.[2] No papers were signed regarding the appointment of his successor owing to the unacceptability to the Soviet government of Prime Minister-designate General S. Rastikis. The document signed by the President on June 15 read:

> Being indisposed, I ask you to substitute for me in my duties as President of the Republic in accordance with Section 71 of the Constitution of Lithuania.[3]

The document was duly countersigned by A. Merkys as Prime Minister and promulgated in *Vyriausybes Zinios* (the Government Gazette) on June 16. In the meantime President Smetona, together with his family and several other people, left for Germany in the afternoon of June 15. They all crossed the "green" frontier at dawn on June 16 and were promptly interned by the *Gestapo*.[4]

The departure of the President created an unexpected legal situation in Lithuania. He was out of reach of the Soviet emissary, Deputy People's Commissar for Foreign Affairs V. G. Dekanozov, who arrived in Kaunas by a special plane in the afternoon of June 15. Dekanozov could not coerce the President into signing documents that would make the Soviet-imposed changes in Lithuania conform to the Lithuanian Constitution. Neither could the latter be forced to resign and yield his office to a more amenable person—a Soviet stooge.

Dekanozov did not fail to show his profound displeasure with the step taken by President Smetona. In his conversation with Professor V. Kreve, who was to become Deputy Prime Minister and Minister for Foreign Affairs in the new "People's" government, Dekanozov complained he was not only surprised, but also deeply offended by Smetona's step. He was at a loss to understand such a lack of confidence in the Soviet government. No one in Moscow had expected it, for the Soviet government had given assurance it harbored no intention of endangering Lithuania's independence or meddling in her internal affairs.[5]

Dekanozov was right about Moscow's reactions. Molotov made no secret of his displeasure with Smetona's departure either, when he had a chance to talk with the German Ambassador in Moscow. He thought the Lithuanian-German frontier was not adequately guarded and promised assistance to the Lithuanian government if so requested. Thus, Molotov tried to convey the impression that the Lithuanian government was still running Lithuanian affairs.[6]

This also was Merkys' contention on June 16, the second day of Soviet invasion, stated in his radio address to the people:

> The Red Army arrived as a friendly allied army . . . There will be no interference with economic and creative work conditions in Lithuania, provided all officials continue in their duties as before and the broad masses heed their directives . . . We shall face the future with confidence. Our internal, social, cultural, and political affairs should not be affected.[7]

The use of the expression "should not be" was symptomatic. After the address, Merkys admitted off the record that he could not do much about what might happen in the future. He believed decisions had already been made without asking Lithuanian consent, and the course of events could be neither slowed down nor arrested.

The man making decisions was Dekanozov. After surveying the situation, he believed he had found a legally unimpeachable solution by having A. Smetona disqualified from holding the office of President of the Republic. His plan was crystallized in the form of a communique issued on June 16 by the Lithuanian Telegraph Agency *Elta.* The communique read;

> Yesterday, June 15, President of the Republic Antanas Smetona left the country. Under the present circumstances, the Government considers the departure as his resignation from the duties of President of the Republic. In accordance with Section 72 of the Constitution of Lithuania, the duties of President of the Republic shall be performed by the Acting Prime Minister, Mr. Merkys.[8]

The legality of this "document" must be seriously doubted. First, the communique was published in the papers, but not in *Vyriausybes Zinios* (the Government Gazette) as required by the Constitution. Second, so far as is known, there was no decision taken by the government (the Council of Ministers) to consider the departure of President Smetona as his resignation; therefore, it is still not clear by whose authority the communique was published. Third, members of the Council of Ministers, appointed by the President, had no right to remove him from an office to which he had been elected by popular representation (electors). Fourth, there was no basis for claiming that Smetona would not return from abroad and resume his duties. Last, no revolution had taken place in the country to create a new legal situation. The civilian and military personnel of the Soviet government on duty in Lithuania had raised no objections to, or refused to recognize the authority of, the Lithuanian government and its agents they had found on their posts upon the invasion of the country. If there were persons acting on orders of the Soviet government or its agents in Lithuania and serving its ends, their deeds created no revolutionary situation in the sense recognized by international law.

In addition to not being a lawful document, the communique arrogated to the Acting President of the Republic rights he had no authority to assume, as he had been appointed to substitute for the President of the Republic within the limits of Section 71 of the Constitution of Lithuania. For Section 71 stipulated the following:

> In the event that the President of the Republic is ill or away from the country, the Prime Minister shall act in his stead. The Prime Minister in charge shall execute for the President acts that are inherent in his powers.

The text clearly implies that the Acting President of the Republic can only perform the ordinary functions of the President who is either ill or abroad. There can hardly be any doubt that President Smetona did not intend to convey to his substitute, A. Merkys, the authority to displace him permanently. Assuming any other interpretation of Section 71, the President of the Republic could be just as easily disqualified when, for example, on official visits to foreign countries.

However, Merkys himself was *persona non grata* to the Soviet government. This had been clearly demonstrated during his discussions with Molotov at the Kremlin and by the fact that the ultimatum of June 15 called for the formation of a *new* government. Molotov openly stated he had no confidence in Merkys' government, which "did not understand the situation, was unfriendly to the Soviets, and had arranged provocations." This he said to the Lithuanian Minister in Moscow while delivering the ultimatum. It was, therefore, highly unlikely that the Soviet government would let Merkys exercise powers inherent in Section 72 of the Constitution of Lithuania. Section 72 stipulated:

> In the event of the death or resignation of the President of the Republic, the Prime Minister shall assume the leadership of the State until a President of the Republic is elected and until he assumes the leadership of the State. While heading the State, the Prime Minister shall have all the powers of the President of the Republic.

It was soon apparent that Merkys, in his new duties, was only needed by the Soviets to perform a single duty—to appoint his own successor. This was accomplished by having him approve the Cabinet submitted by J. Paleckis and then sign his own resignation. Thereby J. Paleckis became "Acting President of the Republic," while Deputy Prime Minister V. Kreve became "Acting Prime Minister" (June 17).

There were no thanks for this service. A month later (July 16), A. Merkys, former Foreign Minister J. Urbsys, and their families were ordered deported. The deportation order, in the form of a letter to "the President of the Republic" (not Acting President of the Republic, as it should have been), read:

> For reasons of State security, I hold that it is necessary to deport from the territory of Lithuania, as persons dangerous to the Lithuanian State, and to settle them in the Soviet Union, the former Prime Minister of the Republic of Lithuania A. Merkys, and Minister of Foreign Affairs, Urbsys, together with their families.[9]

The request signed by M. Gedvila, Minister of Internal Affairs, was immediately approved by J. Paleckis, "President of the Republic." He wrote on the margin: "I approve and consent." Since Lithuania at that time was no part of the Soviet Union, the document is a curiosity in itself. There is no doubt that Dekanozov was behind it.

Dekanozov was also behind Paleckis' appointment to the office of Prime Minister. Merkys had no voice whatsoever in this appointment. This he found out after calling on Dekanozov on June 16 with a list of candidates suggested as his successor.[10] Although not specifically mentioned in the ultimatum, duties assigned to Dekanozov in Kaunas were described by Urbsys, in his wire from Moscow on June 15, as "taking care of the formation of the new Cabinet." [11] In a communication to the German Ambassador in Moscow, Molotov described Dekanozov's duties as "negotiations concerning the formation of the new government." [12] Hence, as Dekanozov himself was looking for candidates who suited him, he flatly rejected all candidates submitted by Merkys.

It became clear that Merkys was unable to appoint a government that would be acceptable not only to the Kremlin, but also to the Lithuanian people. "We tried all tricks, submitted all kinds of proposals, but the only result was that the Bolsheviks rejected them summarily; finally, we had to agree to a composition they forced upon us," Merkys complained to Kreve. [13]

Dekanozov himself confirmed the veracity of Merkys' assertions: [14] "I have been unable to agree with Acting President of the Republic Merkys and his advisors on the composition of the new Lithuanian government," he told Kreve. "You will have to be at the head of the new government, and so I wanted to have a talk with you before Merkys had made you his formal proposal." With these words Dekanozov put on the desk a neatly typed list of all the future "ministers." It showed that J. Paleckis, a pro-Soviet journalist, was to be Prime Minister while Kreve himself was to serve as Deputy Prime Minister and Foreign Minister.

Kreve expressed surprise that his participation in the government was being discussed not by the Acting President of the Republic, but by a Soviet Plenipotentiary at the Soviet Legation. He refused the offer, and remained oblivious to the prospect that he himself would become the actual head of the government, as Merkys would resign and Paleckis would take over the duties of the Acting President of the Republic, and would have no influence on government activities. Nor was he intimidated by Dekanozov's statement that the refusal would offend the Soviet Union. Kreve went home only to receive a call from the Soviet Minister to Lithuania trying to find out whether he had changed his mind. The reply again was in the negative.

After seeing Paleckis, Prime Minister-designate, the following morning, Kreve felt his refusal to go along with Dekanozov was well founded. Paleckis had no freedom of action. He could talk to Kreve only in the presence of the Soviet Minister. In fact, Paleckis spent most of his time at the Soviet Legation, taking and transmitting Dekanozov's orders. When Paleckis was somewhere else, he called the Soviet Legation on the telephone, afraid to take a single step on his own initiative. [15] Kreve could not expect to receive different treatment at the hand of the Soviets either; Merkys and Paleckis were two very good examples.

And yet Kreve ultimately became what Dekanozov wanted him to be—Deputy Prime Minister and Foreign Minister. It seems he was persuaded by Merkys and Kreve's own close friends. Merkys, who invited Kreve to his office for such a persuasion session, was of the opinion that, by satisfying some Soviet demands, however unjustified and humiliating, a far greater danger could possibly be avoided. Finally, Kreve gave in and the new, Soviet-approved government of Lithuania came into being (June 17).

This raises a very important point. As the above facts show, the formal head of the Lithuanian government, Prime Minister and Acting President of the Republic Merkys, had no freedom of action in choosing his successor. The Soviet-favored Prime Minister-designate Paleckis was powerless to act on his own, being a mere tool in Dekanozov's hands. However, the Constitution of Lithuania left to the President of the Republic alone the prerogative of appointing and dismissing the head of the government—the Prime Minister (Section 97). This implies that he was not bound to consult with anyone in discharging this constitutional duty; least of all with a representative of a foreign government.

According to Merkys' admission, he was forced to agree to the composition of the new government of Lithuania as dictated by Dekanozov, who in turn was backed by a strong Soviet armed and police force stationed in Lithuania since October 1939 and greatly reinforced after June 15, 1940. In other words, Merkys acted under duress, and Lithuania was no longer a sovereign state.

But if so, then the new Lithuanian government, being imposed by a military power of a foreign state and serving its political ends—which later on found its expression in an outright incorporation of Lithuania into that state—could not be regarded a true government of Lithuania. It was nothing but a Soviet puppet government, in no way associated with the legal order of Lithuania. To use a term employed by the League of Nations in its resolution of December 13, 1939, condemning the Soviet aggression against Finland,[16] it was "an alleged government which was neither *de jure* nor *de facto* the government recognized by the people of" . . . Lithuania.

This term applied to Kuusinen's government formed in the Soviet occupied Finnish town of Terjoki. The fact that the government of the "Democratic Republic of Finland" requested military assistance from the Soviet Union and even signed a treaty to that effect[17] did not impress the League of Nations. Kuusinen's government remained an organ of the Soviet Union rather than of the Finnish people. There was actually no legal difference between the formation of Kuusinen's government for Finland and Paleckis' government for Lithuania—both were

Soviet puppets. An authoritative study of the constitution and workings of puppet governments, to which various invader states had resorted at one time or another, reaches the following conclusion:

> Puppet governments are organs of the occupant and, as such, form part of his legal order. The agreements concluded by them with the occupant are not genuine international agreements, however correct in form; failing a genuine contracting party, such agreements are merely decrees of the occupant disguised as agreements which the occupant in fact concludes with himself. Their measures and laws are those of the occupant.[18]

Hence, whatever Paleckis' government did has no legal effect whatsoever upon the Lithuanian people. It is the Soviet Union which bears full responsibility and is entitled to full credit for all legal acts since June 17, 1940, the day Paleckis' government was appointed, or even since June 15, 1940, when the constitutional government of Lithuania lost freedom of action.

Outwardly, the new government of Lithuania did not seem so bad.[19] Out of seven members of the Cabinet, three, including the Prime Minister, were Communists; two were Liberal Democrats, among them the Deputy Prime Minister; and two were fellow-travelers. Dekanozov was in such haste with the formation of a new government that he had no time to select suitable candidates for various Cabinet posts. As a result, the Deputy Prime Minister took charge of the Ministry of Foreign Affairs and the Ministry of Public Education; the Minister of Finance doubled as Minister of Communications; the Minister of Agriculture also ran the Ministry of the Interior; and the Minister of Defense was at the same time Commander-in-Chief of the Lithuanian Army.

This situation underwent a change within a few days. Five new Cabinet members were appointed. Yet in this case, too, certain departures were noted from established procedures for such instances. Thus, a newly created post of Minister of Labor was assigned to M. Junca-Kucinskas, a convicted communist who at the time of his appointment was still in prison serving a long-term sentence. Minister of Education A. Venclova was abroad and only upon his return did he receive news that he had been "knighted" in his absence and without his consent.[20]

The declaration of the Dekanozov-selected Prime Minister and Acting President of the Republic Paleckis of June 18 was rather reassuring. Speaking on the foreign policy of the new government, he said:

> In foreign relations, the new government will continue to maintain normal relations with all states. The first task of the government will be the establishment of sincere and friendly relations with the Soviet Union with which Lithuania has a close alliance based on the Mutual Assistance Pact.[21]

The day before he had taken the oath to uphold the Constitution of the Republic of Lithuania. Minister of the Interior M. Gedvila, a seasoned communist, whom Paleckis appointed on June 18, spoke just as reassuringly in his first public address to the Lithuanian people:

> The basic elements of our governmental system remain unchanged. Nobody threatens legally acquired property. The Red Army came to our country with no purpose to change our system of life or to exercise some kind of occupation, but to protect us from the danger of war and to help us maintain our independence.[22]

Later on Gedvila told Kreve the text of his address had been approved by the Central Committee of the Communist Party of Lithuania as well as by Dekanozov. The latter had assured him the Red Army had arrived to assist Lithuania in the preservation of her independence and had no intentions of undertaking a change in her internal affairs. Soon Gedvila became wiser, he said, but there was no way out— his resignation would be regarded as treason to the Party and dealt with accordingly. As a communist he had reached such an impasse that it remained for him either to go crazy, kill himself, or wait until someone else killed him.[23]

Incidentally, Gedvila was not the only high communist in Lithuania deceived by Dekanozov. So was Paleckis. He told Kreve he was assured by Dekanozov that Lithuania's independence was in no danger. When asked by Kreve whether he knew about Moscow's designs on Lithuania, Paleckis admitted he did, but he had lost his mind on learning of Moscow's intentions, and now was sorry at having regained his mental faculties. In his words, there were other high officials in the government apparatus who had been similarly deceived by Dekanozov. Paleckis felt that any resistance would be useless. It only would provoke reprisals against the Lithuanian people, and particularly against the intelligentsia.[24]

The impending danger was sensed all over Lithuania. As rumors spread unabated, little affected by statements such as Gedvila's, the communist-run *XX Amzius* (formerly the organ of Christian-Democrats) published the following emphatic denial of Sovietization intentions:

> There can be no doubt but that agitation against the new government is concealed under slogans, such as: "We shall immediately introduce the Stalin Constitution." Such slogans must be characterized as mistakes. We should understand that such slogans mean the overthrow of the present government. That is what our most hostile enemies want us to do.[25]

And yet *Tiesa*, the organ of the Communist Party of Lithuania, came out with a headline, *Long Live Soviet Lithuania!*[26] The Director

of Radio Kaunas received a severe reprimand for permitting the transmission of a brief address made by Kreve during a wreath-laying cere-
mony at the Tomb of an Unknown Soldier in Kaunas on June 26. The
only objectionable statement must have been Kreve's pledge on behalf
of the entire "People's" government to "fight and work for a happy
and independent Lithuania." [27] By then the opening and closing of
Vilnius and Kaunas Radio programs with a prayer was no longer
permitted.[28] Soon thereafter transmission of Lithuanian music and
patriotic poetry or songs ceased.[29]

Farmers, the mainstay of a predominantly agricultural country
such as Lithuania, likewise received prompt assurance that all rumors
about land nationalization and collectivization were utterly wrong.
"The land saturated with your blood and your sweat is yours and will
remain yours," M. Mickis, Minister of Agriculture, stated on June 22.[30]
Yet a week later (July 2) a high official of Mickis' Ministry revealed in
a public speech the details of the forthcoming land nationalization
currently under discussion. This official was immediately dismissed. The
communist press vilified him for revealing these plans of the communists.[31] In less than three weeks (July 22) land was nationalized
as he had predicted. Nationalization of industrial, commercial, and
other enterprises was also prepared in utmost secrecy under direct
guidance of the Soviet Legation in Kaunas.[32]

Kreve himself soon found that he no longer was working with the
same people he started with. The original composition of the government, with communists in the minority, underwent considerable change
with the addition to the list of four more communists out of twelve
ministers. He also soon found another thing—besides the Council of
Ministers, actually there were four governments in Lithuania, each
defying the new government's orders and working against it. These
were:[33]

(1) *The Central Committee of the Communist Party of Lithuania,*
terrorizing government officials; forcing them to obey its demands; running a blindly destructive propaganda machine (press, radio, public
meetings); organizing strikes; and intimidating peaceful citizens with
the aid of the scum of the population;

(2) *The Soviet Army of Occupation,* setting up its own unenforce-
able regulations; threatening those who "sabotaged" their demands;
taking charge of communist demonstrations; and intimating that the
latter would be given protection, should the government try to prevent
the people from expressing their sympathy for the Soviet Union;

(3) *The Soviet Legation in Kaunas,* demanding the removal of
officials at home and abroad and indicating who should replace them;

indicating which resolutions the Council of Ministers should adopt; outlining proper relations with foreign representatives; and constantly reminding the ministers that, in order to maintain good relations with the
Soviet Union, it was necessary to take Dekanozov's views into account,
since they represented the views of the Soviet government which was
desirous to trust fully the Lithuanian government; furthermore, the
impression was to be avoided that the Lithuanian government was in-
sincere and had secret, possibly even unfriendly designs; and

(4) *The Lithuanian Ministry of the Interior,* an actual state within
a state, completely disregarding the Council of Ministers; jailing and
exiling the people; and running the country as the Minister saw fit.
In no time this Ministry was reorganized from its very foundation; all
officials from top to bottom were replaced by communists or their
sympathizers; higher officials became mere fronts for "advisers" or
"deputies" sent in from Moscow who acted only upon instructions
received from the Soviet government and knew how to enforce them.

As a result of this situation, the Council of Ministers found itself
deprived of all power. Being composed mostly of communists and
fellow-travelers, who strictly followed Soviet policies, and a few patriots,
Kreve being one of them, the Council was split asunder by internal
disagreements. The people blamed "the government" for the rapid
deterioration of the internal order and economic life, although the government was virtually impotent.

Kreve, utterly disgusted, decided that the best he could do was to
resign. His friends dissuaded him, however, on the ground that it was
necessary "to hold out until the bitter end" and that he had no right to
resign under the existing circumstances. They also advised him to go to
Moscow to see Molotov or even Stalin, acquaint them with the situation
in Lithuania, and demand they order their Legation in Kaunas and the
Military Government to stop interfering in Lithuanian affairs and des-
troying the authority of the Lithuanian government and to recall Soviet
citizens who had been unlawfully seated in the Ministry of Internal
Affairs.

Molotov at first rejected the idea of such a meeting on the ground
that the Soviet government had its plenipotentiary in Lithuania who
was authorized to discuss all problems with the Lithuanian government.
Dekanozov also called on Kreve. He wanted to know why Kreve, if he
had something important to discuss with Molotov, did not wish to discuss it first with him, Dekanozov. Kreve retorted that the Lithuanian
government still had its diplomatic representative in Moscow and was
free to appeal to the Soviet government through him; as for discussions
in Kaunas, they already had proved futile. Dekanozov swallowed the

pill. He stressed, however, that Kreve did not evaluate properly the existing conditions which "changed a great deal" after the Soviet troops came in.

Dekanozov was right about changing conditions. On June 22, a week after the occupation of Lithuania and Dekanozov's arrival in Kaunas, the German Minister to Lithuania wired the following report:

> Meanwhile the situation has developed in such a way that today Lithuania is already completely under the domination of the Soviet Union. Soviet commissars are installed in all government offices; the police, especially, are now in the hands of extreme communists. Communist propaganda is developing with such speed and force that presumably already within the next few weeks elections to the Soviets will take place, which will then in all probability soon proclaim annexation by the Soviet Union. For this reason, it is generally expected that Lithuania's formal independence will not last very much longer.[34]

The German Minister's report actually tallies with Kreve's description of the situation in Lithuania. This stood in sheer contradiction to assertions given by Soviet military and political emissaries—General Pavlov and Dekanozov. "Because of Stalin's genial and wise policy, Lithuania will be happy as she will preserve her internal organization and order," General Pavlov assured Lithuanian officers assembled in Gudagojis on June 15 to sign an agreement regarding the entry of Soviet troops.[35] Dekanozov followed the same line during his first meeting with Kreve on June 17:

> The Soviet government has given assurances that it has no intention of doing any harm to Lithuania's independence, interfering in her internal affairs, or attempting to change her internal organization . . . Both Comrade Stalin and I personally have only the best of wishes for Lithuania. We are not affected by the disease of Russian patriotic chauvinism; we like and respect the Lithuanian nation [and] Comrade Stalin has no hidden aims and designs in regard to Lithuania; he only wants to safeguard your country from a possible future German attack in the event of a change in the political situation and in our relations with them. We wish to protect ourselves and indirectly to protect you. We have no other aims here in Lithuania. As soon as the danger recedes, our Army will be immediately withdrawn, and in the future you will live as heretofore. I am glad that we are going to be direct neighbors and that friendly relations between the USSR and Lithuania will be even closer than until now.[36]

Since both Stalin and Molotov had given similar assurances repeatedly in the past, Kreve thought what was happening in Lithuania possibly remained unknown to Moscow. "We were the first victims of the Bolsheviks in Europe," he stated in his memoirs. "We knew neither their tactics, nor methods, nor final ends . . . If eminent diplomats of Western Europe and America allowed themselves to be deceived because they failed to grasp the situation, then God Himself allowed us to be deceived as well." [37]

And so Kreve repeated his request to see Molotov. The latter gave in and set up the appointment for June 30—two weeks after the occupation of Lithuania. Kreve left by train. Dekanozov preceded him by plane and was among the high Soviet officials to meet the train at the flag-bedecked station. "Although you were met in the same way as our high officials used to be met in good times when they came to Moscow," the Lithuanian Minister to the Soviet Union told Kreve after learning the purpose of his coming, "I do not think that Moscow's attitude toward the Baltic States has changed; if it did, then it has become even more unfavorable."

Molotov saw Kreve the same night at 11:00 P.M. He wanted, however, to speak to Kreve alone, despite all protestations. Their conversation lasted for four and a half hours. Here Kreve learned for the first time the naked cynicism of a Soviet statesman. Until then he had encountered at close range only Dekanozov—a cynical and rude man forcing the Soviet Minister in Kaunas to present his belated regrets and apologies wherever Dekanozov went.[38]

Molotov began his all-night exposé of Soviet aims regarding the Baltic States in general and Lithuania in particular by declaring that the Soviet Union had always had the best interests of Lithuania at heart. It had upheld her interests on the international level; had supported her everywhere and always; and had demonstrated its friendship by returning to Lithuania her former capital, Vilnius. Molotov then intimated that the previous government of Lithuania had failed to show gratitude, began persecuting "all that smacked of Russian culture," and showed signs of leaning toward Germany. To support this last claim, Molotov asserted that the delegates of Lithuania, Latvia, and Estonia met in Riga and decided to take a firm stand against the Soviet Union, to resist Soviet influence, and to seek a closer cooperation with the Germans. The Lithuanian Minister in Berlin, upon President Smetona's instructions, even began negotiations with the German government for an agreement directed against the Soviet Union.

Molotov's accusation of the Lithuanian government lacked any basis in fact. As already stated,[39] the Lithuanian Minister in Berlin acted on his own initiative and even in opposition to the express instructions from the Lithuanian government. He was reminded that the policy of Lithuania was to maintain good relations with all states and seek realization of her national aspiration by peaceful means. Hence, the Lithuanian government refused to heed Ribbentrop's suggestion to take Vilnius from Poland and showed no interests in offers of German protection and weapons. There are no indications that the far-reaching German draft of a military and economic convention was ever submitted to the Lithuanian government for consideration.

On the other hand, Molotov admitted that the Soviet Union was very much concerned about the possible developments in German-Lithuanian contacts. He told Kreve:

> We were overtaken unexpectedly by this fact and we were very worried. If Lithuania had listened to the demands of the German government and had thus proved herself an ally of Germany, she would have become a German fortified area extending far to the east, a starting point in the event of war with us. And we would have been unable to take any measures against her without risking war with Germany, which we did not and do not desire. We were able to breathe more freely when we discovered that the Lithuanian government did not dare to listen to the Germans, had refused to occupy Vilnius by force, and had thereby lost the confidence of Germany. In the presence of this dangerous fact, we were forced to change radically our attitude toward the Baltic nations, as well as toward Germany, and take steps which we had neither desired nor anticipated. These steps were necessary in the interests of security. We had no right to give such a situation an opportunity to repeat itself.

What Molotov had in mind were two agreements with Germany, placing Latvia and Estonia, and then Lithuania as well, within the exclusive Soviet zone of influence. However, even these agreements failed to dispel Soviet mistrust of Germany, he said. The Soviet Union "was compelled" to strengthen its armed forces in the Baltic States. Molotov wanted to sweeten the pill:

> I understand that this act of ours seems unpleasant to you, but believe me, it is more advantageous to you than to us; we protect you from danger from the German side, from Germany's attempts to entangle your tiny nation in a world war whose flames lick ever closer.

After listening passively to this exposé, Kreve retorted that neither he nor anyone else was responsible for the policies of the previous government of Lithuania. He feared the people might start to regret the past, if matters in Lithuania continued the same in the future as hitherto; if destruction of economic and legislative systems went on; if Soviet officials in Kaunas maintained their destructive propaganda and caused unrest in the country; and if Soviet officers kept on demoralizing Lithuanian institutions. Kreve ended his frank statement by requesting that the Soviet government instruct its garrison commanders in Lithuania to comply more fully with the local system and conditions, as well as with popular opinion and national psychology.

Molotov repaid frankness with frankness:

> You must take a good look at reality and understand that in the future small nations will have to disappear. Your Lithuania along with the other

Baltic nations, including Finland, will have to join the glorious family of the Soviet Union. Therefore you should begin now to initiate your people into the Soviet system which in the future shall reign everywhere, throughout all Europe, though put into practice earlier in some places, as in the Baltic nations, later in others . . . We shall not use force, but we shall know how to convince your people that their welfare demands this union, since only in this way, under the protection of the entire Soviet Union, can they live in peace, without fear of being drawn into the slaughter of war. You will see that before four months have passed, the people of all the Baltic States will vote for incorporation, which will take place without any disturbances. Lithuania cannot remain an exception, and her future will depend upon the fate of all Europe. Lithuania, as well as the other Baltic States, will be able quietly, even more quietly than ever before, and undisturbed to expand her national culture, only giving it a socialist content.

Kreve was completely abashed by Molotov's revelation. He recalls that his throat went dry, his lips felt sealed, and he remained speechless for some time. Molotov noticed this and ordered some tea served. Kreve, after regaining his composure, warned Molotov that, in such an event, the people in desperation might resort to armed resistance and that Germany might interfere, for she would not tolerate the instigation of the Soviet system on her border. "I can only warn you that when your aims become clear, our people will look to the Germans as possible allies who will help liberate them from your tyranny."

This was definitely too much, but Kreve remembers he no longer realized what he was saying. Molotov was obviously displeased:

Germany swallowed the occupation of the Baltic States without choking, and she will have to digest their incorporation; they are having too much trouble in the West now to want a war with the mighty Soviet Union. . . . If the Russian Tsars, beginning with Ivan the Terrible, were trying to reach the Baltic Sea, they were doing this not for their own personal ambitions, but because this was required for the development of the Russian state and the Russian nation. It would be unpardonable if the Soviet Union did not seize this opportunity which may never recur. The leaders of the Soviet Union have decided to incorporate the Baltic States into the family of Soviet republics.

Molotov dismissed unconcernedly Kreve's reminder that the United States, too, might come to the aid of Western Europe. "Its entry into the war does not worry us in the slightest. All those who put their faith in them will be greatly disillusioned." Molotov's statement could only be interpreted as a direct warning to Kreve, who saw now that the Soviets, stepping over the bodies of vanquished states, would not listen to reasoning in a blind pursuit of their sinister aims. As his last approach, Kreve proposed conclusion of a friendship pact on new terms whereby Lithuania would agree to orient her foreign policy in accordance with Soviet interests and upon Soviet advice.

Molotov rejected the proposal on the ground that World War II would help the Soviet Union gain power throughout all of Europe. "We cannot allow a small island with a form of government that will have to disappear in all of Europe to remain behind our back," he said. There was no use to talk any longer. Kreve rose and declared that Molotov's words did not convince him and that he, whatever his fellow-ministers do, would resign as the head of government. He was bold enough to state his reason:

> I had been mistaken in believing the promises given by the Soviet Union that armed forces came into Lithuania just to protect her neutrality, and not to interfere in her internal affairs. I was mistaken in so believing and, therefore, I must make the proper deductions. Furthermore, I do not wish to participate in the burial of Lithuania's independence.

It was not surprising after this that the leave-taking, in Kreve's words, was cool. Molotov even warned Kreve "to think twice" before deciding to resign, for "such a step on your part at this time would be very unpleasant for us."

It was nearly four o'clock in the morning when the meeting ended. It took till dawn to put all details of the conversation on paper. Nevertheless, the next morning Dekanozov dragged Kreve out of bed to show him around Moscow and continued to elaborate on Molotov's ideas of the night before.[40] He said that Molotov had been very displeased with Kreve, who then accused Dekanozov of falsehoods while trying to enlist his participation in the government. The reply was that the political situation had changed since then. There followed a long discourse on the inevitability of communist rule through Europe in the wake of World War II. It ended with the following summation:

> There are no such forces in the world today that could prevent our party from gaining power throughout Europe [and that is why] our party's aims have changed in regard to the Baltic States. Their incorporation in the Soviet Union is one of the first steps toward those aims. Our party can delay no longer, for such favorable circumstances might not repeat themselves.

In conclusion, Dekanozov reminded Kreve that Molotov had requested him to keep his conversations in Moscow confidential and refrain from making reports either in public or at a Cabinet meeting. Kreve refused: "I shall think about what action I take in this situation," he stated; "but I shall not conceal the fact that I shall act in the best interests of my country."

This second conversation was likewise put on paper. Despite undisguised threats on the part of both Molotov and Dekanozov ,Kreve made an extensive and frank report about his talks in Moscow when he came home. Foreign diplomatic missions were given a hint. At least the German Minister in Kaunas knew by July 5 that Molotov had told Kreve that Lithuania's incorporation was a settled question.[41] Kreve was depicted by the Minister as a man who welcomed a German *démarche* on her economic interests in Lithuania and wanted to establish still closer economic relations between the two countries.[42]

Seeing that he could not change the course of events, Kreve resigned on July 5. Somehow he managed to avoid either arrest or deportation, but he took no chances before the Soviets came back to Lithuania in the summer of 1944. He escaped to the West and came to the United States in 1947 to teach at the University of Philadelphia. He brought along a memo on his conversations with Molotov and Dekanozov and made a document of it in the form of a sworn statement (Philadelphia, Pa., September 15, 1950).

Kreve's 12,000-word statement was subsequently included in its entirety in the House of Representatives *Third Interim Report of the Select Committee on Communist Aggression and the Forced Incorporation of the Baltic States into the USSR* (83rd Congress, 2nd Session). The truthfulness of Kreve's statement is beyond any doubt. His narrative was the result of ten years of thinking about the events and people of that brief period back in 1940 in which he himself played such a prominent role. Furthermore, Kreve did not seek political and material advantages from it and died shortly thereafter.

Chapter Fifteen

ELECTIONS SOVIET-STYLE

Kreve came back from Moscow on July 3. He knew Lithuania's Sovietization was unavoidable. Nevertheless, he made one more attempt to convince Dekanozov of the necessity to conclude a Soviet-Lithuanian friendship treaty. Kreve was not deterred by Molotov's refusal to discuss the matter. On his return from Moscow, he found that the idea of an "Independent Lithuanian People's Republic" had been taken up for discussion by *Lietuvos Zinios,* a press organ of the Peasant Populist Union. The paper considered this as a *sine qua non* condition for support on the part of the "working intelligentsia." They were not opposed to friendly relations with the Soviet Union, yet they wanted freedom in the management of internal affairs and preservation of the country's economic system and culture.[1]

Kreve's attempt to take up the discussion of a Soviet-Lithuanian friendship treaty with Dekanozov fell upon deaf ears. Dekanozov then was already working on the implementation of Molotov's announcement to Kreve that the Lithuanian people would be asked, "in the manner approved by Soviet republics," whether they wish to join the Soviet Union.

Kreve wanted to resign. Yet his colleague, Finance Minister E. Galvanauskas, dissuaded him and talked him into staying for a while. Galvanauskas' argument was that they had to stay on until their dismissal and seek to frustrate Moscow's designs as long as possible.[2]

Dekanozov knew that what Molotov wanted was impossible to accomplish under the existing laws, particularly under the Lithuanian Electoral Law. He, therefore, saw to it that a new law be drafted and submitted for approval to the Council of Ministers by P. Pakarklis, Minister of Justice and an avowed communist.[3]

Kreve refused to put the draft on the agenda, and thereby unexpectedly made Radio Moscow a liar. For it was on July 3 that Radio Moscow, in its noon news release, announced that the Lithuanian People's Government had passed the Electoral Law. Actually, it was not before July 4 that the matter came up for discussion, and only on July 5 Radio Kaunas was able to announce the promulgation of the law.[4] In this case Radio Moscow beat its competitor by 56½ hours. Radio Moscow would undoubtedly have proved correct in announcing events in Lithuania, had not Kreve interfered by refusing to comply with Moscow's orders.

On the other hand, Kreve was unable to hold up the discussion of the law for long. After he refused to put the draft on the agenda, Paleckis, in his capacity as Acting President of the Republic, called a meeting of the Council of Ministers over which he presided. As the Council of Ministers consisted of seven Communists, two fellow-travelers, and two Liberal Democrats, Kreve's efforts, under these conditions, were to no avail. The Council of Ministers passed the Electoral Law to the People's Diet as submitted by Paleckis.

Kreve kept his promise to Molotov and immediately resigned. So did another Liberal Democrat in the Cabinet, Finance Minister E. Galvanauskas (he also fled from Lithuania).[5] Now the Lithuanian government consisted exclusively of communists and fellow-travelers—willing stooges in Moscow's hands.

On July 5 an official communique regarding elections to the "People's Diet" was broadcasted and appeared in the papers. The next day a proclamation "To the Lithuanian People," signed by "J. Paleckis, Prime Minister, Acting President of the Republic," was published in *Vyriausybes Zinios* (the Government Gazette). The proclamation ended with the announcement that the government had resolved to:

(1) enact a new law on election to the People's Diet;

(2) hold the elections of a new People's Diet;

(3) form the Supreme Electoral Commission;

(4) set the date of elections to the People's Diet for July 14, 1940.[6]

Soviet emissary in Latvia, Andrei Vyshinsky, Deputy Chairman of the Council of People's Commissars and Deputy People's Commissar for Foreign Affairs, found his task somewhat simpler than in Lithuania.[7] On his arrival in Riga on June 18, Vyshinsky found Latvian President of the Republic K. Ulmanis at his post. What he needed was to coerce Ulmanis to sign various papers that would make formation of the Latvian government comply with the constitutional requirements. Yet Vyshinsky had to see to it that the new government be "capable of, and ready to, ensure honest execution of the Latvian-Soviet Pact of Mutual Assistance."

Vyshinsky called briefly on President Ulmanis at 10:30 P.M. on the day of his arrival and announced he had been entrusted by the Soviet government with the execution of the stipulations resulting from the Soviet ultimatum. Thereupon Vyshinsky immediately plunged into the actual formation of the new Cabinet. He closeted himself in the Soviet Legation and even refused to talk to Foreign Minister V. Munters. However, the prospective members of the Cabinet, picked by Vyshinsky, were summoned to see him.

Next morning (June 19) the list was complete. Vyshinsky at 11:00 A.M. called once again on the President and presented a list of the new Cabinet members. Ulmanis wanted to know if he would be permitted to make changes or suggest other names, or was this just a matter of "signing on the dotted line." Vyshinsky replied that all the names had been approved by the Soviet government and he did not believe the latter would agree to any changes. "Am I from this moment a prisoner of yours and a prisoner of Moscow?" Ulmanis wondered.

The list comprised only two known communists out of eight suggested Cabinet members. The others were fellow-travelers, including Prime Minister-designate Professor A. Kirchensteins. The pressure exerted upon the President must have been tremendous, for he signed the list despite the fact that three of the new ministers were not even Latvian citizens. The Soviets repaid this service by deporting him, like Merkys, to the Soviet Union.

On June 20, at 10:00 A.M., the new Government of Latvia came into existence. The next day an announcement appeared in *Valdibas Vestnesis* (Official Gazette) to the effect that a new Cabinet had "constituted itself," as the wording was; it already had held its first meeting; and a new Commander-in-Chief of the Latvian Army had been appointed.

However, this announcement was in many respects at variance with the constitutional requirements. There was no indication in the announcement that the Cabinet members were designated by the President of the Republic, as stipulated in Section 56 of the Latvian Constitution. Neither was there indication that the *Saeima* (the Diet) had been asked to pass its vote of confidence or nonconfidence (Section 59). Finally, the announcement was made on behalf of the Secretariat of the President of the Republic, but no one had signed it by his name. But even if all these requirements had been met, the act itself had no legal standing, since it was forced upon the President by a foreign power whose large forces were stationed all over Latvia. All that has been said in regard to the Soviet puppet government of Paleckis in Lithuania firmly applies to Kirchenstein's government in Latvia.

In Riga, as in Kaunas, "spontaneous" demonstrations were staged to show "the enthusiastic endorsement of the new Latvian People's Government." Actually, government employees and factory workers were forced to take part in them. During the demonstrations, shouts were heard: "Long live Soviet Latvia in the Soviet Union!" This evidently was premature and too revealing for Vyshinsky. He called demonstrators "drunk hooligans" and pointedly ended his own speech to the mob beneath the balcony of the Soviet Embassy with the cheer: "Long live independent Latvia and long live the friendship between independent Latvia and the Soviet Union!" [8]

In his statement of policy on June 20, Prime Minister Kirchensteins was just as reassuring as Paleckis in Lithuania:

> It is the firm conviction of the Government that the solid friendship between the nations of the great Soviet Union and the Republic of Latvia will continue in the future to be a mighty and real force, which will ensure the independence of the Latvian state, a common security, and a peaceful and successful collaboration between the two states. In its foreign policy, it is the principle of the Government to assure peaceful and friendly relations with all countries and primarily with the USSR. The Government will see to it that the constitution of the Republic of Latvia is fully realized in accordance with the true will of the people. The Government calls upon the people of the Republic of Latvia to join hands in the common task on behalf of our beloved native land, Latvia.

A promise on behalf of the new Cabinet "to do its utmost to safeguard the free and independent Latvian Republic" was repeated by Kirchensteins in a broadcast on June 21 and again to the members of his Cabinet the day thereafter. A former member of the Latvian (Ulmanis') Government, who actually "saw Vyshinsky Bolshevize Latvia," as the title of his memoirs reads,[9] gave evidence under oath that all these statements were written in Russian by a certain Vetrov, one of the Secretaries at the Soviet Legation in Riga, reputedly an NKVD (People's Commissariat for Internal Affairs) man. He became chief adviser to Vyshinsky on Latvian affairs. Vyshinsky edited Vetrov's writings and gave them for translation to P. Blaus, the new Minister of Public Affairs. Blaus admitted unashamedly that the new Latvian Government "was not taking a step without asking Mr. Vyshinsky's advice."

Possibly Vyshinsky was not telling even Prime Minister Kirchensteins what he had in store for Latvia. He merely told him the Soviet Union had no desire to absorb Latvia; it wanted to establish a common foreign policy, possibly following the pattern established for Outer Mongolia. Yet, in contradiction to Vyshinsky's assurances, it was around the 1st of July that a high NKVD official in Riga, until then disguised as a Secretary at the Soviet Legation to Latvia, bluntly told a former member of the Latvian Government that there will no longer be an independent Latvia.[10]

Vyshinsky was well aware of the Soviet Government's plans in regard to the Baltic States, as revealed by Molotov to Kreve. They provided for asking the Latvian people, "in the manner approved by the Soviet Republics," to join the Soviet Union. Since the Latvian election law did not fall under this category, Vyshinsky's immediate task was to induce his hand-picked Government of Latvia to effect the necessary changes in the law.

On July 5 *Valdibas Vestnesis* published the "Law Concerning Elections to the Diet." It coincided with the day a similar proclamation was issued in Lithuania. A suspicion that the same hand was directing the timing of elections in both Lithuania and Latvia was further emphasized by the fact that the voting date was set up to be July 14 in Lithuania, July 14 and 15 in Latvia.

Although Berlin knew reliably by July 11 that all three Baltic Republics would be absorbed by the Soviet Union after the elections, Kirchensteins denied it categorically when asked by the German Minister in Tallinn.[12]

Estonia figured last in Soviet plans. While Dekanozov landed in Kaunas on June 15 and Vyshinsky came to Riga on June 18, it was June 19 when A. Zhdanov, Member of the Presidium of the Supreme Soviet of the USSR and First Secretary of the Communist Party in the Leningrad region, arrived in an armored railroad car in Tallinn.[13] He was the same man who, back in 1936, threatened the little countries on the northwest frontier of the Soviet Union with "such a crushing blow that the enemy will never again turn his eyes on Leningrad." [14] Now he had his way.

The German Minister to Estonia, who had Zhdanov's arrival watched, reported to his home office that the Soviet emissary drove from the railroad station to the Soviet Legation in an armored car, accompanied by two tanks. The station and the streets leading to the Soviet Legation were closed to all traffic. Soviet soldiers lined them, and armed sentries stood in front of the houses, all of which had been thoroughly searched.[15] Finally the Director of the Police Department had been warned by the Soviet Legation that he would be held personally responsible for Zhdanov's safety.[16]

Zhdanov paid a visit to President of the Republic of Estonia K. Päts the day he arrived. He opened the conversation by repeating his accusation that Estonia had concluded a military agreement with Lithuania. To this President Päts replied that he could state authoritatively this was untrue, and he did not wish any further reference to the charge.

Then the President informed Zhdanov that the Estonian government had resigned on June 16 and that he was ready to appoint a new head of the government who then could confer with Zhdanov on the composition of the Cabinet. His personal choice was Estonian Minister in Moscow A. Rei, and he wondered whether A. Rei would be acceptable to the Soviet government as Prime Minister.

Zhdanov replied in the negative, as he did in regard to the candidacy of M. Pungh, Chairman of the Soviet-Estonian Chamber of Commerce, member of the Soviet-Estonian Friendship Association, and legal adviser of long standing to the Soviet Legation. This prompted the President's inquiry as to who was to appoint the Cabinet, he or the Soviet government. It was the President's privilege, Zhdanov assured him; but it would be necessary to secure Moscow's approval of the candidates. Zhdanov made no suggestions of his own and returned to the Soviet Legation.

This first meeting with Zhdanov aroused some optimism among the Estonians, according to the dispatch of the German Minister in Tallinn, dated June 20.[17] The Minister had gathered that the Estonians were inclined to believe the Soviets were not contemplating either annexation or Bolshevization of their country; in fact, the Estonians had come to the conclusion that the Soviet occupation was really due to Anglo-French promptings in Moscow based on the desire to see Germany rushing her troops to the Soviet frontier and thereby relieving pressure in the West.

This was quite a departure from the earlier (June 17) fears expressed by President Päts. He then feared that the Soviet Union, if offered no resistance, would pursue, step by step, the course it had begun, until the Baltic States were completely incorporated and Bolshevized. On the other hand, he felt that even the slightest expression of German interest in Estonia or in the Baltic States in general would suffice to set a limit to the Soviet advance at once. In an attempt to stop the invasion of Estonia by Soviet troops at the last minute, the President asked the German Minister to submit his considerations to the German government and to suggest that the interest of the Reich in the Baltic States be expressed in Moscow as soon as possible.[18]

Although the Minister's personal opinion was that the Soviet occupation, or even Bolshevization of Estonia would prejudice important German economic interests there, he could only promise to transmit the suggestion; otherwise he had to adopt "a noncommittal attitude on the whole." He could do nothing else in view of the circular letter (already cited) of the State Secretary in the German Foreign Ministry of June 17, stressing that Germany was unconcerned about either unresisted reinforcement of Soviet troops in the Baltic States or reorganization of their governments and requesting German diplomatic representatives to avoid partisan statements likely to give rise to misinterpretation.[19]

In the afternoon of June 21 Zhdanov once again called on President Päts to inform him that neither of the two proposed candidates was acceptable to the Soviet government. He had, however, a suitable candidate, J. Vares. Yet this time Zhdanov came supported by the demands raised during "popular" demonstrations, in which the Soviet Legation and Soviet troops in Tallinn played a prominent part. This constituted a repetition of what had already happened in Kaunas and Riga. The same pattern was to be followed in Bulgaria, Rumania, Hungary, Czechoslovakia, and Poland in 1945–1948. As a student of Soviet methods of penetration in Eastern Europe said: "Whenever needed, workers were used for purposes of mass violence . . . at precisely the decisive moment." [20]

In Estonia in 1940, demonstrations were ordered late on June 20 by the new Board of the Central League of Labor Unions. Emboldened by Zhdanov's presence, a group of Estonian communists broke into the offices of the League, declared the old Board dismissed and replaced by their own Board. Thereupon the latter decided to organize demonstrations. Then the Soviet Legation summoned the Estonian Minister of the Interior and warned him not to interfere with demonstrations. No attention was paid to the objection that such demonstrations would be illegal, since the Commander-in-Chief of the Estonian Army had on June 17 imposed a ban on all public meetings to avoid interference with movements of Soviet troops entering Estonia in force.

At the same time, Soviet troops displayed their strength in the streets of Tallinn. They even showed up—guns, tanks, and all—at the gates of larger factories as a reminder that participation in the demonstrations was a must. They also accompanied the marching columns of demonstrators on their way to the assembly point and thence to the offices of the Prime Minister, to the residence of the President, and to the Central Prison. Among the demonstrators there were hundreds of Soviet construction workers and Estonian citizens of Russian descent—expressly brought for that purpose to Tallinn—and Soviet military personel in civilian clothes. Among the Estonian workers there were communist sympathizers, but the majority were forced to take part in this ostentatious display of the alleged "will of the Estonian people."

The noisy demand to form a new government, plus the release of political prisoners, was the objective of these demonstrations. President Päts became convinced his resistance would be useless, with Soviet tanks and guns so prominently backing up mob demands. He called in Zdanov's choice for the office of Prime Minister, J. Vares.

The latter brought along the list of all Cabinet members. As the President wanted to introduce some changes, Vares said he could not do so without consent of the Soviet Legation, to which he then went for consultation. He came back at 9:00 P.M. to inform the President that no changes were possible. Seeing that he, like Latvian President Ulmanis, must sign "on the dotted line," President Päts gave in and approved Vares' Cabinet as submitted. The new Prime Minister was sworn in then and there and promptly departed to the Soviet Legation. Otherwise, the change in the Estonian government seemed to conform fully to the provisions set forth in the Constitution of Estonia, but in effect it was just another Soviet puppet government, as in Lithuania and Latvia, for which the Estonian people were in no way responsible.

Following the general pattern established in Lithuania and Latvia, the majority of the new Estonian ministers were either politically unknown or known as non-communists. The Prime Minister himself had never been active in political life. He was a poet, known under the pen name of Johannus Barbarus. Vares was described as a person of weak character. He suited remarkably the Soviets, for he willingly took their orders. And there was no shortage of orders.

In fact, the Estonian government was run by the Soviet Legation in Tallinn, with Zhdanov pulling the strings. Zhdanov personally checked Cabinet members' speeches, government declarations, and other documents. Cabinet members were required to submit their reports to the Soviet Legation several times a day. They could make no decisions without previous Soviet approval.

The government's declaration may be cited as an example. It was prepared at the Soviet Legation, which also called up Radio Tallinn and informed its officials that Prime Minister Vares would broadcast the declaration. Vares arrived in the company of the Soviet Minister in Tallinn, who watched the reading. But even then the text was not released to the press; it had to be replaced by a new revision cleared with Zhdanov.

In the final, Zhdanov-approved version published on June 22, the declaration stated the following on the subject of Estonian foreign policy:

> The Government, maintaining and developing normal relations with all states, in the first place will guarantee an honest and scrupulous fulfillment of the mutual assistance pact with the USSR and further development, on the basis of a close alliance, of actually sincere and friendly relations with the USSR.[19]

There was no hint in the declaration that Estonia might be Sovietized or forced to join the Soviet Union. Conversely, there was no promise to preserve Estonian independence and uphold her Constitution. This was left out upon the express desire of Zhdanov, who reasoned that it was superfluous as no one wanted to do away with Estonian independence. Rumors to the contrary were spreading, however. On June 24 Foreign Minister N. Andresen reminded the Estonians that the Soviet troops made no attempt to seize power in the country. This he used as the basis for his statement:

> Management of our affairs in Estonia will now and in the future be our own concern. I am emphasizing all this to refute rumors which are willfully spread that from now on only the benevolence and good will of the Red army are the determining factors.[20]

Andressen's own deeds belied his words. To please his masters, he suggested abrogation of the Estonian-Latvian Treaty of Defensive Alliance of November 1, 1923, and the Treaty of Good Understanding and Cooperation Between Estonia, Latvia, and Lithuania of September 12, 1934. His suggestion was acted upon on June 28 and 30 respectively. (Latvia and Lithuania followed the lead on July 1.)[21] Nevertheless, the Soviet government did not forget those treaties; on December 4, 1952, Vyshinsky, speaking at the United Nations, called them a "military alliance with specific aims . . . engaged, behind the back of the USSR, in hostile activities against the Soviet state.[22]

To satisfy completely the Soviet masters, the new government of Estonia had to ask the people whether or not they wished to join the Soviet Union. It hastened to promise new elections in the declaration of June 22:

> The Government will raise the question of dissolution of the present Chamber of Deputies and the Council of State which at the present time do not represent the will of people, and of holding new elections in order to secure a really popular representation.

On July 4 the Cabinet took up the question of elections. The Minister of Interior, who, on the eve of this Cabinet meeting, had seen Zhdanov with fresh instructions from Moscow, insisted that elections be held on July 14. This was legally impossible, since the Estonian Election Law required an interval of at least 35 days between the proclamation of elections and the voting date. This requirement could only be changed by the Diet. Yet Zhdanov was reluctant to call it into session because the government had promised to dissolve the Chamber of Deputies and the Council of State. He was also sure that the desired change in the electoral law would be rejected.

Another meeting with Zhdanov produced a set of instructions in his own handwriting which called for the following: (1) elections to be held on July 14–15; (2) no court appeals to be permitted; (3) the Central Election Committee to consist of two representatives each from the Minister of Interior and the Communist Party and one representative of each of the labor unions and the Central Statistical Bureau, i.e., the majority, if not all, to be communists. Thereupon President Päts was summoned to the capital from his summer residence to preside over the Cabinet meeting.

The meeting produced two documents. One was a Presidential Decree anouncing elections to a new Chamber of Deputies and formation of a new State Council; it was signed by President Päts and countersigned by Prime Minister Vares.[23] The other was a Governmental Order setting July 14 and 15 for elections to the Chamber of Deputies and promulgating extensive changes in the Electoral Law (31 sections out of 78 were changed); the order was signed by the Prime Minister, the Minister of Interior, and the Secretary of State.[24]

The *New York Times* had no doubt that the new governments in the Baltic States represented mere transition regimes and that the weight of half a million Soviet soldiers would "inevitably entail a gradual Sovietization of these countries." [25] However, as late as July 3 President Päts did not share this view. He stated to the German Minister in Tallinn that he expected neither Sovietization nor incorporation; but his only hope was that Germany would oppose it because of her economic interests in Estonia.[26]

This completed the preparatory election cycle in all three Baltic States. It could not possibly have been a coincidence that decrees proclaiming elections were enacted in Kaunas, Riga, and Tallinn on the same day—July 5—and all of them set up the same dates of voting—July 14 and 15 (in Lithuania only July 14 was designated, but this oversight was corrected by extending voting for another day). Nor could the newly-appointed governments have come together and agreed on these dates. The very idea of their collaboration must have appeared dangerous to them after the soviet government had branded the previous limited contacts among the Baltic States as "not only insufferable and unbearable, but even extremely dangerous and menacing to the security of the frontiers of the Soviet Union." This they demonstrated by hastening to annul the two treaties providing for some collaboration. Hence, only Moscow could have been behind the plan.

Kreve furnished a further proof of the prearrangement of the entire election procedure from Moscow. He stated in his memoirs that Dekanozov had told him the elections must take place in all three Baltic republics on the same date. Dekanozov also threatened that Kreve's "sabotage" would be reported to Molotov and that ways and means would be found to make him consider, adopt, and promulgate the electoral law on time.[27]

Moscow needed rubber-stamp parliaments in the Baltic republics to legalize their incorporation. An outright annexation would have been impossible to justify in any plausible way. Not only had the Soviet Union repeatedly renounced its former sovereignty rights to the Baltic peoples; it could not even claim that there were many "kindred brothers" in the Baltic States—an excuse used for the invasion of Eastern Poland on September 17, 1939. An annexation because of the alleged plotting against the Soviet Union, however clumsy the proofs, would have remained an annexation, incompatible with Lenin's and Stalin's pronouncements on that matter and the continuous lip service to it. The apparent readiness of the puppet Baltic governments to sign any papers submitted by the Soviet emissaries could not be considered a suitable solution either. And so Moscow decided to stage Soviet-type "elections."

Soviet experience with their own yes-parliaments, beginning with the lowest local subdivisions and ending with the Supreme Soviet, was both extensive and encouraging. The Soviet government was quite sure of its ability to cope with the Soviet-type Baltic parliaments, too.

A strict supervision of elections was achieved by stipulating in the new electoral laws that the government in each country was to appoint the Supreme Electoral Commission; the latter was to appoint the district commissions; and these, the precinct commissions. Thus, by appointing communists to the Supreme Electoral Commission, communist control of the whole election machinery from top to bottom was easy to implement. There was no court appeal against the decisions of the Supreme Electoral Commission, as all such provisions were eliminated from electoral laws.

The second objective was to eliminate opposition to the election candidates, according to Soviet practice. In Lithuania this objective was achieved by providing in Section 19 of the Law on the Elections to the People's Diet that "as many candidates for the people's representatives shall be nominated as there are to be elected from the electoral district." This provision deprived the "elections" of the basic ingredient—the choice among the candidates and the programs. Those nominated as candidates were assured automatically of election, so that the net result would have been exactly the same if the machinery had stopped there and then. What was to take place in Lithuania on July 14, 1940, would not be elections in a generally accepted sense. This was publicly admitted by a high official of the People's Government of Lithuania, Director of the Lithuanian Information Bureau K. Korsakas. He said on the day of elections:

Today, the Lithuanian people, following the example of the free peoples of the USSR under the leadership of Great Stalin, are electing the Diet in a most just and democratic way. It is true that these elections are not bourgeois democratic elections.[28]

The travesty was further strengthened by barring all but the Supreme Electoral Commission-approved persons from becoming candidates for "elections." To be sure, the Electoral Law provided that the candidates "shall be nominated at the county meeting of the toiling people convoked by the district electoral commission" (Section 20). Thus, everyone's chances to be nominated were the same. But the law did not specify how this was to be done, for the convocation of the entire electorate in an average county with its 125,000 population scattered over an area of 1000 sq. mi. was a sheer impossibility. As an example, only some 2500 people attended the nomination meeting in Kaunas, a city of 100,000.[29]

On July 8, two days before the deadline for nominations, the Supreme Electoral Commission issued a statement clarifying the situation. Now it was "cultural, educational, labor, or other public organizations or working people's associations, possessing permission established by law to carry on their activities" who had the right to nominate candidates. This eliminated the bulk of the electorate as well as political parties, except the Communist Party. The activities of all other political parties had been suspended as of July 1 by the order of the Minister of the Interior pending issuance of special permits. Their issuance was refused, however, the reason being that the Communist Party received its legitimation on June 25. Official comments on this event, to quote *Lietuvos Aidas* of June 26, ran as follows:

> The Communist Party, which has always fought for the people's interests, will now be the only legal party in liberated Lithuania. There is no place in Lithuania for other parties which for a long time struggled against the people and against the independence of Lithuania.[30]

Consequently, only the Communist Party and a few other legalized organizations could submit their lists of candidates. This they did immediately after the proclamation of "elections." They formed a "Union of Working People of Lithuania" and published on July 7 a joint electoral platform. The latter was signed by the Lithuanian Communist Youth Organization, Central Bureau of Labor Union, Freethinkers' Association, Tenants' Association, and the Lithuanian Communist Party. It would have been impertinent for the latter to run alone in view of the fact that its membership did not exceed 1500 or 0.05 per cent of the population.

The rest was easy.[31] Meetings of the "working people" were called at a county's seat, the former government was denounced, the list of candidates—"the best among the best"—was read and approved by acclamation. No discussion by the "outsiders" was tolerated, and no name substitutions were accepted. Since the law required that "as many people's candidates for representatives shall be nominated as there are to be elected from the electoral district" (Section 19), and since there were three counties in each electoral district, it was more than a pure coincidence that an identical list of candidates was invariably approved at each county's meeting and then automatically became a district's list.

It was the Central Committee of the Communist Party of Lithuania in Kaunas who took care of all the details. They even supplied Radio Kaunas (and presumably the press) with the biographies of nominees before the nomination meetings had taken place. Some of the reporters even managed to supply ahead of time complete descriptions of nomination meetings and to pocket the money for this kind of "reporting."

Just as strange a procedure was used to select the candidates. Several of them, who never in their life were communists, subsequently testified that no one had ever asked their consent (as provided in Section 22 of the law) and that they received news about their nomination either from papers or from other people. Their efforts to refuse to run were not accepted. One "candidate," Dr. A. Garmus, a noncommunist and politically inactive, was told by a prominent party man that "lists have by now been made public, and no one can take your name out." A well-known writer, L. Dovydenas, was advised that withdrawal was impossible after all the publicity in the press. "A very good reason," he was warned, "would be needed, such as death or escape; yet do not try to escape—since last night you are under the supervision and protection of the Security Department." Another high functionary of the Communist Party openly warned him that refusal would endanger his own life and that of his family. "The Communist Party knows what it does and does what it wants," he was told.[32]

It came into the open later that Dekanozov had his final say about the selection of nominees for the "People's Diet" as was the case with the selection of candidates for the "People's Government." Dr. Garmus reveals, for example, that Dekanozov himself told him about having made a mistake and approved of Dr. Garmus' candidacy when it was submitted to him. Consequently, not only the "People's Government," but also the "People's Diet" as well were mere Soviet puppets with all the legal consequences arising therefrom.

In Latvia and Estonia, elimination of opposition to the nominees was achieved in a roundabout way.[33] Electoral laws in both countries, even after introduction of changes desired by Soviet emissaries (as this was exemplified by Zhdanov's hand-written instructions), did not go so far as in Lithuania. Technically, it was possible to have competing lists of candidates.

But for that, electoral laws contained a safeguard—a very brief deadline for nominations; specifically, 5 days. Since the old electoral laws allowed 28 days for the same purpose in Estonia and 30 days in Latvia, the belief must have prevailed that the nominees would not be able to comply with the time limit. This was particularly so in Latvia, where the Central Electoral Commission ruled that the lists of candidates would be accepted from 10:00 A.M. to 12:00 noon on July 8 and 9 and from 10:00 A.M. to 2:00 P.M. on July 10 only. Furthermore, it was decreed on July 8 that all candidates must have their political platform ready, as well as proof it had been brought to the knowledge of the electorate.

Nevertheless, all major Latvian political parties, with the exception of Communists and Social-Democrats, managed to reach an agreement on a joint list of candidates of the Latvian National Union; to work out a joint platform; and to publish it before the deadline. The latter was extremely hard to accomplish because the Latvian National Union was forbidden to hold public meetings; it had no access to either press or radio; and the printing shops were instructed to accept no orders for election material without government approval. And yet some literature hit the streets as early as July 5, the day the election law was promulgated.

It was reasonably expected that the list would draw 75 to 85 per cent of all votes cast. Informed about the adoption of the platform, Vyshinsky wished "every success." But shortly thereafter (July 9), the Latvian National Union's election headquarters were invaded, searched and closed, and all the principal figures in this movement were arrested and deported to the Soviet Union. The press gave the following account:

> Some representatives of the class of wealthy citizens, calling themselves Latvian democrats, have started to organize their own list of candidates, in spite of the fact that all really democratic citizens already joined the Working People's League. They have collected signatures among their fellow citizens. Our safety organs have revealed this political adventure and have, just in time, turned them over to the public prosecutors for investigation and liquidation of this adventure.

There were five electoral districts, however, where the opposition succeeded in submitting its lists of candidates. The endeavor failed because of disqualification of such lists due to "formal defects," as the Central Electoral Committee officially announced. In the final analysis, only one list of candidates, that of the "League of the Working People" was approved for "elections." The basic element of free elections—the choice among the candidates and their platforms—was thereby removed. What was ordered in Lithuania by government decree, was achieved in Latvia by trickery.

But even if all provisions in the Latvian Law on Elections of July 5, 1940, had been fully and conscientiously implemented and the opposition had been permitted to run its own slate of candidates, the "elections" would have been unlawful *per se*. For Section 81 of the Latvian Constitution stipulated that the Council of Ministers was not authorized to enact fundamental laws; electoral laws were specifically enumerated as such laws. Only the Diet could enact them. Yet this provision was disregarded, making the whole undertaking unlawful from the beginning to the end.

In Estonia, where legal "election" prerequisites were similar to those in Latvia, patriotic groups and political parties joined forces and succeeded in nominating in every electoral district from one to three candidates running in opposition to the single candidate of the "Estonian Working People's League." An intimidation campaign against the opposition nominees began at once. It brought only meager results, despite threats of physical violence against the nominee himself and/or his family. Facing impending failure, the Cabinet issued on July 9 a supplement to the electoral law providing for the submission of every candidate's election platform by 2:00 P.M. on July 10. This time the Cabinet again acted on Zhdanov's order, which was translated from Russian into Estonian at the meeting.

Although in many instances but one or two hours remained to comply with the requirement to submit the election platform by the deadline, only four out of all the nominees failed to meet the deadline. Nearly all of the submitted platforms were rejected, however, on various implausible grounds. This was done on orders received from the Communist Party. A score or so of nominees were forced by threats and pressure to withdraw their petitions. Finally, in those instances where the orders for disqualification of opposition nominees arrived too late and the latter were officially accepted as candidates, the electoral commissions had to reverse themselves and invalidate nominations.

As a result of threats and manipulations, by the deadline only as many candidates remained as there were electoral districts. All of them had been pledged to support the Estonian Working People's League platform,[34] prominently published in *Pravda* on July 7 and signed by various Estonian organizations—the Communist Party of Estonia being among them. In this manner, the Estonians, like the Lithuanians and Latvians, were left with no choice regarding either the candidates or political platforms. Nevertheless, this was presented in the press as a great victory.

On July 14, the Communist-dominated *Rahva Haal* in Tallinn depicted the elimination of all opposition to the candidates supported by the Estonian Working People's League as a proof that "the overwhelming majority of the people and all workers had adhered to the League." After the elections, *Pravda* (July 19) stated that the "brilliant victory" of the Estonian Working People's League was in effect a "victory of the Estonian Communist Party" and a proof that the entire Estonian nation was "for the Communist Party." Thus, *Pravda* made, perhaps inadvertently, the admission that there was no distinction between the Working People's League and the Communist Party—a fact which heretofore had received no publicity and was even denied.

Changes in the Law on Elections to the Chamber of Deputees of August 17, 1937, were enacted in violation of the Estonian Constitution. For the only legal procedure to enact the changes was to have them adopted by both houses of the State Assembly and confirmed by the President, or to have them passed by a qualified majority of both houses in the case of a Presidential veto. The President was also empowered by the Constitution to enact laws during the recess of the State Assembly, yet election laws were strictly excluded from such legislation. As for the government, it had no legislative power at all. Its decrees had to conform to existing laws, without effecting changes in them. In changing the electoral law, the government of Estonia not only violated the Constitution, but also the oath of office which required that members of the Cabinet swear "to be faithful to the Republic of Estonia and its Constitution."

A characteristic feature of Soviet-type "elections" is the extremely large percentage of "voters"—usually in the neighborhood of 99 per cent. No effort is spared to bring them out to the polling places. This was also the case in the Baltic States on July 14–15, 1940, where the people had to perform their "sacred duty," as *Pravda* (July 7) called it.

In Lithuania, the new electoral law left no choice for persons 21 years of age or over: "Everyone shall have the duty to vote" (Section 24). Record was also to be kept of those voting and nonvoting: "A note shall be made on the passport . . . that its bearer had voted" (Section 35). The press did its best to make it clear that discharge of this duty was a serious business. On July 9 *Vinliaus Balsas* reminded its readers editorially:

> Persons who do not vote or who do not take part in elections are not concerned with the future of the people. They are the enemies of the people. There is no longer a place for such persons in workers' Lithuania.[35]

This theme was repeated over and over again in the press, over the radio, in candidates' speeches, at endless meetings, etc.[36] The so-called agitators went from house to house and urged the people to "vote"; refusal was accompanied by threats. Slogans were coined and put in circulation: "He Who Does Not Vote Votes for People's Enemies!" "Stalin's Eye Sees Everything!" "The Kremlin Watches the Lithuanian People and Knows Who Are Its Enemies!" Intimidation was actually put into effect on the night of July 11/12, almost on the eve of "balloting," when some 2000 people, political leaders and active members of the suspended noncommunist parties as well as members of the Riflemen's Association (Home Guard) were arrested in the first such mass undertaking. An NKVD order to that effect was signed on July 7, practically on the morrow of proclamation of elections.[37]

In Estonia, *Rahva Haal* published a threatening editorial on the eve of "elections" in which it was said:

> Shirking the elections would be a very imprudent step to take. In the present situation passivity could be viewed by us as hostility towards the working people; only those opposed to the working people will remain passive.

In Latvia, participation was drummed up by a government decree ordering government and office employees, factory workers, shop personnel, and army units to march to the polls in columns, with banners, bands, and all. The *New York Times* saw right through all these elaborate preparations:

> The intensity of the election campaign in the face of the fact that the "Working People's Bloc" is bound to capture all seats in the new Parliaments is due to its effort to roll up as large a vote as possible in order to claim overwhelmingly popular support for what it is proposed to do.[38]

Official polling results received prominent display in *Pravda* (July 17). They showed that the voting percentage ran as high as 81.6 per cent in Estonia, 94.7 per cent in Latvia, and 95.5 per cent in Lithuania; 92.9 per cent of those who had voted in Estonia, 97.6 per cent in Latvia, and 99.2 per cent in Lithuania cast their ballots for "people's candidates." Such high figures have always been a characteristic trait of Soviet-type "elections." Their falseness with respect to the officially announced polling results in the Baltic States on July 14–15, 1940, has been established beyond doubt in several ways.[39]

It is hard to comprehend the contention that so high a percentage of the electorate had voted if anyone was welcome to the polls, regardless of whether or not he was duly registered. In some cases no identification papers were required, so that multiple balloting was entirely possible. Moreover, even complete aliens—Red Army soldiers and officers, *Tass* correspondents, assorted commissars, and other representatives of the "brotherly Russian people"—were permitted to raise the voting percentage. The United States Minister in Kaunas recalls that "some of our own American students in Lithuania managed to arrive with American passports wherein appears the word *Balsavo* (voted)." [40]

No wonder that in many a balloting district participation exceeded 100 per cent of eligible voters. An impartial witness, the United States Minister in Kaunas, knew of an electoral precinct where the participation was as high as 122 per cent.[41] He said before a United States Congressional Committee that his observer saw communist sympathizers voting several times.[42] Even this incredibly high figure was beaten by Radio Kaunas which was able to report the record-breaking participation of 166 per cent in the district of Mazeikiai.

Great laxity prevailed also in computing the ballots cast. Precinct electoral commissions added ballots at will, replaced invalid ballots, or simply raised the number of ballots without any proof. There were numerous precincts where the voting percentage was as low as 10–15 per cent, but the official minutes invariably recorded 80–90 per cent. In Estonia the official percentage of voters, announced on July 17 in all local papers and *Pravda,* was 81.6. Another official announcement, made public on July 18, raised the previous figure to 84.1 per cent.

It has subsequently been established that this correction was a deliberate forgery seeking to raise the voting percentage, which happened to be the lowest among the three Baltic Republics. This was achieved by simply reducing the number of those entitled to vote by 35,119, a procedure that automatically raised the voting percentage to the desired level.[43] Additional documentary evidence also disclosed that the actual voting percentage in all of Estonia did not attain 80 per cent, while in some rural districts only 40–60 per cent of eligible voters went to the polls.

Official figures for Lithuania have subsequently been denied by a number of former members of the Lithuanian People's Diet and members of the Government of the Lithuanian Soviet Republic. In a joint statement signed under oath, they said:

> In order to enhance the effect, it was declared that 95.5 per cent of all the electorate had voted for the list of candidates to the People's Diet, while actually, as confirmed by the members of the People's Diet election committees and as shown by the statements made at secret meetings by the former Chairman of the Council of the People's Commissars, M. Gedvilla, and the former Chairman of the Presidium of the Supreme Soviet, J. Paleckis, only 16 to 18 per cent of the submitted ballots were valid.[44]

Hence, this statement reveals that in Lithuania six to seven voters out of ten, being afraid to abstain from balloting, at least evidenced their opposition by submitting invalid ballots; specifically, by dropping empty envelopes, crossing out the names of the candidates, or scribbling remarks on official ballots. Many a voter showed his contempt by throwing the ballots to the ground. This prompted the Supreme Electoral Commission to issue a warning that no such "provocations" were allowed. In Estonia, the situation must have been just about the same, since even the use of booths was discouraged to prevent placing anything else but the official ballot in the envelope. "Sabotage" at the polls was openly discussed among the top communists, and only later a directive was issued prohibiting any reference to the disappointing election results.[45]

Evidence is also available on the fact that the official polling results did not show the actual figures, but rather those predetermined in Moscow. Due to a mishap in timing, the London *Tass* office anounced election results in the Baltic States as early as July 14. Yet the polls closed only on July 15. It was more than a coincidence that the figures announced by the London *Tass* happened to be exactly the same as those officialy announced by the Moscow *Tass* three days later.[46]

Shortly after the "elections," Molotov, in his speech before the Seventh Session of the Supreme Soviet of the USSR on August 1, referred to them as "free democratic parliamentary elections, based on universal direct and equal voting and secret ballot." (A. Vyshinsky, then Soviet representative to the United Nations, used exactly the same words before the General Assembly of the United Nations on December 4, 1952.)[47]

Molotov's speech was duly reported in *Pravda.* Had he, however, consulted *Pravda's.* files for April 1938, he would have found that the opinion of the mouthpiece of the Communist Party of the USSR was entirely different in regard to similar "voting" held in another country. Having invaded Austria, Nazi Germany was conducting there a plebiscite on April 10, 1938. For six days, beginning with the April 7 issue, *Pravda* spared no space in denouncing the whole undertaking. The plebiscite was called "a comedy" and "an insolent violation of the will of the Austrian people." In reporting on preparations for the plebiscite, *Pravda* described wide-spread purges of voters; mass arrests; jailing and banishment to concentration camps of those likely to mark "nay" on their ballots; use of bribery alongside with terror; a huge demagogic campaign; orders to appear in groups at the polls; suicides and executions; etc. In a dispatch from Berlin dated April 11, *Pravda* had the following to say on the plebiscite (the latter invariably in quotation marks):

> No one had any doubts as to the outcome of the "plebiscite." As was expected, the official results announced today show a nearly 100% "participation" in the "plebiscite" and nearly 100% (99.08%) "voting" in the manner desired by the fascists.

After reporting that Germany had rushed SS troops to Austria "to fight the internal enemies" and after quoting German Propaganda

Minister J. Goebbels, who supposedly stated that "the German Army is the most reliable guarantee for the attainment of objectives," *Pravda* supplied its own comments:

> The seizure of Austria by a robber received a formal seal. The "plebiscite" was carried out in conformity with all the rules of the fascist "craftsmanship": at first the lists of "suicide cases" and then the lists of prison and concentration camp inmates were expanded; thereupon, those remaining free were given ballots with a strict warning to draw appropriate conclusions therefrom. As for the rest—it is a simple matter of statistics. It is only incomprehensible why the fascist statisticians all of a sudden suffered an attack of shamefulness and reported that there was only 100% or nearly 100% voting. Had the fascist statisticians reported there was 200% or 300% voting among the population and that all voted "aye," the world would have been just as little astonished as it is now.
>
> The fascists have already perpetrated many a trick in the course of their five-year practice, yet the present "plebiscite" is indeed a crowning of all the records established by true charlatanry. To occupy militarily a country, impose a satrap viceroy, police, and gendarmery, introduce an occupation army 300,000 men strong, and then arrange for "a free declaration of will" . . . is indeed the most ignominious comedy.
>
> Does it pay for the voter to get excited, weigh the candidates against each other, agitate in their favor, defend them? Goebbels and Company have already given thought to everything: they drew up the list of candidates and determined their precedence according to each "candidate's" rank and position; as for the question who will be sitting in the *Reichstag*, the *Führer* will select them. The comedy of the fascist "plebiscite" causes unanimous ironic comments and jokes about it in the whole international press.

Only the names, places, and dates have to be changed to apply the above comments as they are to the "elections" in the Baltic States on July 14–15, 1940.

Chapter Sixteen

INDEPENDENCE EXTINGUISHED

Following a pattern established in the Soviet Union, the announcement of very high percentages of the electorate who allegedly went to
the polls in the Baltic States on July 14–15, 1940, was immediately ex-
ploited by the Soviet propaganda machine. It was presented as an
indication of the overwhelming approval of electoral platforms sub-
scribed to by the people's representatives and their nominating organizations—the Working People's Leagues. Mass meetings were staged in
Tallinn, Riga, and Kaunas as soon as the "election" results were made
public (July 17). This time, a new note was injected in speakers' pronouncements. As an illustration, the Secretary of the Communist Party
of Estonia, addressing such a meeting in Tallinn, said:

> In giving such a big vote to the candidates of the Estonian Working People's
> League, the Estonian people has expressed its greatest confidence in the
> land of socialism, the Soviet Union, and in the great Stalin, the leader of
> the peoples of the Soviet Union and of the working people of the whole
> world . . . It wishes to live together with the peoples of the Soviet Union,
> under guidance of the great Stalin, a life of peace, freedom, and happiness.
> We see today, here at the meeting, slogans which have been advanced by
> workers. These demand that Estonia should join as a member of the
> Union of Soviet Socialist Republics.[1]

Another high-ranking communist, Secretary of the Central Council
of Estonian Labor Unions, gave an interview to *Pravda* in which he
made the following reference to the "election" results:

> It is completely obvious in the light of the electoral campaign that the
> bourgeois-democratic forms of government no longer hold the trust of the
> masses. No one believes any longer in bourgeois parliamentarism—not even

those interests which would force Estonian workers to believe in it. The masses demand true democracy and a complete reorganization of the governmental apparatus.[2]

In Latvia, posters appeared reading: "We Demand Establishment of Soviet Latvia as the 14th Soviet Republic," and the Secretary of the Latvian Communist Party hastened to give assurance that the people's demands would be met. So did Soviet emissary Vyshinsky who expressed hope that the Latvian People's Diet would "fulfill the wish, cherished for long years by the Latvian people, to create close, indestructible ties of friendship with the Soviet Union and to establish a new life under the Red Labor Flag." [3]

In Lithuania, all of a sudden, speakers began throwing around slogans, such as: "We Demand Introduction of Soviet System"; "Let Us Join the Mighty Socialist Union"; "Long Live Socialist Lithuania"; "We Shall Not Stop Half-way"; "The People's Diet Must Heed the People's Demands"; "The People Demand Assurance of Indestructible Friendship Between Lithuania and Her Best Friend—the USSR"; etc.[4]

The communist-run press invariably presented the speeches and the communist-advocated demands and resolutions as an expression of popular will. *Rahva Haal* had this comment on July 18, following a huge mass rally in Tallinn:

> Demonstrations which took place on July 17 in the entire country, and which in their extent surpassed the great preelection meetings, put forward new political demands—the formation of Workers' Soviets, the transformation of the bourgeois Estonian Republic into an Estonian Soviet Socialist Republic, entry of Estonia into the Union of the Soviet Socialist Republics.[5]

Comments in the Moscow press were exactly the same. It could not be otherwise, since the entire communist press received then, as it does now, its instructions ("the general line") from the same command post. Taking *Pravda* as an example, the July 17 issue, which prominently displayed "election" results for all three Baltic States, had the following to say:

> During the period of preparation for elections throughout the whole of Estonia, from one end to the other, there grew the demand for the attainment of a more elaborate form of accord with the Soviet Union than was made possible by the present mutual assistance pact.

What the paper failed to mention, however, was the fact that the demonstrations provided the Estonians with an opportunity to display their real feelings. An Estonian flag was unfurled at the precise moment when a column was marching past the balcony where Zhdanov and his two guests, Vyshinsky and Dekanozov, were standing and waving at the marchers; a battle between the latter and the police ensued; and only the Red Army assistance could restore order. The same happened on the following day, during a soccer match between the Estonian and Latvian teams. This time Estonian flags appeared everywhere, patriotic songs resounded, and Soviet tanks and armored cars were needed to quiet the crowd down.[6] If a display of a real Estonian attitude toward the hated Soviet puppet government was needed, none better could be found.

With the "elections" over, the stage was set for another act of the Moscow-directed play: "Joining the Glorious Family of The Soviet Union." The plot had been revealed by Molotov to Kreve long before anyone spoke about elections or incorporation. Soviet emissaries in Kaunas, Riga, and Tallin were charged with staging the second act in all of its details. Since no date for the convocation of People's Diets had been set in electoral laws nor announced officially by the time the "election" results became known, this evidently constituted the purpose of the meeting of all three emissaries in Tallinn on July 17.[7]

Nothing has become known of what they talked about, yet the same evening Zhdanov summoned Estonian Prime Minister Vares to tell him that the People's Diet would have to convene on July 21 and pass a resolution requesting admission of Estonia to the Soviet Union. The day before he had merely suggested to Vares that the People's Diet consider joining the Soviet Union. The announcement on July 17 represented quite a change from the previous position.

Evidently this must have been the essence of the agreement reached by the three Soviet emissaries. For it was the next day—July 18—that government decrees were publishd in Tallinn, Riga, and Kaunas. The *New York Times* summed up the situation:

> Obviously at a signal from a higher authority and in preparation for assembly of the newly elected Baltic Parliament, the entire Baltic press today began a campaign for incorporation of the three Baltic States, Lithuania, Latvia, and Estonia, into Soviet Russia.[8]

The meeting of the Soviet emissaries must likewise have decided on the fate of the constitutional heads of both Latvia and Estonia. Both were forced to resign on July 21 and appoint respective Prime Ministers as successors,[9] a repetition of what happened in Lithuania during the first days of Soviet occupation. Their usefulness to the Soviets was over, and they could now be discarded.

Shortly thereafter Estonian President Päts and Latvian President Ulmanis were deported to the Soviet Union. But even here the Soviets could not abstain from low trickery. Thus, Ulmanis was asked by the Soviet Minister in Riga what his preference would be for a place of exile—the Soviet Union or a Western country. The reply was—

Switzerland. Nevertheless, Ulmanis was exiled to the Soviet Union. Hence, only President Smetona of Lithuania succeeded in avoiding deportation and ultimately reaching the free West (he died in Cleveland, Ohio, in 1943).

Seeing that the stage was set for incorporation of Lithuania, one of the People's representatives, Dr. A. Garmus, very popular personally, but inactive politically and definitely not a communist, decided to speak about the future of Lithuania with Dekanozov.[10] In doing so, he acted not only on his own behalf, but also on behalf of a group of similarly thinking representatives. He bluntly asked Dekanozov what were Soviet plans regarding Lithuania and told him there was general concern about her independence. Dekanozov took Dr. Garmus to the window and said:

> You inquire about Lithuania's independence, don't you? But do you see what's going on outside? Do these tanks and these crowds say anything to you? You realize what's going on all over the country, but you dare speak about the independence of Lithuania. You realize that if it is not for those crowds who swept away your independence, these tanks show that Lithuania can no longer be independent . . . These crowds are begging for Lithuania's incorporation into the Soviet Union.

Outside the Soviet Legation where this conversation took place tanks rattled incessantly, and noisy crowds marched by with red flags, banners, and portraits of Soviet leaders. Dr. Garmus realized Dekanozov had already made up a devilish plan—the Lithuanians themselves would have to beg the Soviet Union for incorporation, or in his words, they would have to "dig their grave with their own hands and bury themselves." He let Dekanozov know he and those sharing his views would not vote in favor of incorporation. Dekanozov's reply left no doubt that he would stop at nothing:

> I see. It is too bad I made a mistake in approving of your candidacy when it was submitted to me. It is indeed bad. But you better not try to: there are means to achieve what we want, and we have plenty of such means at our disposal.

Evidently Dekanozov told Kreve about his warning ("I will get that Garmus," Dekanozov said).[11] Kreve in turn cautioned Dr. Garmus to weigh his decision in view of possible ruthless reprisals not only against him, but also against the Lithuanian intelligentsia as a whole.[12]

Kreve's apprehension was fully confirmed shortly thereafter by A. Snieckus, Chief of the Soviet-Lithuanian Police and First Secretary of the Communist Party of Lithuania. He found it necessary to warn the reluctant People's representatives on the eve of the convocation of the Diet. He was quite open-minded in saying that orders had been received from Moscow requesting the Baltic People's Diets to ask the

Supreme Soviet of the USSR to admit their countries as members of the Soviet Union. As the representatives' dissatisfaction became apparent during the briefing, Snieckus added that every representative who dared to vote against the motion would be shot along with all members of his family, and the entire intelligentsia would be subjected to repressions.[13]

H. Kacinskas, a noted dramatic actor, but utterly uninterested in politics, was one of such reluctant People's representatives. He stated subsequently he would not have agreed to vote for incorporation, had he not been forced by terror and deception[14] (he later escaped to the West and came to live in the United States). The use of intimidation was also confirmed collectively by a group of former People's representatives who signed an affidavit to that effect. The affidavit read:

> A number of members of the People's Diet, who were not members of the Communist Party, were compelled by threats to become members and vote for incorporation into the Soviet Union . . . Not a single member of the People's Diet dared express a protest against the use of force, as in view of the circumstances, such protest would have involved danger to his life. Moscow's representative G. Dekanozov and the members of the Soviet Legation openly threatened all those members of the People's Diet and their families who had dared to announce that they would not vote for incorporation into the Soviet Union.[15]

Intimidation was also used in Estonia. Zhdanov threatened Prime Minister Vares he would jail him if he brought up for discussion on the floor a draft resolution by which Estonia would secure for herself extensive self-government patterned after that of Mongolia, yet within the framework of the Soviet Union.[16] There was no need to look for a better case of parliamentary voting under duress.

After having scared into submission both people's representatives and members of the government, Soviet emissaries took care that nothing went wrong at the last minute. Not mentioning strict double and triple checking of all those admitted to the premises where Baltic People's Diets convened on July 21, the premises and the surrounding area were guarded as if for a top secret military conference. In Kaunas, for example, the State Theater was guarded by some 50 Soviet tanks; armed sentries were posted everywhere; plainclothesmen sat among the representatives and guests; and nearly 200 Red Army men hid behind the curtains and under the large table cloth.[17] In Tallinn, Soviet tanks were likewise stationed in front of the Parliament Building; uniformed, heavily armed Soviet troops were everywhere inside and outside the building.[18]

Inside, representatives were not seated as a group. On the contrary, plainclothesmen and reliable communists surrounded each representative's seat on all four sides. As a result, the chair was unable to determine who was a representative and who was not. Counting votes was virtually impossible. But on the other hand, the peculiar seating arrangement provided for a foolproof control of each representative's actions. And it was easy to stop him if he, disregarding all threats, should depart from the assigned role.

There is ample evidence that the entire procedure of voting for adherence to the Soviet Union had been worked out in all its details in Moscow. It was furnished by V. Zalvis, former announcer of Radio Kaunas, who was commissioned to transcribe the July 21 meeting of the Lithuanian People's Diet at the State Theater. He subsequently escaped to Western Europe, carrying prepared speeches, tape recordings, and other similar material.[19] According to Zalvis, not only was the text of main speeches approved by Moscow, but even the order of business and the names of representatives to be nominated to serve on various committees were neatly typed both in Russian and Lithuanian on letterheads of the Soviet Legation to Lithuania.

The failure of a plane to arrive on time from Moscow with the approved text of a speech to be delivered by Minister of Justice P. Pakarklis caused considerable consternation among the organizers of the gathering, including the Soviet Minister in Kaunas. The latter kept running back and forth from the President's box in the State Theater, where Dekanozov was seated, to backstage, where the performers were pushing buttons. The Minister even put through a long distance call to Riga, thinking that the missing paper might have been dispatched there by mistake instead of to Kaunas. To everybody's relief, the okayed text was delivered on the chairman's desk only fifteen minutes late; it was initialed: *V.G.D.* [V. G. Dekanozov].

Other participants at the meeting corroborate V. Zalvis' story. Furthermore, in the State Theater Dr. Garmus found himself repeatedly refused the floor, since the Chairman knew what Dr. Garmus' attitude was toward the whole undertaking.[20] Practically none of the representatives had heard anything about the drafts of laws they were to vote on. The drafts were prepared by the Communist Party, and there was no discussion whatsoever. Dr. Garmus summarized his conclusions on the proceedings at the People's Diet in these words:

> The whole People's Diet was generally a parody of a Diet. Being constituted through terror and deceit, it was only because of terror that it brought to formal implementation the objectives sought by the Bolsheviks. The People's Diet absolutely did not state the will of the people. It could only state the will of a few hundred of Lithuanian communists and their masters in Moscow.

Another representative, L. Dovydenas, under oath told the United States Congressional Committee that the first meeting of a Diet committee to draw up the constitution of the Lithuanian Soviet Socialist Republic, of which he was a member, could not get under way because the draft of the constitution had not been translated in time from the Russian; it was the Soviet Minister in Kaunas who made an announcement to that effect.[21] Dovydenas was also severely reprimanded for his idea of preserving intact the old Lithuanian anthem and flag: "If you fall out of line during the meeting of the People's Diet, you will be declared insane . . . there will be slaughter." [22] Dovydenas' opinion of the role played by the People's Diet was just as low as that of Dr. Garmus':

> Everybody, the blind, the deaf, and the feeble-minded, could become convinced during the first meeting of the People's Diet that the latter was nothing but trickery and deception staged for propaganda purposes and for foreign consumption.[23]

The meeting itself provided Radio Kaunas announcer Zalvis with an intimate view of the workings of a Soviet-type "parliament." The organizers knew beforehand that Zalvis would see many strange happenings and admonished him "not to see many things and not to talk about what he would see." But the announcer could not help wondering when Acting President of the Republic Paleckis informed him as to who would speak when and where, and gave other details that could never be predicted in a democratic parliament. "Our people just cannot agree with our guests from Moscow," Paleckis explained apologetically. "The latter have had much more experience in these things, while we only start to learn."

But for all that, the Soviet Legation in Kaunas was well versed in such things. A former representative, R. Juknevicius, testified that he was summoned to the Legation and handed a slip of paper with instructions as to how he should behave at the third meeting of the People's Diet. When a particular speaker had finished, Juknevicius was told to raise his hand for the purpose of making a motion, which was also prescribed for him in Russian on another slip of paper.[24]

It was simply impossible for Zalvis not to overhear complaints about representatives' speeches not being checked or not being translated from the Russian on time. Representatives kept coming backstage and asking for their okayed speeches, but even here the lack of experience became manifest when one of the representatives was handed the text of his speech in everybody's view while he was walking toward the rostrum. The role of a people's representative seemed to be deprived of any mental strain; he was instructed where to sit, when to speak, what to say, and there existed but a single way to vote—yes.

No one cared about formalities when it actually came to adopt a crucial resolution proclaiming Lithuania a Soviet Republic. As the Chairman asked those in favor to raise hands, Zalvis recalls that "both the representatives and the public raised hands; those sitting in the rear rows raised both." No one cared about counting votes or even announcing whether or not the resolution had been carried. Seventy-nine representatives simply disappeared in a sea of nearly a thousand "guests." This has been attested to not only by Zalvis, but also by several former members of the Lithuanian People's Diet.[25]

The very same procedure was repeated when the adherence of the Lithuanian Soviet Socialist Republic to the Soviet Union was "voted" on. This time even Red Army soldiers present in the theater raised their hands. Somebody on the stage shouted, again without counting "ayes" and "nays," "Passed!", and another "unanimous" decision was put on record. What Molotov had predicted three weeks earlier became a frightening reality. Radio Vilnius and Kaunas discontinued playing the Lithuanian anthem; the yellow-green-red flag was hauled down.

In their joint affidavit, former members of the People's Diet of Lithuania had this to say on the manner of their "election" and "voting";

> When voting on the incorporation into the Soviet Union took place, the votes of members were not counted: together with them voted all strangers present at the meeting . . . It is my sincere belief [former representative H. Kacinskas added] voting or abstaining on my part as well as on the part of other representatives would have produced no effect whatsoever upon the course of events.[26]

Prearrangement of the entire "voting" may also be deduced from the fact, witnessed by Zalvis, that the editors of *Tiesa,* the mouthpiece of the Lithuanian Communist Party, were so sure of the ultimate outcome that they put both "unanimous" resolutions in their paper even before the People's Diet convened. Copies of *Tiesa,* still smelling of printer's ink and featuring minute descriptions of the entire July 21 session, were circulated backstage in the State Theater well before the representatives started "discussing" the matters. Moscow Radio likewise hastened to announce the passage of the law on land nationalization two hours before it happened.[27]

No such extensive evidence is available on the prearrangement of the sessions of the People's Diets either in Latvia or Estonia. Instructions emanating from Moscow must have been the same, however, as one may assume from Snieckus' reference to identical orders sent from Moscow to all three Baltic States. In Tallinn, as in Kaunas, the resolution in favor of incorporation of Estonia into the Soviet Union passed "unanimously" in the open vote, by a simple showing of hands.[28] There was probably no difference in Riga, either.

The Soviet-appointed Baltic People's Diets, being agents of the Soviet Union rather than duly elected parliamentary representatives of the Baltic peoples, could not promulgate binding laws. Moreover, constitutional changes the Baltic People's Diets voted on lay outside their prerogatives, even if they had been elected without violating constitutions in force.

Assuming that the decision to join the Soviet Union was a treaty of federation, none of the Baltic Parliaments, People's or not People's, was empowered to enter into bilateral agreements with foreign states. The constitutions in force expressly stated that this was a prerogative of the government; the only way for the Parliament to express its approval or disapproval of all the treaties the government had concluded remained open in ratification procedure. On the other hand, while the People's Diets, disregarding constitutional provisions, took upon themselves the right to conclude a federation treaty with the Soviet Union, they failed to exercise their unquestionable right of ratification. But the latter, in accordance with international law, was indispensable to put such a treaty in effect.

This alone made null and void the resolutions passed by the Baltic People's Diets and requesting admission of the Baltic Soviet Republics into the Soviet Union on federation principles ("on the same basis as the Ukrainian Soviet Socialist Republic, the Byelorussian Soviet Socialist Republic, and other constituent republics," as the resolution of the Estonian People's Diet, for example, stated). Hence, no binding agreements to this effect between the Baltic States, on the one hand, and the Soviet Union, on the other, could possibly have been concluded. By virtue of international law, their mutual relations are still regulated by unexpired bilateral and multilateral treaties (including peace treaties) concluded before the occupation. The Baltic countries have remained what they had been before their forcible incorporation in the Soviet Union in 1940—sovereign and independent states. Ever since 1940 this has been the general attitude of western democracies, exemplified by their governments and courts.

The legality of the decision to join the Soviet Union taken by the Baltic People's Diets can likewise be questioned on the ground of incompatibility with constitutional provisions in each country. In essence, such decisions amounted to the renunciation of sovereignty, and none of the three constitutions in force permits the Diet to do so.

In Estonia, the Constitution of 1938 provided for two houses of the National Assembly—the Chamber of Deputies and the State Council. A law could take effect only if acted on by both Houses and signed by the President of the Republic. The illegally constituted Estonian People's Diet could only exercise the functions of the Chamber of

Deputees. As for the State Council, its dissolution was declared on June 21 and its formation on July 5; yet neither a new State Council was formed nor the old one called for a joint session with the Chamber of Deputies on July 21–23. Consequently, the People's Diet could not enact laws binding the Estonian people. This was all the more true of the far-reaching constitutional changes which could only be effected through a complex and lengthy procedure (Sections 146–150). Both chambers of the National Assembly could agree only on the wording of the constitutional amendments, whereupon the President of the Republic was bound to call new elections to the Chamber of Deputies and re-constitute the National Council. And only if both chambers of the new National Assembly confirmed the proposed amendments, could the latter be promulgated as a law.

In Lithuania, the Constitution of 1938 expressly stated (Section 1) that sovereignty was inherent in the Lithuanian nation, thus implying that even a legally constituted Diet—not to speak of a puppet People's Diet of 1940—had no right to renounce what belonged to the nation as a whole. To be sure, amendments were possible by a three-fifths majority of the Diet members (Sections 153–154), but renunciation of sovereignty is not an amendment—it is a complete abandonment of the most cherished right of every nation.

In Latvia, the Constitution of 1922 required that any modification of its provisions contained in Sections 1 and 2 (Latvia is an independent democratic republic . . . The sovereign power of the Latvian State is vested in the Latvian people) be submitted to referendum to become valid (Section 77). In this case the question can be raised as to whether or not the decision of the Latvian People's Parliament did modify Sections 1 and 2 of the Constitution in force; that is, whether the principles of independence, democracy, and sovereignty, rigidly anchored in the Constitution, were affected by the decision. The same question equally applies to the constitutional changes in Estonia and Lithuania.

There is no doubt that the adoption of a Soviet model of the Constitution meant a complete abandonment of the above principles. Taking the 1940 Constitution of the Latvian SSR as an example, its Section 2 states that "the political basis of the Latvian SSR are the Soviets of deputies of the working people which have been formed . . . after the establishment of a proletarian dictatorship in Latvia." In other words, the Latvian SSR is a dictatorship—not a democracy. This fundamental change could not be enacted without a referendum, as required by Section 77 of the Constitution in force at the time of such change.

The same holds true of the loss of independence and sovereignty. Section 13 of the Constitution reads: "The Latvian SSR wields its state power independently, retaining its sovereign rights in all their entirety."

Yet this declarative statement is preceded by a qualification: ". . . with the exception of the limitations of Section 14 of the Constitution of the USSR." Limitations, neatly arranged in 23 subdivisions of Section 14, leave practically no field in which a member-republic could exercise its rights independently.

National defense and foreign relations of "independent" Soviet republics were expressly included under Section 14. This alone made their independence a fiction in accordance with the Soviet's own interpretation of an arrangement between Italy and Albania (*Pravda,* April 10, 1939). It is hard to comprehend why the management of national defense matters and foreign relations by Italy in Albania and by the Soviet Union in the Baltic republics should be treated differently.

The merger between the Baltic republics and the Soviet Union entailed further restrictions of their independence and sovereignty so as to make it completely illusory. Pursuing the same example of the Latvian SSR, its 1940 Constitution acknowledged the laws of the Soviet Union as mandatory in Latvia (Section 17); granted equal rights to the citizens of all the other federated republics (Section 18); and accepted the Soviet Union's participation in the management of its agriculture, industry (except that of local significance), forests, commerce, internal affairs, state security, justice, health protection, and state control (Sections 48–49).

Furthermore, although the Constitution stated that "all power in the Latvian SSR belongs to the urban and rural working people vested in the body of the Soviets of deputees of the working people" (Section 3), yet the latter were empowered to adopt decisions and give orders only "within the limits of the rights granted them by the laws of the USSR and the Latvian SSR" (Section 55). People's Commissars of the Latvian SSR could issue decrees and instructions in their jurisdiction and check the execution "in accordance with the laws of the USSR and the Latvian SSR, and with the regulations and orders of the Soviet of People's Commissars of the USSR and the Soviet of People's Commissars of the Latvian SSR, as well as with the decrees and instructions of the federal People's Commissariats of the USSR" (Section 47). The laws of the USSR and the regulations and orders of the Soviet of People's Commissars of the USSR were also mandatory for the legislative and administrative activities of the Soviet of People's Commissars of the Latvian SSR (Section 41), termed by the Constitution "the supreme executive and administrative organ of the Latvian SSR" (Section 39). Thus, the imperial principle of *Reichsrecht bricht das Landesrecht* reduced the notion of sovereignty of the member-republic and its organs to a pure illusion.

Just as illusory is the alleged right to "free secession from the

Union of Soviet Socialist Republics" (Section 15). The so-called Stalin Constitution of the Soviet Union of 1936 assures each member-republic of its "right of free withdrawal from the USSR" (Section 17). However, owing to the fact that no procedure is outlined to make effective use of this right, it is a clear case of *lex imperfecta*. One may, of course, presume that a decision to secede from the Soviet Union, if duly adopted by the Supreme Soviet of the member-republic ("the supreme state authoritative organ," according to Section 20 of the Constitution of the Latvian SSR), ought to be considered representative of popular will as it would amount to a repetition in reverse of what had taken place in 1940. Moscow in 1940 did not question the validity of a decision to join the Soviet Union adopted by the similarly constituted People's Diets. Why should things be different now?

The decision to secede is, however, dependent not on a republic's desire alone, but rather on the Soviet Union's agreement to let it do so. On one occasion during World War II (February 8, 1943), *Pravda* made it clear that the Baltic republics had no right to decide alone whether to remain members of the Soviet Union or withdraw from it. They, the paper claimed, were "parts of the Soviet territory, bound by the country's constitution to the other republics of the Soviet Union." The article received further prominence by being broadcasted over the Moscow and Leningrad radio.

Consequently, an attempt to vote in favor of secession would undoubtedly be regarded as treason. According to the Soviet Constitution, treason is defined as any action injurious to the military might, state independence, or territorial integrity of the USSR (Section 133). Who may doubt that a decision to sever part of the Soviet territory can always be considered injurious to the military might, state independence or territorial integrity of the USSR? Once accused of treason, the "people's deputies" would come under the Soviet Criminal Code which decrees "capital punishment"—death by shooting—for such crimes (Section 58, 1a).

This is, of course, much too hypothetical. First, it would never be possible to bring up for discussion such an idea before the Supreme Soviet of a member-republic in view of prearrangement of debates, as this was revealed in Lithuania in 1940. If someone started speaking in favor of it or distributing leaflets (no paper would ever print anything unwelcome to Moscow), he likewise would face a firing squad by virtue of Section 58 of the Soviet Criminal Code declaring "capital punishment" for similar actions based on exploitation of "religious or national superstitions." Or he could be declared insane and locked up—an obstinate nominee for the People's representatives in Lithuania, L. Dovydenas, was actually subjected to such a threat. Lenin himself, as early as 1922, had serious doubts about the "freedom to withdraw from the Union." He feared it might prove to be "nothing but a scrap of paper, incapable of defending the minorities in Russia from incursions of that 100% Russian, the Great Russian, the chauvinist, in reality, the scoundrel and despoiler which the typical Russian bureaucrat is." [29]

And so, in the final analysis, an independent state joining the Soviet Union in the hope of seceding from it whenever it chooses should think first of Dante's inscription over the gate to Hades: "All hope abandon, ye who enter here!"

Of course, restrictive constitutional provisions would not have been applicable to the decision to join the Soviet Union had a revolution taken place. This was not the case. Attempts were made, on the contrary, to effect the transition from one system of government to the other in strict compliance with constitutional provisions. In Lithuania, even a nonapplicable article of the constitution was involved to appoint a new head of the state, who then was forced to appoint a Soviet-puppet government. The heads of the Latvian and Estonian republics did the same, although under duress, yet in compliance with constitutional provisions. The newly appointed prime ministers swore to uphold the respective constitutions. The fact that the puppet governments paid little attention to the constitution thereafter does not alter the legal situation—they never claimed a revolution had taken place. In fact, a revolution would not have had legal bearing in view of the military occupation of the Baltic States by the Soviet Union at the time the constitutional changes were put into effect and in the presence of Soviet emissaries who directed all affairs.

All these facts make invalid the constitutional changes undertaken in the Baltic States in 1940. They have no binding effect upon the Baltic peoples and other states. This view has found full recognition in western democracies and their courts.[30]

The Soviet government itself was very much concerned about the legality of such profound changes in the life of other countries when changes ran against Soviet interests or where it could pose as a champion of justice in international relations. The note to the German government presented on March 18, 1938, on the occasion of the establishment of the German protectorate over Czechoslovakia may be quoted as an example:

> In signing in Berlin the Act of March 15th, Dr. Hacha, President of Czechoslovakia, had no authority from his people for doing so and acted in manifest contradiction with Art. 64 and 65 of the Czechoslovak Constitution and the will of the people. Consequently, the aforesaid act cannot be considered legally valid.[31]

Yet contradictions with various articles of the Lithuanian, Latvian and Estonian constitutions were in 1940 dismissed as irrelevant by the Soviet government which went ahead with the implementation of incorporation plans in the Baltic States.

The last act was transferred to Moscow. After having heard delegations of the Lithuanian, Latvian, and Estonian "people," who overreached one another in vilifying their own countries, the Supreme Soviet of the USSR "granted the request." Accordingly, Lithuania became the fourteenth; Latvia, the fifteenth, and Estonia, the sixteenth of the Soviet Socialist Republics (August 3, 5, and 6, respectively). In a speech on that occasion, Molotov did not conceal his joy:

> We can note with satisfaction that the peoples of Estonia, Latvia, and Lithuania voted solidly for their representatives who unanimously pronounced in favor of introducing the Soviet system and the incorporation of Lithuania, Latvia, and Estonia in the Union of Soviet Socialist Republics.[32]

What Molotov really wanted to say was that a referendum in favor of Sovietization and a merger with the Soviet Union had actually taken place in the Baltic States and that the people's representatives had in fact received from the electorate an unrestricted (imperative) mandate to do so. Nothing can be farther from truth, however.

First, circumstances under which the "referendum" or "plebiscite" was held were far from being normal by any standards. To quote Sarah Wambaugh, an authority on the subject,

> no plebiscite, even if it is held under an agreement between the two states, can command serious consideration, if it is held under the control of one of them . . . such plebiscite could only be considered valid should the party in control be defeated.[33]

There is no doubt that the 1940 "referendum" in the Baltic States was held under the strict control of the Soviet Union—a party highly interested in the results foretold by a member of its government—Molotov—at the time when no one knew such a "referendum" would be held. The Soviet control locally was exercised through the Moscow emissaries who directed every step of the puppet governments to deprive the Baltic States of every vestige of independence. Their role was sufficiently elucidated by ample testimony given by the people who chanced to meet them in action.

The emissaries were backed by a very strong contingent of Soviet troops and police. According to Soviet admission, issued by *Tass* on June 22, the strength of Soviet troops brought into the Baltic States was estimated at 18 to 20 divisions (200,000 men).[34] Although foreign estimates ran as high as 100 to 150 divisions, even the Soviet's own estimate indicates that purely numerically the invading force was several times stronger than the combined armed forces of all three Baltic States, not to speak of great superiority in armaments. It should also be kept in mind that the *Tass* figure referred to the situation a week after the opening of invasion. As reinforcements continued to pour in, the total strength of Soviet troops by July 14–15 must have grown further. Moreover, the *Tass* figures presumably did not include a strong police contingent which arrived at the same time.

The role played by the Red Army in the matter of Sovietization of the Baltic States was readily acknowledged by the local communist bigwigs, the puppet governments, and the people's Diets. "Aided by the friendly and mighty Workers' and Peasants' Army, Lithuanian laborers, working peasants, and intelligentsia have torn to pieces their slave chains," M. Sumauskas, an ardent communist and President of the Chamber of Labor, stated at a mass meeting in Kaunas on June 24. A telegram to Stalin, which he suggested at the conclusion of the meeting, ended with the most servile expressions of "deepest gratitude for aid in our struggle against the bloody regime." A crudely painted sign held up in front of the speaker's platform read "Hail Our Liberator— the Red Army." [35]

Glorification of, and gratitude to, the Red Army kept pouring in on the bewildered participants in compulsory gatherings, on the readers of the Communist-run press and on the radio listeners. Government members readily joined in it. Taking again Lithuania as an example, People's Minister for Agriculture M. Mickis openly admitted in a public address that "it was Comrade Stalin, leader of all peoples, who gave us victory," he immediately corrected himself, "who helped us to achieve victory." Acting President of the Republic Paleckis excelled everyone else in his expression of servility:

> Unlimited is our gratitude toward those of our friends, Red Army men, whose arrival has opened up the prison gates. All our attempts to achieve liberation by our own forces would hardly have been successful. But today we have attained this goal without difficulty. Thanks to what and to whom? Thanks to the neighbor, the Soviet Union; thanks to the Red Army.

Paleckis' personal gratitude to the Soviet Union for putting him in the saddle in 1940 and keeping him there for an incredibly long time remained truly "unlimited." Writing in 1958—nearly two decades later, with him still as Chairman of the Presidium of the Supreme Council of the Lithuanian SSR—he admitted that the "fascist regime" in Lithuania had been "swept away with the assistance of the sister-Soviet nations." [35a]

It was only a logical conclusion therefrom that the Lithuanian People's Diet could not omit in its resolution on joining the Soviet Union the following paragraph:

Now the people, helped by the mighty Red Army, have overthrown the yoke of enslavers and established at home the Soviet rule . . . If the people have been able to establish in their own country the only just order —the Soviet order—it is all due to the Soviet Union.[36]

Official pronouncements on the role of the Red Army sounded entirely different right after the invasion. "The Red Army came to our country not to change our system of life or to exercise some kind of occupation, but to protect us from the danger of war and to help us maintain our independence," M. Gedvilas, Lithuanian Minister of the Interior, stated a week after the arrival of Soviet troops (June 22).[37] "We should not close our eyes to the fact that the Red Army did not attempt to seize power in Estonia; management of our affairs in Estonia will now and in the future be our own concern," N. Andresen, Estonian Foreign Minister, declared on June 24.[38] "The Red Army is assisting us in the defense of our freedom and the preservation of our state," A. Kirchensteins, Latvian Prime Minister, declared on July 6.[39] Yet the emphasis on noninterference of the Red Army in domestic affairs was completely abandoned after the July 14–15 "elections" and replaced by the expressions of deep gratitude for the interference.

This was only for local consumption. The official line ever since has been to deny completely any part taken by the Red Army in the Baltic States in 1940. To quote the *New Times* (August 12, 1953), aimed at the English-speaking readers:

All the world knows that there was no seizure of Lithuania, Latvia, and Estonia by the Soviet Union . . . They joined it voluntarily; the decision to do so was adopted by their parliaments and wholeheartedly approved by their people in 1940.

The same line of defense has been maintained by the Soviet and their satellite representatives at the United Nations whenever the Soviet Union is attacked for enslavement of the Baltic peoples. The Soviet people are told to believe the following story:

The Baltic toilers overthrew their reactionary Governments and hoisted the Soviet flag. Latvia, Lithuania, and Estonia were declared Soviet republics. They requested the Supreme Soviet of the USSR to admit them into the Soviet Union. The request was granted.[40]

Soviet views on voting held in the presence of foreign troops were emphatic in the first days of their rule in Russia. "If a nation is not given the right to determine the form of its state life by free voting and completely free from the presence of the troops of the annexing or stronger state and without the least pressure," the Bolshevik *Decree on Peace* of November 8, 1917, read, "then the adjoining of that nation by the stronger state is annexation, that is, seizure by force and violence."

Since the Soviets had not abrogated this Decree, there was, even by their own standards, no "free voting" in the Baltic States where the Red Army, representing "the troops of the annexing or stronger state," had remained during the "voting." The same views were strongly reiterated during the peace negotiations at Brest-Litovsk in 1917–1918[41] and on the occasion of the Nazi-held plebiscite in Austria in 1938.[42]

A referendum of the 1940 Soviet "elections" in the Baltic States must also be declared invalid because of concealment of the basic issue. The political platforms of the only admitted lists of candidates in the Baltic States contained no reference whatsoever to the intended conversion of the latter into Soviet republics and their incorporation in the Soviet Union. "Our demands in the field of foreign policy are friendship between the peoples of Estonia and the Soviet Union and a close alliance of the Estonian Republic with the USSR," the election platform of the Estonian Working People's League stated. There was no slightest hint in the long statement that any Sovietization was contemplated in the field of domestic relations either. "Nobody has the right to infringe upon the property rights of the peasants and to force the peasants to join the collective farms," it was stated, for example. "Long live free Estonia!" [43]

The Estonian government categorically denied there was any plebiscite contemplated. In a cable to the Estonian Consul General in New York on the eve of "elections," Foreign Minister N. Andresen gave the following reply to the inquiry whether a plebiscite to join the Soviet Union would be held in Estonia on July 15:

> There is no plebiscite, only elections to the Chamber of Deputees according to the Constitution. Rumors about joining without foundation.[44]

In an earlier (July 1) letter to the Estonian Minister in London, Andresen gave assurance that, in spite of far-reaching changes in domestic policy and social structure now under way, Estonia would remain an independent state whose sovereignty had been guaranteed by the Soviet Union.

The electoral platform of the Union of Working People in Lithuania likewise avoided mentioning any Sovietization or incorporation into the Soviet Union.[45] All it said on the subject of foreign policy was that the nominees would strive to strengthen "the friendship and unshakeable alliance of the Republic of Lithuania and the Soviet Union." No far-reaching changes were announced in the field of domestic policy. The same held true of numerous speeches made by Acting President of the Republic Paleckis, several ministers, and high functionaries of the Communist Party during a huge meeting in Kaunas on July 11.[46] Nearly all speakers found it necessary to express their gratitude to the

Red Army which had "opened prison gates," "liberated," "chased away the ghosts with its tanks," etc.; there were scattered references to the Soviet Union and Stalin; however, no one said a word about changing the social structure in Lithuania or joining the Soviet Union. A few posters such as: "Long Live Stalin's Constitution," "Long Live the 13th Soviet Republic!", and "Long Live the 16th Soviet Republic!", brought along by some enterprising demonstrators, were disregarded as out of line.

The same was repeated on July 13 over the radio: "The Red Army has come here to protect us from enemies, not to enslave us. It brought us peace and tranquility"; "No one intends to force the peasants to join collective farms"; "The people demand assurance of unshakeable friendship between Lithuania and her best friend—the Soviet Union"; "As we continue cooperation with the Soviet Union and its leaders, we will make really big strides toward economic welfare and cultural progress." Speeches were even more freely interspersed with declarations of gratitude to "the friendly Soviet Union," and "the mighty Red Army." [47]

In Latvia, the same travesty prevailed until after the "elections." The electoral platform of the League of Working People was innocuous. So were the comments. Addressing the Latvian people, Prime Minister Kirchensteins said on July 6:

> We are able to give you this ballot so soon only thanks to the friendly support received from our mighty neighbor, the Soviet Union. Let us, therefore, be grateful to the Soviet Union and pledge help to defend her frontiers against the enemy. Once again I salute freedom and independence of the Latvian Republic. We are and will remain free, for we believe in the promises of Stalin, the highest authority of the Soviet Union.[48]

Soviet emissary Vyshinsky likewise spoke in identical terms. Rumors about the impending annexation to the Soviet Union were vigorously denied by other government officials attributing such rumors to the "enemies of the people."

All these statements clearly indicate that the pre-"election" campaign carefully avoided any reference to the eventuality of Sovietization of the Baltic States and their incorporation into the Soviet Union. How can one, under such conditions, speak of a referendum in favor of Sovietization and incorporation, if the people, who were virtually driven to the polls, were not told about the basic issues involved and the issues were deliberately concealed, or misrepresented? And how can one speak of international legality of a referendum held in the presence of huge masses of troops and police of a foreign power in favor of which the referendum was decided? If the Soviets denounced a referendum held in Austria in 1938 under the exactly same conditions as in the Baltic States in 1940, they have to agree that the Austrian people were at least told what the basic issue was.

It is just as deceptive to claim that the alleged enthusiastic participation of the electorate in the "elections" was tantamount to granting the so-called imperative mandate, i.e., a blank check, to their representatives. For hardly anyone could be expected to grant such far-reaching authority to representatives imposed on him, in full awareness, by the Communist Party. The Communist Party in turn could not claim to represent the people because of its extremely small popularity among the Baltic peoples. Thus, in Lithuania, a nation of about 3 million people, there were, at the time of Soviet invasion, less than 1500 registered communists; the majority of them were ethnically non-Lithuanians (mostly Jews and Russians).[49] Neither could the Baltic peoples give an imperative mandate to representatives, most of whom—workers, farmers, soldiers, craftsmen, school teachers, and the like—were totally unknown politically and unheard of by anyone beyond the confines of their narrow local communities.

Finally, the referendum argument is invalid for the simple reason that its results were precisely the same as spelled out in Soviet-German agreements in the fall of 1939 (particularly Molotov's confirmation of the Soviet intent to occupy Lithuania, dated October 8th)[50] and as foretold by Molotov to Kreve several weeks before the alleged referendum took place. Only if the results of the referendum held in the presence of foreign troops run against the wishes of the occupying power can such a referendum be regarded as valid.[51]

Molotov, in his recommendation of the approval of the so-called petition of the Baltic Soviet Socialist Republics for admission, made at the Seventh Session of the Supreme Soviet of the USSR on August 1, 1940, conveniently forgot that only a year prior to the occupation of the Baltic States the Soviet press was extremely scornful of the occupation of Albania by Italy.

Reporting on the invasion of Albania in 1939, *Pravda* (April 8 through 14) used terms such as: "A New Act of Aggression"; "Ciano is Forming a Puppet Government in Tirana"; etc. The paper spoke disdainfully of the Italian-controlled "Albanian Provisional Administrative Council," "Constituent Assembly," "delegates," "acceptance" of the Albanian crown by the King of Italy, etc. (invariably in quotation marks). It ridiculed Italian reasons for the occupation of Albania and gleefully reported the refusal of Albanian legations abroad to recognize the Italian occupation. The fact that the new Albanian government was to have neither foreign nor defense ministries was interpreted as indicative of its complete dependence on Italy.

But if Molotov had taken a closer look at the events in Albania in 1939 and in the Baltic States in 1940, he would have found no difference whatsoever between the Soviet and the Italian actions and the subsequent clumsy attempts at legalization of a brutal occupation by force. The Soviet government was also highly critical of the Italian attitude toward Ethiopia; it even attempted to impose its views upon the League of Nations. This may be seen from an address made by People's Commissar of Foreign Affairs M. Litvinov on May 12, 1938:

> It must be made clear that the League of Nations has no intention of changing its attitude whether to the direct seizure and annexation of other people's territory, or to those cases where such annexations are camouflaged by setting up of puppet "National" Governments, allegedly independent, but in reality serving merely as a screen for, and an agency of, the foreign invader.[52]

Molotov could also have taken a look at the Soviet attitude toward the occupation of Austria by Germany ("armed invasion and forcible deprivation of the Austrian people of their political, economic, and cultural independence . . . violence perpetrated in the center of Europe"),[53] as well as toward the occupation of Czechoslovakia (both in 1938). In this latter case, the Soviet government dispatched a note to the German government on March 18, the contents of which so strikingly applied to the loss of independence by the Baltic peoples two and a half years later:

> It is hard to admit that any people will voluntarily declare themselves in agreement with the destruction of their independence and with their incorporation into the body of another state; much less such a people who for centuries have fought for their independence and already for twenty years have preserved their independent existence.[54]

It is indeed hard to admit that the Baltic peoples could have felt differently. The United States Department of State evidently entertained the same views when it, on July 23, 1940, issued the much-quoted statement on the impending incorporation of the Baltic States into the Soviet Union:

> During these past few days the devious processes whereunder the political independence and territorial integrity of the three small Baltic Republics— Estonia, Latvia, and Lithuania—were to be deliberately annihilated by one of their more powerful neighbors, have been rapidly drawing to their conclusion . . . The policy of the government is universally known. The people of the United States are opposed to predatory activities no matter whether they are carried on by the use of force or by the threat of force. They are likewise opposed to any form of intervention on the part of one state, however powerful, in the domestic concerns of any other sovereign state, however weak . . . The United States will continue to stand by

these principles, because of the conviction of the American people that unless the doctrine in which these principles are inherent once again governs the relations between nations, the rule of reason, of justice, and of law—in other words, the basis of modern civilization itself—cannot be preserved.[55]

The United States kept its word even in World War II, when the Soviet Union—an ally!—felt entitled to demand acknowledgment of its claims to the Baltic peoples and their land. The attitude of the United States undoubtedly served as an example to other democracies which have steadfastly refused to accept the Soviet-intimated finality of the fate of the Baltic peoples.

A continuous adherence of the United States to the high principles expressed in the above statement represents the only hope sustaining the Lithuanians, the Latvians, and the Estonians in their unrelenting resistance to national oppression and in their burning desire to regain the independence which they enjoyed from 1918 to 1940.

1) Frank A. Golder, *Documents of Russian History, 1914–1917* (New York /London, 1927), p. 307.
2) *Ibid.,* pp. 308–309.
3) *Ibid.,* pp. 311–313.
4) *Ibid.,* p. 329.
5) *Ibid.,* p. 330.
6) *Ibid.,* p. 354.
7) *Ibid.,* p. 561.
8) *Ibid.,* p. 369.
9) *Ibid.,* p. 646.
10) *Select Committee on Communist Aggression. Investigation of Communist Takeover and Occupation of the Non-Russian Nations of the U.S.S.R.* (hereafter *Select Committee on Communist Aggression*). House of Representatives, 83rd Congress, 2nd Session (Washington, 1954), III, 12–18.
11) *Eesti Vabadussoda 1918–1920* (2 vols., n.p., 1948–1951), I, 27–28.
12) August Rei, *Nazi-Soviet Conspiracy and the Baltic States: Diplomatic Documents and Other Evidence* (London, 1948), pp. 20–21.
13) Alfred Bilmanis, *Latvian-Russian Relations: Documents* (Washington, 1944), pp. 39–42; *Select Committee on Communist Aggression,* III, 50.
14) M. Walters, *Lettland: seine Entwicklung zum Staat und die Baltischen Fragen* (Rome, 1923), pp. 340–341.
15) Petras Klimas, *Le développement de l'Etat Lithuanien* (Paris, 1919), p. 142; *Select Committee on Communist Aggression,* III, 78–79; T. Norus and J. Zilius, *Lithuania's Case for Independence* (Washington, 1918), pp. 76–80; *Russian Poland, Lithuania and White Russia.* Handbooks prepared under the direction of the Historical Section of the Foreign Office, No. 44 (London, 1920), p. 141; Antanas Jusaitis, *The History of the Lithuanian Nation and Its Present National Aspirations* (Philadelphia, 1919), pp. 173–174; Vaizgantas, *Rastai* (Kaunas, vrs. yrs.), XVI, 212.
16) *Leninskii sbornik* (Moscow/Leningrad, 1924 ff.), II, 42–50 (par. 7, p. 46).
17) *Ibid.,* p. 144.
18) *Ibid.,* pp. 153–160 (par. 9 substituted for par. 7).
19) *Ibid.,* pp. 161–170.
20) V. I. Lenin, *Sochineniia,* 4th ed. (36 vols., Moscow/Leningrad, 1941–1951), VI, 294.
21) *Ibid.,* VIII, 531.
22) *Vsesoiuznaia Kommunisticheskaia partiia (b) v rezoliutsiiakh i resheniiakh s''ezdov, konferentsii i plenumov TsK (1898–1932).* Part I: 1898–1924 (hereafter *VKP (b) v rezoliutsiiakh).* (Moscow, 1933), p. 121.
23) Lenin, *op. cit.,* XVIX, 213–221.
24) *Ibid.,* pp. 30, 386.
25) *Ibid.,* p. 92.
26) *Ibid.,* p. 213; XX, 365–424; XXII, 135.
27) *Ibid.,* XX, 365–424.
28) *Ibid.,* p. 4.
29) *Ibid.,* pp. 265, 286–287.
30) Leon Trotsky, *The Real Situation in Russia* (London, n.d.), pp. 297–298; Bertram D. Wolfe, *Khrushchev's and Stalin's Ghost* (New York, 1957), pp. 271–279.
31) Lenin, *op. cit.,* XXIII, 1–9, 16–64.
32) *Ibid.,* XXII, 132–145, 153; XXIII, 77–78.
33) *VKP(b) v rezoliutsiiakh,* p. 733.

34) Lenin, *op. cit.*, XXII, 132–145.
35) *Ibid.*, pp. 306–344.
36) *Ibid.*, XXI, 86, 265.
37) *Ibid.*, XXIV, 51, 267.
38) *Ibid.*, XXII, 314.
39) *Ibid.*, p. 177.
40) *Ibid.*, XXIV, 16.
41) *Ibid.*, p. 231.
42) *Ibid.*, pp. 16–17.
43) Bilmanis, *op. cit.*, p. 33.
44) Constantine R. Jurgela, *History of the Lithuanian Nation* (New York, 1948), p. 352.
45) *Naujienos*, April 16, 1957.
46) I. V. Stalin, *Sochineniia* (13 vols., Moscow, 1946–1951), II, 310–311, 360.
47) *Ibid.*, III, 51.
48) *Ibid.*, IV, 3.
49) Edward Hallet Carr, *The Bolshevik Revolution 1917-1923* (3 vols., London, 1950–1953), I, 417.
50) *VKP(b) v rezoliutsiiakh*, p. 22.
51) *Ibid.*, p. 121.
52) *Ibid.*, p. 201.
53) *Ibid.*, pp. 239–240.
54) *Ibid.*, p. 271.
55) Lenin, *op. cit.*, XXIV, 435.
56) *Ibid.*, p. 320.
57) *VKP(b) v rezoliutsiiakh*, p. 280.
58) *Ibid.*, p. 308.
59) *Ibid.*, p. 312.
60) *Ibid.*, pp. 314–315.
61) James Bunyan and H. H. Fisher, *The Bolshevik Revolution 1917–1918. Documents and Materials* (Stanford/ London, 1934), pp. 121–122.
62) *Ibid.*, p. 125.
63) *Pravda*, November 16, 1917.
64) *Soviet Documents on Foreign Policy;* Jane Degras, ed. (3 vols. London/New York/Toronto, 1951–1953), I, 4.
65) *Ibid.*, pp. 9–10.
66) *Ibid.*, p. 4.
67) *Ibid.*, pp. 11–12.
68) A. Ioffe (ed.), *Mirnye peregovory v Brest-Litovske* (Moscow, 1920), pp. 6–8.
69) *Ibid.*, pp. 28–29.
70) *Ibid.*, pp. 29–30.
71) *Ibid.*, p. 44 ff.
72) V. Bartuska, *Lietuvos nepriklausomybes kryziaus kelias* (Klaipeda, 1937), p. 211.
73) Ioffe, *op. cit.*, 255–258
74) *Ibid.*, p. 31.
75) *Ibid.*, p. 203.
76) *Ibid.*, p. 77.
77) *Ibid.*, p. 92.
78) Bilmanis, *op. cit.*, pp. 44–49.
79) *Soviet Documents on Foreign Policy*, I, 98.
80) *Ibid.*, p. 129.
81) *League of Nations, Treaty Series*, XI, 30, No. 289.
82) *Ibid.*, III/2, 106, No. 94.
83) *Ibid.*, II/3, 196, No. 67.
84) *Pravda*, August 2, 1940.
85) Lenin, *op. cit.*, XXVI, 408.
86) Leon Trotsky, *My Life* (New York, 1930), p. 383.
87) Ioffe, *op. cit.*, p. 179.

NOTES TO CHAPTER 2

1) Ioffe, *op. cit.*, pp. 94–95.
2) *Ibid.*, pp. 151–155.
3) *Papers Relating to the Foreign Relations of the United States* (hereafter *Foreign Relations of the United States*); *1918, Russia* (3 vols., Washington, 1931), I, 420.
4) Lenin, *op. cit.*, VI, 412, 414.
5) *VKP(b) rezoliutsiiakh*, p. 239.
6) Lenin, *op. cit.*, XIX, 453, 476, 492.
7) *Ibid.*, XX, 92, 202.
8) *Ibid.*, XXII, 331–332; XXIV, 52; XXVI, 149.
9) V. A. Maklakov, *Vlast' i obshchestvennost' na zakate staroi Rossii. Vospominaniia sovremennika* (n.p., n.d.), p. 226.
10) *VKP(b) v rezoliutsiiakh*, p. 273.
11) Lenin, *op. cit.*, XXII, 136–137.
12) *Ibid.*, p. 135; XXIV, 52, 62.
13) *Ibid.*, XXIV, 267.
14) Stalin, *op. cit.*, III, 16–19, 53, 208; IV, 31–32.
15) *Ibid.*, III, 52, 208.
16) *Ibid.*, p. 52.
17) *VKP(b) v rezoliutsiiakh*, pp. 271–272.
18) *Ibid.*, p. 288.
19) Bunyan and Fisher, *op. cit.*, pp. 282–283.
20) *Ibid.*, p. 397.
21) *Ibid.*, pp. 394–396.
22) Stalin, *op. cit.*, IV, 168–170, 177–185.
23) E. I. Pesikina, *Narodnyi komissariat po delam natsional'nostei i ego deiatel'nost' v 1917–1918 g.g.* (Moscow, 1950), pp. 32–33.
24) Bunyan and Fisher, *op. cit.*, p. 394.
25) Lenin, *op. cit.*, XXIII, 56.
26) *Ibid.*, XXIV, 265.
27) *Select Committee on Communist*

Aggression, III, 16–31; Rei, *op. cit.,* pp. 20–26; Hampden J. Jackson, *Estonia* (London, 1941), pp. 127–134; Stanley W. Page, "Lenin, the National Question and the Baltic States, 1917–1919," *The American Slavic and East European Review,* VII, No. 1 (1948), 20–26.
28) S. Chudenok, "Iz vospominanii ob Oktiabr'skoi revoliutsii v Estliandii," *Proletarskaia revoliutsiia,* X (1927);

quoted by Page, *op. cit.,* pp. 20–21.
29) *Select Committee on Communist Aggression,* III, 386.
30) *Izvestiia,* January 25, 1918.
31) *Ibid.,* February 14, 1918.
32) Lenin, *op. cit.,* XIX, 491.
33) *Eesti Vabadussoda,* I, 39.
34) *Select Committee on Communist Aggression,* III, 386–387.
35) Walters, *op. cit.,* p. 341.

NOTES TO CHAPTER 3

1) Bilmanis, *op. cit.,* pp. 44–48; *Foreign Relations of the United States, 1918, Russia,* II, 442 ff.
2) Ioffe, *op. cit.,* pp. 229–231.
3) Lenin, *op. cit.,* XXVII, 157, 159, 163.
4) Bilmanis, *op. cit.,* pp. 51–56.
5) Pesikina, *op. cit.,* pp. 18–19; S. I. Iakubovskaia, "K voprosu ob obrazovanii SSSR," *Voprosy istorii,* No. 1 (1947), 55–61; R. Sarmaitis, *Amerikos-Anglijos imperialistu intervencija Lietuvoje 1918–1920* (Vilnius, 1955), pp. 31–32.
6) Z. Angarietis, "Ar viskas taip buvo?", *Komunaras,* No. 6 (1922), p. 167.
7) P. Ruseckas, "Kaip augo ir stiprejo musu kariuomene," in *Kareivis Lietuvos Gynejas* (Kaunas, 1926), p. 20.
8) *Izvestiia,* April 27, 1918.
9) Pesikina, *op. cit.,* p. 74.
10) *Soviet Documents on Foreign Policy,* I, 124–125.
11) *Izvestiia,* December 13, 1918.
12) *Politika Sovetskoi vlasti po natsional'nomu voprosu za tri goda: 1917–XI–1920* (n.p., 1920), pp. 134–135.
13) *Soviet Documents on Foreign Policy,* I, 126–127; *Mezhdunarodnaia politika noveishego vremeni v dogovorakh, notakh i deklaratsiiakh;* Yu. V. Kliuchnikov and A. Sabanin, eds. (hereafter *Mezhdunarodnaia politika*) (4 vols., Moskva, 1925–1929), II, 206–207.
14) Pesikina, *op. cit.,* p. 91.
15) *Izvestiia,* December 10, 1918.
16) *H. Lauterpacht, Recognition in International Law* (Cambridge, 1947), p. 95.
17) *League of Nations Official Journal,* 1937, Special Supplement, No. 175, p. 63.
18) Stalin, *op. cit.,* IV, 184.
19) Sarmaitis, *op. cit.,* pp. 17–18; A. Snieckus, "Vincas Mickevicius-Kapsukas—izymus Lietuvos revoliucinio

judejimo veikejas," *Komunistas,* No. 4 (1955), 25.
20) *Izvestiia,* December 24, 1918.
21) *Ibid.,* December 22, 1918.
22) Cf. map, p. 14.
23) Sarmaitis, *op. cit.,* p. 16.
24) *Komunistas,* 1919, Nos. 1–3 & 22.
25) V. Kapsukas, "Sovietu valdzia Lietuvos sodziuj 1919 m.," *Komunaras,* No. 5 (1922), 136–137.
26) V. Mitskevich-Kapsukas, "Revoliutsiia v Litve (1918) i sozdanie vremennogo rabochekrest'ianskogo pravitel'stva," *Istorik Marksist,* No. 2/3 (1935), p. 44.
27) *Select Committee on Communist Aggression,* III, 440; *Mezhdunarodnaia politika,* II, 208.
28) Iakubovskaia, *op. cit.,* p. 14.
29) *Select Committee on Communist Aggression,* III, 440–442.
30) Vaizgantas, *op. cit.,* IV, 236–237.
31) *Istorik Marksist,* No. 2–3 (1935), p. 46.
32) Z. Angarietis, "Litva i Oktiabr'skaia revoliutsiia," *Zhizn' natsional'nostei,* No. 1 (1923), 219.
33) *Komunistas,* 1919, No. 2.
34) Angarietis, *op. cit.,* p. 219.
35) *Komunistas,* 1919, No. 31.
36) *VKP(b) v rezoliutsiiakh,* I, 354.
37) Germantas, *Der Kommunismus—das Unglück der Menschheit* (Berlin, 1938), p. 3.
38) *Izvestiia,* December 24, 1918.
39) Iakubovskaia, *op. cit.,* p. 19.
40) *Ibid.,* p. 14.
41) *Soviet Documents on Foreign Policy,* I, 129.
42) *Ibid.,* pp. 124–125.
43) Iakubovskaia, *op. cit.,* p. 15; and *Ob"edinitel'noe dvizhenie za obrazovanie SSSR* (Moscow, 1947), p. 57.
44) *Politika Sovetskoi vlasti po natsional'nomu voprosu za tri goda: 1917–XI–1920,* p. 54.
45) *Ibid.,* p. 69.

46) *Pravda*, January 16, 1919; *Komunistas*, 1919, No. 2.

47) S. I. Iakubovskaia, "K voprosu ob obrazovanii SSSR," p. 14.

48) *Sovetskaia Litva*, July 19, 1952.

49) *Pravda*, August 30, 1957.

50) *League of Nations Official Journal*, *loc. cit.*, p. 63.

51) Stalin, *op. cit.*, IV, 183.

52) A. Golubev, *Grazhdanskaia voina 1918–1920 g.g.* (Molodaia Gvardiia, 1932), pp. 151–161.

53) Iakubovskaia, *op. cit.*, pp. 16–17.

54) *Politika Sovetskoi vlasti po natsional'nomu voprosu za tri goda: 1917–XI–1920*, p. 163.

55) Pesikina, *op. cit.*, pp. 78–79; A. A. Tille, "Obrazovanie Latviiskoi Sovetskoi Sotsialisticheskoi Respubliki —akt suverennoi voli latyshskogo naroda," *Sovetskoe gosudarstvo i pravo*, No. 4 (1955), p. 19.

56) *Grazhdanskaia voina 1918–1921* (A. S. Bubnov, S. S. Kamenev, M. N. Tukhachevskii, and R. P. Eideman, eds.). Vol. III: *Operativno-strategicheskii ocherk boevykh deistvii Krasnoi Armii* (hereafter *Grazhdanskaia voina 1918–1921*) (Moscow/Leningrad, 1930), p. 60.

57) *Politika Sovetskoi vlasti po natsional'nomu voprosu za tri goda: 1917–XI–1920*, p. 175.

58) Rei, *op. cit.*, pp. 25–26.

59) Golubev, *op. cit.*, p. 156; *Grazhdanskaia voina 1918–1921*, p. 58.

60) Iakubovskaia, *op. cit.*, pp. 15–16.

61) *Leninskii sbornik*, XXXIV, 170.

62) Stalin, *op. cit.*, IV, 168–170.

63) Rei, *op. cit.*, p. 25.

64) Kapsukas, *op. cit.*, p. 136; Angarietis, *op. cit.*, p. 168.

65) Rei, *op. cit.*, p. 25.

66) *Ibid.*, pp. 25–26.

67) Cf. the map, p. 14.

68) Iakubovskaia, *op. cit.*, p. 15; *Politika Sovetskoi vlasti po natsional'nomu voprosu za tri goda: 1917–XI–1920*, pp. 55–57; Page, *op. cit.*, pp. 26–30.

69) *Komunistas*, 1919, No. 14.

70) Iakubovskaia, *op. cit.*, p. 9.

71) *Izvestiia*, February 22, 1919.

72) *Ibid.*, February 16, 1919.

73) *Komunistas*, 1919, Nos. 23 & 32.

74) Iakubovskaia, *Ob"edinitel'noe dvizhenie za obrazovanie SSSR*, p. 52.

75) Iakubovskaia, *K voprosu ob obrazovanii SSSR*, pp. 18–23; Mezhdunarodnaia politika, II, 253–254.

76) *VKP(b) v rezoliutsiiakh*, pp. 331–332.

77) *Izvestiia*, January 8, 1919.

78) *Politika Sovetskoi vlasti po natsional'nomu voprosu za tri goda: 1917–XI–1920*, p. 133.

79) Lenin, *op. cit.*, XXVIII, 205.

80) Kapsukas, *op. cit.*, p. 138.

81) Angarietis, *op. cit.*, p. 167.

82) K. A. Baginian, "K voprosu ob opredelenii agressii," *Sovetskoe gosudarstvo i pravo*, No. 1 (1955), p. 63.

83) Golubev, *op. cit.*, pp. 152–157; Sarmaitis, *op. cit.*, p. 35.

84) *Grazhdanskaia voina 1918–1921*, pp. 60–61.

85) R. Mikker, "Bor'ba za Sovetskuiu vlast' v 1917–1919 g.," *Istoricheskii zhurnal*, No. 11 (1940), p. 55.

86) P. Dauge, "Oktiabr'skaia revoliutsiia v Latvii," *Istoricheskii zhurnal*, No. 11 (1940), pp. 42–43.

87) Sarmaitis, *op. cit.*, p. 33; Snieckus, *op. cit.*, p. 26; Kapsukas, *op. cit.*, pp. 138–140; Angarietis, *op. cit.*, pp. 167–169; *Izvestiia*, January 15 and May 3, 5, 8, 1919.

88) Kapsukas, *op. cit.*, pp. 136–140; Angarietis, *op. cit.*, pp. 166–169.

89) Angarietis, *op. cit.*, p. 168.

NOTES TO CHAPTER 4

1) B. E. Shtein, *Russkii vopros na parizhskoi mirnoi konferentsii, 1919–1920 gg.* (Moscow, 1949), pp. 265–266; V. P. Potemkin, ed., *Istoriia diplomatii* (3 vols., Moscow/Leningrad, 1941–1945), III, 70–73; *Vestnik Narodnogo Kommissariata Inostrannykh Del R.S.F.S.R.*, No. 3 (1920), pp. 1–6; *Mezhdunarodnaia politika*, II, 344–346, 387–390, 392–394, 424–425.

2) *Soviet Documents on Foreign Policy*, I, 167–168.

3) *Ibid.*, p. 169.

4) *The Estonian Review*, I, 161–162; quoted by Malbone W. Graham, *New Governments of Eastern Europe* (New York, 1927), pp. 673–675.

5) Malbone W. Graham, *The Diplomatic Recognition of the Border States. Part III: Latvia.* (Berkeley, 1941), pp. 434, 511 n. 1.

6) Malbone W. Graham, *The Diplomatic Recognition of the Border States. Part II: Estonia* (Berkeley, 1939), p. 282.

7) Shtein, *op. cit.*, pp. 272–273.

8) *Soviet Documents on Foreign Policy*, I, 171–175.
9) *Papers Relating to the Foreign Relations of the United States, 1919, Russia* (Washington, 1937), p. 710; *Vestnik Narodnogo Kommissariata Inostrannykh Del R.S.F.S.R.*, No. 3 (1920), pp. 3–4, and No. 1–2 (1921), p. 11.
10) *League of Nations, Treaty Series*, XI, 30, No. 289.
11) *Izvestiia*, February 5, 1920.
12) Lenin, *op. cit.*, XXX, 279.
13) *Ibid.*, pp. 320, 350.
14) *Ibid.*, pp. 292–302.
15) A. I. Denikin, *Ocherki Russkoi smuty* (5 vols., Paris-Berlin, 1922–1926), IV, 26.
16) *Izvestiia*, February 4, 1920.
17) *Ibid.*, February 8, 1920.
18) *League of Nations, Treaty Series*, III/2, 106, No. 94.
19) *Ibid.*, II/3, 196, No. 67.
20) *Izvestiia*, August 8, 1920.
21) Lenin, *op. cit.*, XXX, 363.
22) *Vestnik Narodnogo Kommissariata Inostrannykh Del R.S.F.S.R.*, No. 3 (1920), p. 1.
23) *Ibid.*, No. 1–2 (1921), p. 11.
24) *Leninskii sbornik*, XXIV, 197.
25) *Foreign Relations of the United States, 1919, Russia*, pp. 710–711, 742–743.
26) *Izvestiia*, January 28, 1920.
27) Lenin, *op. cit.*, XXVII, 90.
28) *Ibid.*, XVII, 334.
29) Arved Berg, *Latvia and Russia* (London/Toronto, 1920), p. 30.
30) *Naujienos*, April 16, 1957.
31) *Gosudarstvennoe soveshchanie* (Moscow/Leningrad, 1930), p. 12.
32) *Revoliutsiia 1917 goda: Kronika sobytii*, I (Moscow /Leningrad, 1923), p. 100.
33) *Gosudarstvennoe soveshchanie*, p. 5.
34) Isaac Deutscher, *Stalin: A Political Biography* (London/New York, 1949), p. 243 n. 1.
35) *Denikin, op. cit.*, V, 139.
36) *Izvestiia*, July 15, 1920.
36a) League of Nations, *Official Journal, Special Supplement No. 4: Documents Concerning the Dispute Between Poland and Lithuania* (Geneva, 1920).
37) Petras Maciulis, "Lietuvos ir Sovietu Sajungos santykiu raida istorijos sviesoje," *Tevynes Sargas*, No. 4 (1948), p. 280; *Vestnik Narodnogo Kommissariata Inostrannykh Del R.S.F.S.R.*, No. 8 (1920), pp. 132–133.
38) Cf. T. A. Taracoucio, *War in Soviet Diplomacy* (New York, 1940), 280–281.
39) Petras Maciulis, "Sovietu Sajungos smurtas pries Lietuva," *Draugas*, June 10, 1950.
40) *League of Nations, Treaty Series*, VI, 52, No. 149.
41) *Soviet Documents on Foreign Policy*, I, 379–381.
42) *Conférence de Moscou Pour la Limitation des Armaments* (Moscow, 1923), p. 100.
43) *Soviet Documents on Foreign Policy*, I, 371–372, 381–383.
44) *League of Nations, Treaty Series*, LX, 145, No. 1410.
45) L. Fischer, The Soviets in World Affairs (2 vols., Princeton, 1951), II, 717–718.
46) *Soviet Documents on Foreign Policy*, II, 282–283.
47) James T. Shotwell and Max Laserson, *Poland and Russia, 1919–1945* (New York, 1945), p. 51.
48) *Soviet Documents on Foreign Policy*, I, 283–287.
49) *League of Nations, Treaty Series*, XI, 168, No. 296.
50) Potemkin, *op. cit.*, III, 158–166.
51) *Conférence de Moscou*, pp. 239–241.
52) *Soviet Documents on Foreign Policy*, I, 301–303.
53) *Ibid.*, pp. 303–304.
54) *Ibid.*, p. 300.
55) *Ibid.*, pp. 318–319.
56) Potemkin, *op. cit.*, III, 166.
57) *Conférence de Moscou*, pp. 5–25.
58) *Ibid.*, pp. 46–238.
59) *Ibid.*, pp. 125–127.

NOTES TO CHAPTER 5

1) *Soviet Documents on Foreign Policy*, I, 421; *Godovoi otchet za 1923 g. Narodnogo Kommissariata Inostrannykh Del SSSR*, pp. 59–60.
2) *Soviet Documents on Foreign Policy*, I, 417; *Godovoi otchet za 1924 g. Narodnogo Kommissariata Inostrannykh Del SSSR*, p. 74.
3) *Soviet Documents on Foreign Policy*, I, 358–359, 377–383, 417, 429–430.
4) *League of Nations, Treaty Series*, XXIII, 82, No. 578.
5) *Soviet Documents on Foreign Policy*, I, 421.
6) Bilmanis, *op. cit.*, p. 17; Georg

von Rauch, "Die baltischen Staaten und Sowjetrussland," *Europa-Archiv*, Nos. 17, 20, 22 (1954), p. 6862; K. V. Ozols, *Memuary poslannika* (Paris, 1938), p. 163.

7) Rauch, *op. cit.*, pp. 6863–6864; Jackson, *op. cit.*, pp. 181–182; Ruth Fisher, *Stalin and German Communism* (Cambridge, 1948), p. 463. The Soviet version: *Godovoi otchet za 1924 g. Narodnogo Kommissariata Inostrannykh Del SSSR*, pp. 92–93.

8) *Soviet Documents on Foreign Policy*, II, 49; *Izvestiia*, January 3, 1926.

9) *Draugas*, January 12, 1957.

10) *Naujienos*, January 17, 1957.

11) K. Bilevicius, "Is revoliucinio pogrindzio," *Pergale*, Nos. 10–11 (1956), pp. 70, 73.

12) *Naujienos*, January 17, 1957.

13) *League of Nations, Treaty Series*, XXXVIII, 357, No. 991.

14) Fischer, *op. cit.*, II, 518; *Godovoi otchet za 1924 g. Narodnogo Kommissariata Inostrannykh Del SSSR*, pp. 73–74.

15) *Soviet Documents on Foreign Policy*, I, 467.

16) Fischer, *op. cit.*, II, 519.

17) *Soviet Documents on Foreign Policy*, II, 32–33.

18) *Ibid.*, I, 467.

19) *Ibid.*, p. 421.

20) Jackson, *op. cit.*, p. 219; Ozols, *op. cit.*, pp. 180–189.

21) *Pravda*, December 29, 1925; *Deutsche Allgemeine Zeitung*, December 30, 1925.

22) *Soviet Documents on Foreign Policy*, II, 112.

23) *Izvestiia*, December 12, 1926.

24) *Soviet Documents on Foreign Policy*, II, 190–191.

25) *League of Nations, Treaty Series*, LX, 145, No. 1410.

26) *Soviet Documents on Foreign Policy*, II, 145.

27) *Select Committee on Communist Aggression*, III, 318–332.

28) Fischer, *op. cit.*, II, 718.

29) *Soviet Documents on Foreign Policy*, II, 113.

30) *Ibid.*, pp. 135–136.

31) *Izvestiia*, October 8, 1926.

32) *Ibid.*, October 13, 1926.

33) *Ibid.*, September 29, 1926.

34) *Soviet Documents on Foreign Policy*, II, 142–143.

35) Jonas Budrys, "Generolas Klescinskis—Maskvos snipas," *Dirva*, Nos. 6–9 (1957); *New York Times*, May 25, 1927.

36) Fischer, *op. cit.*, II, 726.

37) Alfred Bilmanis, *A History of Latvia* (Princeton, 1951), p. 384.

38) *League of Nations, Treaty Series*, LIV, 155, No. 1283.

39) *Ibid.*, CXXII, 349, No. 1648.

40) *Soviet Documents on Foreign Policy*, II, 217–221, 339–340.

41) *Ibid.*, II, 355.

42) *Izvestiia*, August 28, 1928.

43) *Soviet Documents on Foreign Policy*, II, 335–339.

44) *Ibid.*, p. 346.

45) Bilmanis, *op. cit.*, pp. 167–168.

46) *Soviet Documents on Foreign Policy*, II, 356–358.

47) *Ibid.*, p. 374.

48) *League of Nations, Treaty Series*, LXXXIX, 669, No. 2028.

49) *Soviet Documents on Foreign Policy*, II, 372–374.

50) *Ibid.*, p. 429.

51) Rauch, *op. cit.*, p. 6867.

52) *League of Nations, Treaty Series*, CXLVIII, No. 3045.

53) A. Tarulis, "Pirmojo bolsevikmecio nuotrupos," *Naujoji Ausra*, No. 3 (1948), p. 72.

54) *Soviet Documents on Foreign Policy*, II, 505–507.

55) *Ibid.*, p. 522.

56) *League of Nations, Treaty Series*, CXLVIII, 113, No. 3408.

57) *Ibid.*, CXXXI, 297, No. 3020.

58) *Ibid.*, CXXXII, 309, No. 3021; CXLVIII, 129, No. 3409.

59) *Soviet Documents on Foreign Policy*, III, 1–8.

60) *Ibid.*, pp. 28–29.

61) *League of Nations, Treaty Series*, CXLVII, 67, No. 3391.

62) *Ibid.*, CXLVIII, 79, No. 3405.

63) Taracoucio, *op. cit.*, p. 122.

64) *Soviet Documents on Foreign Policy*, III, 29–31.

65) *Izvestiia*, October 29, 1933.

66) *Soviet Documents on Foreign Policy*, III, 47.

67) Oscar Halecki, *Borderlands of Western Civilization: A History of East Central Europe* (New York, 1952), pp. 433–434.

NOTES TO CHAPTER 6

1) *Soviet Documents on Foreign Policy*, III, 46–48.
2) *Ibid.*, p. 22.
3) *Ibid.*, p. 66.
4) *Ibid.*, p. 70.
5) *Ibid.*, p. 80.
6) *Ibid.*, p. 70.
7) *Official Documents Concerning Polish-German and Polish-Soviet Relations 1933–1939 (The Polish White Book)* (London/Melbourne, n.d.) p. 19.
8) *Ibid.*, pp. 20–21.
9) W. W. Hartlieb, *Das politische Vertragssystem der Sowjetunion 1920–1935* (Leipzig, 1936), p. 175.
10) W. P. and Z. Coates, *World Affairs and the U.S.S.R.* (London, 1939), p. 19.
11) *Soviet Documents on Foreign Policy*, III, 79–83.
12) *League of Nations, .Treaty Series*, CL, 87, No. 3455 (Estonia); CLXXXVI, 267, No. 4315 (Lithuania).
13) *Soviet Documents on Foreign Policy*, III, 78.
14) *Ibid.*, p. 79.
15) Hartlieb, *op. cit.*, pp. 175–176.
16) *Soviet Documents on Foreign Policy*, III, 78–83.
17) *Ibid.*, pp. 83–85.
18) Hartlieb, *op. cit.*, p. 178.
19) *New York Times*, July 24, 26, 29, 1934.
20) *Izvestiia*, July 30, 1934.
21) *Ibid.*, August 3, 1934.
22) *Official Documents Concerning Polish-German and Polish-Soviet Relations 1933–1939*, pp. 25–26.
23) Joseph E. Davies, *Mission to Moscow* (New York, 1941), pp. 218, 576.
24) Hartlieb, *op. cit.*, pp. 180, 183.
25) *League of Nations, Treaty Series*, CL, 103, No. 3457.
26) *Ibid.*, CLIV, 93, No. 3540.
27) V. Sidzikauskas, "Our Tradition of Cooperation," *The Baltic Review*, No. 1 (1953), pp. 40–42.
28) *Soviet Documents on Foreign Policy*, III, 103–116.
29) Hartlieb, *op. cit.*, p. 203.
30) Rauch, *op. cit.*, p. 6968.
31) *Soviet Documents on Foreign Policy*, III, 151–158.
32) Rauch, *op. cit.*, p. 7089.
33) *Soviet Documents on Foreign Policy*, III, 226.
34) Rauch, *op. cit.*, p. 6969.

35) *Draugas*, May 22, 1951.
36) Rauch, *op. cit.*, pp. 7089–7090.
37) *Le Temps*, December 26, 1936.
38) Rauch, *op. cit.*, pp. 6969–6970; M. M. Beloff, *The Foreign Policy of Soviet Russia 1929–1941* (2 vols., London/New York/Toronto, 1947–1949), II, 77–78.
39) Anicetas Simutis, *The Economic Reconstruction of Lithuania After 1918* (New York, 1942), pp. 126–127; Jean Szembek, *Journal 1933–1939* (Paris, 1952), pp. 293–297.
40) Stasys Rastikis, *Kovose del Lietuvos laisves: Kario atsiminimai* (2 vols., Los Angeles, 1956–1957), I, 515–521.
41) Maciulis, *Lietuvos ir Sovietu Sajungos santykiu raida istorijos sviesoje*, p. 280.
42) Davies, *op. cit.*, p. 294.
43) *Documents on German Foreign Policy 1918–1945. Series D: 1937–1945* (10 vols., Washington/London, 1953–1957), V, 488.
44) Davies, *op. cit.*, p. 578.
45) *Documents on German Foreign Policy*, V, 436–437.
46) *Ibid.*, pp. 438–439.
47) *Ibid.*, VII, 639.
48) Department of State, Microfilms 11/0474–0475.
49) *Documents on German Foreign Policy*, V, 438–439.
50) *Soviet Documents on Foreign Policy*, III, 279.
51) *Ibid.*, p. 303.
52) *Ibid.*, p. 305.
53) *Ibid.*, pp. 304–311.
54) *Documents on British Foreign Policy. Third Series: 1933–1939* (9 vols., London, 1946–1951) III, 153–154.
55) *Soviet Documents on Foreign Policy*, III, 319.
56) *Documents on German Foreign Policy*, V, 488.
57) Szembek, *op. cit.*, p. 373.
58) Robert Machray, "The Baltic Trends," *Fortnightly*, CXLV (1939), p. 77; quoted in *Select Committee on Communist Aggression*, III, 190.
59) Davies, *op. cit.*, p. 518.
60) *Documents on German Foreign Policy*, V, 460–462.
61) *Documents on British Foreign Policy*, III, 638–639.
62) *Ibid.*, p. 640.
63) *Ibid.*, pp. 644–645.

64) *Ibid.,* IV, 52.
65) *Ibid.,* p. 378.
66) *French Documents (French Yellow Book)* (New York, 1940), p. 77.
67) *Soviet Documents on Foreign Policy,* III, 322–323.
68) *Documents on German Foreign Policy,* V, 525.
69) *Documents on British Foreign Policy,* IV, 475–476.
70) *Ibid.,* pp. 430–431.
71) *Ibid.,* pp. 474–475.
72) *Ibid.,* p. 464.
73) *Ibid.,* pp. 517–519.

74) L. B. Namier, *Diplomatic Prelude, 1938–1939* (London, 1948), p. 88.
75) *Foreign Relations of the United States, 1939, I, General* (Washington, 1956), p. 89.
76) *Documents on German Foreign Policy,* V, 530.
77) E. V. Weizsäcker, *Erinnerungen* (München/Leipzig/Freiburg i Br., 1950), p. 77. Boris Meissner, *Die Sowjetunion, die Baltischen Staaten und das Völkerrecht* (Köln, 1956), pp. 17–23, disagrees that there was any coercion on the part of Germany.

NOTES TO CHAPTER 7

1) Szembek, *op. cit.,* p. 443.
2) Potemkin, *op. cit.,* III, 673–691.
3) *Documents on German Foreign Policy,* V, 228.
4) *Documents on British Foreign Policy,* V, 349–350.
5) *Ibid.,* pp. 448, 487; *Documents on German Foreign Policy,* V, 330.
6) *Documents on British Foreign Policy,* V, 650.
7) *Ibid.,* p. 590.
8) *Ibid.,* p. 564.
9) *Ibid.,* pp. 404–405.
10) *Documents on German Foreign Policy,* V, 330–331.
11) *Documents on British Foreign Policy,* V, 572–573.
12) Davies, *op. cit.,* p. 443.
13) *British Documents on Foreign Policy,* V, 464.
14) *Ibid.,* p. 462.
15) *Ibid.,* pp. 648–649.
16) *Ibid.,* p. 669.
17) *Ibid.,* pp. 679–680.
18) *Ibid.,* pp. 693, 698.
19) *Ibid.,* p. 689.
20) *Ibid.,* p. 711.
21) *Ibid.,* p. 680.
22) *Ibid.,* pp. 701–702, 710–712.
23) *Ibid.,* pp. 722, 725–727.
24) *Ibid.,* p. 737.
25) *Ibid.,* p. 564.
26) *Ibid.,* pp. 727, 737.
27) *Documents on German Foreign Policy,* V, 332–340.
28) *Documents on British Foreign Policy,* V, 736.
29) *Documents on German Foreign Policy,* V, 341.
30) *Documents on British Foreign Policy,* VI, 35.
31) *Ibid.,* pp. 95–96.
32) *Ibid.,* pp. 48–49.
33) *Ibid.,* V, 803.

34) Bilmanis, *A History of Latvia,* p. 351.
35) *Documents on British Foreign Policy,* V, 787–788.
36) *Parliamentary Debates,* 5th Series, H. of L., v. 113, cols. 350–364 (quoted in *Documents on British Foreign Policy,* VI, 15).
37) *British Documents on Foreign Policy,* VI, 85–87, 89–91.
38) *Ibid.,* p. 141.
39) *Ibid.,* p. 152.
40) *Ibid.,* pp. 160–163.
41) *Documents on German Foreign Policy,* V, 352–354.
42) Mairin Mitchell, *The Maritime History of Russia, 848–1948* (London, 1949), pp. 301–302.
43) *Documents on British Foreign Policy,* VI, 251, 272–273.
44) *Ibid.,* pp. 276–277.
45) *Ibid.,* pp. 279–281.
46) *Ibid.,* pp. 311, 313.
47) *Ibid.,* pp. 325–327.
48) *Ibid.,* p. 301.
49) Bilmanis, *Latvian-Russian Relations,* p. 191.
50) *Documents on British Foreign Policy,* VI, 256–257.
51) Kazys Skirpa, *Vilnius—nepriklausomybes raktas* (a manuscript).
52) *Documents on British Foreign Policy,* V, 737; VI, 85–87, 89–91.
53) *Ibid.,* VI, 448.
54) *Ibid.,* p. 405.
55) Georges Bonnet, *Fin d'un Europe* (Geneva, 1948), II, 401–403.
56) *Documents on British Foreign Policy,* VI, 577–578.
57) *Documents on German Foreign Policy,* V, 356.
58) *Documents on British Foreign Policy,* VI, 570–575.
59) *Ibid.,* p. 592.

60) *Ibid.,* VII, 42–45.
61) *Ibid.,* p. 74.
62) *Documents on German Foreign Policy,* V, 359.
63) *Documents on British Foreign Policy,* VII, 114–115.
64) *Documents on German Foreign Policy,* V, 359.
65 *Documents on British Foreign Policy,* VII, 225, 237.
66) *Documents on German Foreign Policy,* V, 363–371.
67) *Documents on British Foreign Policy,* VII, 426.

NOTES TO CHAPTER 8

1) *Documents on British Foreign Policy,* V, 463, 594–595, 646.
2) *Ibid.,* p. 724.
3) *Ibid.,* p. 775.
4) *Documents on German Foreign Policy,* VI, 630.
5) *Ibid.,* p. 586.
6) Weizsäcker, *op. cit.,* pp. 186–187.
7) *Documents on German Foreign Policy,* V, 321.
8) *Ibid.,* V, 530.
9) *Ibid.,* pp. 457–458.
10) Rastikis, *op. cit.,* I, 589.
11) *Documents on German Foreign Policy,* V, 530.
12) *Ibid.,* p. 321.
13) *Ibid.,* p. 246.
14) *Documents on British Foreign Policy,* V, 215.
15) *Documents on German Foreign Policy,* VI, 238, 246; Rastikis, *op. cit.,* I, 589.
16) Bilmanis, *op. cit.,* p. 189.
17) *Foreign Relations of the United States: The Soviet Union 1933–1939* (Washington, 1952), p. 935.
18) *Documents on German Foreign Policy,* VI, 401–402.
19) Rastikis, *op. cit.,* I, 539–568.
20) *Ibid.,* p. 465; Skirpa, *op. cit.*
21) *Documents on German Foreign Policy,* VI, 639.
22) *Ibid.,* p. 554; Rastikis, *op. cit.,* pp. 569–580; Skirpa, *op. cit.*
23) *Documents on German Foreign Policy,* VI, 244, 264–265, 283–284, 286–287, 309.
24) *Ibid.,* pp. 315–317, 323–324.
25) *Ibid.,* pp. 359–360.
26) *Ibid.,* pp. 394–395.
27) *Ibid.,* pp. 651–655.
28) *League of Nations, Treaty Series,* CXCVIII, 105, No. 4629 (Latvia); CXCVIII, 49, No. 4622 (Estonia).
29) *Documents on German Foreign Policy,* VI, 1076.
30) *Foreign Relations of the United States: The Soviet Union 1933–1939,* p. 937.
31) *Documents on British Foreign Policy,* V, 158–159.
32) *Ibid.,* p. 698; *Documents on German Foreign Policy,* VI, 736.
33) *Documents on German Foreign Policy,* VI, 806.
34) *Ibid.,* p. 643.
35) *Ibid.,* pp. 728–729, 736.
36) *Ibid.,* VII, 76–77, 87–90.
37) *Ibid.,* VI, 1006–1009.
38) *Ibid.,* pp. 659–662.
39) *Ibid.,* X, 347.
40) *Ibid.,* VI, 1015–1016.
41) *Ibid.,* p. 1052.
42) *Ibid.,* p. 1002.
43) *Ibid.,* pp. 1003–1004.
44) *Ibid.,* pp. 1048–1049.
45) *Ibid.,* pp. 1049–1050.
46) *Ibid.,* pp. 1059–1062.
47) *Ibid.,* p. 1076.
48) *Ibid.,* VII, 553.
49) *Ibid.,* pp. 62–64.
50) *Ibid.,* pp. 76–77, 87–90.
51) *Ibid.,* pp. 84–85.
52) *Ibid.,* pp. 114–116.
53) *Ibid.,* pp. 121–123.
54) *Ibid.,* pp. 134, 149–151.
55) *Ibid.,* pp. 156–157.
56) *Ibid.,* pp. 167–169.
57) *Ibid.,* pp. 149–151.
58) *Ibid.,* p. 152.
59) *Ibid.,* pp. 220, 225–229.
60) Peter Kleist, *Zwischen Hitler und Stalin: 1939–1945* (Bonn, 1950), pp. 51–52.
61) *Documents on German Foreign Policy,* VII, 221, No. 206.
62) *Ibid.,* p. 221, No. 207.
63) *Ibid.,* pp. 245–247; V, 359–361.
64) *Ibid.,* VIII, 130.
65) *Ibid.,* p. 147.
66) *Ibid.,* p. 148.
67) *Ibid.,* p. 244.

NOTES TO CHAPTER 9

1) *Foreign Relations of the United States: The Soviet Union 1933–1939,* p. 936.
2) *Ibid.,* p. 935.
3) *Documents on German Foreign Policy,* VII, 404.
4) *Ibid.,* pp. 411–412.
5) *Ibid.,* pp. 423, 450.
6) *Ibid.,* pp. 566–567.
7) Rastikis, *op. cit.,* I, 560; Skirpa, *op. cit.*
8) Rastikis, *op. cit.,* I, 456, 591.
9) *Documents on German Foreign Policy,* VII, 450.
10) *Ibid.,* p. 467.
11) Rastikis, *op. cit.,* I, 592.
12) *Documents on German Foreign Policy,* VII, 467.
13) *Ibid.,* VIII, 35.
14) *Ibid.,* p. 34, No. 36.
15) *Ibid.,* p. 34, No. 35.
16) *Ibid.,* pp. 38–39; Skirpa, *op. cit.;* Rastikis, *op. cit.,* I, 591.
17) *Documents on German Foreign Policy,* VIII, 55 n. 2.
18) *Ibid.,* pp. 54–55.
19) *Ibid.,* p. 56; Rastikis, *op. cit.,* I, 592.
20) *Documents on German Foreign Policy,* VIII, 83–84.
21) *Ibid.,* pp. 55 n. 3, 75.
22) Skirpa, *op. cit.*
23) *Documents on German Foreign Policy,* VIII, 76–77.
24) *Foreign Relations of the United States: The Soviet Union 1933–1939,* p. 938.
25) *Ibid.,* p. 435.
26) Skirpa, *op. cit.;* confirmed in a communication by Dr. A. Trimakas, Consul General of Lithuania in Vilnius in 1939.
27) Owen J. C. Norem, *Timeless Lithuania* (Chicago, 1943), p. 160; Rastikis, *op. cit.,* I, 601.
28) *Documents on German Foreign Policy,* VIII, 112.
29) *Ibid.,* pp. 121–123; Supreme Lithuanian Committee of Liberation, *Memorandum on the Restoration of Lithuania's Independence* (n.p., 1950), pp. 26–28.
30) *Select Committee on Communist Aggression,* III, 444.
31) Rastikis, *op. cit.,* I, 605.
32) *Documents on German Foreign Policy,* VIII, 130.
33) Communication from Dr. Peter Kleist, former Specialist for Eastern Europe in the *Dienststelle Ribbentrop.*
34) *Documents on German Foreign Policy,* VIII, 90, 103, 109–110.
35) *Ibid.,* pp. 159–160.
36) *Ibid.,* p. 166.
37) Bilmanis, *op. cit.,* p. 197.
38) Supreme Lithuanian Committee, *op. cit.,* p. 28.
39) Cf. p. 119 *supra.*
40) *Select Committee on Communist Aggression,* I, 379.
41) *Nazi-Soviet Relations 1939–1941* (Washington, 1948), pp. 226–254.
42) A photostat in *Documents on German Foreign Policy,* VIII, 974.
43) *Ibid.,* pp. 215–216; Rastikis, *op. cit.,* I, 610.
44) *Documents on German Foreign Policy,* VIII, 199.
45) *Ibid.,* p. 207.
46) *Ibid.,* pp. 212–213.
47) *Ibid.,* pp. 213–216.
48) *Ibid.,* p. 219.
49) *Ibid.,* p. 244.
50) Department of State, Microfilm 115/117640.
51) *Documents on German Foreign Policy,* X, 23.
52) *Ibid.,* p. 113.
53) *Ibid.,* pp. 167–168, 192.
54) *Ibid.,* p. 201.
55) Alfred Berzinsh, *I Saw Vyshinsky Bolshevize Latvia* (Washington, 1948), p. 9.
56) *Documents on German Foreign Policy,* VIII, 266.
57) *Ibid.,* X, 167–168.
58) *Ibid.,* p. 201.
59) *Ibid.,* pp. 396–397.
60) *Ibid.,* p. 450.
61) *Ibid.,* p. 588.
62) *Ibid.,* p. 470.
63) *Ibid.,* pp. 587–588.
64) *Nazi-Soviet Relations,* p. 184.
65) *Ibid.,* pp. 182–183.
66) *Ibid.,* pp. 186–187.
67) *Ibid.,* pp. 276–286.

NOTES TO CHAPTER 10

1) *Foreign Relations of the United States: The Soviet Union 1933–1939,* pp. 936–937.
2) *Documents on German Foreign Policy,* VII, 373–374.
3) *Ibid.,* p. 412.
4) *Ibid.,* p. 464.
5) *Ibid.,* p. 455.
6) *Ibid.,* p. 464.
7) *Ibid.,* pp. 491, 521.
8) *Ibid.,* p. 543.
9) *Ibid.,* p. 404.
10) *Ibid.,* pp. 519–520.
11) *Ibid.,* VIII, 3.
12) *Soviet Documents on Foreign Policy,* III, 376.
13) *Documents on German Foreign Policy,* VIII, 101.
14) *Foreign Relations of the United States: The Soviet Union 1933–1939,* p. 938.
15) *Documents on German Foreign Policy,* VIII, 91.
16) *Ibid.,* pp. 110–111.
17) *Ibid.,* p. 101.
18) *Ibid.,* pp. 246–247.
19) *Nazi Conspiracy and Aggression* (10 vols., Washington, 1946–1948), VI, 977.
20) *Documents on German Foreign Policy,* VIII, 130.
21) *Select Committee on Communist Aggression,* III, 216–220; IV, 1429–1440.
22) *New York Times,* September 20, 1939.
23) *Select Committee on Communist Aggression,* III, 216–218 (Documented by witness' statements).
24) *Documents on German Foreign Policy,* VIII, 107–108, 119–120.
25) *Foreign Relations of the United States: The Soviet Union 1933–1939,* p. 941.
26) *Documents on German Foreign Policy,* VIII, 147.
27) *Foreign Relations of the United States: The Soviet Union 1933–1939,* pp. 939–1940.
28) *Select Committee on Communist Aggression,* III, 221.
29) Rei, *op. cit.,* p. 41.
30) *Select Committee on Communist Aggression,* III, 221, n.
31) *Documents on German Foreign Policy,* VIII, 129–130.
32) *Ibid.,* pp. 200–201.
33) *Nazi-Soviet Relations 1939–1941,* p. 240.
34) *Documents on German Foreign*

Policy, VIII, 147.
35) *Ibid.,* p. 174.
36) *Foreign Relations of the United States: The Soviet Union 1933–1939,* p. 943.
37) *League of Nations, Treaty Series,* CXCVII, 223, No. 4643.
38) *Foreign Relations of the United States: The Soviet Union 1933–1939,* p. 944.
39) Rei, *op. cit.,* pp. 40–41.
40) *Select Committee on Communist Aggression,* III, 245 n. 15.
41) *Ibid.,* I, 1433.
42) *Documents on German Foreign Policy,* VIII, 174.
43) *Foreign Relations of the United States: The Soviet Union 1933–1939,* pp. 950–951.
44) *Documents on German Foreign Policy,* VIII, 162–164.
45) *Ibid.,* p. 198.
46) *Ibid.,* pp. 198–199.
47) Bilmanis, *op. cit.,* pp. 192–198.
48) *Foreign Relations of the United States: The Soviet Union 1933–1939,* p. 946; Rastikis, *op. cit.,* I, 606.
49) *Select Committee on Communist Aggression,* III, 211.
50) *Documents on German Foreign Policy,* VIII, 206.
51) Bilmanis, *op. cit.,* pp. 198–199.
52) *Foreign Relations of the United States: The Soviet Union 1933–1939,* pp. 958–964.
53) *Documents on German Foreign Policy,* VIII, 182 n. 1.
54) *Lithuanian Bulletin,* New York, Nos. 1–2 (1948), pp. 26–27; Rastikis, *op. cit.,* I, 606–625.
55) *Documents on German Foreign Policy,* VIII, 212–213.
56) *Ibid.,* pp. 213–215.
57) *Ibid.,* pp. 219–220.
58) *Lithuanian Bulletin,* loc. cit., p. 27.
59) Rastikis, *op. cit.,* I, 613–614.
60) Simutis, *op. cit.,* pp. 128–131; *Select Committee on Communist Aggression,* I, 488–489.
61) *Foreign Relations of the United States: The Soviet Union 1933–1939,* pp. 972–974, 979; V. Zalvis, "Pries 10 metu," *Britanijos Lietuvis,* London, Nos. 1–34 (1950); Rastikis, *op. cit.,* I, 638.
62) *Foreign Relations of the United States: The Soviet Union 1933–1939,* p. 976.
63) *Official Documents Concerning*

Polish-German and Polish-Soviet Relations 1933–1939, p. 194.
64) *Foreign Relations of the United States: The Soviet Union 1933–1939*, p. 973.
65) *Draugas*, March 25, 1958.

66) Shotwell and Laserson, *op. cit.*, pp. 73–79; Edward J. Rozek, *Allied War Diplomacy: A Pattern in Poland* (New York/London, 1958), pp. 183–412, *passim*.

NOTES TO CHAPTER 11

1) October 6, 1939.
2) *Foreign Relations of the United States: The Soviet Union 1933–1939*, p. 967.
3) *Izvestiia*, November 1, 1939.
4) *Foreign Relations of the United States: The Soviet Union 1933–1939*, pp. 964–965.
5) *Ibid.*, pp. 982–984.
6) *Ibid.*, p. 961.
7) *Ibid.*, pp. 949–952, 969–970; *Documents on German Foreign Policy*, VIII, 174–175.
8) *Documents on German Foreign Policy*, VIII, 284–285.
9) *Foreign Relations of the United States: The Soviet Union 1933–1939*, pp. 974–975.
10) *Ibid.*, p. 968.
11) *Ibid.*, p. 966; Rastikis, *op. cit.*, I, 619–620.
12) *Foreign Relations of the United States: The Soviet Union 1933–1939*, pp. 951, 957–958, 961, 963, 974.
13) Rastikis, *op. cit.*, I, 609.
14) *Documents on German Foreign Policy*, VIII, 284.
15) *Foreign Relations of the United States: The Soviet Union 1933–1939*, p. 964.
16) *Ibid.*, p. 962.
17) *Ibid.*, pp. 945, 954, 955; *Select Committee on Communist Aggression*, III, 229–233.
18) *Foreign Relations of the United States: The Soviet Union 1933–1939*, pp. 975, 978.
19) *Select Committee on Communist Aggression*, I, 26.
20) Maciulis, *Lietuvos ir Sovietu Sajungos santykiu raida istorijos sviesoje*, p. 281.
21) Rastikis, *op. cit.*, I, 627–630.
22) *Foreign Relations of the United States: The Soviet Union 1933–1939*, pp. 978, 981.
23) Norem, *op. cit.*, p. 173.
24) Berzinsh, *op. cit.*, pp. 12–13.

25) *Select Committee on Communist Aggression*, III, 241.
26) Berzinsh, *op. cit.*, pp. 14–15.
27) *Foreign Relations of the United States: The Soviet Union 1933–1939*, p. 970.
28) *Ibid.*, pp. 982–984.
29) *Ibid.*, p. 984.
30) *Pravda*, March 17, 1940.
31) *Select Committee on Communist Aggression*, III, 240; *New York Times*, March 17, 1940.
32) *Pravda*, March 30, 1940.
33) Davies, *op. cit.*, p. 466.
34) *Select Committee on Communist Aggression*, III, 470–472, 495–497; a photostat in *Lithuanian Bulletin*, No. 3 (1946), p. 27.
35) *Select Committee on Communist Aggression*, IV, 1433–1434; a photostat in Supreme Lithuanian Committee, *op. cit.*, p. 36.
36) *Select Committee on Communist Aggression*, III, 236–237.
37) *Documents on German Foreign Policy*, VIII, 92.
38) Communication from General M. Reklaitis (Liaison Officer with Soviet Garrisons).
39) *Select Committee on Communist Aggression*, III, 318.
40) *Nazi Conspiracy and Aggression*, VI, 983.
41) *Documents on German Foreign Policy*, IX, 134–136.
42) *Select Committee on Communist Aggression*, III, 238–239, 318; Berzinsh, *op. cit.*, p. 15.
43) Rastikis, *op. cit.*, II, 50.
44) *Select Committee on Communist Aggression*, III, 235–236.
45) *Ibid.*, p. 240.
46) Cordell Hull, *The Memoirs* (New York, 1948), p. 810.
47) Davies, *op. cit.*, p. 450.
48) *Documents on German Foreign Policy*, X, 11–12.

NOTES TO CHAPTER 12

1) *Select Committee on Communist Aggression,* I, 40; III, 318–332; VIII, 264–266; Supreme Lithuanian Committee of Liberation, *op. cit.,* pp. 65–66; Rastikis, *op. cit.,* I, 697.
2) *Documents on German Foreign Policy,* IX, 475 n.
3) *Ibid.,* pp. 474–475.
4) Zalvis, *op. cit.,* No. 2.
5) Kazys Skirpa, "Diplomatijos kompetencijos ir V.L.I.K-o veikla," *Nepriklausoma Lietuva,* Montreal, Canada, Nos. 37–46 (1956).
6) Bilmanis, *op. cit.,* pp. 201–202.
7) *Foreign Relations of the United States: The Soviet Union 1933–1939,* p. 980.
8) *Select Committee on Communist Aggression,* III, 242.
9) *Documents on German Foreign Policy,* IX, 475, n. 3.
10) Maciulis, *Sovietu Sajungos smurtas pries Lietuva,* p. 1.
11) *Select Committee on Communist Aggression,* III, 322–332; Maciulis, *op. cit.* pp. 1–2.
12) Rastikis, *op. cit.,* II, 23.
13) *Select Committee on Communist Aggression,* I, 294, 654; III, 334; Maciulis, *op. cit.,* pp. 1–2.
14) *Select Committee on Communist Aggression,* VIII, 266.
15) *Ibid.,* I, 57, 59; *Documents on German Foreign Policy,* IX, 574–575, 589; Berzinsh, *op. cit.,* pp. 16–23.
16) *Select Committee on Communist Aggression,* III, 242–243.
17) *Documents on German Foreign Policy,* IX, 475, n. 3.

NOTES TO CHAPTER 13

1) *Select Committee on Communist Aggression,* III, 332–334.
2) Supreme Lithuanian Committee of Liberation, *op. cit.,* pp. 63–70.
3) Bilmanis, *op. cit.,* p. 202.
4) *Documents on German Foreign Policy,* IX, 593–595.
4a) Rastikis, *op. cit.,* pp. 1, 355, 366.
5) *Select Committee on Communist Aggression,* III, 239, 321.
6) *Ibid.,* pp. 292–294.
7) Cf. Chs. 11–12 *supra.*
8) Zalvis, *op. cit.,* No. 2.
9) *Select Committee on Communist Aggression,* I, 40.
10) *Ibid.,* I, 39–42; III, 334–335; *Naujienos,* March 20–21, 1957; Rastikis, *op. cit.,* II, 19–26.
11) Rastikis, *op. cit.,* II, 23–24, 35–36.
12) *Select Committee on Communist Aggression,* I, 540.
13) Maciulis, *op. cit.,* p. 2.
14) Norem, *op. cit.,* p. 175.
15) General Reklaitis' communication.
16) *Documents on German Foreign Policy,* IX, 574.
17) *Ibid.,* p. 560.
18) *Ibid.,* p. 583.
19) *Ibid.,* pp. 579–580.
20) *Ibid.,* p. 578, n. 4.
21) *Ibid.,* p. 584.
22) *Ibid.,* pp. 593–595.
23) *Select Committee on Communist Aggression,* I, 294, 654 (General J. Cernius' estimate).
24) General Reklaitis' communication.
25) Berzinsh, *op. cit.,* p. 17.
26) *Select Committee on Communist Aggression,* I, 294.
27) Cf. p. 183 *supra.*
28) Bilmanis, *op. cit.,* pp. 202–203.
29) *Select Committee on Communist Aggression,* I, 77, Berzinsh, *op. cit.,* pp. 17–18.
30) Cf. p. 153 *supra.*
31) *Select Committee on Communist Aggression,* III, 456.
32) *Documents on German Foreign Policy,* VIII, 219–220.
33) *Ibid.,* IX, 595–596.
34) *Ibid.,* p. 688.
35) *Ibid.,* p. 583.
36) *Ibid.,* pp. 594–595.
37) Bilmanis, *op. cit.,* pp. 193, 196.
38) *Select Committee on Communist Aggression,* I, 59.
39) Berzinsh, *op. cit.,* p. 18.
40) *Ibid.,* p. 22.
41) *Select Committee on Communist Aggression,* I, 57–62.
42) *Ibid.,* p. 69.
43) *Ibid.,* III, 243.
44) Rei, *op. cit.,* pp. 47–48.
45) *Select Committee on Communist Aggression,* III, 244.

46) *Ibid.,* pp. 249–251.
47) *Documents on German Foreign Policy,* IX, 600.
48) *Ibid.,* p. 599.
49) *Ibid.,* p. 599 n. 1.
50) *Ibid.,* X, 11–12.

51) Bilmanis, *op. cit.,* p. 191.
52) *Documents on German Foreign Policy,* IX, 548–550.
53) Norem, *op. cit.,* p. 175.
54) Berzinsh, *op. cit.,* p. 18.

NOTES TO CHAPTER 14

1) *Select Committee on Communist Aggression,* III, 335.
2) Zalvis, *op. cit.,* No. 3 (it appears in *Vyriausybes Zinios,* No. 710 (1940), however).
3) *Select Committee on Communist Aggression,* III, 336; Rastikis, *op. cit.,* II, 25.
4) *Documents on German Foreign Policy,* IX, 577–580; *Select Committee on Communist Aggression,* III, 451; V. Kreve-Mickevicius, "Vyriausybes sudarymas," *Nemunas,* Nos. 3–4 (1950), p. 11.
5) *Documents on German Foreign Policy,* IX, 599–600.
6) Zalvis, *op. cit.,* No. 4.
7) *Select Committee on Communist Aggression,* III, 337.
8) *Lithuanian Bulletin,* Nos. 9–10 (1947), p. 5.
9) *Select Committee on Communist Aggression,* III, 335.
10) *Ibid.,* p. 337.
11) *Documents on German Foreign Policy,* IX, 599–600.
12) Kreve, *op. cit.,* p. 15.
13) *Ibid.,* p. 12; *Select Committee on Communist Aggression,* III, 451–452.
14) Kreve, *op. cit.,* pp. 17–18.
15) *League of Nations Official Journal,* Council, 1939, p. 540.
16) *Ibid.,* p. 512.
17) Krystyna Marek, *Identity and Continuity of States in Public International Law* (Geneva, 1954), p. 514.
18) *Select Committee on Communist Aggression,* III, 338.

19) Zalvis, *op. cit.,* No. 5.
20) *Ibid.,* No. 5.
21) *Select Committee on Communist Aggression,* III, 339.
22) V. Kreve-Mickevicius, "Bolseviku invazija i Liaudies Vyriausybe," *Lietuviu archyvas,* III (Kaunas, 1942), p. 14.
23) *Ibid.,* p. 15.
24) *Select Committee on Communist Aggression,* III, 339.
25) Zalvis, *op. cit.,* No. 11.
26) *Ibid.,* No. 9.
27) *Ibid.,* No. 7.
28) *Ibid.,* No. 17.
29) *Ibid.,* No. 7.
30) *Ibid.,* No. 10.
31) *Select Committee on Communist Aggression,* III, 452–454.
32) Tarulis, *Pirmojo bolsevikmecio nuotrupos,* p. 72.
33) *Documents on German Foreign Policy,* IX, 688.
34) General Reklaitis' communication.
35) *Select Committee on Communist Aggression,* III, 451.
36) *Ibid.,* p. 454.
37) *Ibid.,* pp. 455–460; Kreve-Mickevicius, *op. cit.,* pp. 10–13.
38) Kreve-Mickevicius, *op. cit.,* p. 9.
39) Cf. pp. 131–133 *supra.*
40) *Select Committee on Communist Aggression,* III, 460–463.
41) *Documents on German Foreign Policy,* X, 126.
42) *Ibid.,* p. 221.

NOTES TO CHAPTER 15

1) Rastikis, *op. cit.,* II, 50; J. Pajaujis, "Darbo inteligentijos uzdaviniai Liaudies respublikoje," *Lietuvos Zinios,* June 28, 1940.
2) Kreve-Mickevicius, *op. cit.,* pp. 13–16.
3) *Select Committee on Communist Aggression,* III, 344.
4) Zalvis, *op. cit.,* No. 11.

5) *Select Committee on Communist Aggression,* III, 344.
6) *Ibid.,* p. 248.
7) *Ibid.,* pp. 298–303; I, 61–64.
8) *Ibid.,* I, 69, 335.
9) *Ibid.,* p. 64; Berzinsh, *op. cit.,* p. 32.
10) *Select Committee on Communist Aggression,* I, 72.

11) *Documents on German Foreign Policy*, X, 189–191.
12) *Ibid.*, pp. 197–198.
13) *Select Committee on Communist Aggression*, III, 252–268 (documented by depositions in Committee files).
14) Cf. pp. 92–93 *supra*.
15) *Documents on German Foreign Policy*, IX, 628.
16) *Select Committee on Communist Aggression*, III, 252.
17) *Documents on German Foreign Policy*, IX, 627–628.
18) *Ibid.*, pp. 600–601.
19) *Select Committee on Communist Aggression*, III, 393–394.
20) Stephen Kertesz, "The Method of Soviet Penetration in Eastern Europe." In *The Soviet Union: Background, Ideology, Reality* (Notre Dame, 1951), p. 99.
21) *Select Committee on Communist Aggression*, III, 303; Kreve-Mickevicius, *op. cit.*, p. 14; Zalvis, *op. cit.*, No. 19.
22) *Select Committee on Communist Aggression*, I, 55.
23) *Ibid.*, p. 394.
24) *Ibid.*, pp. 394–397; Meissner, *op. cit.*, pp. 83–90, furnishes additional evidence based on copies of official documents made available to him (cf. n. 303, p. 83).
25) June 23, 1940.
26) *Documents on German Foreign Policy*, X, 107–108.
27) Kreve-Mickevicius, *op. cit.*, p. 16.
28) *Select Committee on Communist Aggression*, III, 349.
29) Pranas Mickus, "Liaudies Seimo rinkimu duomenu klastojimas," *Lietuviu*

archyvas, III, (Kaunas, 1942), pp. 17–34.
30) *Select Committee on Communist Aggression*, III, 339.
31) A. Garmus, "Lietuvos ijungimas i SSSR—Maskvos diktatas," *Lietuviu archyvas*, III (Kaunas, 1942), pp. 36–41; Zalvis, *op. cit.*, No. 12.
32) Liudas Dovydenas, "Mano kelias i Liaudies Seima," *Lietuviu archyvas*, III (Kaunas, 1942), pp. 47–59.
33) *Select Committee on Communist Aggression*, III, 268–273, 303–306 (with further documentation).
34) *Ibid.*, pp. 397–399.
35) *Ibid.*, p. 352.
36) Mickus, *op. cit.*, pp. 19–20; Zalvis, *op. cit.*, Nos. 12–17.
37) *Select Committee on Communist Aggression*, III, 468–470.
38) July 14, 1940.
39) *Select Committee on Communist Aggression*, I, 461; III, 275–276, 306, 355–358; Mickus, *op. cit.*, pp. 17–34; Zalvis, *op. cit.*, No. 18.
40) Norem, *op. cit.*, p. 82.
41) *Ibid.*, p. 182.
42) *Select Committee on Communist Aggression*, I, 575–576.
43) August Rei, *Have the Baltic Countries Voluntarily Renounced Their Freedom?* (New York, 1944), p. 35.
44) *Lietuviu archyvas*, III, 5.
45) Dovydenas, *op. cit.*, p. 56.
46) Bernard Newman, *Baltic Background* (London, 1948), p. 163; quoted in *Select Committee on Communist Aggression*, III, 306.
47) *Select Committee on Communist Aggression*, I, 55.

NOTES TO CHAPTER 16

1) *Select Committee on Communist Aggression*, III, 277.
2) *Ibid.*, pp. 277–278.
3) *Ibid.*, p. 306.
4) Zalvis, *op. cit.*, Nos. 18–19.
5) *Select Committee on Communist Aggression*, III, 278.
6) *Ibid.*, pp. 279–280.
7) *Ibid.*, p. 278.
8) July 20, 1940.
9) *Select Committee on Communist Aggression*, III, 284–285, 307.
10) Garmus, *op. cit.*, pp. 42–43.
11) Rastikis, *op. cit.*, II, 11.
12) Garmus, *op. cit.*, p. 44.
13) *Select Committee on Communist Aggression*, VI, 39; Rei, *op. cit.*, p. 42.
14) Juknevicius, *op. cit.*, p. 61.

15) *Lietuviu archyvas*, III (Kaunas, 1942), pp. 5–6.
16) *Select Committee on Communist Aggression*, III, 285.
17) *Ibid.*, IV, 1240–1245; VI, 40–41; Zalvis, *op. cit.*, Nos. 19–22.
18) *Select Committee on Communist Aggression*, I, 51–52.
19) Zalvis, *op. cit.*, Nos. 19–25; Lord Vansittart, *Even Now* (London, n.d.), pp. 159–160.
20) Garmus, *op. cit.*, p. 45.
21) *Select Committee on Communist Aggression*, VI, 38.
22) Dovydenas, *op. cit.*, pp. 54–55.
23) *Ibid.*, pp. 57–58.
24) Juknevicius, *op. cit.*, p. 63.
25) *Select Committee on Communist*

Aggression, IV, 1240–1245; VI, 39.

26) *Lietuviu archyvas,* III, 5–6; Juknevicius, *op. cit.,* p. 61.

27) Zalvis, *op. cit.,* No. 27.

28) Rei, *op. cit.,* p. 41.

29) Wolfe, *op. cit.,* p. 272.

30) Marek, *op. cit.,* pp. 369–416.

31) *Documents on German Foreign Policy,* VI, 54.

32) *Select Committee on Communist Aggression,* III, 415–416.

33) Sarah Wambaugh, *Plebiscites Since World War* (Washington, 1933), p. 498.

34) *Documents on German Foreign Policy,* X, 11–12.

35) Zalvis, *op. cit.,* No. 10.

35a) J. Paleckis, "18 kovos ir statybos metu," *Komunistas,* No. 7 (1958) p. 3.

36) *Select Committee on Communist Aggression,* III, 360–361.

37) *Ibid.,* pp. 338–339.

38) *Ibid.,* p. 260.

39) *Ibid.,* p. 303.

40) N. N. Mikhailov, *Nad kartoi rodiny, 1917–1947* (Moscow/Leningrad, 1947), p. 15.

41) Cf. pp. 13–17 *supra.*

42) Cf. pp. 234–235 *supra.*

43) *Pravda,* July 7, 1940.

44) *Select Committee on Communist Aggression,* III, 277.

45) *Ibid.,* pp. 353–354.

46) Zalvis, *op. cit.,* Nos. 14–16.

47) *Ibid.,* No. 16.

48) *Select Committees on Communist Aggression,* III, 303.

49) Garmus, *op. cit.,* p. 35.

50) *Documents on German Foreign Policy,* VIII, 244.

51) Wambaugh, *op. cit.,* p. 498.

52) *League of Nations Official Journal,* 1938, p. 341.

53) *Soviet Documents on Foreign Policy,* III, 726–727.

54) *Ibid.,* VI, 54.

55) *The State Department Bulletin,* III, No. 57 (1940), p. 48.

INDEX

Aggression, Soviet concept of, 50; London Convention, 81–83; "indirect," 87, 109–113
Albania and the Baltic States, 254–255
Andresen, N., 224, 251, 252
Angarietis, Z., 35, 39, 40, 50, 52
Annexation, Bolshevik view of, 7–8, 17; of Eastern Lithuania, 134–135
Anvelt, J., 27–28, 71
Appeal to the Lithuanian and White Russian Workers and Peasants, 39
Appeal to the Peoples of Belligerent Countries, 13
Arbitration, at Moscow Conference, 68; treaty, 73
Astakhov, G., 120-122
Austria and the Baltic States, 234–235, 255

Balodis, General J., 184
Baltic Foreign Ministers' Conferences, 165–166
Baltic Sea, Bolshevik goals, 47
Barthou, L., 88
Beck, J., 88
Berkis, General, 184
Berzinsh, A., 197
Bilmanis, A., 165, 167, 174
Birk, A., 74
Bizauskas, K., 129, 133, 145, 162
Bonnet, G., 111
Brauchitsch, General, 130
Brest-Litovsk Peace Conference, 13–17, 32
Briand-Kellogg Pact, 78–83
British-French-Soviet negotiations, 101–113
Butaev and others, disappearance, 170–173, 182–183
Butler, R., 111

Catherine II, Empress of Russia, 8, 12
Cernius, General J., 130, 133
Chamberlain, N., 104, 107, 128
Chicherin, G., 55, 56, 58, 70, 74, 78, 80
Churchill, W., 137
Ciano, G., 120
Clemenceau, G., 54
Commissariat for: Latvian Affairs, 34; Lithuanian Affairs, 34–35; Nationality Affairs, 34–37, 44; Stalin and, 34

Communist activities in Lithuania, 72, 77
Communist abortive revolt in Estonia, 71–72
Cordon sanitaire, 58, 64
Czechoslovakia, Soviet refusal to come to aid, 96–97

Davies, J. E., 89, 97
Daugava River, limit of German interests, 125–126
Declaration of the Rights of Peoples of Russia, 12, 24
Decree on Peace, 11
Decree on Recognition of Independence of the: Estonian Soviet Republic, 37, 45; Lithuanian Soviet Republic, 40; Latvian Soviet Republic, 41
Decree on the Temporary Organization of Administration and Local Self-Determination in the Province of: Estonia, 2, 27; Livonia and Kurland, 3
Dekanozov, V. G., 180, 189, 201–215, 237, 239, 241
Denikin, General A., 58, 60
Department of State, 161, 255–256
Deportation of Baltic Presidents, 238–239; Lithuanian Ministers, 203
Directive No. 001223, application to Baltic States, 166–167
Disarmament Convention 1922, proposed, 67–68, 76
Dovydenas, L., 228, 241–242

Eastern Pact, 91
Egorov, Marshal A. I., 93, 184
Elections to Baltic Diets: preparations, 225–238; polling results, 232–234; parallels in Austria under Nazis, 234–235
Estonian National Council, 3, 27–31; Constituent Assembly, 28; Declaration of Independence, 31; Workers' Commune, 30–31
Exteritoriality for Soviet Trade Missions, 79

Finland and the Baltic States, 65, 205
Franco, General F., 38, 43
Frohwein, German Minister in Tallinn, 147